War Plans and Alliances in the Cold War

This important new volume reviews the threat perceptions, military doctrines, and war plans of both the NATO alliance and the Warsaw Pact during the Cold War, as well as the position of the neutrals, from the post-Cold War perspective.

Based on previously unknown archival evidence from both East and West, the 12 essays in this collection focus on the potential European battlefield rather than the strategic competition between the superpowers. They present conclusions about the nature of the Soviet threat that previously could only be speculated about and analyze the interaction between military matters and politics in the alliance management on both sides, with implications for the present crisis of the Western alliance. By focusing on the potential European battlefield rather than the strategic competition between the superpowers, the book explores the Cold War roots of the different American and European approaches to security.

The conclusions about the strengths and weaknesses of the two alliances highlight the importance of political, rather than merely military, determinants of the cohesion of NATO in the post-Cold War security environment.

This new book will be of much interest to students of the Cold War, strategic studies, and international relations history.

Vojtech Mastny directs the Parallel History Project on NATO and the Warsaw Pact, based at the Center for Security Studies in Zurich and the National Security Archive in Washington. His latest book, *The Cold War and Soviet Insecurity: The Stalin Years*, won the American Historical Association's 1997 George L. Beer Prize.

Sven G. Holtsmark is a senior fellow at the Norwegian Institute for Defence Studies, part of the National Defence Educational Centre. He is the author of *Soviet-Norwegian Relations 1917–1995* and other works on diplomatic history and relations between the Nordic countries and the Soviet bloc.

Andreas Wenger is Director of the Center for Security Studies at the Swiss Federal Institute of Technology in Zurich. His latest publications include *International Relations: From Cold War to the Globalized World* (2003).

CSS Studies in Security and International Relations
Edited by Andreas Wenger and Victor Mauer
Center for Security Studies,
Swiss Federal Institute of Technology (ETH), Zürich

War Plans and Alliances in the Cold War
Threat perceptions in the East and West
Edited by Vojtech Mastny, Sven G. Holtsmark, and Andreas Wenger

War Plans and Alliances in the Cold War

Threat perceptions in the East and West

**Edited by Vojtech Mastny,
Sven G. Holtsmark, and
Andreas Wenger**

Routledge
Taylor & Francis Group

LONDON AND NEW YORK

First published 2006
by Routledge
2 Park Square, Milton Park, Abingdon, Oxon OX14 4RN

Simultaneously published in the USA and Canada
by Routledge
270 Madison Ave, New York, NY 10016

Routledge is an imprint of the Taylor & Francis Group, an informa business

Transferred to Digital Printing 2006

© 2006 Vojtech Mastny, Sven G. Holtsmark, and Andreas Wenger

Typeset in Times New Roman by
Newgen Imaging Systems (P) Ltd, Chennai, India

British Library Cataloguing in Publication Data
A catalogue record for this book is available from the British Library

Library of Congress Cataloging in Publication Data
    War plans and alliances in the Cold War: threat perceptions in the
East and West / edited by Vojtech Mastny, Sven Holtsmark, and
Andreas Wenger.
        p. cm. – (CSS studies in security and international relations)
    Includes bibliographical references and index.
        1. North Atlantic Treaty Organization – Military policy. 2. Warsaw
Treaty Organization – Military policy. 3. Military planning – Europe.
4. Military planning – North America. 5. Cold War. I. Mastny, Vojtech,
1936– II. Holtsmark, Sven. III. Wenger, Andreas. IV. Title. V. Series.

UA646.3.W38 2006
355'.0335409045–dc22   2005025833

ISBN10: 0–415–39061–3 (hbk)
ISBN10: 0–415–39564–X (pbk)

ISBN13: 978–0–415–39061–3 (hbk)
ISBN13: 978–0–415–39464–9 (pbk)

Contents

PART II
The politics of alliance management   163

Contributors

Jonathan Søborg Agger is head of section at the Danish Institute for International Studies (DIIS) in Copenhagen. He has published several articles on Danish nuclear policy during the Cold War. Since 2001, he has been a member of a team working on the White Book on Denmark's security policy during the Cold War commissioned by the Danish government.

Wilhelm Agrell is associate professor in history at Lund University, Sweden. He has written a number of books on Swedish security and defense policy in the twentieth century, covering such aspects as the Swedish nuclear weapons program and the Swedish intelligence liaison with the Western powers during the Cold War, including the participation in the *Venona* project. He is a member of the Royal Swedish Academy of War Sciences.

Kjell Inge Bjerga has been a research fellow at the Norwegian Institute for Defence Studies since 1999. He is candidatus philologiae from the University of Oslo, 1999. He has published the book *Enhet som våpen: Øverstkommanderende i Nord-Norge 1948–2002* [Unity as a Weapon: The Joint Commander Armed Forces North Norway 1948–2002] as well as several articles on Norwegian security and defense policies, military organizations, and civil–military relations.

William Burr is a senior analyst at the National Security Archive, George Washington University, where he has directed document declassification projects on the Berlin Crisis (1958–62), US nuclear weapons policy, US–China relations, and Nixon–Ford administration national security policy. He has written for a variety of scholarly and popular journals on topics in Cold War history. In 1999, he edited *The Kissinger Transcripts: Top Secret Talks with Beijing and Moscow* (New York: New Press). His current research centers on nuclear weapons policy during the Nixon administration.

Beatrice Heuser is the director of research at the Military History Research Institute of the Bundeswehr in Potsdam. She also holds a professorship at the University of Potsdam, and previously held the chair for International and Strategic Studies at the Department of War Studies, King's College,

University of London. In 1997–98, she worked in NATO's International Staff as a consultant/intern with a Balkans portfolio. She has published widely on NATO and nuclear history, and is currently working on a monograph on *The Evolution of Strategy since Machiavelli.*

Jan Hoffenaar is head of the Research and Publications Office of the Institute of Military History in The Hague. He has published books and articles on the military history of the Netherlands, and is the co-author of the history of the Dutch army during the Cold War, *Met de blik naar het Oosten.* His current research and publications are focused on the military–political relations between NATO and the Netherlands during the Cold War.

Sven G. Holtsmark is a senior fellow and head of international studies at the Norwegian Institute for Defence Studies/National Defence Educational Centre. He has published books and articles on the history of Norwegian foreign and security policy and on Soviet and East German policy toward Norway. His current research includes contributions to a history of Nordic Communism and a documentary project on the relations between the Soviet and Norwegian Communist parties.

Frede P. Jensen is a senior research fellow at the Danish Institute for International Studies (DIIS) in Copenhagen. His interests include Scandinavian diplomatic and military history as well as Cold War studies. He has published books on the Northern Seven Years War (1563–70) and on the Western European Union. Since the 1980s he has contributed to a number of official reports and White Books commissioned by the Danish government covering aspects of the Cold War.

Lawrence S. Kaplan is university professor emeritus of history and director emeritus, Lyman L. Lemnitzer Center for NATO and European Union Studies at Kent State University. He is currently professorial lecturer in history at Georgetown University. A former president of the Society for Historians of American Foreign Relations (1981) he is the author of a number of books on NATO including *The Long Entanglement: NATO's First Fifty Years* (1999) and *NATO Divided, NATO United: The Evolution of an Alliance* (1994).

Petr Luňák is a Czech foreign service officer, currently working for the Public Diplomacy division of NATO in Brussels. He is also a faculty member of the School of Social Sciences of Charles University in Prague where he has taught history of the Cold War and security studies. He has published articles on Cold War history and edited a number of volumes of documents from the Czech archives.

Vojtech Mastny directs the Parallel History Project on NATO and the Warsaw Pact, based at the Center for Security Studies in Zurich and the National Security Archive in Washington. He was NATO's first Manfred Wörner Fellow in 1996. He has been professor of history and international relations at Columbia University, University of Illinois, Boston University, and the Johns Hopkins School of Advanced International Studies as well as professor of strategy at US Naval War College. His latest book, *The Cold War and Soviet Insecurity: The Stalin Years*, was the winner of the American Historical Association's 1997 George L. Beer Prize.

Trine Engholm Michelsen has been a research fellow at the Danish Institute for International Studies (DIIS) in Copenhagen. She is now an analyst in the Danish Security Intelligence Service. Her interests include history of international relations, history of mentality, European studies, and Cold War studies. She holds a PhD in political philosophy and has published a book on the French sociologist of international relations, Raymond Aron.

Kjetil Skogrand is a research fellow at the Norwegian Institute for Defence Studies. He holds an MA from the University of Sussex, 1992, and is candidatus philologiae from the University of Oslo, 1994. He just submitted his doctoral thesis to the University of Oslo. Skogrand has also been a research fellow at the Norwegian Institute of International Affairs and assistant professor at the Department of History, University of Oslo. He has published several works on Scandinavian and international security issues. His last major work is *Norsk forsvarshistorie*, vol. 4: *Alliert i krig og fred, 1940–1970* [The History of Norwegian Defense, vol. 4: Allied in War and Peace, 1940–1970].

Matthias Uhl studied history, East European history and political science from 1990 to 1995 in Halle/Saale and Moscow. From 1996 to 2000 he was a researcher in the faculty of East European History at the Martin Luther University in Halle-Wittenberg, where he received his PhD in 2000. From 2000 to 2005 he was a senior researcher at the Institute of Contemporary History in Munich and Berlin. Since July 2005, he has been working at the German Historical Institute in Moscow.

Andreas Wenger is professor of international security policy and director of the Center for Security Studies (www.css.ethz.ch) at the Swiss Federal Institute of Technology (ETH) in Zurich. He was a guest scholar at Princeton University (1992–94, 2000), Yale University (1998), the Woodrow Wilson Center (2000), and at Georgetown University and George Washington University (2005–06). He is author of several books, including *Living with Peril: Eisenhower, Kennedy, and Nuclear Weapons* (Lanham, MD: Rowman & Littlefield, 1997) and *International Relations: From the Cold War to the Globalized World* (Boulder, CO: Lynne Rienner, 2003).

Introduction

New perspectives on the Cold War alliances

Vojtech Mastny

This is a book about a history made fresh by the decay of the Western alliance aggravated by disputes about the Iraq War. The history is that of the alliance and its former rival – the Warsaw Pact – during the Cold War, and the freshness is in what the story tells us about two important topics addressed in the book in a historical perspective. The first is military threats and their perceptions as well as misperceptions, along with the war plans that were drawn as a result. The second is the management of the alliances that were formed to cope with those real or imaginary threats – the Western alliance that has survived, albeit with clouded future, and the Soviet one that has disintegrated.

The twelve studies that comprise the book have not been written to draw lessons but are well suited the make the reader draw them. The research was originally undertaken for a conference intended to review the threat perceptions, military doctrines, and war plans during the Cold War from the post-Cold War perspective. The conference was organized by the Norwegian Institute for Defense Studies as a partner in the Parallel History Project (PHP) on NATO and the Warsaw Pact – an international scholarly network dedicated to the study of the Cold War's military aspects and their political implications. It met in June 2003 – three months after the Iraq war started – in Longyearbyen on Norway's Spitzbergen islands.

A committee, consisting of the three editors of the present volume, has selected the twelve essays from among the twenty-six prepared for the conference. The original texts were first reviewed, then rewritten, and finally edited in several stages according to the editors' guidelines, to emphasize what is new and important in the larger picture. It is for this reason that the resulting presentations, now printed here, illuminate some of the main issues that darken the American–European alliance relationship fifteen years after the Cold War had been won. Three fourths of the presentations are by Europeans.

Not intended to be comprehensive, the book is distinct in focusing on topics bearing not only on military but also on other aspects of security – or insecurity – and in so doing inviting comparisons between NATO and the Warsaw Pact by using new evidence. The evidence presented tends to downgrade the role of nuclear weapons, suggesting that their importance for both waging war and keeping peace has been overrated, and upgrade the significance of conventional forces, whose indispensability has been vindicated since the end of the Cold War and as a result of it. Most of the authors concentrate on the Cold War's potential European battlefield, where the prospect of war had an air of reality, rather than on the intercontinental strategic competition between the superpowers, whose speculative nature often defied common sense.

Besides Europe's crucial "central front," the contributions explore especially its northern flank, more important than the southern one because of its greater potential for conflict and thus also for conflict management. In looking at the workings of each of the alliances, the different chapters examine not only relations between the dominant superpower and its clients but also the varieties of interaction between the big and the small within the two military groupings. In addition, the book highlights the ambivalent role of the neutrals and nonaligned in the strategic competition between NATO and the Warsaw Pact.

The book is divided into two sections – one mainly on threat perceptions and war plans, the other on alliance management. They each start with an interpretive overview of the main issues in the strategy of the two sides, followed by case studies exploring the wider implications of their rivalry. All of the authors use previously unknown evidence – from the archives of NATO, the United States, United Kingdom, Germany, Norway, Denmark, the Netherlands, Poland, the Czech Republic, Hungary, Bulgaria, Romania, Finland, and Sweden – including many documents made available through the PHP's efforts. Although the evidence is still incomplete – the restrictions on access to archival material less than thirty years old have been the reason for limiting the scope of inquiry to 1949–79 – it allows for new conclusions about some of the tantalizing old questions that previously could only be speculated about.

The most important of those conclusions concern the nature of the Soviet threat and its policy consequences – which is what the Cold War was about. Not only can we tell better than before how accurate Western perceptions of the threat were but we can also understand better how the Soviet Union believed itself to be threatened and why. Even though the relevant files of its former defense ministry and general staff remain inaccessible, they can be largely substituted by those from the mostly open archives of its former Eastern European allies. Thus, for example, voluminous records of the Soviet-designed Warsaw Pact exercises as well as some of the alliance's actual war plans made in Moscow are available in those archives – far more of such material than is available from NATO.

The interaction between military matters and politics can be better documented on the Western side, but only within the thirty-year limit, whereas from the communist side the evidence is available, if unevenly, for the entire Cold War period. In particular, Eastern European records show what Moscow wanted its allies to do or not to do and how military considerations figured in its and their calculations. American archives remain unsurpassed in their richness as well as their openness, but for that reason also account for the "America-centrism" of the bulk of Cold War studies. This is a bias the present book is designed to avoid.

* * *

Introducing the first section, Vojtech Mastny reviews the military aspects of the Soviet Union's European strategy in the light of new evidence. He finds the strategy more attuned to other than strictly military considerations – to intentions rather than capabilities – than was typical of American, though less of European, strategic concepts. The Soviet approach conformed to the Marxist doctrine, whose emphasis on conflict of interest made the Kremlin leaders more "sensitive to the interaction between the military and the political balance than their Western, especially American, adversaries usually were. Because of the flaws of the doctrine, however, their perceptions and resulting policies were also more likely to be wrong."

According to Mastny's analysis, the changes in Soviet strategic posture reflected primarily the internal dynamics of the Soviet system and only secondarily an external pattern of action and reaction driven by the military competition with the West. Inspired by the ideological proposition that the Western capitalist system was inherently aggressive and bent on the destruction of the "socialist commonwealth" by exploiting its vulnerabilities, Soviet strategy betrayed an inherent sense of insecurity that was to be offset by overwhelming military power. The Soviet military, whose ideological commitment remained strong while the political leadership was faltering, were increasingly influential in shaping the Warsaw Pact's offensive planning although it was their Kremlin superiors who controlled it.

The close dependence of policy on the personalities of the supreme leaders, documented by new evidence, made Soviet management of military power less predictable than suggested by the image of the Cold War's bipolar stability. Stalin's reputed realism and sense of caution did not prevent him from imposing the Berlin blockade and sanctioning the aggression in Korea – blunders that gave the Cold War the military dimension it had originally lacked. Khrushchev's restless drive for innovation and desire to demilitarize the conflict did not prevent him from achieving the opposite effect, leading to the Cold War's most dangerous crises over Berlin and Cuba. And Brezhnev, though more averse to risk than either of his predecessors, tolerated out of weakness and corruption excessive militarization of Soviet power, which was wrought with unprecedented dangers.

From what is now known about the workings of the Soviet system, the Western strategy of nuclear deterrence, often credited with having kept the Cold War cold, thus appears as largely misguided. Irrelevant to deterring a major war that the enemy did not wish to launch in the first place, it was at the same time ineffective in preventing the miscalculations that led to limited war in Korea, in discouraging Khrushchev's attempts to manipulate nuclear weapons for political gain, or in averting the acceleration of the arms race regardless of détente. In the end, it was not the pointless nuclear posturing but the advances of NATO's conventional forces that impressed upon the Soviet Union its inability to compete with the West in high technology, thus preparing the ground for the Cold War's peaceful resolution. "In the longer run, the fallacies of deterrence muddled rather than clarified the conditions under which the use military power can be both legitimate and effective."

The abuse of military power contemplated by the Soviet Union at the height of the second Berlin crisis is the subject of Matthias Uhl's account of the Warsaw Pact's "Buria" exercise in 1961. The account, based on records found in former

East German archives, suggests that the situation was more precarious than generally believed. There was a disturbing correlation between the starting point of the exercise, which simulated a massive attack on Western Europe, and the date Khrushchev originally considered for signing a separate peace treaty with East Germany, which by terminating the Western powers' right of access to Berlin would have risked triggering their military response.

"Buria" was the first Warsaw Pact exercise testing the concept of a swift offensive thrust deep into Western Europe, amid prodigious use of nuclear weaponry by both sides. The concept, with its simplistic assumptions about the ability to fight and win a nuclear war, was symptomatic of the "nuclear romanticism" that held sway of Soviet strategists longer than of their Western counterparts. Uhl notes that Soviet military planners considered an all-out nuclear offensive as the only acceptable option because they believed – in contrast to NATO's own estimates – that the adversary was quite capable of defense by conventional means. He cites contemporary assessments by both the CIA and the East German intelligence that NATO was superior to the Warsaw Pact in nuclear-capable aircraft and about equal to it in the number of nuclear warheads.

Intended to confirm the validity of the all-out strategy, "Buria" left critical questions unanswered. It never clarified which side would be the first to launch a nuclear strike. Nor did it consider an intervention by US strategic forces once the fighting in Europe had begun. It revealed potentially insuperable difficulties in coordinating the different Warsaw Pact armies. Uhl concludes that such uncertainties "obviously contributed" to Khrushchev changing his mind and deciding not to sign the treaty with East Germany after all.

In examining the pivotal role of Czechoslovakia in Soviet planning, Petr Luňák analyzes actual war plans rather than exercises. Such plans are more readily available from Czechoslovakia than from other countries of the former Soviet bloc. They are all the more revealing since they date as far back as the early Cold War years, when Western fears of Soviet attack were at their highest. The surprise is that under Stalin they were unequivocally defensive, providing for operations only on home territory, and that their defensive character remained the same after his death for several more years. It was only the Berlin crisis that brought about their reversal as evident not only in the "Buria" exercise but in later Czechoslovak plans as well.

Luňák discusses the plans against the background of the military buildup Stalin ordered in January 1951 – the time when American defeat in the Korean War seemed most likely. He explained his reasoning to his Eastern European lieutenants at a secret meeting by telling them that he wanted to have powerful armies ready to take advantage of a favorable situation which he expected to arise in Western Europe in two years' time. Although he did not clarify what exactly he had in his mind the increasingly irrational streak in it during the last years of his life did not rule out an adventure that would have given substance to the Western apprehensions.

The strategic importance of Czechoslovakia stemmed from both its location and its vulnerability. Although a conflict on its Western border would have inevitably entailed a clash with US forces there were no Soviet troops stationed on its territory until 1968, and it was impossible to predict how its army and its people would have acquitted themselves had push come to shove. In such a situation, it made more sense for Stalin to keep the country's war plans defensive than it did for his successors to drag it into their offensive plans, which – as pointedly stressed by Luňák – the subservient Czechoslovak leaders supported unreservedly to their discredit.

What applied to Soviet strategy under Stalin in Czechoslovakia did not necessarily apply to it at other times and in other places. Frede Jensen, using Polish and East German documents, breaks new ground by demonstrating that Denmark occupied a special place in Warsaw Pact planning, being treated as the easiest target. Whether this was in fact true or not remains so important a question in that country that in 2001 the Danish parliament commissioned a major research project to answer it. In any case, an attack on Denmark leading to its "liberation" remained a constant in Soviet strategy from Stalin to Gorbachev, with a pivotal role in the operation assigned to the Poles.

In discussing the general question of how important records of exercises are in relation to war plans, Jensen finds them complementary. The Warsaw Pact's operational plans preserved in the Eastern European archives were authentic components of the master plans drawn up at the Moscow general staff because of their "structural congruity." They also interacted, as the war plans defined and influenced the exercises while the exercises served to update and refine the war plans.

According to Jensen, the Warsaw Pact's offensive strategy did not necessarily imply aggressive intentions. With its implementation dependent on political decisions to be taken in situations that could not be predicted, it was not incompatible with defensive priorities and a status quo foreign policy. Both Warsaw Pact and NATO plans presumed highly hypothetical crisis scenarios. After 1965, Soviet strategists began to move away from their preferred "all-out" nuclear scenario but never found a suitable substitute.

What the planners did find out on the example of Denmark was that the landing operations they envisaged would be increasingly risky because of NATO's growing capacity to defend itself by conventional means. Moreover, the Polish army – the linchpin of the operation – was not strong enough even numerically to be certain of success. The prospective attackers never achieved – nor did they try to achieve – the 3:1 superiority that the rule of thumb requires for an attack to have a chance to succeed.

If preparing for war in Europe involved too many uncertainties for both sides – but especially for the one wed to an offensive strategy – the same was true even more about planning for a nuclear confrontation between the superpowers. The futility of such planning comes out clearly from William Burr's analysis of the Nixon administration's quest for "limited options" from 1969 to 1975. The recently declassified US documents that he uses provide the kind of detailed insight into the complexities and subtleties of high-level strategic thinking that we have from Washington but not from Moscow – in part because the Soviet thinking was never so complex and subtle.

This may have been for the better rather than the worse. It was at the high tide of détente with Moscow that US policymakers, led by Henry Kissinger, felt the need to search for ways that would make nuclear weapons politically more useful – just as their Soviet counterparts were, more sensibly if not more successfully, trying to reduce the dependence of their strategy on nuclear threats. Kissinger thought it was needed to give the president a wider range of options to deter war more effectively, or else reduce its destructiveness. Burr dissects the bureaucratic wrangling that resulted in the adoption of the "Schlesinger doctrine" and the presumably more rational SIOP-5 master plan for nuclear targeting, supposedly less damaging to civilian population. Whatever the supposed damage, the real damage was to détente, since Soviet leaders were given reason to suspect that "Washington was interested in concepts of nuclear options as a way to coerce Moscow while avoiding a general war."

The idea that nuclear threats, much less their implementation, could be controlled was an illusion of civilian "defense intellectuals" – more influential in Washington than in Moscow – rather than of military professionals. Kissinger's belief in the feasibility of "graduated use of force" did not impress the Pentagon and CIA, where most doubts about limited options were raised. In opposing the perils of militarized thinking of civilians, the US military advocated sanity, whereas on the other side the situation was reversed. Soviet generals kept elaborating and refining their offensive war plans until they were forced to discard them by Gorbachev and his civilian advisers.

In its own way, the peaceful outcome of the Cold War vindicated the position of the neutrals whose aim was by definition to stay out of it. Wilhelm Agrell's study is a reminder of how important neutrality was in Europe. When the Second World War ended, there were only occupied and neutral states on the continent, and once the two hostile military groupings came into existence, the new concept of nonalignment supplemented the old notion of neutrality. The strategic position of states that were not members of either alliance introduced an element of unpredictability into the rivalry that both NATO and the Warsaw Pact had to take into account.

In NATO's early years, the mostly nonaligned southern Europe was critical for the US plans that counted on keeping there a foothold necessary to turn back the expected Soviet onslaught. Later on the defense-minded Yugoslavia figured prominently in the calculations of both alliances – more as a "hostile neutral" than a "silent ally," in Agrell's terms. Most of other countries – Switzerland, Austria, Sweden, and Finland – were "silent allies" – of NATO rather than the Warsaw Pact, significantly – although their governments have remained to this day notably reluctant to reveal the extent of the collusion. The Swedish and Warsaw Pact sources utilized by Agrell leave no doubt that Sweden, militarily the strongest of the nonaligned, always counted in the Soviet eyes as a potential NATO ally that should not be unnecessarily provoked. Operations against Sweden are conspicuously absent from any of the Warsaw Pact planning documents we have.

Just as the Cold War gave a new meaning to neutrality, the concept largely lost any meaning once the confrontation ended and one of the alliances vanished. The prevailing trend in Europe has since been not toward neutrality but toward joining the remaining alliance, despite the fact that the old security threats have vanished, too, and the new ones could not compare. The main issues in the enlargement of NATO have been its accommodation to the changes in both the substance and the perception of security as well as accommodation of its new members, whose previous alliance experiences had been radically different. The differences in alliance management that kept NATO whole while its rival fell apart are those particularly pertinent in view of the Western alliance's transatlantic rift. They are addressed in the second part of the book.

* * *

Andreas Wenger starts the part with an overview of NATO's strategic planning, in which the interplay of military and political factors made its politics more important than its substance. The three main stages in the development of NATO strategy he identifies are not the same as those described by Mastny with regard to Soviet strategy, thus indicating how much each of the alliances evolved by own dynamics rather than by interaction with the other. NATO's problems, however, were conducive to their solution whereas the Warsaw Pact's problems eventually brought it down.

Wenger finds NATO's strategy during its formative first decade determined overwhelmingly by nuclear weapons. The weakness of the alliance's conventional forces led to its nuclearization after the controversial decision to equip it with tactical nuclear weapons. The decision was intended to buy time but its main effect was to spur arms race by multiplying the number of NATO's nuclear warheads out of any reasonable proportion. The failure of the strategy that was to make the West more secure but achieved the opposite became evident once the Soviet Union acquired the capability to hit the United States on its own territory, thus raising doubts about the credibility of the American commitment to the defense of Europe – the bedrock of NATO.

The 1958 Sputnik shock, followed by the Berlin crisis, inaugurated a period in which the politics of military planning increasingly dominated the alliance's strategy. The uncertainties of the planning fueled disputes that plunged NATO into the deepest crisis in history prior to the current one – a crisis, however, described by Wenger as a catharsis from which the alliance emerged stronger and more functional than before. The disputes, during which the United States tried to impose its strategic preferences on reluctant allies and the French took the lead in resisting, presaged what would happen again half a century later. Wenger explains why the disputes had a happy ending.

The crisis ended in 1967 with the adoption of the Harmel report that married NATO's military and political purposes by defining its dual goal as defense *cum* détente. Its new strategic concept was as subtle as it was effective. As summed up by Wenger, its implementation provided for leadership by persuasion rather than by control, flexibility rather than chain of command, political consultation rather than agreement on operational details. Once the allies agreed on NATO's political role, a compromise on strategy became possible. The ambiguities of the strategy may not have been very helpful in case of a war, but short of it they were what the alliance needed to maintain its political cohesion and help preserve peace as well.

Beatrice Heuser examines how NATO managed to accommodate its contentious members on the central issue of its military planning – nuclear deterrence. This was an issue the allies discussed continuously and vigorously, in a telling contrast with their Warsaw Pact counterparts, inhibited by the Soviet Union. The absence on the Eastern side of an equivalent of NATO's Nuclear Planning Group as a forum of meaningful discussion was one of the signal differences between the two military groupings. Heuser attributes the wide range of views permeating the Western debate to differences in the NATO nations' political cultures and decision-making mechanisms. Their commitment to common democratic values nevertheless ensured that the alliance's decisions reflected respect for those differences rather than power politics, as the "realist paradigm" would have it.

Heuser cites abundant instances of American "unilateralism" in dealing with the allies, only to show how it was repeatedly tempered by respect for their particular concerns. The Carter administration's abrupt cancellation of the neutron bomb program, Reagan's proclamation of the "Star War" strategy without prior consultation with the Europeans, or his casual readiness during his Reykjavik meeting with Gorbachev to discard the nuclear weapons that they needed for reassurance were all annoyances that strained the alliance but did not break it.

One reason was that the United States, in sharp contrast to the Soviet Union, tolerated "an impressive degree of anti-hegemonic behavior." Despite the overwhelming importance Washington attached to nuclear weapons, it deferred to the wishes of those of its allies who preferred to keep them out of their territories. The American supreme commanders of NATO, quite unlike their Soviet opposite numbers, tended to be sympathetic to the allies' concerns, even to the extent of becoming advocates of their causes in Washington. Because of the public nature of the decision-making process there, however, US political representatives in NATO often had little room for compromises, but then the British were usually ready to step in to broker them. This is how Heuser describes the remarkably open political setting conducive to trust that allowed NATO to function as well as did.

Managing to overall satisfaction not only the relations between the superpower and its dependents but also the relations between the big and the small within the alliance was a notable accomplishment, analyzed by Kjell Inge Bjerga and Kjetil Skogrand on the example of Norway. This was a staunch ally but also one with reservations, notably veto on the introduction of nuclear weapons to Norwegian territory and insistence on control over any allied forces operating there. With regard to NATO, the Norwegians pursued both integration and "screening"; with regard to the Soviet adversary, both deterrence and reassurance. The clarity of their policies commanded respect.

The structures NATO designed to accommodate its smaller allies by striking a balance between national control and alliance integration may seem cumbersome and bureaucratic. This is what they certainly were in peacetime, but they served the good purpose of providing channels through which the allies could shape common decisions. And they could be expected to perform efficiently in wartime as well by fostering cooperative attitudes. The placement of NATO's northern regional command in Norway, for example, helped to make Norwegian officials feel more comfortable with the alliance's bureaucratic system than they would have been with the casual ways in which it had made its decisions in its early years. The close personal relations "on the level *below* presidents, cabinets, and secretaries general" were what made the system conducive to pragmatic solutions. "If the alliance is searching for a lesson of history in the present situation," the authors suggest, "it might be here."

In a companion piece to Jensen's earlier discussion of the Warsaw Pact plans, Jonathan Agger and Trine Engholm Michelsen consider how Denmark, the "footnote country" reputed as NATO's laggard because of its propensity to attach reservations to its decisions, actually responded to the threats the plans posed. The question is important because, in the last analysis, the alliance could only be as strong as its weakest link. Denmark was vulnerable not only because of its exposed geographical location but also because of the anti-militarist leanings of its public, both of which bred skepticism about the possibility of defending the country.

The authors distinguish between the threat inherent in the Warsaw Pact's offensive plans, which remained on paper, and Soviet political pressure, which was real. While the Danish governments did not have to worry about the appeal of communism among their citizenry, they had to cope with Moscow's psychological warfare aimed at influencing the public opinion. They had to be nimble in navigating between the people's preferences and NATO's demands. Tolerant of the alliance's domestic critics but firm in resisting insidious Soviet disarmament schemes, they were astute political managers of security.

In Agger's and Engholm's opinion, "Moscow failed in its attempt to effect changes in Denmark's security policy." It succeeded, however, in some of its specific campaigns, particularly those aimed at excluding foreign military aircraft from Danish territory, keeping NATO away from the Bornholm Island, and restricting Danish–West German military cooperation. Arguably, the Danes would have willingly assumed such restrictions by themselves, but this can never be proved. What is proved by the authors is that the appeasement of the Soviets had no negative political consequences internally – no small tribute to the vitality of the Danish democracy.

Nor did the Danish constraints seriously damage but merely rankled NATO. Its other members assumed that in an emergency the constraints would be removed; more importantly, this is what the enemy had to assume too. On balance, political signals thus mattered more than military prowess although the latter certainly helped in making the former more credible. In a different way, this also applied to the outcome of the controversy about the defense of the bulk of the Netherlands' territory, discussed in the chapter by Jan Hoffenaar.

The issue came into the open in 1952, when it became a public secret that NATO would give up on defending the Rhine–IJsel line, thus allowing the

Netherlands to fall to the enemy if war came. The decision was not prompted by any change in Soviet military posture but by French desire to divert the alliance's resources to the Mediterranean, where France was fighting to save the remnants of its colonial empire in North Africa. This was the reason why the Dutch thought the appointment of French marshal Alphonse Juin as NATO's commander in Central Europe was "dangerous for the Netherlands from the strategic point of view."

Defending the nation's soil was important psychologically and politically for a country whose precipitous collapse under the onslaught of the Nazi invaders remained fresh in memory. Hoffenaar notes that the Dutch tried hard using their skills in hydraulic engineering to make the Rhine–IJsel line defensible. Their governments, "Janus-like," had to "adopt two faces" – a reassuring one toward their "people, who wanted to be protected and defended, [and]..., another, more an assertive one... needed to confront NATO, which was, as yet, incapable of providing the protection."

Fortunately for the Dutch, before the Soviet strategy turned offensive in the early 1960s, NATO had grown strong enough to acquire the will to defend them. It moved its defense line even farther east into West Germany. Reassured, the Dutch became the alliance's most enthusiastic supporters, supplying it not only with troops but, perhaps more importantly, also with a disproportionately high number of its high officials including secretaries general.

Another attempt to divert NATO's attention "out of the area" is the theme of the book's last and in some ways most timely chapter. The chapter by Lawrence Kaplan is about a famously ambitious and arrogant US defense secretary, who managed to antagonize not only Europeans but also much of the high US military by pressing for the deployment of troops for a war in a distant country that was being widely opposed as misconceived. The secretary was Robert S. McNamara and the country was Vietnam.

The divisive episode occurred in 1965–68 as increased need for troops in Vietnam led Washington to demanding a substantial reduction of US personnel in Europe, thus raising among the allies doubts about the constancy of American commitment to its defense – NATO's fundamental article of faith. In trying to reassure Europeans, it was American civilian strategists rather than military experts, who typically disparaged the enemy's numerical strength and exalted the West's technological superiority. The "dual basing" of troops in both the United States and Europe, introduced on the controversial assumption that their combat readiness would not suffer, remained, according to Kaplan, the most important legacy of the unilateralist episode even after its other effects had been overcome.

If the European fears of abandonment were eventually dispelled – most of the troops stayed and the US commitment continued – this was largely because of the 1968 invasion of Czechoslovakia that brought Soviet forces closer to the NATO lines, thus serving as "a sober reminder of the importance of US troops in Europe." Although "European hopes for détente with the Soviet bloc revived quickly, as did Senate complaints against Europeans," so did also the basic trust within the alliance, which remained its indispensable glue for the rest of the Cold War and in its aftermath until it began to dissolve in a different international setting.

* * *

Any reader of this book will notice how different the security environment was during the Cold War than it is today. It would be a mistake to assume, however, that the differences make anything that can be learned from the experience irrelevant to today's concerns. Although the Cold War was a historical anomaly because of its intensity, duration, as well as bipolarity, it offers for those very reasons unique insights into the ways conflict can be avoided or mitigated despite formidable odds. It also helps to understand why the American and European perceptions of threats to security, utility of military power in countering them, and indispensability of alliances have diverged so much and what can be done about this.

As the Cold War took its course, the American concepts of security may have become deeper in the military sense but the European ones were getting wider. By casting doubt on the validity of established notions of power politics, the Cold War experience led to a redefinition and expansion of security beyond the military realm, with lasting and probably irreversible consequences. The experience shaped the characteristically European approaches that account not only for Europe's remarkably stable "security architecture" since the Cold War but also for much of the concurrent instability in transatlantic relations.

The two relevant conclusions that can be drawn from the findings in this book should be obvious. The first is that military threats are not always what they seem to be nor can they be reliably estimated. The second is that, whatever the threats might be, they can be held at bay by sound alliance management, which heeds not only the interests but also the sensibilities of all involved. This is not only how NATO could best hope to avoid joining its erstwhile Soviet adversary in the proverbial dustbin of history, but also how the United States could best command respect for its continued primacy.

Part I

Threat perceptions and war planning

1 Imagining war in Europe

Soviet strategic planning

Vojtech Mastny

The Cold War was by definition a potential real war in the making, and imagining such a war was what the belligerents' military strategy was about. It concerned their respective threat perceptions, military doctrines, and war plans which, however, were very different in East and West. Focusing on the Soviet side, this essay tries to explain why they differed and what with consequences. In doing so it centers less on the US–Soviet rivalry than on the potential European battlefield. Although the two theaters of conflict were interrelated, there was always an air of unreality about the intercontinental confrontation whereas on the Old Continent long memories made war all too imaginable.

We still cannot tell how close the seemingly unreal may have actually come to passing, since the high-level evidence of the superpowers' nuclear planning remains scarce, but we now have abundant evidence about the confrontation of the two military groupings in Europe. Some of this record casts a new light on the old questions that during the Cold War seemed to be those of life a death but could only be speculated about. In the happy absence of such an existential predicament, the answers to them may be less consequential today but more likely to be accurate. There are also new questions, those arising from the different post-Cold War perspective, which make the Cold War experience particularly relevant. This is especially true about questions made topical by the emergence of international terrorism and the ensuing crisis of the Western alliance.

The evidence now available about the Cold War's military dimensions is vastly better than it used to be but is still incomplete as well as asymmetrical. It tells us more about internal decisionmaking on the western than on the Soviet side but only up to the time limit of thirty years back from now imposed in most western archives; by contrast, former communist records are often open, if unevenly, for the entire Cold War period. On the military side, we have documents from exercises and even war plans of the Warsaw Pact – much more than we have from NATO. What we do not have are the files of the Soviet general staff, where those plans were made. But since their implementation depended to a significant degree on the participation of the Warsaw Pact allies, what remains in Moscow under lock and key can be largely substituted for by documents from the more readily accessible Eastern European archives.

The resulting picture is necessarily different from that which can be drawn by using mostly English-language sources, as has been the case with much of the literature about the Cold War written by mostly monolingual specialists on US foreign policy, often with the intention of making a case for or against it. Drawing on multi-archival evidence, the discussion that follows tries to avoid this pitfall by interpreting Soviet strategy in Europe in its own terms and judging it accordingly. The judgment gives its architects the benefit of the doubt though not necessarily absolution.

Stalin and his legacy

There is no doubt anymore that early western estimates of Soviet military threat, summarized since 1950 in NATO's annual assessments of the enemy's "strength and capabilities," were wildly exaggerated. Those images of 175 "active line divisions," ready to strike at a moment's notice simultaneously in central, northern, and southern Europe, against the British Isles and Africa, the Middle East and Far East, even Alaska, while still leaving enough reserves to defend the Soviet homeland, were products of both fear and ignorance. They rested on the dubious assumption that a division "existed unless there were three pieces of evidence to the contrary."[1]

Although the Soviet forces facing the West in Stalin's lifetime were not nearly so large as NATO feared, they were still much larger than their western counterparts. However, the two documents from the Cold War's formative period that the Russian authorities have thus far chosen to release show a strictly defensive posture. If this was so at that time, then the failure to release any further such documents from later years may indicate that, once the Cold War started in earnest, the posture was no longer so benign. Or, in view of America's overwhelming nuclear superiority, Stalin's contingency plans may have embarrassingly called for appeasement. He had been capable of it before.[2]

The dark Stalin years still leave us much in the dark about what Soviet strategy really was at that time. The weight of the fragmentary evidence lends support to its defensive rather than offensive character. According to a retrospective description by Czechoslovak military experts from 1968, it was "based on the slogan of defense against imperialist aggression, but at the same time assuming the possibility of transition to strategic offensive with the goal of achieving complete Soviet hegemony in Europe" – just as the West feared. The plans prepared under Stalin that have been found in Eastern European archives were nevertheless unequivocally defensive. The 1951 operational plan of the Polish army, then under direct command by his favorite Soviet marshal Konstantin K. Rokossovskii, did not mention an offensive, but only defensive operations leading to the defeat of western invaders within the home territory rather than beyond. The same was true about contemporary Czechoslovak plans.[3]

According to western critics of NATO, the Soviet Union had reasons to fear its aggressive intentions. The most perceptive of the critics, George F. Kennan, wrote in 1952 of a "cosmic misunderstanding" in suspecting the Soviets "precisely of the one thing they had not done, which was to plan, as yet, to conduct an overt and unprovoked invasion of Western Europe." In his view,

> Observing … that the [NATO] pact was supported publicly by a portrayal of their own intentions and strength that they did not recognize as fully accurate – it was no wonder that the Soviet leaders found it easy to conclude that the Atlantic Pact project concealed intentions not revealed to the public, and that these intentions must add up to a determination on the part of the Western powers to bring to a head a military conflict with the Soviet Union as soon as the requisite strength had been created on the Western side.[4]

Although the hypothesis is persuasive, there is no evidence that Stalin actually thought that way. The creation of NATO in 1949 did not elicit a significant Soviet military response, only political countermeasures. Despite his monumental suspiciousness, at least Stalin was in a position to know from his well-placed spies that no western attack was imminent. By providing him with this critical margin of reassurance, the unintended transparency of the western plans may thus have been a blessing in disguise at a time when Western Europe remained militarily most vulnerable and the deterrent effect of America's atomic supremacy at best uncertain.

Ruminations about the inevitability of war figured prominently in Stalin's private and public pronouncements. Their ambiguity, however, was suggestive of a muddle in his mind. He never made it clear whether the looming war was the one among capitalist powers that Lenin had prophesized or a Soviet–American war. If the latter, the Soviet prospects were bound to be discouraging because of the enemy's vast superiority in resources – a good reason for trying to postpone the inevitable war, perhaps indefinitely, by political means. These included Moscow's sponsorship of the massive "peace" movement calculated to undermine western will to fight. Ultimately, Stalin placed his bets on the "general crisis of capitalism" that might take its course before war would become topical.

As most generals are said to do, Stalin imagined the next war could be like the last one. His theory of "permanently operating factors" attributed the decisive importance in warfare to the factors that had supposedly allowed him to lead his country to victory in the Second World War – superior command, firepower, and equipment, besides the high morale of the troops backed by a supportive home front. Because of his discounting the importance of nuclear weapons, sophisticated western observers chided the theory as simplistic and naive. Yet the American plans from that period, too, followed the Second World War model in assuming that the few atomic weapons the United States had could not prevent Soviet conquest of Western Europe, which would only be reversed later by its liberation from overseas. If Stalin knew these plans his doctrine was actually "quite perceptive and realistic."[5]

Short of the test of war, Stalin's reputed realism nevertheless left much to be desired. Although he had every reason not to provoke the much more powerful United States, this is precisely what he did by turning the originally political and ideological conflict into a potentially military one. He acted as if he were ready to risk a military confrontation when he imposed the 1948 Berlin blockade, which prompted the creation of NATO and US commitment to the defense of Europe. A year later, when he gave the green light to the communist invasion of Korea after much hesitation, he took the calculated risk that the Americans would not intervene but miscalculated again.

The Korean War did not have a sobering effect on Stalin. In successfully prodding the reluctant Chinese to enter the war against the United States, he asked their supreme leader Mao Zedong rhetorically: "Should we fear this?" He answered that "we should not, because together we will be stronger than the USA and England, while the other European capitalist states ... do not present serious military forces. If war is inevitable, then let it be waged now."[6] Although the statement was self-serving, it was consistent with Stalin's disposition to take greater risks in Europe when the military situation in East Asia looked unfavorable to the United States.

From the first-hand record of Stalin's secret meeting with Eastern European party and military leaders in January 1951, whose aggressive thrust had previously been imperfectly documented, we now know what exactly he told his minions at a time when the Americans seemed to be on the verge of defeat in Korea. In a reversal of his previous neglect of Eastern European armies as insufficiently reliable, Stalin ordered their massive expansion, to be accomplished within the two years during which he expected the United States to become bogged down in a loosing war in Asia. He referred to the need to exploit to communism's advantage the favorable situation he believed would develop in Europe, and although he did not explain – nor did he necessarily know – how this should be done, the massive buildup, sustained by growing militarization of the economy, ensued.[7]

The favorable conditions Stalin expected to occur in Europe never materialized, as the Korean War prompted the Americans and West Europeans to rally and transform NATO from a paper alliance into a military force to reckon with. Stalin underestimated its vigor, particularly its ability to integrate West Germany, and showed contempt for American guts. After the unexpected setbacks of US forces in Korea and Washington's similarly unexpected failure to press for victory after their subsequent successes, he told Chinese premier Zhou Enlai that

> Americans don't know how to fight.... They are pinning their hopes on the atomic bomb and air power. But one cannot win a war with that. One needs infantry, and they don't have much infantry; the infantry they do have is weak. They are fighting with little Korea, and already people are weeping in the United States. What will happen if they start a large-scale war?[8]

Tantalizing bits and pieces found in Russian sources suggest that during Stalin's last sickly years his propensity for risk-taking and possible catastrophic miscalculation may have grown into bizarre proportions. He is said to have ordered the production of 10,000 Il-28 long-range bombers, to be stationed on the

Arctic ice and ready to take off to drop atomic bombs on US targets, presumably in support of an amphibious assault on Alaska. The NATO estimates that Stalin was in a position to know presumed such Soviet capability and may have even implanted the wild ideas in his mind. There was enough madness in it as his death was approaching.[9]

Acting on Stalin's military legacy became the top priority of his successors. Not only did they publicly reassure the West of their readiness to resolve any conflict peacefully but they also secretly decided to terminate the Korean War he had artificially been prolonging – all within days after his death. Disposing of the despot's legacy, however, was a formidable task. Having acquired an empire in Europe as an indispensable safeguard of Soviet security as he understood it, he had done so in a way that provoked confrontation with the world's most powerful nation, thus making the Soviet Union less secure as a result. With the mastermind gone and no one capable of fitting into his shoes, the Soviet strategy was bound to change. Just how much it would change, however, depended again on the personalities of the Kremlin leaders, besides the behavior of the adversary and accidental factors beyond anybody's control.

Khrushchev's innovations

The revision of Stalin's military doctrine was spearheaded by the Soviet military rather than the embattled political leaders, beset with their power struggle besides other pressing issues. Criticism focused on Stalin's dismissal of the importance of surprise in warfare that had been for him a reminder of his having been caught by surprise by the German attack with nearly catastrophic results. Rather than adapting the doctrine to political expediency, the critics now sought to adapt it to the advent of the nuclear era, as their western counterparts had long been doing. The Kremlin leaders initially discouraged a revision which, in contrast to their efforts to mitigate Stalin's political legacy, had aggressive military implications.[10]

On the pages of the confidential military journal *Voennaia mysl*, Soviet authors began to argue that the only reliable defense against a nuclear attack is preempting it and that the only reliable way of making the attack successful is launching it before the enemy could preempt. This was the same discouraging conclusion that NATO's planners had reluctantly reached in trying to resolve an irresolvable dilemma.[11] Their Soviet counterparts, however, resisted such a conclusion, incompatible with their Bolshevik militancy. They argued that surprise was the answer and preemption was not only possible but also necessary.

By early 1955, the Kremlin had endorsed this dangerous notion by allowing an article that defended it to be published. It had to come to terms somehow with the Soviet progress in the acquisition of nuclear weapons and their means of delivery that was the delayed effect of Stalin's investment in their research and development.[12] But how it would come to terms with it was determined by the emergence by that time of Nikita S. Khrushchev as the supreme leader. Khrushchev was not as effectively in control of Soviet strategy as Stalin had been but could still shape it in fundamental ways, for better or for worse.

The emotional Khrushchev differed from his cynical predecessor by his faith of a true believer in the ideals of communism and its ultimate victory. His impulsive spirit of innovation distinguished him from the calculating Stalin, whose reputed realism made him more cautious. In fact, they were both singularly prone to miscalculation. The ultimate fate of Khrushchev's otherwise admirable attempt to "demilitarize" the Cold War, which ushered in the "first détente," was a case in point.

By initiating unilaterally cuts in Soviet conventional forces – the mainstay of Soviet power under Stalin – Khrushchev astonished western observers, predisposed to believe that the reductions were pretended rather than real. They could not find these consistent with his rattling of nuclear weapons. But there was no inconsistency in his mind, as evident from the secret exposé of his strategy he made to top Polish communists in March 1956, when the détente seemed most promising:

> We have to smartly lead this policy and move toward disarmament. But, we should never cross the line, which would endanger the survival of our conquests. We have to do everything to strengthen defense, to strengthen the army. Without these things, nobody will talk to us. They are not hiding the fact that they have the hydrogen bomb, nuclear arms, and jet-propulsion technology. They know that we have all these things, and therefore they have to talk to us, fight with us; but not be afraid..., this is a game, in which nobody will be a winner. If Lenin would arise he would have been pleased to see his cause become so strong, that the capitalistic world admits being unable to win the war against the socialist countries.... We must work...to reduce the troops and increase defense.... It is difficult to agree with marshals on this matter, they're rather hot-tempered.[13]

There was a downside to Khrushchev's trying to demilitarize the Cold War. Unlike Stalin, he was quite ready to imagine a war different from any in the past, or at least pretend that he was. He never ceased to remind his audiences that the next war would be an all-out nuclear one, and drew an optimistic conclusion from it. He went beyond Stalin in his belief that nuclear weapons could not only be held for deterrence but also manipulated – "as a factor in political battles, a method of exerting pressure, threats, and even blackmail," in the words of his son.[14] That belief was fatal to his striving to demilitarize the East–West conflict and would prove his own undoing as well.

The first moment of truth came in November 1956 when Khrushchev prodded the Soviet decision to resort to force in suppressing the Hungarian revolution once it became obvious that a political solution would not work. He made matters worse by choosing to gratuitously threaten London and Paris with nuclear obliteration unless their governments stopped their intervention against Egypt during the concurrent Suez crisis – after they had already decided to do so under American pressure. Although he had been bluffing, he nevertheless convinced his politburo colleagues that it was because of his "showing teeth" that the West relented. This was a perilous precedent, with baneful consequences for Soviet military thinking.[15]

In March 1957, defense minister Marshal Georgii A. Zhukov, the preeminent practitioner of Stalin's military doctrine during the Second World War, expatiated on the implications of the doctrine's revision by explaining to select military audiences what the inevitable use of nuclear weapons in a future war would mean. Releasing the doctrine from the constraints of Stalin's aversion to surprise, Zhukov dwelt on the need to take the enemy by surprise by striking first, which he claimed would allow the Red Army to get all the way to the English Channel in forty-eight hours. He enjoined his listeners that this was "not to be discussed openly," but the Soviet decision about this time to create nuclear support systems for troops on the battlefield suggests that he meant what he was saying

Despite Stalin's demotion as military thinker – he came to be caricatured as planning the Second World War operations on a globe in his office – as late as 1956 Soviet forces preserved their defensive posture. The posture only began to change once the crisis Khruschchev provoked over Berlin defied his hopes for a speedy resolution and started spinning out of control. Only now can the gravity of the crisis be appreciated from documents in Soviet and East European archives showing its importance for the reversal of Soviet strategy.

In April 1959, the Warsaw Pact's supreme commander Marshal Ivan S. Konev supervised its first major command exercise rehearsing the thrust into Western Europe described by Zhukov, on the assumption that it would be initiated in order to preempt an imminent surprise attack by NATO. More to the point, in the same month the Soviet Union began to install, near the East German town of Fürstenberg, intermediate-range nuclear missiles targeted at US strategic air force bases in Great Britain.[17] Although those missiles were capable of reaching London or Paris as well, this time Khrushchev did not boast about them; their deployment only became known once the Cold War was over.

Three months later, however, the Fürstenberg missiles were uninstalled as surreptitiously as they had previously been installed, and shipped away back to the Soviet Union. This was the time Khrushchev was preparing for the Camp David talks with President Dwight D. Eisenhower, from which he expected western concessions leading to the solution of the Berlin question on Soviet terms. From the talks, he gained the impression that such concessions were forthcoming, and on this assumption he went the farthest in preparing, after his return, for radical reductions of Soviet troops and armaments. In December 1959, he memorably harangued the party presidium:

> Should we have such a big army as we have now? This doesn't make sense. Our assumption is that we don't want war and are not preparing for an attack but for defense. If one accepts this assumption, as we do, our army should be capable of defending the country and repelling enemies who might try to attack our Motherland or our allies. We have these powerful armaments, such as rockets. This is what they are for. What country or group of countries in Europe would dare to attack us?[18]

Khrushchev even raised the prospect of moving toward the "territorial system" of substituting a militia for the standing army. He slashed expenditures on civil defense and announced the most substantial reductions thus far of Soviet ground and naval forces, to the growing dismay of his generals and admirals.[19]

This was Khrushchev's finest hour, but it did not last. Even before he decided on the spur of the moment to break up his May 1960 summit meeting with Eisenhower that he had long striven for, he had realized that he had misjudged western readiness for concessions on Berlin. Without backup options, he allowed the crisis to escalate by its own momentum, bringing the Cold War's militarization, which he had initially tried to reverse, to dangerous new heights. This made his strategy more dependent on the Soviet military than he had originally wanted.

From defensive to offensive strategy

Czechoslovakia played a pivotal role in Soviet strategy because of the country's geographical position, made more vulnerable by the absence until 1968 of Soviet troops on its territory. Its army was not held in high regard by either its Soviet supervisors or NATO analysts, but it was an indispensable link of the Warsaw Pact's front line. As late as April 1960, its Soviet supervisors still "unequivocally emphasized" to its leading officers that "in view of the political situation" – a reference to the still promising prospects for a favorable Berlin settlement – the Czechoslovak army would only receive ground-to-air rather than ground-to-ground missiles, meaning defensive rather than offensive weaponry. Six months later, however, an amendment to its long-term procurement program envisaged providing it with a variety of equipment for mainly offensive use, including tactical missiles capable of bearing Soviet nuclear warheads. The change was indicative of the turning point that had been reached in the interval.[20]

It is difficult to pinpoint a precise moment at which the turning point may have been reached. The reorientation of Soviet strategy occurred gradually rather than suddenly by Khrushchev's default rather than his design as he was losing control of the situation. Like Stalin before him, he was again taking a calculated risk when he assumed that his intended conclusion of a separate peace treaty with East Germany, which would have abolished the western powers' right of access to West Berlin, would not trigger their armed response. Before leaving for the June 1961 summit with President John F. Kennedy in Vienna, he tried to reassure his presidium colleagues that he was "95 percent" certain there would be no war. He thus assumed a 5 percent risk of provoking a possibly nuclear war when he tried to intimidate the president by threatening to go ahead with the East German treaty.[21]

Fulminating that, if the United States wanted to go to war over Germany, "let it begin now," Khrushchev sounded like Stalin ten years before, except that Stalin was then deliberately trying to force the Chinese hand in Asia whereas Khrushchev was now unwittingly forcing his own hand in Europe. He brushed away Kennedy's warnings: "All I ever hear from your people . . . is that damned word, miscalculation! You ought to take that word and bury it in cold storage and never use it again! I'm sick of it!" He vowed "to sign the peace treaty with [East] Germany by the end of this year," and if the previously unknown record of Soviet military preparations is any indication, he meant it.[22]

The possibility of miscalculation that Kennedy warned against is what made the six months that followed the most dangerous period of the Cold War in Europe. There was no crisis management center in the Kremlin that we know of. Khrushchev's casual instructions left it largely up to the generals how to prepare for the possible military repercussions of the conclusion of a separate peace with East Germany. Marshal Rodion Ia. Malinovskii, Zhukov's successor as defense minister, ventured the opinion that a preemptive strike by conventional means could knock out NATO's nuclear forces. Consistent with Khrushchev's presumption that the West would shy away from using nuclear weapons for the sake of Berlin, it was the disposition of the Warsaw Pact's conventional forces in Central Europe that was changed. A document written five years later in the Czechoslovak defense ministry thus describes what exactly happened:

> The former strategic concept that gave our armed forces the task to "firmly cover the state border [and] not allow penetration of our territory by enemy forces..." was changed...and the Czechoslovak People's Army was assigned an active task.[23]

The new task was assigned to the Czechoslovak army by a document signed by Grechko and Malinovskii on July 11, which the defense committee of the party central committee in Prague then dutifully endorsed. The army's new manual defined its mission as "securing a line of advance into the depth of enemy territory." The particulars were eventually spelled out in a summary of the army's war plan approved at the highest level in October 1964, which was only discovered in the Prague archives in 1999 – the only such plan of either of the Cold War alliances that has come to light thus far.[24]

The Soviet preparations for a military conflict in Europe likely to be provoked by what one of the planning documents obliquely refers to as "measures in connection with the solution of the German and Berlin questions" were ominous. They were being implemented through the structure of the Warsaw Pact, thus giving the alliance a military substance it had been lacking before. A week after the initial version of the Czechoslovak war plan was approved, the Prague party leadership at Malinovskii's direction ordered secret emergency measures to put the country on war footing by October 1. They included the draining of reservoirs behind the Vltava River dams above Prague in anticipation of their breach by enemy bombing to prevent the inundation of the city.[25]

Even after he gave the green light to start building a barrier on August 13 that would block the crossings to West Berlin, Khrushchev appears to have been undecided about whether he should take the risky next step of signing the separate East German peace treaty. Rather than being the final solution of the Berlin question, the building of the barrier in stages served to test what the western reaction to the conclusion of the treaty might be. The ongoing Soviet military preparations did not stop but continued, with October 1 as the target date for their completion. This was the peak period of danger. On September 8–9, the Warsaw Pact defense ministers, meeting for the first time as a group, approved measures to be taken to achieve the requisite level of readiness for war. For Czechoslovakia, for example, these included the assignment of three battalions to secure airfields and of a special brigade for river-crossing as well as preparations for a swift reception of Soviet nuclear ammunition and for the prepositioning of Soviet forces on the country's territory. At the end of September, Poland mobilized its forces along the East German border.[26]

The huge "Buria" maneuvers, which impressed western observers as being intended mainly for show, actually served as a dry run for what the Soviet high command was preparing to do in case the conclusion of the treaty with East Germany provoked a military conflagration. The opening date of the exercise's scenario, October 1, was the date of the putative signing of the treaty, and the action that would follow was rehearsed on maps by senior Soviet commanders during a meeting with their Eastern European subordinates conducted in deep secrecy at the headquarters of the Soviet forces in Germany at Wünsdorf.[27]

Polish general Tadeusz Pióro, who was at the meeting, later testified that the exercise envisaged the invasion of Western Europe, including Norway, though not the British Isles. The Polish army would take Hamburg – or what would be left of it after a hydrogen bomb has been dropped on the city – and move on to seize Denmark. According to Pióro, the Warsaw Pact forces were supposed to march all the way to the Pyrenees; according to the confidential information provided at the time by East German defense minister Heinz Hoffmann to his country's top military, only as far as Paris. Whatever the finish line – and the insistence by the Soviet director of the war game that Luxembourg was the capital of Belgium showed that its organizers' geography was somewhat shaky – this was by no means an idle game.[28]

In a sense, the Berlin crisis was more serious than even the Cuban missile crisis that followed a year later. The confrontation in the Caribbean would flare up but pass quickly, whereas the one in Central Europe festered on. Even after Khrushchev had abandoned the separate peace treaty project and the emergency measures had been lifted by the end of 1961, the planning for a European war by his generals continued unabated – perhaps in the absence of his decision to the contrary that left the initiative in their hands. This was another setback to Khrushchev's original ambition to demilitarize the Cold War, a setback further compounded by the Cuban adventure and not any less painful for having been self-inflicted.

The adoption by Moscow of an offensive European strategy proved a lasting legacy of the Berlin crisis for a quarter of a century until the strategy was discarded under Gorbachev. In addition, the Soviet–American showdown over Cuba, though not related to Europe in its origins, had important repercussions for the potential European battlefield. General Anatolii I. Gribkov, who had been one of the organizers of the Cuban operation before becoming the Warsaw Pact's chief of staff, later described the conclusion drawn by Soviet strategists from the outcome of the confrontation. The conclusion was that, since neither superpower could use its nuclear weapons against the other globally, they could be used more readily in a "game of nerves" at the "theater level," namely, in Europe, while keeping the respective homelands inviolate. Abundant evidence from Warsaw Pact archives illustrates what the game was about.[29]

The "romantic" times

Khrushchev's abortive attempt to demilitarize the Cold War having gone full circle, he tried belatedly to break out of that vicious circle by curbing the ambitions of the Soviet military. According to recollections of his son Sergei, he told Grechko that "two [nuclear] cannons are enough for you, marshal, and for the Americans." "We don't need an unlimited number" of targets for nuclear missiles, Khrushchev argued, "ten or so [being] sufficient to make even [the] thought of war senseless."[30] Unimpressed by a display of expensive new conventional gadgetry either, he asked rhetorically: "Are we planning to conquer anyone? No! Then why do we need the weapons that we saw today?"[31]

Whatever the exact wording of Khrushchev's pertinent exhortations, he was fighting a loosing battle. The growth of the Soviet military establishment during his last two years in power paralleled the erosion of his authority in the aftermath of the Cuban fiasco. The palace coup that toppled him in October 1964, supported even if not engineered by the military, removed a leader whose desire to reduce his country's bloated defense establishment as not only redundant but also counterproductive presaged the Soviet reasoning that would eventually make the ending of the Cold War possible. In the meantime, however, the successor regime of Leonid I. Brezhnev, an admirer and darling of the military, reversed the trend initiated by Khrushchev, thus giving the generals more opportunity to influence policy and the Cold War a new lease on life. It was a tragic development.[32]

The middle and late 1960s were the heyday of what former Soviet general Valentin V. Larionov retrospectively dubbed the "romantic" period of naive belief in the nuclear arms' capacity to "achieve any political or military objective, even the most extreme ones." The image of Warsaw Pact forces marching through a nuclear pandemonium to victory, as drawn in the 1964 Czechoslovak war plan, was reenacted in countless exercises. "It was like in the fairytale," the irreverent general Pióro remembered from the exercises he used to attend. "At the time of the battle, clouds burst, and the downpour made the enemy troops soaking wet while our own became pleasantly refreshed."[33]

With hundreds of nuclear bombs blasting away, the Poles would roll through West Germany alongside their Soviet allies at breakneck speed, smashing the Dutch and Belgian armies and not stopping until they have reached the English Channel. On their way, they would receive the surrender, to cite but one example, of the city of Hannover where they would install a "progressive" administration including pliable Social Democrats. The Czechoslovak army would have by then reached Lyon in a nine-day sweep, having dropped along the way leaflets urging NATO soldiers to lay down their arms and posted orders to the local populace to welcome its "liberation."[34]

The daily rates of advance anticipated in the successive exercises were actually getting shorter even though Warsaw Pact analysts acknowledged that the enemy's ability to block it was getting better. NATO's own estimate in 1964 was that it could stop the invaders in 4–7 days and push them back in ten. According to US estimates, it would take the enemy at least thirty days after the opening of hostilities to build an invasion force, by which time its offensive thrust would be weakened by a half as a result of NATO interdiction.[35]

In the southern theater of operations, the records of Hungarian army exercises, believed by local experts to be the closest to the actual war plans, show that nuclear incineration was in store for Munich, Verona, and Vicenza, as well as for Vienna, the capital of neutral Austria. The Warsaw Pact's planning documents took the violation of Austrian neutrality for granted – ostensibly first by NATO moving into the country "under the cover of the Austrian armed forces," and subsequently by invading Hungarian and Czechoslovak troops as well. At least one field manual, however, envisaged unprovoked passage of those troops through a "neighboring territory" in order to bypass NATO's nuclear minefields in West Germany.[36]

The Warsaw Pact scenarios assumed that enemy nuclear bombs would be falling on East Europe, but not on the Soviet Union itself – whether because Moscow wanted to keep the allies in dark about how it would cope with such a calamity or because of the presumptuous expectation that the war would be over before the fighting on the ground would reach Soviet territory. This was an improbable expectation, but no less so than another assumption underlying all the exercises. This was the assumption that NATO would foolishly attack despite its inferiority in both manpower and firepower – rated to be in the order of 2:3 – and that it would be so incompetent in concealing its preparations as to allow the Warsaw Pact forces to detect them in time to achieve full combat readiness by the moment of the attack. "Having declared alarm," the outline of a 1965 Czechoslovak war game fantasized, the Warsaw Pact commanders "were able to lead the bulk of their forces away from the impact of the enemy nuclear strike, took advantage of the favorable situation, and turned into offensive operation according to the previously prepared plan."[37]

In real life, to be sure, Czechoslovakia, East Germany, Poland, and Hungary would have had to bear the brunt of the western assault. They were woefully unprepared. According to Pióro, Polish "army chemists, posing as nuclear experts with but preschool knowledge of the subject," calculated what would happen in meaningless but reassuring detail in order to show that the expected damage would be tolerable. The official assessments admitted that millions would die or be dying and most industries would be destroyed, but pretended that production would not be seriously impaired. With grim stoicism, the troops would go on fighting and citizens would go about their daily tasks. Rare was the honest admission of what was most likely to happen, such as that by the Hungarian analysts who concluded that the enemy's goal to paralyze the economy, cut off supplies to the army, and demoralize the population would be "largely achieved."[38]

Although similar delusions existed in the West as well, there was a difference. There the "thinking of the unthinkable" was a specialty of "defense intellectuals," illustrative of the perils of militarized thinking of civilians. By contrast, the Soviet planning of the unplannable was in the hands of the generals, who tried to influence and sometimes manipulate their political superiors. Such was notably the case of Admiral Sergei Gorshkov, the father of the Soviet nuclear navy designed to challenge US maritime supremacy. The dictum that war is too important a business to be left to generals was particularly pertinent in the Soviet case.

In the absence of the records of the Soviet general staff, where the war plans were made, we at least have a unique account of the thinking behind them. This is General Petr I. Ivashutin's remarkable secret study of the conduct of war in nuclear conditions, prepared in 1964 at the request of Marshal Matvei V. Zakharov, the head of the General Staff Academy, for the education of the nation's military elite that was being trained there. As the chief of military intelligence, Ivashutin was by virtue of his position the Soviet Union's best informed person about the conditions under which war might be fought, thus giving a special air of authority to the ideas his study was intended to instill into the minds of that elite.[39]

Ivashutin's argumentation is startling in its cynicism. He describes war as a welcome opportunity rather than a deplorable necessity. He contends that, thanks to the availability of nuclear weapons, "complete annihilation of the imperialist coalition within a short time" is no longer "pure adventurism" but "an entirely realistic task." There will always be "enough time to launch the required massive number of combat-ready missiles before the first detonations of enemy nuclear missiles on the territory of the socialist countries" would take place, he assures Soviet strategists. Even though a few of the missiles might get through, most of them supposedly would not, since the Soviet Union had – in his view if not in reality – solved the problem of how to destroy ballistic missiles in flight. In any case, whatever the damage either side would suffer, the "imperialistic camp is more sensitive to strikes against [nonmilitary] targets than is the socialist community."[40]

Self-deception was integral to Soviet planning. All Warsaw Pact scenarios presumed a war started by NATO although Soviet intelligence was well aware that its exercises practiced defense. Even for internal purposes, disingenuous arguments were used to circumvent the contradiction. In his highly classified study, Ivashutin dismissed the enemy's defensive posture as nothing but a "not very clever propaganda trick. By no means are NATO forces preparing for defense," he wanted his elite audience to believe. In a convoluted fashion, Konev reasoned that since NATO was training on the wrong assumption that the Warsaw Pact was planning an attack, the Warsaw Pact must train on the right assumption that NATO was planning it. Or, as Ivashutin put it in Marxist terms, whatever defensive plans the West might have, "objectively" they did not matter, since a capitalist alliance was aggressive by its nature regardless of any "subjective" disposition of those who directed it.[41]

Such were the operational, rather than merely doctrinal, consequences of the Marxist–Leninist ideology that inspired the Soviet military – the most ideologically committed, as well as the most disciplined, part of the country's establishment.

Because of the interpenetration of the military and party structures in the Soviet system as well as the traditional loyalty of the Russian military to the ruling autocrats, the generals were not predisposed to act on their own. But in the absence of the necessary directives from their political superiors – whose grip on the system was progressively weakening – they would have been guided by the doctrine in deciding what to do. There cannot be a doubt that, regardless of the feasibility of the plans they had drawn, they would have had no qualms about trying to put them into effect. Herein was a clear and present danger.[42]

Making Europe safe for conventional war

The political science paradigm of "action–reaction," which attributes the decisive role to changes in western strategy, is an inadequate explanatory model for the development of Soviet strategic thinking. Not only did Moscow strategists pride themselves at the originality of their own assumptions and the supposedly "scientific" nature of Soviet policy, but they also acted primarily for their own reasons – such as when they were ready for a revision of Stalin's military theory as a result of his death. They had options to choose from. If their choices depended on their estimates of the adversary's intentions, the pattern was that of "anticipatory reaction," in which the accuracy of the estimates was largely determined by ideological preconceptions. This made the Cold War's armed standoff less stable than the "realist" theory would have it.[43]

NATO's transition from the doctrine of "massive retaliation" to that of "flexible response" was its most important strategic innovation in the 1960s. Based on the American concept of "limited war" – a war short of total defeat of the enemy that could be fought without resort to nuclear weapons – the transition occurred gradually, though with a predictable outcome, over a decade prior to 1968, when the new doctrine was enshrined in NATO's document known as MC 14/3. All this time, the Soviet Union had the opportunity to adapt its own doctrine and strategy in an anticipatory fashion.[44]

The crucial change in Soviet strategy that occurred at the time of the Berlin crisis, however, was in response to Khrushchev's mismanagement of the crisis rather than to anything that happened on the western side. Conversely, the US enunciation of the strategy of flexible response in 1961 by the incoming Kennedy administration, which NATO did not endorse until six years later, failed to elicit a change in the Soviet doctrine or military dispositions in Europe. Moscow rejected the theory of limited war, which underlay the new US strategy, as spurious because of its questionable assumption that a war in Europe could be won, or at least terminated satisfactorily, without resort to nuclear weapons. Soviet analysts asked themselves the pertinent question of how NATO could possibly expect to win in a limited war while its conventional forces remained inferior. Their inferiority invited the conclusion that the West counted on a nuclear first strike as its only chance to win. In fact, as may be concluded from the "Buria" records, the Warsaw Pact planners themselves saw such a strike as their only option because they did not believe NATO was so weak as being unable to defend itself against their planned offensive by conventional means alone.[45]

Noting that the theory of flexible response did not preclude the use of nuclear weapons but merely postulated lesser need for them – while NATO's arsenal of tactical nuclear missiles kept growing – Soviet spokesmen insisted publicly that any military conflict in Europe was bound to escalate into an all-out nuclear exchange. This was a more sensible assumption than that which motivated western quest for "controlled escalation." Nevertheless, the winning potential of the Warsaw Pact's numerically superior conventional forces in a European war exerted irresistible attraction on its strategists as rising political inhibitions in the West against any use of nuclear weapons were for anyone to see.

According to British expert Michael MccGwire, the strategy of defeating NATO by conventional means was adopted at the plenary meeting of the Soviet party central committee in December 1966. It entailed the creation of "operational maneuver groups" that would paralyze NATO's command and communication system by seizing its neuralgic points before its political leaders could make up their minds about resorting to nuclear weapons. In the absence of firm evidence that such a momentous decision was entrusted to a body of more than two hundred people, the Soviet striving to make Europe safe for conventional war was more likely the effect of the evolving plans by the military encouraged, or at least not discouraged, by the post-Khrushchev party leadership.[46]

In any case, the resulting change in the Soviet bloc's military posture was incremental rather than sudden and kept the plans for nuclear mayhem intact. In fact, the plans were getting, if anything, more "realistic." New agreements provided for the installation of Soviet nuclear missiles in Poland, Hungary, and Czechoslovakia. A growing number of the Warsaw Pact's command post exercises enacted an offensive into Western Europe in ever greater detail. To better find the way, in 1966 the scale of the maps printed for use on the battlefield was changed from 1:100,000 to 1:50,000.[47]

The plans envisaged greater sacrifices for the Soviet allies than for the Soviet Union itself. Because of their much smaller territorial size, a war turned nuclear would have meant not only their extensive devastation but also possible extinction as nations. The Czechoslovak army would have borne the brunt of NATO's nuclear blow while the Soviet Union was preparing a counterblow. Czechoslovak officers were appalled at finding out that in the first few days their troops' casualty rate would be as high as 60–70 per cent. Even the country's normally subservient government began to question the merit of increased military expenditures demanded by Moscow.[48]

This was the background of the Warsaw Pact's most severe crisis in the latter part of the 1960s, coinciding with NATO's parallel crisis. On both sides, disputes about threat perceptions, doctrines, and deployments revealed fundamental differences between the views of the respective superpowers and their allies about how or whether a war was to be fought in Europe. By testing the alliances' preparedness for such a war, the moment of truth came in 1968 as a result of the events in Czechoslovakia.

Perceptive minds among the Czechoslovak military cautioned against the perils of limited war as well as of deterrence as practiced by the superpowers. In a pep talk to his subordinates, Czechoslovakia's chief of general staff Otakar Rytíř described the theory of limited war as a clever invention of western strategists that "fooled our Soviet comrades" by forcing them into competition in "classical" armaments. That competition, he prophesied presciently, "we cannot win, comrades," since it is something that only "the capitalist system can afford. Because its economy, whether we like it or not, is superior." Czechoslovak reformers were also ahead of their time by condemning nuclear deterrence as possibly helpful to the superpowers in maintaining their special status but detrimental to everyone else. They called for a "European security policy" that would supersede the Cold War's armed standoff.[49]

The Soviet invasion of Czechoslovakia cut short such unorthodox thinking until a different Kremlin leadership would itself embrace it under Gorbachev twenty years later. The invasion became a strategic watershed by exposing the shortcomings of both alliances' planning for a European war. Even as Soviet troops were about to roll into the country, the Moscow high command did not rule out the possibility that NATO might move to stop them, and instructed them to hold fire in case of an encounter – a very different scenario from those that the Warsaw Pact had been practicing. The Western allies, to be sure, had no intention to move into Czechoslovakia and estimated that the Soviet Union would not either, although they knew that it was positioned to do so at a moment's notice. Both sides were caught unprepared. NATO's top officials were absent from their posts and the alliance's communication system did not function properly. Nor did the Soviet army acquit itself with flying colors; although unopposed by the Czechoslovak forces, it ran into bottlenecks and its supply lines became strained in ways that could be fatal in combat conditions. This was the army supposedly capable of reaching the Rhine in a week![50]

The conduct of the opposing alliances in a potentially confrontational situation was thus quite different from the scenarios they had been exercising. NATO initially feared that the advance of Soviet forces closer to its defense lines had tilted the military balance in Europe, but soon concluded that this was not the case. The Soviet troops were kept reassuringly distant from the West German border and the token Eastern European forces, on which Moscow chose not to rely in conducting the invasion, were sent home expeditiously. The installation of Soviet nuclear warheads in Czechoslovakia, to which its government had already agreed before, was an incidental military benefit of an operation undertaken for political reasons, and made no practical difference. Despite all the planning to make war more feasible, the outcome of the Czechoslovak crisis suggested that Europe was not so much safe *for* war as safe *from* war. The dawning of détente in the aftermath of the crisis cast added doubts not only on the feasibility but also on the merit of the military plans.

Imagining war at a time of détente

The implications of détente for the Soviet military posture in Europe were not immediately clear. There was no urgency to change the posture once Moscow in March 1969 achieved its long-standing goal of reorganizing the Warsaw Pact to make it into a more effective military instrument. The institutionalization and consolidation of the alliance made its military leaders more confident of its capabilities as well as more dismissive of NATO's than they had been before. Warsaw Pact assessments in the early 1970s dwelt on the weakness rather than strength of the enemy – its weak flanks in relation to the center, vulnerability of the supply lines, lack of strategic depth, inadequate command and control systems, besides continued budgetary strains and the chronic US–European disagreements.[51]

In December 1969, Grechko told the Warsaw Pact defense ministers that the international situation was "complex." He claimed that it was the Soviet military superiority that had forced Washington to start negotiating about limitations of strategic armaments. The superiority, according to Grechko, was the reason why there was no immediate danger of war. In his view, NATO was too weak to attack unless backed by US strategic missiles, which he admitted was improbable. All the same, he and other high Soviet military warned most vociferously against lowering the guard, not to mention lowering the generous defense budgets from which they were benefiting. They insisted that détente could not be trusted.[52]

Little is known about the specifics of the high-level Soviet debate about the merits and demerits of détente. A bargain was reportedly struck between Brezhnev and Grechko during military maneuvers in Belorussia that followed the December 1969 party plenum, as a result of which the military promised to support arms control in return for increased funding of their programs. Whatever may or may not have been agreed, the Strategic Arms Limitation Talks (SALT) about the reduction of strategic armaments went ahead and so did the programs, while the Warsaw Pact's offensive strategy remained unchanged. Exercises continued enacting a blitzkrieg deep into Western Europe, ostensibly in defense against NATO's hypothetical attack and not excluding a massive use of nuclear weapons.[53]

Not everything remained the same. Big maneuvers with troops, calculated to instill awe, became less and command post exercises with maps more frequent as well as more sophisticated. They began to make allowance for a "period of threat" likely to precede any outbreak of hostilities, thus making preparations for NATO's hypothetical surprise attack less imperative and those for the Warsaw Pact's own surprise attack less topical – no negligible advance beyond the "romantic" period. Still, there was nothing but make believe in the new concept of a "converging strike" (*встречный удар*, *Begegnungsschlag*) which presumed the release of nuclear weapons by both sides at exactly the same time, thus fudging the question of who would fire first.[54]

The concepts of Soviet strategists were not as subtle and recondite as those of their adversaries; in particular, they were "many years behind in the application of the techniques of systems analysis" that informed the American thinking. According to a leading US analyst, Raymond Garthoff, the Soviet thinking was "predicated more on the domination of political judgments than on mechanistic calculations, and...these political judgments are very conservative..... We are probably more sophisticated military technical analysts; despite general ideological distortions, they may well be the better political historians." Better though Soviet leaders may have been in relating military power to politics in theory, however, they were not good enough at translating it into practice.[55]

In November 1969, the Soviet Union began to negotiate with the United States about limitations of strategic armaments – the détente's first tangible accomplishment. The chief Soviet negotiator, Vladimir S. Semenov, surprised his US counterparts by taking a favorable view of Washington's concept of strategic stability based on "mutual assured destruction" – a "mechanistic" calculation that led to the conclusion of the politically sterile antiballistic missile (ABM) treaty. At the same time, Moscow welcomed US acquiescence in the further development of its own offensive missiles, which were not only militarily useless but also politically counterproductive. The same was true about starting, in 1970, the construction of the first Soviet nuclear attack carrier and the SS-20 intermediate-range missile system directed specifically against Western Europe. Betraying poor reading of "political history," such programs could not easily be reconciled with détente, and would in fact contribute substantially to killing it.[56]

Different views about which way the "correlation of forces" was moving separated Brezhnev from the Soviet military. At the April 1971 party congress, the general secretary was upbeat about a forthcoming "restructuring of international relations" that would justify reductions of not only nuclear but also conventional forces, and further elaborated on that theme in public speeches. A month before, Grechko struck a very different note by telling the Warsaw Pact allies that "the international situation had deteriorated," "having been hardly more serious, tense, and turbulent than it is now." In September, Brezhnev confided in visiting West German Chancellor Willy Brandt Soviet readiness to initiate mutually advantageous cuts of troops and armaments in Europe. But the readiness was not translated into action.[57]

Referring to the possibility of reducing the Warsaw Pact's conventional forces, Brezhnev in January 1972 told its Political Consultative Committee (PCC) that "unfortunately the situation is such that we cannot yet do it," adding cryptically that the Soviet party central committee was studying the matter. Four months later, détente blossomed at the Brezhnev–Nixon summit, producing the SALT I treaty and other agreements that mitigated, but also legitimized, the armed competition between the superpowers. Washington and Moscow agreed on the "basic principles" that were supposed to stabilize their relationship, including the coveted US recognition of the Soviet Union's questionable "right to equal security."[58]

In advance of the summit, supreme commander Marshal Ivan I. Iakubovskii at a meeting of the Warsaw Pact's military council had disparaged the "various peace negotiations" that were under way. He told its members that if the question of troop reductions "were to be addressed we would be given the assignment in time by the central committees of our communist parties." Although no such assignment followed the summit, at the council's next meeting five months later Soviet chief of general staff Sergei M. Shtemenko made the surprise announcement that the planned 1973 annual "Shield" exercise and all other exercises rehearsing the offensive into Western Europe had been cancelled. This, however, was the only known change of Soviet military posture that may be attributed to the spirit of détente emanating from the recent US–Soviet agreements.[59]

If further steps in that direction depended on Moscow's overall assessment of the international situation, the indications seemed promising. The progress of the Soviet project for a Conference on Security and Cooperation in Europe (CSCE), in which Brezhnev had deeply invested his prestige, bolstered his optimistic view of the benefits of détente. The project aimed at securing Soviet ascendency in Europe by political rather than military means, particularly by steering the conference and its periodic follow-up sessions in ways that would position Moscow as the main guarantor and arbiter of European security, thus achieving by diplomacy what Khrushchev had failed to achieve by bluster. To obtain US consent to the conference, the Soviet Union agreed to the American demand for parallel negotiations on "mutual and balanced" reductions of conventional forces (MBFR) in Europe. Such reductions would be easier for Moscow to contemplate once its political ascendency appeared irresistible.

Preliminaries for both conferences had already been set on course when Brezhnev hosted Warsaw Pact leaders for their annual working vacation in the Crimea in August 1973. In his *tour d'horizon*, he outlined to them his vision of a world in which the West has been forced to accept the "rules of the game" defined by the Soviet Union. In bringing the vision within reach, Brezhnev explained that "our defense potential of course has not been the least important . . . , and should be further increased." But the rules of the game, as he saw them, required that continued political warfare must not be allowed to foment military confrontation. He confided in his audience his intention to reduce substantially the Soviet bloc's nuclear as well as conventional forces, starting with 5–10 percent cuts in Central Europe.[60]

This was, as far as the available evidence goes, the closest between Khrushchev and Gorbachev that the Kremlin ever came to acting on dismantling the military confrontation in Europe. But it did not actually act on it by the time the Yom Kippur War in the Middle East had intervened two months later and détente subsequently started to crumble for reasons Brezhnev found baffling. Indeed, the reasons were not easy to grasp.

The elusive "military détente"

Brezhnev understood that there was a connection between the overall détente and its missing component, termed in Soviet parlance "military détente." This is what he had called for as early as January 1972 when trying to justify his forthcoming summit with Nixon to the Warsaw Pact allies. Although Moscow's spokesmen never clarified what exactly the concept meant, it implied both sides' diminished reliance on military power in their ongoing political competition. Military détente was not the same as arms control, pursued by the United States on the dubious assumption that the arms race was the cause rather than a symptom of mutual insecurity. While the Soviets found it in their interest to cooperate, they understood better than Americans that the root causes of their insecurity were internal.

Hence they tried to compensate by military strength for their system's increasingly glaring deficiencies in other measurements of power. This was what spelled trouble for détente.

Détente's decline has usually been traced to the October 1973 Yom Kippur War in the Middle East, which prompted a naval confrontation in NATO's Mediterranean backyard. The harassment of the US 6th Fleet by the nuclear-armed Soviet squadron exposed shortcomings of the 1972 agreement on prevention of "accidents at sea." It made a potentially disastrous clash more likely than any time since the Cuban missile crisis. Unlike then, however, this time Moscow emerged politically victorious by being able to demonstrate its ability to interdict vital US supply lines to NATO while establishing its own supply lines to its Arab clients through the airspace of NATO member Turkey. The episode revealed cracks within the Western alliance just as America's defeat in Vietnam was approaching."[61]

The outcome of the Middle Eastern crisis did not immediately wreck détente, but neither did it discourage the Soviets from assuming that flexing their military muscles need not endanger it. Their arms diplomacy in parts of the Third World strategically more important to the West than to them eventually proved fatal to it. Brezhnev nevertheless continued to be committed to détente longer than the US government was, largely because of the satisfaction he received from the fulfillment of his favorite CSCE project, culminating in the conclusion of the 1975 Helsinki "Final Act." This was regarded by Moscow as the European equivalent of the 1972 "basic principles" agreement with the United States, which was supposed to put the Cold War on a new footing by securing the Soviet Union's global ascendancy. Reflecting Moscow's faith in achieving a dominant position in Europe by diplomatic means, the CSCE did not include military components. It did include the discussion and implementation of "confidence-building measures" concerned with the deployment and movements of troops – measures necessary to nurture the elusive military détente.

Moscow's readiness for military détente came to be tested once the "Helsinki process" had confounded Soviet expectations by giving political substance to the Final Act's ostensibly paper provisions on human rights. As soon as political dissidents began to effectively invoke them, the internal foundations of Soviet security were threatened. A heightened sense of insecurity permeated the November 1976 meeting of the Warsaw Pact's political consultative committee, the first after Helsinki, although nothing militarily significant had happened in the meantime. Brezhnev deplored an "intensified ideological struggle concerning the substance and perspectives of the process of international détente," blaming the turn of events on the Western-instigated "stir about the so-called 'humanitarian contacts.' "[62]

The committee responded by calling for military détente, but the proposal to achieve it by issuing a NATO–Warsaw Pact declaration ruling out the first use of nuclear weapons was disingenuous. If adopted, the verbal statement would have made no difference in a dire military emergency but all the difference in the current political situation. It would have nullified the US nuclear guarantee indispensable for the cohesion of NATO but would have had no such disruptive effect on the Warsaw Pact. Not surprisingly, it was ignored, and the vaunted military détente did not occur. Nor was there an indication that the Soviet military had been preparing for it.[63]

At the same PCC meeting, Gribkov read a secret report that outlined the prospects of the alliance in view of the expected Soviet achievement of "strategic nuclear parity" by 1979. This was not the parity most Western experts believed had already been achieved earlier in the decade and many feared was now being threatened by Moscow's ongoing military buildup. From its perspective, the balance was actually tilting in the opposite direction and the parity to be achieved was therefore to be understood as the rectification of an incipient imbalance brought about by NATO's growing challenge to Soviet strategic superiority. This was precisely the opposite reading of what Western critics of détente perceived as a "clear and present danger" of the Kremlin's drive for strategic superiority, which could enable it to dictate its terms to the West, and thus win the Cold War.[64]

Moscow had a special reason to be concerned by the emergence of China, in the Soviet mind even through not in reality, as a military rather than merely ideological threat, evoking the nightmare of a two-front war. "We are weighing our every step," Brezhnev tried to reassure the Polish party chief Edward Gierek, "taking into account our responsibility and the consequences of a possible direct armed confrontation between the USSR and China." China had allied itself with NATO, defense minister Marshal Dmitrii F. Ustinov charged alarmingly in a briefing of top Soviet generals, and was receiving massive technological assistance from West Germany, besides the United States and Japan. He insisted that NATO had never been so dangerous. From intelligence reports, he was in a position to know about its exercises that simulated a war in which China would take the Western side and the Soviet Union would be forced to negotiate after an unsuccessful attempt to invade Western Europe had turned it back without NATO even having to resort to nuclear arms.[65]

The military implications of the West's growing technological edge increasingly preoccupied the Warsaw Pact. At the December 1978 meeting of its defense ministers, none other than General Ivashutin – the one who had exalted his country's supposed nuclear invincibility fourteen years before – painted an alarming picture of NATO approaching the "technological surprise moment," which would allow it to "influence decisively the course and outcome of future operations" because of its "development and deployment of new weapons systems." He meant conventional systems capable of making nuclear weapons redundant. Such a prospect made pointless Brezhnev's assurances that the Soviet Union did not seek nuclear superiority, as he maintained in his 1977 speech in Tula.[66]

In that year, the Soviet Union began to train on Western Europe its SS-20 intermediate-range nuclear missiles of which NATO had no equivalent. According to a retrospective assessment by Poland's general Wojciech Jaruzelski, this was a "desperate attempt to somehow compensate for the West's ever more obvious superiority in advanced technology." At the time, the deployment of the missiles seemed to support the Western belief that a crucial strategic decision had been made in Moscow, but it was rather the absence of any such decision that was disconcerting. No one in the aging and increasingly embattled leadership was likely to take the responsibility for reversing the ongoing programs, which consequently threatened to get out of hand because of the "inertia of past requirements."[67]

The Warsaw Pact's assessments of the adversary in the second half of the 1970s contrasted sharply with the dismissive views during the first half of NATO's capacity to even defend itself, much less successfully attack. The revised estimates conveyed grudging respect and growing alarm. Intelligence analysts scrutinized anxiously the alliance's annual maneuvers in Germany as a possible ruse for a surprise attack, the "nearly even" balance of forces notwithstanding. Now the Warsaw Pact's alert times were getting shorter, while NATO could afford to make its own more leisurely.[68]

Estimates based upon East German spies' all but complete access to NATO's secrets left no doubt that the capabilities of the alliance were getting better and better. In the command post exercises that rehearsed the Warsaw Pact offensive into Western Europe, the expected rates of daily advance and its estimated depth were diminishing; gone were the visions of rolling on to the English Channel in six days or to Lyon in nine. East Germany's Admiral Theodor Hoffmann recalls that in the 1960s he had believed his navy's brand new ships were better than NATO's but a decade later no longer considered them to be a match even to the Danish navy, equipped in the meantime with state-of-the-art Western technology.[69]

Gribkov relates that once most Western European targets had been covered with Soviet nuclear-tipped missiles, "the question had come up: what to do next?" One answer was creating special forces and giving them the best technology the country could produce, thus trying to cope with NATO's innovative forward strategy, the Follow-on Forces Attack (FOFA), by launching preemptive commando raids against its nerve centers deep in Western Europe. Iakubovskii's successor as the Warsaw Pact's supreme commander, Viktor G. Kulikov, introduced organizational improvements while increasing the alliance's combat and mobilization readiness.[70]

Kulikov's tried to finalize the project, stalled since 1973, that would supplement the statute on the Warsaw Pact's command in peacetime with one for use in wartime. This would give its Soviet supreme commander wide discretionary powers to deploy Eastern European armies as he would see fit – the reason why some of the allies had been procrastinating. The Poles introduced as many as 60 amendments. The eventual adoption of the statute in March 1980 showed the alliance's weakness rather than strength. Not only did Romania refuse to sign, but also the division of responsibility between the supreme commander and the chief of the Soviet general staff, who happened not to be on the best of terms, remained unclear.[71]

By the late 1970s, serious doubts were cast on the viability of Moscow's offensive strategy. NATO, having weathered France's withdrawal from its integrated command and perhaps even gained from the loss, found a coherent and sensible new strategy in FOFA, which reduced its dependence on nuclear weaponry. It made strides in streamlining its organization and absorbing high technology for conventional warfare – an achievement the static Soviet system could not match. The "revolution in military affairs," trumpeted by the Soviet military as a break-through, heralded the advantages of defense over the offensive strategy they had been committed to. According to former East German colonel Joachim Schunke, who was in charge of monitoring NATO's innovations and interpreting them, the Moscow general staff never drew radical conclusions from the turn in the technological battle, nor could it easily afford to.[72]

As the 1970s drew to a close, a relapse to Stalinist thinking, with its emphasis on morale and ideological commitment rather than professional competence, was an unmistakable sign of decay. The phraseology of "permanently operating fac-tors" and "irresistible laws of history" began to creep again into the military discourse, just as the tide of history was turning against the Soviet Union.[73] Admonitions for ideological hardening were increasingly heard at Warsaw Pact gatherings as the country was drifting into the suicidal war in Afghanistan. Its invasion dealt a coup de grace to superpower détente, not to mention military détente – an outcome all the more ominous since the fatal decision was made by a small clique within the politburo, unopposed by the top generals despite their misgivings. Misperceived threats, misguided doctrines, and misconceived war plans presaged the looming collapse of the Soviet Union's seemingly formidable military machine.

* * *

The Soviet Union was neither a 10 foot giant nor a paper tiger. While predisposed to invest prodigiously in military power and sometimes inclined to manipulate it at risk, the successive Kremlin leaders found translating it into political gain dif-ficult and often counterproductive. Because of their ideological way of thinking, which ran deeper and lasted longer than it appeared, they may have been more sensitive to the interaction between the military and the political balance than their Western, especially American, adversaries usually were. Because of the flaws of the doctrine, however, their perceptions and resulting policies were also more likely to be wrong.

In the autocratic Soviet system, the susceptibility to miscalculation was mag-nified by the close dependence of policymaking on the foibles of the supreme leaders. As their exclusive grip on power progressively weakened, the influence of the military, by nature the ideologically most committed as well as the most disciplined segment of the establishment, increased, though never to the extent of taking the ultimate decisions out of the hands of their political superiors. This was fortunate, given the generals' propensity to draw far-fetched and potentially cata-strophic plans for war.

If the West's containment strategy ultimately succeeded, this was due more to the superiority of its "soft power," which Western, though not Soviet, strategists tended to underestimate, than to the workings of military power. Moreover, nuclear weapons, sometimes credited with keeping the Cold War cold, influenced those workings less than conventional forces did. It was their development that accentuated the West's technological superiority in ways conducive to the Cold War's eventual peaceful resolution.

The Western theory and practice of deterrence, with its pointless nuclear posturing divorced from political realities, appears in retrospect as irrelevant in preventing a major war – which the enemy did not intend to start in the first place – as well as ineffective in preventing lesser abuses of military power. In the longer run, the fallacies of deterrence muddled rather than clarified the conditions under which the use of military power can be both legitimate and effective in a different international environment. The redefinition and expansion of security beyond the military realm has endured as the Cold War's unique legacy.

Acronyms and abbreviations

AAN [Archiwum Akt Nowych]: Modern Records Archives, Warsaw; AÚV KSČ [Archiv Ústředního výboru Komunistické strany Československa]: Archives of the Central Committee of the Communist Party of Czechoslovakia, Prague; BA–MA: Bundesarchiv–Militärarchiv, Freiburg im Br.; *FRUS*: *Foreign Relations of the United States* (Washington, DC: US Government Printing Office); IMS: NATO International Military Staff; LC: Library of Congress, Washington, DC; KC PZPR [Komitet Centralny Polskiej Zjednoczonej Partii Robotniczej]: Central Committee of the Polish United Workers' Party; NARA: National Archives and Records Administration, College Park, MD; NATO-A: NATO Archives, Brussels; NSA: National Security Archive at the George Washington University, Washington, DC; OSA: Open Society Archives at Central European University, Budapest; RGANI [Российский государственный архив новейшей истории]: Russian State Archives of Contemporary History, Moscow; VÚA [Vojenský ústřední archiv]: Central Military Archives, Prague; ZPA: Zentrales Parteiarchiv [der Sozialistischen Einheitspartei Deutschlands]

Many of the archival documents cited below are available in facsimile on the PHP Web site, www.isn.ethz.ch/php, as indicated.

Notes

1 Series SG 161, IMS, NATO-A. John Duffield, "The Soviet Military Threat to Western Europe: US Estimates in the 1950s and 1960s," *Journal of Strategic Studies* 15 (1992): 208–27. Philip A. Karber and Jerald A. Combs, "The United States, NATO, and the Soviet Threat to Western Europe: Military Estimates and Policy Options, 1945–1963," *Diplomatic History* 22, no. 3 (1998): 399–429. Matthew Evangelista, "Commentary: The 'Soviet Threat': Intentions, Capabilities, and Context," *Diplomatic History* 22, no. 3 (1998): pp. 439–49. Ernest May, John Steinbrunner, and Thomas Wolfe, *History of the Strategic Arms Competition, 1945–1972*, ed. Alfred Goldberg (Washington, DC: Office of the Secretary of Defense, 1981), p. 81, NSA. For e representative selection of US estimates, see *CIA's Analysis of the Soviet Union, 1947–1991: A Documentary*

Collection (ed.), Gerald K. Haines and Robert Leggett (Washington, DC: Center for the Study of Intelligence, 2001), especially pp. 227–310.

2 Matthew A. Evangelista, "Stalin's Postwar Army Re-appraised," *International Security* 7, no. 3 (1982–83): 110–38. Although semi-motorized and more involved in nonmilitary duties than Western armies, the Soviet army could still have been capable of an offensive thrust, as it had proved to be in the Second World War: Gilberto Villahermosa, "Stalin's Postwar Army Reappraised: Déjà Vu All Over Again," *Soviet Observer* [Harriman Institute] 2, no. 1 (1990): 1–5. "Оперативный план действий Группы советских оккупационных войск в Германии" [Operational Plan of the Group of Soviet Occupation Forces in Germany], November 5, 1946, *Voennoistoricheskii zhurnal*, no. 2 (1989): 26–31. "Приказ Главнокомандующего Группой советских оккупационных войск в Германии" [Order of the Supreme Commander of the Group of Soviet Occupation Forces in Germany], January 19, 1946, *Voennoistoricheskii zhurnal*, no. 8 (1989): 21–4.

3 Memorandum by thirty members of the academic staff of the Military Political Academy and Military Technical Academy for the Czechoslovak communist party central committee, June 4, 1968, Vojtech Mastny, " 'We Are in a Bind': Polish and Czechoslovak Attempts at Reforming the Warsaw Pact, 1956–1969," *Cold War International History Project Bulletin* 11 (1998): 230–50, at p. 245. "Plan operacyjny rozwinięcia 1 i 2 Armii Wojska Polskiego na wypad działań wojennych w 1951 r." [Operational Plan for the Deployment of the 1st and 2nd Polish Armies in the Event of Hostilities in 1951], microfilm (o) 96/6398, reel W-15, LC, http://www.isn.ethz.ch/php/documents/collection_1/docs/warplan2-I.pdf. On the Czechoslovak war plans, see the contribution by Petr Luňák in this volume.

4 "The Soviet Union and the Atlantic Pact," September 8, 1952, in George F. Kennan, *Memoirs, 1950–1963* (London: Hutchinson, 1973), pp. 327–51, at p. 336.

5 The American war plans from the Stalin era are published in Steven T. Ross, *American War Plans, 1945–1950* (New York: Garland, 1988). The evaluation of Stalin's doctrine is from the classified communist history of the Polish army, "Kształtowanie się doktryny wojennej Polski" [The Shaping of Poland's Military Doctrine], in *Ludowe Wojsko Polskie 1945–1955, "Dzieło I"* [The Polish People's Army, 1945–1955: Part One] (Warsaw, 1986), 199–313, at p. 228, microfilm (o) 96/6398, reel W-80, LC.

6 Kathryn Weathersby, "To Attack or Not to Attack? Stalin, Kim Il Sung, and the Prelude to War," *Cold War International History Project Bulletin* 5 (1995): 1–9, and Kathryn Weathersby, " 'Should We Fear This?' Stalin and the Danger of War With America," Working Paper no. 39, *Cold War International History Project* (Washington, DC: Woodrow Wilson International Center for Scholars, 2002), p. 18.

7 Notes by Emil Bodnăraş on meeting with Stalin, January 9–12, 1951, C. Cristescu, "Ianuarie 1951: Stalin decide înarmarea Românei" [January 1951: Stalin Decides to Arm Romania], *Magazin Istoric* [Bucharest], no. 10 (1995): 15–23.

8 Conversation between Stalin and Zhou Enlai, August 20, 1952, *Cold War International History Project Bulletin* 6–7 (1995–96): 9–14, at p. 13. Translation edited.

9 Presentation by Vladimir Naumov at the conference "Stalin and the Cold War," Yale University, September 23–26, 1999. Sergei Khrushchev, "The Cold War through the Looking Glass," *American Heritage*, October 1999: 34–50, at p. 36. "The Soviet Bloc Strength and Capabilities, 1953–56," SG 161/3 (Revised Final), approved by the Military Representatives Committee on January 27, 1953, p. 117, IMS, NATO-A.

10 Georgi Arbatov, *The System: An Insider's Life in Soviet Politics* (New York: Random House, 1992), pp. 109–10. Raymond L. Garthoff, *The Soviet Image of Future War* (Washington, DC: Public Affairs Press, 1959), pp. 64–73, presents a more sympathetic account of the Soviet doctrinal debate than does Herbert Dinerstein, *War and the Soviet Union: Nuclear Weapons and the Revolution in Soviet Military and Political Thinking* (New York: Praeger, 1962), pp. 167–214.

11 "Report by the Military Council to the North Atlantic Council on 'The Improvement of the Posture of SACEUR's Air Force Units to Ensure Detention of an Adequate Operational Capability under Enemy Atomic Attack'," MC 60, February 9, 1956, IMS, NATO-A.

12 Raymond L. Garthoff, *Deterrence and the Revolution in Soviet Military Doctrine* (Washington, DC: Brookings, 1990), pp. 42–3.

13 Excerpt from speech by Khrushchev at closed session of the Polish party central committee, March 20, 1956, *Cold War International History Project Bulletin* 10 (1998): 31.

14 Sergei N. Khrushchev, *Nikita Khrushchev and the Creation of a Superpower* (University Park: Penn State Press, 2000), p. 670

15 Record of the party central committee plenum, June 24, 1957, "Последняя 'антипартийная"группа: Стенографический отчет июньского (1957 г.) пленума ЦК КПСС" [The Last "Antiparty" Group: Stenographic Record of the June 1957 CPSU CC Plenum], *Istoricheskii Arkhiv*, no. 3 (1993): 5–45, at p. 33.

16 Central Intelligence Agency reports on Zhukov's meetings with senior Soviet officers in East Germany on March 12–16, 1957, March 29, 1957, Svend Aage Christensen and Frede Jensen, "Superpower under Pressure: The Secret Speech of Minister of Defence Marshal Zhukov in East Berlin, March 1957," http://www.isn.ethz.ch/php/collections/coll_19.htm. Cf. David E. Murphy, Sergei A. Kondrashev, and George Bailey, *Battleground Berlin: CIA vs. KGB in the Cold War* (New Haven, CT: Yale University Press, 1997), pp. 270–72. "Из выступления маршала Жукова на научной конференции, май 1957 г." [From Marshal Zhukov's Statement at the Scientific Conference in May 1957], May 1957, MNO/SM 1957, box 16, sig. 4/1–1, VÚA. Matthew Evangelista, *Innovation and the Arms Race: How the United States and the Soviet Union Develop New Military Technologies* (Ithaca, NY: Cornell University Press, 1988), p. 266.

17 "Rozbor operačního velitelského cvičení" [Analysis of the Operational Command Exercise], April 7, 1959, MNO/GŠ-OS, 1959, kar. 300, sig. 17/3–8, čj. 009083, VÚA. Matthias Uhl and Vladimir I. Ivkin, " 'Operation Atom': The Soviet Union's Stationing of Nuclear Missiles in the German Democratic Republic, 1959," *Cold War International History Project Bulletin* 12–13 (2001): 299–307, at pp. 302–3.

18 Memorandum by Khrushchev to party presidium, December 8, 1959, *Cold War International History Project Bulletin* 8–9 (1996–97): 418–20, at p. 418. Translation edited from the original, 2/1/416/3–11, RGANI.

19 Report for the Military Defense Commission of the Czechoslovak party central committee, December 5, 1960, 14/3 VKO, VÚA. Raymond L. Garthoff, "On Estimating and Imputing Intentions," *International Security* 2, no. 3 (winter 1978–79): 22–32.

20 "Průběh informace náčelníka generálního štábu o důsledcích konsultace" [Information by the Chief of General Staff on the Results of the Consultation], October 15, 1960, GŠ-OS, 1960, 0039030/22, VÚA. "Zpráva o návrhu změn v plánu výstavby ČSLA na léta 1961–1965" [Report on the Proposed Changes in the Development Plan of the Czechoslovak People's Army for 1961–1965], November 19, 1960, VS, OS (OL), krab. 7, čj. 39030/19, VÚA.

21 Minutes of Soviet party presidium meeting, May 26, 1961, *Президиум ЦК КПСС, 1954–1964* [Presidium of the CC CPSU, 1954–1964], vol. 1: *Черновые протокольные записи заседаний, Стенограммы* [Draft Minutes and Stenographic Records of Meetings], ed. Aleksandr A. Fursenko (Moscow: Rosspen, 2004), pp. 500–7, at p. 503.

22 Memorandum of Kennedy–Khrushchev conversation, June 4, 1961, *FRUS*, 1961–1963, vol. 5, p. 223. Kennedy's account of the conversation to Kenneth O'Donnell, cited in William Taubman, *Khrushchev: The Man and His Era* (New York: Norton, 2003), p. 497. Soviet record of the Khrushchev–Kennedy meeting, June 4, 1961, ZK SED, J IV/202–331 Bd 2, p. 27, SAPMO.

23 "Rede des Verteidigungsministers der UdSSR, Marschall Rodion Jakovlevič Malinovskij, zur Auswertung einer Kommandostabsübung von GSSD und NVA," May 1961, DVW-1/5203, Bl. 7, BA–MA. "Materiály k otázce Spojeného velení" [Materials Concerning the Issue of Unified Command], undated [early 1966], GŠ-OS 0039042/1, VÚA.

24 Resolution by Military Defense Committee, September 2, 1961, 18/4, VKO, VÚA. "Organizační principy ČSLA" [Organizational Principles of the Czechoslovak People's Army], November 22, 1962, GŠ-OS, 1962, 0010081, VÚA. "План использования чехословацкой народной армии на военное время" [Plan for the Deployment of the Czechoslovak People's Army in Wartime], October 14, 1964, discussed by Petr Luňák elsewhere in this volume, is reproduced in "Taking Lyon on the Ninth Day? The 1964 Warsaw Pact Plan for Nuclear War in Europe and Related Documents," http://www.isn.ethz.ch/php/collections/coll_1.htm, where also a discussion about its authenticity and significance may be found. Its English translation is reprinted in *Cold War International History Project Bulletin* 12–13 (2001): 292–7.

25 Czechoslovak politburo resolutions, July 18 and 25, 1961, VKO 1961, 18/4 and inv. č. 61, čj. 8460, box 16, VÚA . Karel Sieber, "Vltavská kaskáda, hospodářská krize Novotného režimu a hrozba jaderné války po druhé berlínské krizi: K širším souvislostem československého obranného plánování na začátku šedesátých let" [The Vltava Cascade, the Economic Crisis of the Novotný Regime, and the Threat of Nuclear War during the Second Berlin Crisis: Implications of the Czechoslovak Defense Planning in the Early 1960s], *Pražský web pro studenou válku* [The Prague Cold War Web], http://www.coldwar.cz/obrana.htm.

26 "Schválení opatření nařízených Hlavním velitelem Spojených ozbrojených sil států-účastníků Varšavské smlouvy dne 8.9.1961 ke zvýšení bojové pohotovosti" [Authorization of the Measures of Increased Combat Readiness Ordered on September 8, 1961, by the Supreme Commander of the Unified Armed Forces of the Member States of the Warsaw Treaty] September 14, 1961, 17/4, VKO, VÚA. Paweł Piotrowski, "Cel: Zachód" [Target West], *Polska Zbrojna*, May 2000: 39. Further documentation in Aleksandr A. Fursenko, "Как была построена берлинская стена" [How the Berlin Wall Was Built], *Istoricheskie zapiski*, no. 4 (2001): 73–90, and *Ulbricht, Chruschtschow und die Mauer: Eine Dokumentation*, ed. Matthias Uhl and Armin Wagner (Munich: Oldenbourg, 2003).

27 For details on the "Buria" exercise, see Matthias Uhl's contribution to this volume.

28 Remarks by Hoffmann, undated [October–November 1961], VA-01, 6103, BA–MA. Tadeusz Pióro, *Armja ze skazą: W Wojsku Polskim 1945–1968 (wspomnienia i refleksje)* [The Defective Army: In the Polish Army, 1945–1968 (Memories and Reflections)] (Warsaw: Czytelnik, 1994), pp. 341–8.

29 Statement by Gribkov, March 25, 1995, *Global Competition and the Deterioration of U.S.–Soviet Relations, 1977–80: The Carter–Brezhnev Project: A Conference of U.S. and Russian Policymakers and Scholars Held at the Harbor Beach Resort, Fort Lauderdale, Florida, 23–26 March 1995* (Providence: Watson Institute for International Studies, Brown University, 1995), p. 186.

30 Sergei Khrushchev, *Nikita Khrushchev and the Creation of a Superpower*, 672–6.

31 Ibid., p. 719.

32 Werner Hahn, "Who Ousted Nikita Sergeyevitch?" *Problems of Communism* 40 (May–June 1991): 109–15. William P. Tompson, "The Fall of Nikita Khrushchev," *Soviet Studies* 43, no. 6 (1991): 1101–21.

33 Larionov quoted in William E. Odom, *The Collapse of the Soviet Military* (New Haven, CT: Yale University Press, 1998), p. 70. Pióro, *Armja ze skazą*, p. 191.

34 General Florian Siwicki to the Commander of the 5th Army, October 28, 1971, 152448/74/42, collection Political Administration of the Military District of Silesia, Archives of the Ground Forces, Wrocław, and other documents from Polish exercises on http://www.isn.ethz.ch/php/collections/coll_12.htm, with English translation of

42 *Vojtech Mastny*

Paweł Piotrowski, "Desant na Danię" [The Landing Operation in Denmark], *Wprost* [Warsaw], June 25, 2002. The texts of the orders and appeals in MNO 1964, kr. 101, 17/1/1,3, VÚA.

35 "Tankové a automobilní technické zabezpečení boje a operace bez použití jaderných zbraní," [The Technical Support of Combat by Means of Tanks and Automotive Vehicles in Operations without the Use of Nuclear Weapons], 1964, sg. 17/1–2, MNO-TAS, VÚA. "Auswertung der Ergebnisse der NATO-Kommandostabsübung 'Fallex 64'," VA-01/14850, BA-MA. John Duffield, "The Soviet Military Threat to Western Europe: US Estimates in the 1950s and 1960s," *Journal of Strategic Studies* 15 (1992): 208–27, at pp. 210–12.

36 "Documents Relating to the Organization and Preparation of the Front-Army War Game of 21–26 June 1965," Records of the Hungarian People's Army Headquarters First Group Directorate, 1969, 68/014/185, War History Archive, Budapest, also at http://www.isn.ethz.ch/php/collections/coll_4_english_content.htm, with commentary by Imre Okváth, "European Cities Targeted for Nuclear Destruction: Hungarian Documents on the Soviet Bloc War Plans, 1956–71." Róbert Széles, "Die strategischen Überlegungen des Warschauer Paktes für Mitteleuropa in den 70-er Jahren und die Rolle der Neutralen," in *Österreichs Neutralität und die Operationsplanungen des Warschauer Paktes* (Vienna: Landesverteidigungsakademie/ Militärwissenschaftliches Büro, 1999), pp. 35–52. "Jaderné miny americké armády, jejich zjišťování a zneškodňování" [US Army Nuclear Mines: Their Detection and Incapacitation], February 15, 1967, p. 52, Vševojsk-2–5, VÚA.

37 "Úvodní přednáška řídícího cvičení VESNA" [Introductory Lecture by the Director of the "Vesna" Exercise], September 6, 1965, MNO-1967, HSPV, sg. 4/4–21/106, VÚA. "Výsledky schválení zámyslu VESNA" [The Results of the Intended Aim of the "Vesna" Exercise], MNO. GŠ-OS 1967, HSPV; sg. 4/4–21/29, čj. 0017600/29/19, VÚA.

38 Pióro, *Armja ze skazą*, p. 191. "Doświadczenia i wnioski z ćwiczenia 'Mazowsze'," [Experiences and Lessons from the "Mazowsze" Exercise], 18–22 April 1963, KC PZPR 5008, AAN, parts translated at http://www.gwu.edu/~nsarchiv/NSAEBB/ NSAEBB14/doc18a.htm. "Předběžné vyhodnocení atomových úderů...." [Preliminary Evaluation of the Effects of Atomic Strikes....], MNO 1963, GŠ/VD, sg. 5/2/6, VÚA. Report on the consequences of nuclear strikes against Hungary, June 6, 1963, Records of the Hungarian People's Army Headquarters First Group Directorate, 1964, box 9 unit 3, War History Archive, Budapest, also at http://www.isn.ethz.ch/php/documents/ collection_4/docs/11.pdf.

39 "Материал по развитии военного искусства в условиях ведения ракетно-ядерной войны по современных представлениях" [Material Concerning Contemporary Views of the Application of Military Art in the Conduct of Nuclear War], Ivashutin to Zakharov, August 28, 1964, pp. 326–444, copy of excerpts from the original at the Central Archives of the Ministry of Defense of Russia, in the Volkogonov collection, container no. 30, Manuscript Division, LC also at http://www.isn.ethz.ch/php/documents/collection_1/docs/ivashutin-I.pdf.

40 Quotes from pp. 338–40, 345, 358, 370, 373–4 of the Ivashutin study.

41 Ibid., p. 396. Speech by Konev at Czechoslovak command exercise, April 7, 1959, VS, OS (OL), krab. 1, čj. 12426, VÚA.

42 For a critique of models of Soviet "civil–military relations," see Odom, *The Collapse of the Soviet* Military, pp. 218–22, 456–7.

43 Kimberly Marten Zisk, *Engaging the Enemy: Organization Theory and Soviet Military Innovation, 1955–1991* (Princeton, NJ: Princeton University Press, 1993), pp. 56, 68, 78–84. Barry Buzan, *An Introduction to Strategic Studies: Military Technology and International Relations* (New York: St Martin's Press, 1987), p. 87.

44 MC 14/3, January 16, 1968, *NATO Strategy Documents, 1949–1969*, ed. Gregory W. Pedlow (Brussels: NATO, 1997), pp. 371–99.

45 "Závěry z operačně-taktické přípravy ozbrojených sil Severoatlantického paktu na středoevropském válčišti v roce 1964" [Conclusions from the Operational and Tactical Preparations of the Armed Forces of the North Atlantic Pact in 1964], 1965, MNO-GŠ/05, 1965, sg. 31/1–8, VÚA. The conclusion from "Buria" records is drawn by Matthias Uhl elsewhere in this volume.

46 Michael MccGwire, *Military Objectives in Soviet Foreign Policy* (Washington, DC: Brookings, 1987), pp. 381–405.

47 Interviews with generals Siwicki and Jaruzelski, "Warsaw Pact Generals in Polish Uniforms: Oral History Interviews," http://www.isn.ethz.ch/php/documents/ collection_9/texts/Nuclear_Delusions.htm. Rytíř to Dubček, May 1968, VS, OS-OL, čj. 00671/20, VÚA. Mark Kramer, "The 'Lessons' of the Cuban Missile Crisis for Warsaw Pact Nuclear Operations," *Cold War International History Project Bulletin* 5 (1995): 59, 110–15, 160.

48 Interviews cited in A. Ross Johnson, Robert W. Dean, and Alexander Alexiev, *East European Military Establishments: The Warsaw Pact Northern Tier* (Santa Monica: RAND, 1980), p. 137. Jaromír Navrátil, "K otázce výstavby Československé armády před rokem 1968" [The Building of the Czechoslovak Army before 1968], *Historie a vojenství* [Prague], no. 5 (1992): 101–25.

49 Remarks by Rytíř, March 13, 1968, *Cold War International History Project Bulletin* 11 (1998): 243–4. Retranslated from the original text in *Vojenské otázky Československé reformy, 1967–1970: Vojenská varianta řešení čs. krize (1967–1968)* [Military Problems of the Czechoslovak Reform, 1967–1970: The Military Option in the Solution of the Czechoslovak Crisis], ed. Antonín Benčík, Jaromír Navrátil, and Jan Paulík (Brno: Doplněk, 1996), p. 79. Memorandum by the staff of the military academies, June 4, 1968, *Cold War International History Project Bulletin* 11 (1998): 244–9, at p. 248.

50 S.M. Zolotov, "Шли на помощь друзьям" [They Went to Help Friends], *Voennoistoricheskii zhurnal* 1994, no. 4: 14–23, at p. 18. Viktor Suvorov, *Освободитель* [The Liberator] (St Petersburg: Konets veka, 1993), pp. 175–6. Leo Heiman, "Soviet Invasion Weakness," *Military Review*, August 1969: 38–45. Vojtech Mastny, "Was 1968 a Strategic Watershed in the Cold War?" *Diplomatic History* 29, no. 1 (2005): 149–77.

51 Evaluations of the "Wintex-71" and "Wintex-73" exercises in reports, respectively, by Kessler and Streletz to National Defense Council, February 17, 1971 and May 17, 1973, DVW1/39497 and DVW1/39500, BA–MA.

52 Speech by Grechko, December 22, 1962, AZN 32855, 18–28, BA–MA, also in http://www.isn.ethz.ch/php/documents/collection_3/CMD_docs/01-043–I.pdf.

53 Edward L. Warner III, *The Military in Contemporary Soviet Politics* (Westport, CT: Praeger, 1977), p. 53. Andrei M. Aleksandrov-Agentov, *От Коллонтай до Горбачева: Воспоминания дипломата, советника А.А. Громыко* [From Kollontai to Gorbachev: Memoirs of a Diplomat Who Assisted Gromyko] (Moscow: Mezhdunarodnye otnosheniia, 1994), pp. 210–11.

54 "Материалы разбора оперативно-стратегического коммандно-штабного учения 'Запад-77'" [Materials from the Analysis of the Strategic and Operational Staff Command Exercise "Zapad-77"], VS, OS-OL, 1977, krab., 29–999–155, čj. 22013/23, pp. 30–32, VÚA. Beatrice Heuser, "Warsaw Pact Military Doctrines in the 1970s and 1980s: Findings in the East German Archives," *Comparative Strategy* 12, No. 4 (1993): 437–57, at pp. 439–40.

55 "How the Soviets View the Strategic Balance," May 1969, NSSM-24, RG-273, NARA. Memorandum by Raymond L. Garthoff, end 1969, quoted in his *A Journey through the Cold War: A Memoir of Containment and Coexistence* (Washington, DC: Brookings Institution Press, 2001), pp. 265–6.

56 Kissinger to Nixon, 22 January 1970, NSCF, box 840, ABM System Vol. III, also at http://www.gwu.edu/~nsarchiv/NSAEBB/NSAEBB60/abm02.pdf. Aleksandr G.

Savelyev and Nikolay N. Detinov, *The Big Five: Arms Control Decision-Making in the Soviet Union* (Westport, CT: Praeger, 1995), pp. 71–125. Cf. Odom, *The Collapse of the Soviet Military*, pp. 71, 85, 436.

57 Raymond L. Garthoff, *Détente and Confrontation: American-Soviet Relations from Nixon to Reagan* (Washington, DC: Brookings Institution, 1994), pp. 49, 133. Report on meeting of Warsaw Pact Committee of Ministers of Defense, March 2–3, 1971, DVW 1/71027, BA–MA, also in http://www.isn.ethz.ch/php/documents/ collection_3/CMD_docs/03-104-I.pdf. Egon Bahr, *Zu meiner Zeit* (Berlin: Blessing, 1996), pp. 498–503.

58 Speech by Brezhnev, January 26, 1972, ZPA, DY/30/526, SAPMO. Coit D. Blacker, "The Kremlin and Détente: Soviet Conceptions, Hopes and Expectations," in *Managing U.S.–Soviet Rivalry: Problems of Crisis Prevention*, ed. Alexander L. George (Boulder, CO: Westview Press, 1983), pp. 119–37. Alexander L. George, "The Basic Principles Agreement of 1972: Origins and Expectations," in *Managing U.S.–Soviet Rivalry*, pp. 107–17.

59 Statement by Iakubovskii at meeting of Military Council, May 16–17, 1973, Rusov to Štrougal, GŠ-OS 1973, May 24, 1973, 0036034/22, VÚA. Report on 7th meeting of the Warsaw Pact Military Committee in Minsk, October 17–20, 1972, dated October 23, 1972, GŠ-OS 1972, 0036034/11–13, VÚA.

60 Speech by Brezhnev, August 1, 1973, 1-B, 35, 4300. TsDA, also at http://www.isn. ethz.ch/php/documents/collection_16/docs/1_Crimea_1.pdf.

61 Lyle J. Goldstein and Yuri M. Zhukov, "A Tale of Two Fleets: A Russian Perspective on the 1973 Naval Standoff in the Mediterranean," *Naval War College Review* 57, no. 2 (Spring 2004): 27–63.

62 Speech by Brezhnev at meeting of the Political Consultative Committee, November 25–26, 1976, KC PZPR, XIA/588, pp. 49–69, AAN, also at http://www.isn.ethz.ch/ php/documents/collection_3/PCC_docs/1976/1976_8_I.pdf.

63 Draft treaty on no-first use of nuclear weapons, November 26, 1976, Radio Free Europe/Radio Liberty archives, Warsaw Treaty, 80-1-109, OSA, also at http:// www.isn.ethz.ch/php/documents/collection_3/PCC_docs/1976/1976_14_I.pdf.

64 Summary of report by Iakubovskii, presented by Gribkov, November 25, 1976, VS, OS (OL) krab. 8, čj. 36033/4, VÚA, also at http://www.isn.ethz.ch/php/documents/ collection_3/PCC_docs/1976/1976_4.pdf. Statement by Gribkov, March 25, 1995, *Global Competition*, p. 182–3.

65 Record of Brezhnev–Gierek meeting, 12–13 March 1979, KC PZPR, XIB/130, AAN. Information by General Shadrov on meetings held in November 1978 on May 28–June 2, 1979, VA-01/40406, 294–317, BA–MA. "Bericht über die Hauptergebnisse der strate-gischen NATO-Kommandostabsübung 'Wintex 77'," May 20, 1977, DVW1/ 39510, BA–MA.

66 "Stand und Entwicklungsperspektiven der NATO-Streitkräfte," December 4–7, 1978, pp. 60–83, p. 82. AZN 32865, BA–MA, also at http://www.isn.ethz.ch/php/ documents/collection_3/CMD_docs/11-060-I.pdf. Tula speech in *Pravda*, January 19, 1977.

67 Wojciech Jaruzelski, *Mein Leben für Polen: Erinnerungen* (Munich: Piper, 1993), p. 201. MccGwire, *Military Objectives in Soviet Foreign Policy*, p. 510.

68 "Wichtigste Entwicklungsrichtungen und Zustand der NATO-Streitkräfte in der Westlichen und Südwestlichen Richtung," December 10–11, 1976, AZN 32863, BA-MA, also at http://www.isn.ethz.ch/php/documents/collection_3/CMD_docs/09–088-I.pdf. "Материалы разбора оперативно-стратегического командно-штабного учения 'Запад-77'" [Materials from the Analysis of the Strategic and Operational Staff Command Exercise "Zapad-77"], May 30–June 9, 1977, VS, OS-OL, 1977, krab. 29–999–155, čj. 22013/23, pp. 9–10, VÚA. "Direktive zur operativen und Gefechtsausbildung der Vereinten Streitkräfte der Teilnehmerstaaten des Warschauer

Vertrages für 1976," October 28, 1975, VA-01/35940, BA–MA. Drew Middleton, "Haig Lifts Estimate of NATO Alert Time," *New York Times*, September 15, 1977. The time was extended from 8 to 15 days.

69 Interview with Admiral Theodor Hoffmann, Berlin, October 24, 2002.

70 Statement by Gribkov, March 25, 1995, *Global Competition*, pp. 183. Kulikov to Hoffmann, September 5, 1977, VA-01/40414, BA–MA.

71 "Grundsätze über die Vereinten Streitkräfte der Teilnehmerstaaten des Warschauer Vertrages und ihre Führungsorgane (für den Krieg)," March 18, 1980, pp. 85–120, AZN 32854, BA–MA, also at http://www.isn.ethz.ch/php/documents/collection_9/docs/Statute_180580.pdf. Interviews with generals Skalski and Jasiński, in "Warsaw Pact Generals in Polish Uniforms: Oral History Interviews," http://www.isn.ethz.ch/php/documents/collection_9/docs/6Skalski.pdf, pp. 23–34 and http://www.isn.ethz.ch/php/documents/collection_9/docs/3Jasinski.pdf, p. 6. Anatoli Gribkow, *Der Warschauer Pakt: Geschichte und Hintergründe des östlichen Militärbündnisses* (Berlin: Edition Q, 1995), pp. 46–7.

72 Joachim Schunke, "Zur Bedrohungsanalyse der militärischen Führung der DDR," in *Landesverteidigung und/oder Militarisierung der Gesellschaft der DDR?*, ed. Günther Glaser and Werner Knoll (Berlin: Trafo, 1995), pp. 34–48, at pp. 47–8.

73 Vadim L. Tsymburskii, *Военная доктрина СССР и России: Осмысления понятий 'угрозы' и 'победы' в второй половине XX века* [The Military Doctrine of the USSR and Russia: Understanding the Notions of "Threat" and "Victory" in the Second Half of the Twentieth Century] (Moscow: Rossiiskii Nauchnyi Fond, 1994), pp. 52–5.

2   Storming on to Paris

The 1961 *Buria* exercise and the planned solution of the Berlin crisis

Matthias Uhl

Introduction

This chapter discusses the Warsaw Pact's plans in the event of an armed conflict in Central and Western Europe on the basis of the operational and strategic command post exercise *Buria*. The exercise took place during the Second Berlin Crisis between September 28 and October 10, 1961.

Buria was the first combined command post exercise of the Warsaw Pact that comprehensively rehearsed the actions of the Unified Armed Forces in the Western European theater of war in the event of an all-out nuclear war. With the exercise, the command structures of the Soviet Army, the Polish Army, the Czechoslovak People's Army, and the East German National People's Army (EGA) tested for the first time the strategic, operational, and tactical interaction of their staffs under the direction of the commander-in-chief of the Unified Armed Forces. At the same time, the armed forces of the eastern military alliance were trained in how to use their troops during the initial period of a nuclear missile war. Some important elements of the exercise, such as the forcing of rivers or landing operations, were also practiced with combat troops up to the strength of a division. *Buria* was thus more than a "normal" command post exercise. It was a command post exercise with elements of a field training exercise. Accordingly, western military experts saw *Buria* as the first large-scale joint field maneuvers of the Warsaw Pact.[1]

Analyzing the exercise afterwards, the military leadership of the Warsaw Pact concluded that the alliance could defeat the NATO troops deployed in Western Europe in a very short time. *Buria* seemed to reflect the view then held by the Soviet General Staff that all continental Europe could and must be brought under the control of the Warsaw Pact within 10–15 days by means of massive use of nuclear weapons.[2]

In the first part of this chapter, the emergence of the Soviet doctrine of all-out nuclear war is discussed on the basis of Soviet sources of military doctrine and strategy from the Cold War; the second part examines the course of the command post exercise. The chapter is based on East German, West German, and, to some extent, Soviet files from the Military Archive of the German Federal Archives. The most important documents for the analysis of the *Buria* command post exercise are lectures, speeches, and analyses by the commander-in-chief of the Unified Armed Forces and by the Soviet and East German ministers of defense. The files provide detailed information about the strategic views of the Warsaw Pact and about Soviet war plans for Western Europe. For the first time, recently released documents from the Armed Forces Staff of the Bundeswehr are evaluated in this chapter. In conclusion, this chapter demonstrates, on the basis of documents from the Russian State Archive of the Economy, the significance *Buria* had for the military restructuring of the Warsaw Pact at the beginning of the 1960s.

The source documents show that *Buria* was of outstanding importance in confirming the Soviet Armed Forces' new doctrine of "all-out nuclear war," which was in force from 1960 until 1969. The interplay between Soviet, East German, Polish, and Czechoslovak forces in the Western European theater of war was rehearsed. For the first time, these Warsaw Pact countries conducted a joint large-scale test of their preparations for and execution of a strategic attack operation in the initial period of a nuclear war.[3] *Buria* thus clearly marks the strategic shift of the Warsaw Pact from the defensive to the offensive at the beginning of the 1960s.

At the same time, however, *Buria* also served as a military–political warning from Soviet head of state and party leader Nikita Khrushchev during the Second Berlin Crisis. The command post exercise not only increased the operational and war readiness of Warsaw Pact troops in Central Europe but it was also intended to serve as an important instrument of pressure in the Soviet–western foreign policy poker game concerning Berlin.[4]

Background of the Soviet military strategy of "all-out nuclear war"

At the end of the 1940s, Soviet military strategy was reoriented toward the new enemy, the USA and the European NATO countries. Initially, the Soviet Union juxtaposed its conventional superiority to the nuclear superiority of the USA. Although the first Soviet atomic bomb test had already been carried out in 1949, nuclear weapons became available to military units on a massive scale only much later. The Soviet air force got its first atomic bombs in 1954, the land forces and navy did not receive nuclear warheads until the end of the 1950s, and the air defense forces got theirs even later.[5]

After the foundation of the Warsaw Treaty Organization in May 1955 and the formation of the Unified Armed Forces of the Warsaw Pact with the Joint High Command at its head, the military–political confrontation between the USSR and the USA developed into a confrontation between the NATO and Warsaw Pact military blocs. Starting in the mid-1950s, this conflict was determined primarily by the rapid development of military technology. The most important goal was the creation and development of strategic nuclear forces. For this purpose, the USSR came to depend primarily on strategic missile forces. At the same time, a new military strategy, the strategy of all-out nuclear-missile warfare, was developed. As a result, the Soviet views about the conditions, the nature, the course, and the outcome of armed conflict changed radically.[6]

The buildup of the Soviet Strategic Missile Forces, first established in 1959, led to heated discussions about the priority of the various types of forces and their roles in a future war. Numerous Soviet army commanders and military theorists, including many military district commanders, held to the view that the land forces would remain the most important branch of the armed forces, even in a nuclear war, since a war in Europe, they believed, could only be brought to a conclusion through the occupation of the enemy's territory. By contrast, Nikita Khrushchev and the leadership of the Soviet General Staff were convinced that the strategic missile forces would play the leading role in a future war, particularly in accomplishing the main strategic mission. Khrushchev and the leadership of the Ministry of Defense around Marshal Rodion Ia. Malinovskii were ultimately able to prevail over the conservative officers in the armed forces and raised their strategic concept to the official military doctrine of the USSR. As a result, the Soviet military was equipped with various types of missiles, used primarily as carriers for nuclear warheads. Among these weapons, intercontinental ballistic missiles (ICBMs) and intermediate-range ballistic missiles (IRBMs) played a key strategic role.[7]

With the introduction of nuclear missiles, a revolutionary development took place in the Soviet forces that led to a complete change in the existing war scenario, and the relationship between strategy, operations, and tactics changed fundamentally.

First, in connection with the development of the Strategic Missile Forces, the role of strategic weapons grew. Soviet military think tanks believed that the Strategic Missile Forces would be able to have an immediate effect on the course of a war and to achieve decisive results. There was a high probability that the primary military and political goals of a war could be reached with strategic weapons. If this were the case, the operational level would expand upon the success of the strategic level, and the tactical level would realize the results obtained by operational art.[8]

Second, the existing timeframes for the strategic actions of the forces changed. It now appeared possible to achieve the envisaged war aims in a single operation or even with a single strike. Accordingly, previous assumptions that war was a more or less lengthy period of a continuation of politics by violent means were overthrown. There was an increasing tendency to see the path to war as an instantaneous act.

Third, strategic operations acquired a greater spatial range in comparison to their role during the Second World War. The ranges of weapons now included all continents and oceans. The distinction between the front and the hinterland was definitively abolished: "From the outset, the conduct of combat operations extends deep into the hinterland of the combatant countries, and there is no strategic space that is not already exposed to attack within the first minutes of the war."[9]

Hence, Soviet military strategy, like that of the USA, became directly dependent on the use of strategic nuclear weapons. Soviet military strategy initially developed in two directions:

- A strategy of deep nuclear missile strikes emerged, in connection with actions by all forces for the simultaneous attack upon and destruction of the economic and military potential of the enemy throughout his entire territory. The goal was to end the war in the shortest possible time.

- A strategy of warfare using conventional weapons was developed, with a series of combat operations aimed at attacking and destroying the forces and the main elements of the economic potential of the enemy, thus gaining victories both in a rapid and an extended battle.[10]

Khrushchev's public presentation at the 4th Session of the Supreme Soviet in January 1960 of the strategy of all-out nuclear missile war as the new military doctrine of the USSR shows that by the beginning of the 1960s the strategic use of exclusively conventional forces was no longer considered a real option. Missiles and nuclear weapons had altered the operational capability of military forces too radically. The atomic firepower had reached a new dimension which made it possible "to deliver a crushing defeat to any aggressor on his own territory."[11]

The new ideas on the nature and content of military strategy in the nuclear age, which resulted from the technological revolution in the armed forces, had already been developed at the beginning of the 1950s in the USSR.[12] However, the new thinking did not become an essential component and dominant area determining Soviet military science until the beginning of the 1960s. The General Staff, the main staffs of the branches of the armed forces, the military academies, and the scientific research organizations of the Ministry of Defense played a key role in the development of these new concepts of military strategy.

The drafting of new regulations for the command and control of strategic operations was decisive in this regard. After the Second World War, Soviet military strategy developed much faster in practice than in theory. The party and the state leadership, therefore, never confirmed the corresponding military directives for the command and control of operations with a strategic character drafted in 1948, 1952, and 1955. The first official guide to strategy in the nuclear age was *The Operations of the Forces of the USSR*, published in 1961 by the Soviet Ministry of Defense.[13]

The fundamental problems resulting from this strategy were analyzed in continual exercises and developed and examined theoretically in numerous academic works, textbooks, monographs, articles, and essays. The whole spectrum of new strategic questions had already been reflected in the book *The Character of Modern War and its Problems*, written in 1953 by authors from the General Staff Military Academy. In 1959, the publication of *Modern Warfare and Military Science* followed. An important contribution to the development and implementation of the strategy of nuclear warfare was the seminal work, *Modern Warfare*, 1960–61, also a product of the General Staff. *Military Strategy*, published in 1962 by a group of authors under the leadership of Soviet First Deputy Minister of Defense Marshal Vasilii D. Sokolovskii, developed into the real sensation, however. Particularly in the two last works, leading Soviet military figures expounded for the first time in a concentrated manner on the nature of the new Soviet military strategy and the methods of nuclear warfare.[14]

During the 1950s and 1960s, the most important principles of strategy were revised almost completely. In previous wars, military success could not be attained other than by an amassment of troops and equipment at the most important sections of the front in order to achieve superiority over the enemy in the axis of the main thrust. Under the conditions of nuclear warfare, according to Soviet military theorists around Marshal Sokolovskii, this principle not only lost its significance but was, in fact, dangerous, since strong troop concentrations represented enticing targets for the nuclear weapons of the enemy. Hence, such factors as maneuvers with nuclear-missile strikes and fire and the definition of the correct order in which targets were to be struck gained vital significance.[15]

The Soviet General Staff also revised the principle of the management of forces and material. As opposed to earlier views, which presupposed gradual reinforcements of forces at the operational level, the need to concentrate all forces and equipment at the outset of a war was now theoretically justified. In the opinion of military theorists, the first strikes and the first operations of a war would be decisive. Consequently, the principle of partial victory also changed. The old principle that the final victory in war was the result of many partial victories on the various fronts and in the various fields of combat was replaced by the notion that victory is the result of the one-act application of the entire potential of a state built up before the war.[16]

The theory of all-out nuclear war was further elaborated at the end of the 1950s. Although various military figures had previously expressed individual ideas about the radical change in the character of warfare, these ideas were not brought together into a single system until 1960. The development of a new theory of nuclear warfare began with a lecture by Chief of the General Staff Marshal Sokolovskii at the General Staff Academy. The General Staff and the main staffs of the branches of the forces had based this lecture on comprehensive strategic and operational research in their military think tanks. It contained, on the one hand, a sharp criticism of the main principles of the old strategy, and, on the other, new ideas on the character and methods of the conduct of war and operations, the strategic and operational use of forces, and the organization of rear-area support of combat operations.[17] The essential ideas of this lecture were later to be developed in the previously mentioned book *Military Strategy* as well as in other Soviet military writings. The most important type of combat operation, according to the authors of these works, was nuclear-missile strikes by the belligerents. They thus rejected the necessity for an early development of forces and regarded the smashing of the enemy's economic potential as the most important objective of military operations.[18]

In connection with the new assessment of the nature of a future war, the General Staff also revised its views on the forms and methods of conducting strategic operations by Soviet forces. Under the previous theory of strategic operations, land forces had played the leading role; however, this no longer corresponded to the demands of nuclear missile warfare. The leading role in warfare now shifted to the Strategic Missile Forces, the strategic long-range air units, and the nuclear-powered missile submarines. In addition, the economy, the system of governmental administration, the strategic nuclear weaponry, and the armed forces of the belligerents were vulnerable at every point on earth and could be destroyed not only in the theater of war but also in the hinterland and within a very short time.[19]

Given these conditions, the need in strategic operations to distinguish between strategic offensive and strategic defense had become superfluous. Defense operations were permissible only at the operational or tactical levels. Soviet military theorists stated clearly that in nuclear warfare there were only the alternatives of attack or defeat:[20]

> Soviet military doctrine sees determined attack operations as the only acceptable form of strategic action in a nuclear war, and stresses that strategic defense contradicts our view of the character of a future nuclear war and of the present state of the Soviet forces. [...] Under modern conditions, passive operations are out of the question at the start of a war, since they would be equivalent to destruction.[21]

For this reason, the following major types of strategic combat operations were at that time assigned a pivotal role: missile operations, operations for the protection of the territory of the country and friendly forces from nuclear strikes by the enemy, strategic attacks in the continental theaters of war, and naval warfare.[22]

Massive nuclear-missile strikes were aimed at destroying the strategic nuclear forces and the most important objects of the enemy's economic war-making potential, demolishing his system of governmental and military administration, and crushing his main concentrations of forces. The strategic actions provided for this purpose were to take the form of nuclear response by the strategic missile forces as well as air strikes by the long-range aviation of the Soviet Air Force with nuclear cruise missiles or atomic bombs.[23]

The strategic efforts to protect friendly territory and friendly forces from enemy nuclear strikes were of special importance. The system developed for this purpose was to minimize the losses from nuclear strikes by the enemy against the most important political and economic centers, troop concentrations, and other targets. The Soviet General Staff understood these actions as involving primarily defensive operations of the country's air defense units, with the support of antiballistic missile (ABM) defense.[24] Soviet ABM research started in 1948 but did not begin in earnest until 1955. The first successful interception of one missile by another occurred on March 4, 1961, when the warhead of a V-1000 Griffon missile destroyed the warhead of a R-5 (SS-3 Shyster) target-missile at an altitude of 25 km. But as the first Soviet ABM system, code-named A-35 Galosh, was very expensive and plagued by technical problems, it was deployed only around Moscow. The A-35 system was designed to deal with an attack by 6–8 ICBMs, a plausible scenario at the end of the 1950s but woefully inadequate in later years. Thus, strategic missile defense was an unresolved problem.[25]

The offense strategy in the continental theaters of war was to ensure the complete disintegration of the enemy forces, the taking of strategically important enemy objectives and terrain, and the occupation of the enemy's territory.[26]

Naval combat operations had the goal of crushing enemy fleets, disrupting enemy sea-lanes, and protecting friendly sea-lanes.[27]

The aforementioned discussion provides a picture of Soviet military doctrine as it stood at the beginning of the 1960s. The command post exercise *Buria* thus fitted into a larger overall strategic framework aimed at defeating the enemy by heavy use of nuclear weapons. Unfortunately, the overall operational plans of the Soviet forces are currently in the archives of the Russian General Staff and are not accessible at the time of writing. Hence, even today, the strategic targets of the long-range bombers and intercontinental missiles aimed primarily at the USA can only be guessed at. Access to Soviet strike plans for intermediate-range and theater weapons is no better. By analyzing the command post exercise *Buria*, however, the operational plans of the Warsaw Pact can be partly deduced, at least those against NATO forces present in the West European theater of war.

The command post exercise *Buria*

The scenario for the exercise assumed an outbreak of hostilities between NATO and the Warsaw Pact in the fall of 1961 and was based on the then current Berlin Crisis. The planning of *Buria* thus reflected the state of NATO and Warsaw Pact forces in the western theatre of operations. The command post exercise was held in an operations area that included Poland, Czechoslovakia, and East Germany. The officers involved in the exercise studied possible hostilities in West Germany, Denmark, Belgium, Netherlands, and France.[28]

The Joint High Command of the Unified Armed Forces postulated the unilateral signing of a peace treaty between the USSR and East Germany on October 4, 1961 as the starting point for the *Buria* scenario. This would have meant that the Allies' access to West Berlin would have been dependent on East German agreement. In the scenario, the German Democratic Republic (GDR) had closed all checkpoints and prohibited Allied aircrafts from using the air corridors to West Berlin. Attempts by the Western Allies in the afternoon of October 5, 1961 to re-open access to West Berlin using military force had, according to the exercise scenarios of the Joint High Command of the Unified Armed Forces, developed into a war involving the use of nuclear missiles as of midday on October 6, ending with the occupation of Paris by Warsaw Pact troops on October 16, 1961.[29]

The main goals of the command post exercise *Buria* were (1) to deploy large troop units from the rear areas to the front over a distance of more than 1,000 km, (2) to prepare for and execute the first operations in the initial period of a war, (3) to commit the fronts and armies to the battle, (4) to assess the interaction of Warsaw Pact forces, (5) to use nuclear missiles at the start of the war and to exploit nuclear strikes, (6) to organize and execute attacks under nuclear conditions, and (7) to secure logistical and medical support for combat operations.[30]

Since the area of the exercise was to encompass the entire Western European theater of war, the staffs of all Warsaw Pact fronts committed to this theater took part in the command post exercise. At the start of the exercise, the 1st Central

Front, consisting of the Group of Soviet Forces in Germany (GSFG) (four combined-arms armies and one tank army) and the EGA (one combined-arms army and one army corps), and the South-Western Front which included the Czechoslovak Army (one combined-arms army) and the Soviet Forces (two combined-arms armies and one tank army), were in full combat readiness, that is, they were capable of immediately entering into combat operations with the NATO troops facing them. The Warsaw Pact forces thus had a total of forty-two full combat ready divisions at their disposal on the first day of combat operations. In the course of the planned operations, another three fronts, the 2nd Echelon, were brought into battle within 2–5 days. These were the Coastal Front, consisting of the Polish army, the 2nd Central Front, and the Western Front, which operated from Czechoslovak territory and consisted of Soviet forces. With the introduction of these three additional fronts, more than 100 divisions would have been at the disposal of the Joint High Command of the Unified Armed Forces for the attack on Western Europe as early as the fifth day of operations.[31]

These 100 divisions were subdivided into a total of 5 tank armies and 20 combined-arms armies. The order of battle of a tank army at that time included three armored divisions and one motorized rifle division. It boasted 12–14 launchers for guided operational-tactical surface-to-surface missiles (SCUD) and unguided tactical rockets (FROG), 1,300 tanks, 850 armored personal carriers (APCs), and 210 artillery pieces. The tank armies were regarded as the most important assault force of the fronts. In the eyes of the Soviet military leadership, they had great power, high mobility, and low vulnerability to enemy nuclear weapons. After the first nuclear strike, they were to act as an armored fist, penetrating deeply into the operational structure of the enemy, tearing up the enemy's strategic front, and destroying NATO's capability for further organized resistance. With an average attack speed of 100 km per day, the tank armies of the Warsaw Pact were to deliver deep and devastating strikes against the NATO defense system. The goal was to reach the Atlantic coast quickly. However, in the course of the exercise, Soviet Minister of Defense Malinovskii was forced to observe that the staffs of the fronts were not able to use the full combat capabilities of the Soviet tank armies. In Malinovskii's view, the tank armies did not reach the Atlantic fast enough.

While the tank armies had the capability to seize strategic objectives in the entire depth of front operations, the military leadership of the Warsaw Pact planned for the combined-arms armies to seize operational objectives as far as 400 km away. Here, too, the attack speed was to be no less than 100 km per day. To this end, a combined-arms army included three motorized rifle divisions and an armored division, with a total of 14 launchers for SCUDs and FROGs, more than 1,000 tanks, about 1,300 APCs, and 350 artillery pieces and mortars. With the aid of the nuclear weapons at their disposal, they were able to independently destroy large enemy troop concentrations and to "sweep away everything in their way that might offer resistance to their advance or hinder them."[32]

All in all, the Unified Armed Forces thus had about 35 tanks and 65 motorized rifle divisions in the Western European theater of war. More than 350 launchers for SCUDs and FROGs with ranges of between 30 and 200 km could be brought to bear against NATO here. Moreover, some one million soldiers were available for the planned attack operation, equipped with 26,000 tanks, 30,000 APCs, and 8,000 artillery pieces. From the air, three Soviet air armies and the air forces of East Germany, Poland, and Czechoslovakia supported this force. They had about 3,000 airplanes and 500 launchers for surface-to-air missiles (SAMs); the former included 1,500 fighter planes and 1,000 bombers and fighter-bombers, of which more than 100 were equipped for dropping atomic bombs.[33]

According to information from the East German military intelligence service, NATO could marshal some 29 divisions with somewhat more than 682,000 men, including 7 armored divisions, against this force on the first day of combat. Its nuclear weaponry included 300 nuclear-capable artillery pieces and 334 missile launchers – 212 Honest John, 68 Lacrosse, 50 Corporal/Sergeant, and 4 Redstone-type missiles. In addition, the equipment of NATO troops included about 6,370 tanks, 3,460 artillery pieces and mortars, and 1,735 anti-tank weapons. The East German intelligence believed that by the fifth day of combat, these troops could be reinforced by another 8 divisions, so that on the tenth day of combat NATO, reinforced by another 10 divisions, could have deployed 47 divisions with about 1.3 million men in the Western Europe theater.[34] For the execution of air operations, NATO forces had 3,526 aircraft at their disposal in Western Europe, including 220 strategic bombers, 1,550 bombers and fighter-bombers, and 1,340 fighter planes. More than 800 of all these planes were equipped for nuclear weapons; further, NATO air forces could marshal 36 launchers for nuclear cruise missiles.[35]

With the command post exercise *Buria*, the Joint High Command of the Warsaw Pact tried for the first time to simulate a military conflict between the forces of NATO and the Warsaw Pact by means of an extensive maneuver. The initial position adopted for *Buria* was based on one of the variants regarded by the Soviet General Staff as possible in the Central European theater of war in the initial period of a nuclear war.

The following scenario was drafted in the staffs of the participating armies for the exercise, which ran from September 28 to October 10, 1961: The international situation continues to deteriorate after the construction of the Berlin Wall in August 1961 and Soviet efforts to conclude a peace treaty with the GDR. As a result, NATO carries out a covert mobilization in Central Europe at the end of September 1961. At the same time, strategic air force elements are redeployed from the USA to Europe. In the western Atlantic and in the North Sea, NATO moves aircraft carriers and assault groups into position, while West Berlin serves as the "center of provocation and as a launching point for aggression."[36] Once it becomes apparent that the signing of the peace treaty is imminent, the Joint High Command assumes that a military clash between the two blocs is inevitable. The EGA units are therefore brought into heightened combat readiness on September 30, 1961, and the active troops are placed under the command of the commander-in-chief of the 1st Central Front, Marshal Ivan S. Konev, on October 1, 1961.[37] The mobilization order is issued at the same time. Immediately after that, the EGA units under the command of the 1st Central Front leave their peacetime garrisons and are deployed in areas near the border, where they occupy their initial combat positions for the forthcoming attack together with the troops of the GSFG.[38]

The Soviet Union signs a peace treaty with the GDR at the beginning of October 1961. As of 2400 hours on October 4, 1961, the lines of communication of the Western powers with their garrison in West Berlin are open only with the approval of the GDR. As a result, the checkpoints and air corridors of the Western powers are interdicted. The Western powers respond by trying to open their lines of communication with West Berlin by military force. Starting at 1500 hours on October 5, elements of a US division push toward Berlin along a motorway; at the same time, cargo aircrafts, later supported by fighter planes, try to break through to West Berlin. After the West is forced to realize that this violent assault toward West Berlin has been resisted by the GSFG and the EGA, it unleashes a war in Europe with a nuclear strike at 1200 hours on October 6.[39]

On the basis of the documents now available, it is not possible to say which side would have carried out the first nuclear strike in *Buria*. An East German National Defense Council paper states that the "Westerners" began the war "with a nuclear missile strike on 6.10 at 1200 hours."[40] In contrast, East German Defense Minister Heinz Hoffmann's personal notes describe the following scenario:

> The war was started by the "Westerners" on Oct. 6th at 1208 hours, with air force and ballistic missile attacks. All the "Easterners" reconnaissance showed the approach of large strategic and tactical air force formations from airfields in Europe and the US, so the "Easterners" responded at 1205 hours with the first large-scale nuclear missile attack.[41]

This first Warsaw Pact attack with strategic, operational-tactical, and tactical missiles was intended to prevent a shift of the balance of forces in NATO's favor:

> The primary objective of the first strategic nuclear weapon blow is to very substantially weaken the military and economic power of the enemy, to seize the strategic initiative from the outset of the war, to eliminate countries or groups of countries of the opposing coalition even within the first hours of the war, and to create favorable conditions for successful strategic operations on the theaters of war and the attainment of the political war aims within as short a time as possible. [...] Because of its importance, the first strategic nuclear strike should involve as many rocket launching facilities, submarines, airplanes and other systems as possible.[42]

In their work for *Buria*, the military planners at the Soviet headquarters assumed that more than 2,200 nuclear weapons would be used in the Western theatre. Some 1,200 nuclear devices were available to the "Westerners," while the "Easterners" had 1,002 nuclear devices in their armies and at their fronts. The total mega-tonnage of nuclear weapons used by NATO and the Warsaw Pact would have been approximately equal.[43]

The Bundeswehr assumed that the Warsaw Pact forces, in their first strategic nuclear strike, would attack a total of 1,200 stationary NATO targets in the European theater of war within a space of thirty minutes. Of these targets, 422 would be in West Germany; in addition, there would be approximately 400 nuclear attacks on mobile targets such as troop concentrations and nuclear weapons. As a result of this large number of nuclear attacks, the political and military leadership of the Federal Republic of Germany would be completely paralyzed for 8–10 days. The administrative structure of West Germany would disintegrate completely in such a situation, the population would be paralyzed or would panic and flee, and the entire transportation system would come to a halt for 2–3 weeks. Within this sea of chaos, there would be only a few islands where minimum functions of public order would operate. The enormous number of dead, injured, and radiation-diseased persons would confront both the military and civilian medical services with insoluble problems.

NATO forces would suffer serious losses in the first nuclear strike. Seventy-five percent of the nuclear weapons stationed in West Germany would be immediately destroyed, as would 90 percent of the radar stations and airfields. In areas where nuclear weapons were used, 40 percent of the military personnel would fall victim to them. The losses in weapons, equipment, and technology would be up to 60 percent. Active NATO divisions in West Germany would be reduced to such an extent that they would no longer be capable of active combat.[44]

On the first day of combat operations, the "Westerners" detonate sixty-eight surface explosions of nuclear weapons in the Oder-Neisse area and the Sudeten Mountains in order to create a nuclear barrier to interdict the strategic reserves of the "Easterners." Overall, an area of more than 140,000 km^2 suffers radiation of 100 roentgens per hour and more. At the same time, heavy initial battles take place between the Baltic Sea and the Austrian border. The 41st Army Corps of the EGA fends off a breakthrough by the "Westerners" along the motorway from Helmstedt to West Berlin. Since the "Easterners" "respond" to the "Western" nuclear attack with an early nuclear counterstrike, NATO does not succeed in changing the balance of forces in its favor.

October 7 – second day of combat operations: Using operational and tactical nuclear weapons, the "Easterners" seize the initiative and advance 80–160 km toward the Ruhr, Frankfurt, and Munich. At the same time, "Western" forces advance along the coast and toward the Leipzig area, pushing 40–50 km into East German territory. They also strike at the flanks of the 1st Central Front with the goal of smashing the attack of the Warsaw Pact's 1st Strategic Echelon.[45] The "Easterners" then commit the Coastal Front (Polish troops). While the 51st Polish Army is to advance through Hamburg, Cuxhaven, and Wesermünde toward the Dutch border, the 52nd Polish Army is to occupy Bremen and to finally push forward through Enschede to Brussels. At the same time, the 50th Polish Army receives orders to occupy Schleswig-Holstein and to push through the Jutland Peninsula into Denmark. Simultaneously, two Polish divisions undertake air and marine landings on the Danish island of Falster. Airborne troops also occupy the strategically important bridge at Nyköbing and thus safeguard the advance toward the island of Zealand.[46]

October 8 – third day of combat operations: The "Easterners" commit the Western Front and the 2nd Central Front as the 2nd Strategic Echelon. While the Western Front advances toward the Ruhr, the 2nd Central Front moves into the Stuttgart area. The Warsaw Pact thus changes the balance of forces further in its favor, and by the end of the day, its troops have reached a line running from the Danish border along the Weser to the Ruhr district, and the first bridgeheads have been established on the west bank of the Rhine as well as in the Main area and at Worms. At the same time, the "Eastern" forces occupy Nuremberg and Munich. The "Westerners," however, switch to defensive holding operations in order to get their troops across the Rhine and to hold off the attack of the "Easterners" there.

October 9 – fourth day of combat operations: The "Easterners" continue their attacks.

October 10 – fifth day of combat operations: Supported by nuclear strikes, the tank grouping of the 1st Central Front crosses the Rhine between Bonn and Mannheim with two tank armies and advances 140 km further to the west. At the same time, the forces of the Coastal and Western Fronts occupy the northern part of the Jutland Peninsula, Zealand and reach the borders of Holland and Belgium. Meanwhile, the "Westerners" try to concentrate their still available reserves: 3 army corps are placed in readiness in the Netherlands and Belgium, 2 in the Nancy area, and 2 in the Paris area. Their mission is to restore the situation on the Rhine. At the end of the day, the Joint High Command orders the five fronts of the Warsaw Pact to continue the battle and by the tenth day of combat operations to reach the line running from Calais along the Seine and the Burgundian Canal to Chalon-sur-Saône and Morez. The war game is terminated with the order to further smash NATO forces on the territory of the Benelux countries and France.[47]

The *Buria* exercise shows that in the early 1960s, the Soviet military leadership believed that the large-scale use of nuclear weapons, combined with attacks by powerful conventional forces, would lead to a decisive defeat of NATO forces in Western Europe. The only "defense" doctrine of the Warsaw Pact at the time was the sweeping strategic attack, destroying the potential enemies' forces on their own territory:

> Only by means of a determined attack of several fronts in a strategic operation can the results of nuclear strikes be exploited most effectively in the theater of war and can the opponent be crushed completely and his territory occupied within a short time.[48]

It is also obvious that the Soviet armed forces had not thought through some of the decisive points of a NATO–Warsaw Pact conflict. For example, documents on *Buria* found to date contain no references to the role of the US strategic forces in the conflict. However, it must be assumed, on the basis of a secret manual on the strategy of nuclear warfare issued in 1964 by the Soviet Minister of Defense, that the General Staff of the Soviet Army hoped to largely eliminate the strategic potential of the Americans during the initial phase of the war. The military leadership of the Soviet Union assumed it would be able to cut off Western Europe from its supply lines from the American continent and thus to prevent any reinforcements of NATO forces in Europe.[49]

The concrete military and civilian effects that the massive use of nuclear weapons in Europe would have on military operations was also not thought through. But it was clear to the General Staff officers conducting the command post exercise that the 2nd Strategic Echelon would suffer devastating losses, primarily from NATO air raids. Soviet army doctors reckoned in 1961 that 300–400 atomic bombs would be used against Soviet forces during the initial period of nuclear missile warfare. Along the main vectors of combat, these bombs would eliminate more than 50 percent of the strength of the fronts. An orderly medical treatment of those injured would therefore be out of the question: "The scope of medical aid must therefore be drastically limited and made available only to those injured persons who still show signs of life and who can be expected to return to their units."[50]

The exercise demonstrated that many important problems of mobilization, transportation, and logistical support of the advance of such large numbers of troops were still completely unresolved. Moreover, considerable weaknesses and flaws in the combat training and control of the forces involved were revealed. However, the flaws in cooperation between the armies of the individual Warsaw Pact countries were even more serious. Communications between neighboring fronts and armies could be established only with very great difficulty, and they were repeatedly interrupted. Thus, no coordinated combat command was possible; the national commanders hardly knew what was going on in the adjacent front sections. For example, during the exercise the East German People's Navy had no knowledge of the intentions of the 50th Army of the Coastal Front, which operated in its segment, despite repeated efforts to obtain such information. Language problems were the main reason for these communication problems, in addition to faulty communication technology. Only very few East German commanders were able to hold conversations with Soviet or Polish general staffs without interpreters. Some of the EGA staff officers could not even read the Russian markings on maps. The troops deployed in the exercise therefore hardly corresponded to the Soviet idea of "unified forces."[51]

One point is clear, however: At the peak of the Second Berlin Crisis, the military leadership of the Warsaw Pact believed that a nuclear war could be fought and, in fact, saw nuclear war as the key instrument for destroying the supposed enemy.

The creation of Warsaw Pact forces for "all-out nuclear war"

Buria made it clear to the Joint High Command of the Unified Forces that not only the Soviet Army but also the forces of its allies would have to reorient themselves to the conditions of "all-out nuclear war." The Joint High Command had established the important foundations for this by 1961.[52]

In the summer of 1965, a study carried out by the US intelligence service, the CIA, came to the conclusion that in just a few years, the Warsaw Pact had been transformed from an organization existing only on paper into an important element of Soviet security and military policy. Moreover, the report showed that since the beginning of the 1960s, the USSR had been engaged in a successful program to boost the military potential of its Eastern European allies and had turned the Warsaw Pact into an effective military structure.[53]

The most important foundations for the radical transformation of the Warsaw Pact were laid at the meeting of the Political Consultative Committee (PCC) in Moscow on March 28 and 29, 1961. At that meeting, Nikita Khrushchev, Walter Ulbricht, and the other communist bloc party leaders and heads of state, discussing the increasingly acute crisis in Berlin, also decided to implement a comprehensive program to rearm and modernize the armies of the Eastern European member states of the Warsaw Pact.[54]

The goal was to bring the armed forces of the USSR's European allies in line with the Soviet Union's new military strategy. Since the mid-1950s, dramatic advances had been made in the Soviet defense research, primarily owing to extremely rapid developments in atomic and missile technology.[55] As discussed earlier, Soviet General Staff planners assumed that the crucial factor in a future war, envisaged as a world conflict involving the mass use of nuclear weapons, would be the initial phase. Accordingly, the combat readiness of the Warsaw Pact armed forces, and their access to the latest technology and weaponry, had to be such that the "imperialist enemy" would be unable to achieve a significant initial advantage through a sudden attack with nuclear weapons and missiles. Instead, the Warsaw Pact's own troops would carry out "*Blitzkrieg*-fast" operations to destroy the enemy's nuclear weapons and to immediately go on the offensive. This meant that the Soviet army and the Warsaw Pact forces had to be prepared "for offensive actions to crush the enemy as quickly as possible in its own territory."[56] To achieve this goal, however, it would be necessary to modernize the armies of the USSR's allies and to equip them with the most modern Soviet armaments.

To that end, between 1962 and 1965 the armed forces of East Germany, Czechoslovakia, Bulgaria, Romania, Poland, and Hungary were to be provided with more than 880 fighter aircraft, 555 helicopters, 6,075 tanks, 17,312 APCs, 554 radar stations, and 41,440 radio sets. At the same time, on instructions from the USSR, a start was made to equip the armies of these countries with state-of-the-art missiles for the first time. This was to involve supplying them with S-75 Dvina/SA-2 Guideline AA missiles, 3M6 Shmel/AT-1 Snapper anti-tank missiles, S-2 Sopka/SSC-2b Samlet coastal defense missiles, K-13/AA-2 Atoll air-to-air missiles, and P-15 Termit/SS-N-2 Styx ship-to-ship missiles.[57]

In total, the armies of the USSR's European allies were to use these weapons to establish the following new units equipped with guided missiles by the end of 1965: 104 AA missile units, 84 anti-tank missile batteries, and 5 coastal defense missile batteries. At the same time, the navies of Poland, Bulgaria, Romania, and East Germany received a total of 28 missile patrol boats from the 205/OSA-1 project, serving as delivery systems for the P-15 Termit/ SS-N-2 Styx sea-target missile. The total value of these predominantly Soviet arms deliveries to the Warsaw Pact nations between 1962 and 1965 has been estimated at over 2.8 billion rubles.[58] To place this figure in context, in 1961, the USSR State Planning Committee estimated the value of the total Soviet arms production for that year at 4.1 billion rubles.[59]

In spite of this major expenditure, these planned arms deliveries fell far short of the requirements determined by the Warsaw Pact Joint High Command which believed that an expenditure of over 4.4 billion rubles between 1961 and 1965 would be required for the rearmament and modernization of the armed forces. With that sum, the Soviet military heads of the Warsaw Pact aimed to supply more than 2,334 fighter aircraft, 880 helicopters, 9,040 tanks, and 22,017 APCs to the armed forces of the USSR's alliance partners.

To purchase these armaments was beyond the economic and financial capacity of the Warsaw Pact member states. Accordingly, the Armaments Commission of COMECON met in Moscow on March 17, 1961 with leading officials from the State Planning Commissions and the Chiefs of Staff of the Warsaw Pact nations to discuss arms deliveries between 1962 and 1965. At the end of the meeting, the participants had agreed on the aforementioned figure of 2.8 billion rubles and had formulated a draft resolution for the meeting of the PCC scheduled for late March, which was then duly approved by the committee.[60]

The presumption that this historic decision represented an attempt by the political and military leadership of the Warsaw Pact to make significant changes and improvements to the military potential of the eastern alliance, regarded as inadequate at that time, is confirmed by further documents from the Russian State Archives of the Economy. These documents show that the measures implemented by the Soviet General Staff and Joint High Command to boost the capacity of the Warsaw Pact armies were not restricted to conventional weapons. In its resolution of March 29, 1961, the PCC also stated that for the first time the armed forces of the Soviet Union alliance partners would be equipped with theater and tactical nuclear weapon carriers.[61]

To ensure the nuclear combat capability of all Warsaw Pact forces, the resolution of March 29, 1961 of the PCC provided for 14 R-11/SCUD missile brigades and 40 Luna/FROG missile units to be made available to Warsaw Pact member states. Each R-11/SCUD brigade had a total of six launching pads from which missiles could be fired, with the capacity of carrying nuclear warheads with an explosive force of up to 40 kilotons over a distance of 200 km. Hungary and East Germany were each to receive one such brigade (costing 4.8 million rubles); Romania and Bulgaria were to receive two, Poland and Czechoslovakia four.

Whereas the purpose of the R-11/SCUD was to deliver nuclear weapons at the army command level, the Luna/FROG missile complex was intended for delivery at the divisional level. Soviet planning allocated one Luna/FROG missile unit to each Warsaw Pact division. Each unit would have two launch pads and would cost 190,000 rubles. The USSR charged its allies 18,000 rubles per missile. The launching devices shot unguided missiles capable of carrying nuclear warheads with an explosive force of up to 20 kilotons over a range of 40 km. Since the

USSR clearly had supply problems, given the higher priority of equipping its own forces, it was initially possible to fully equip only the six East German divisions with the missile complex. In the other Warsaw Pact countries, the numbers of weapon systems delivered were initially insufficient to equip all the units under the Joint High Command. In Poland, for example, which according to the protocol had 14 divisions under Warsaw Pact command, only 8 Luna missiles units were allocated, and Romania received only 5 of the required 8 units.[62]

The apparent preferential treatment of East Germany in the supply of nuclear missile delivery systems was clearly associated with its particularly important position within the alliance. This can also be discerned in the area of theater missiles. As early as the beginning of December 1960, the Joint High Command informed the EGA leadership at a joint meeting that East Germany would be receiving R-11 missiles and launching systems in 1962. Special training in the USSR for the officers and troops began as early as February 1961, that is, before the relevant resolution had been adopted by the PCC. Already at the beginning of 1963, the "Independent Artillery Brigade 2" missile unit was included in the group of EGA units placed under the command of the Joint High Command of the Warsaw Pact.[63]

The supply of delivery systems for tactical nuclear warheads for the EGA proceeded even more rapidly. The process of establishing the first Luna/FROG missile unit, in the guise of "Independent Artillery Unit 9," began in May 1962 and was completed after the delivery of Soviet hardware on September 30, 1962. Just a few weeks later, during the Cuban Missile Crisis, the unit was already in "heightened combat readiness" and was among the EGA troops under the command of the Warsaw Pact Joint High Command.[64] By the end of 1962, two more tactical missile units had become operational, and by May 1963, all six of the active EGA divisions were fully equipped with the Luna weapon system.[65]

In contrast to the GDR, most of the other Warsaw Pact member states did not get approval from the Soviet Union for the supply of theater and tactical nuclear missile delivery systems until 1962. However, the supply of nuclear weapon delivery systems required not only a resolution by the PCC, but also another two resolutions from the USSR Council of Ministers and the relevant bilateral government-to-government agreements.[66] The Soviet Head of State and Party Chairman then notified the First Secretaries of each of the "fraternal states" of the Warsaw Pact in writing of the forthcoming delivery.[67]

However, while this meant that the Warsaw Pact countries had acquired nuclear weapon carriers, decisions on the use of atomic warheads remained the sole preserve of the USSR. In the early 1960s, Soviet Defense Ministry plans envisaged the following scenario for the use of nuclear weapons by the Warsaw Pact allies: In a period of tension, the nuclear warheads – until then stored in the Soviet Union – would be taken by Soviet special commando units to the various countries and would be distributed to the missile units of the allied forces. Specialists from the USSR would then supervise the loading of the warheads in the missiles and clear their use in combat. Thus, the nuclear weapons of the Warsaw Pact armies would remain under Soviet control at all times, right up to the moment of launch.[68] The decision on the initial use of nuclear weapons was the exclusive responsibility of the commander-in-chief of the Soviet armed forces, that is, the General Secretary of the Communist Party of the Soviet Union (CPSU); detailed operational planning for tactical and theater/tactical atomic weapons was carried out by the national command structures of the Warsaw Pact member states in consultation with Soviet commanders and advisers.[69]

Conclusion

The command post exercise *Buria* was not only a demonstrative military measure of the USSR after the construction of the Berlin Wall, but, it also provided for the first time a test of the new operational role of the Unified Armed Forces in the western theater of war. The commander-in-chief of the Unified Armed Forces believed that the arena of both world wars would also be the main theater of war in a conflict between NATO and the Warsaw Pact: "It has special economic significance, especially great human reserves, it has a state like West Germany, the two global systems face each other here along their national frontiers, here is where NATO's greatest reserves have been developed."[70]

In the eyes of the Joint High Command of the Warsaw Pact, despite all the problems that emerged during the exercise, *Buria* seemed to confirm the validity of the "all-out nuclear missile war" for the Western European theater of war. As Soviet Minister of Defense Malinovskii emphasized in his speech evaluating the war games, the exercise showed that "under modern conditions, the main mission of smashing the enemy is fulfilled by nuclear strikes. And it is subsequently the mission of the land forces to complete the task of destroying them."[71]

It was exactly this mission that the top leadership of the Soviet, Polish, Czechoslovak, and East German armies had tested in *Buria*. During the exercise, the land forces had successfully exploited the results of the nuclear strikes by the strategic missile forces and of their own nuclear weapons and had advanced with determination into the depth of the theater of war, where the enemy's staffs, communication sites, missile positions, and troop concentrations were smashed. The 2nd Echelon, brought into battle subsequently, destroyed by means of flank and rear attacks those enemy units still offering resistance. In these attacks, the operational-tactical nuclear weapons of the fronts and armies committed to the theater of war were used on a large scale, since the mass of strategic nuclear weapons had already been used up within the first days of operations.[72]

However, in his evaluation of the exercise, the Soviet Minister of Defense found fault with the fact that the operational-tactical use of nuclear weapons was still based on obsolete artillery patterns. The commanders-in-chief of the fronts used 60 percent of the nuclear weapons available to accomplish the initial assault missions and 30 percent to accomplish the so-called additional missions. A mere 10 percent were held in reserve. According to Malinovskii, the South-Western Front consumed all its available nuclear weapons in the first two combat-operation days of the command post exercise. The Soviet Minister of Defense noted critically that the fronts of the 2nd Echelon had also planned a similar use of nuclear weapons, although they had faced an already weakened enemy. As a result, nuclear weapons would be lacking for offensive missions in depth, where the forces might encounter great operational and strategic enemy reserves.[73]

These statements confirm again that *Buria* was the Warsaw Pact's first strategically oriented command post exercise under the conditions of nuclear-missile war. In 1961, as shown, Soviet military strategy recognized only one form of use for nuclear weapons: the massive strategic nuclear strike, executed by the joint use of nuclear weapons at all order-of-battle levels. This nuclear strike was directed simultaneously against targets in the strategic and continental spheres, and also at those in the theater of war and on the battlefield. The attack by superior conventional forces in Europe that followed immediately was to completely destroy the available NATO forces in Europe with the use of further nuclear weapons. The Soviet General Staff seemed to reckon with an overwhelming success of Warsaw Pact forces in the Western European theater of war in a war with the United States and NATO. At the same time, *Buria* also showed to the military leadership of the Unified Armed Forces that despite the increased significance of missiles, strong conventional forces were still required to implement its offensive strategy. Marshal Malinovskii therefore emphasized at the XXII Party Congress of the CPSU at the end of October 1961 that "definite victory can be obtained against the aggressor only by the unified action of all types of forces."[74]

However, to the overall strategic leadership of the Warsaw Pact, the military position of the United States in a conflict remained an unsolved issue, as the Cuba Crisis was to show a year later. Neither the Soviet Union nor the Warsaw Pact had any real strategic instruments of power to counter the United States. Therefore, it was extremely unrealistic to assume in the planning for *Buria* that the United States would simply accept a defeat of its NATO partners. Nevertheless, in the documents for *Buria* and in those of later Warsaw Pact command post exercises there is no mention of how the strategic use of nuclear weapons by the United States in the Western European theater might be countered.

On the basis of the documents accessible, it seems that *Buria* was no abstract exercise, but rather that it served primarily to check the practicability of the operational plans of the Soviet General Staff for Central Europe. Certainly, the strategic aims stated in the 1961 Operation Plan (OP 61) of the Polish army seem to coincide clearly with the exercise targets for the Polish Coastal Front during the command post exercise *Buria*. The only discernible differences are the assignment of the operational targets to the individual armies and insignificant shifts in the planned time schedules. Thus, the 50th Army assumed the role of the 4th Army of the OP 61. Since it was already fully mobilized, it pushed forward through Schleswig-Holstein toward Denmark on the second operational day. Yet, the missions of the 1st and 2nd Armies provided under the Operational Plan were assumed by units of 51st and 52nd Armies which, because of their longer deployment routes, joined the offensive only on the third operational day.[75] The Soviet General Staff evidently also reviewed the operational plans drafted for the East German National People's Army but turned these over to the East Germans only in the summer of 1962. Czech files should also be examined to determine exactly to what extent the Czechoslovak exercise targets agreed with the operational plans, which were likewise confirmed in the summer of 1961 by the Soviet High Command.[76] Also, in the final judgment of Marshal Grechko, who conducted the command post exercise, *Buria* could be regarded as a goal-oriented Warsaw Pact exercise corresponding to the combat missions to be implemented in this theater of war.[77] The fact that the staffs of 15 armies and more than 60 divisions of the Warsaw Pact participated in the command post exercise *Buria* supports this. During the exercise, the 1st Strategic Echelon alone, which trained to be the spearhead of a Soviet offensive against Western Europe, consisted of 3 fronts, with 28 Soviet, 9 Czechoslovak, 6 East German, and 15 Polish divisions.[78]

Buria proved to be an important and also effective military threat against the West at the climax of the Berlin Crisis. As General Gerhard Wessel, G-2 – Chief of Intelligence – of the Armed Forces Staff of the Bundeswehr, stated:

> The war of nerves has achieved an absolute climax with the nuclear and missile test series and the war games of the Warsaw Pact countries' forces. This climax serves as an instrument of military pressure to force the initiation of negotiations about Berlin and Germany and to lead them to a result positive for the USSR. It must therefore be assumed that the climax of the war of nerves thus reached will remain constant over a long period of time. The danger that the concentration of forces initially created for the war games will lead to an offensive against Central Europe cannot be dismissed, even if there are no signs of an immediately forthcoming attack. However, the considerable augmentation and readiness of enemy forces of recent weeks makes the potential early recognition of enemy intentions more difficult. This serious and difficult situation should be taken into account in formulating our own measures – in the military as in the civilian realm, in the material as in the intellectual realm.[79]

At the same time, however, the flaws and serious weaknesses that appeared during *Buria*, especially concerning the cooperation between the individual Warsaw Pact countries, obviously contributed to a change of opinion of the political and military leadership with regard to the conclusion of a unilateral peace treaty with East Germany. Particularly because Khrushchev could not be sure of the military strength of his own forces and those of his allies, as the command post exercise demonstrated, he moved away from his original political goal in the late fall of 1961. The signing of the peace treaty was in any case no longer on the agenda. In the end, in the evaluation of *Buria* the Soviet General Staff in Moscow even dispensed with major Warsaw Pact exercises planned for November 1961, which the West had repeatedly expected.[80]

In conclusion, the following can be stated: During the 1960s, the authors of Soviet military doctrine, strategy, and operational planning thought that the Warsaw Pact was fully prepared for smashing the European NATO forces in fast, deep operations with a daily attack speed of 80–100 km and the conquest of territory up to the Atlantic within 12–16 days. Only the political, economic, and technological developments of the 1970s and 1980s led to a more realistic assessment of the operational possibilities of the Warsaw Pact. The strategic planning for the European theater of war in the 1980s aimed at forcing frontline NATO countries out of the war. Only in 1987 did the Warsaw Pact receive a military doctrine that clearly excluded any attack option and first use of nuclear weapons and that provided only for the defense of its own territory. But by the time the defensive restructuring of the Warsaw Pact began, the alliance's days were already numbered, and no half-hearted changes in structure, strength, or strategy could arrest its decline.[81]

Notes

1 Cf. Hans-Christian Pilster, *Rußland – Sowjetunion. Werden, Wesen und Wirken einer Militärmacht* (Herford: Mittler & Sohn, 1981), pp. 200–1; Hannes Adomeit, *Soviet Risk-Taking an Crisis Behaviour* (London: George Allan & Unwin, 1982), p. 213.

2 Cf. G. Khetagurov, "Preparation and Conduct of a Front Offensive Operation on a Maritime Axis in the Initial Period of a War," *Military Thought – Special Collection*, no. 4 (1961) in *Lt Col Oleg Penkovsky: Western Spy in Soviet GRU*, http://www.foia.cia.gov/penkovsky.asp (April 21, 2004).

3 Cf. Starting position for the command post exercise *Buria*, September 26, 1961, p. 16, DVW-1/6289, Bundesarchiv–Militärarchiv (Federal Military Archive) in Freiburg i. Br. (hereinafter referred to as: BA–MA).

4 Cf. Situation report of the Armed Forces Staff of the Bundeswehr (Fü B II 3), October 18, 1961, BW-2/2226, BA–MA; Hannes Adomeit, *Die Sowjetmacht in internationalen Krisen und Konflikten. Verhaltensmuster, Handlungsprinzipien, Bestimmungsfaktoren* (Baden-Baden: Nomos Verlagsgesellschaft, 1983), pp. 328–33. See also Penkovskii, Meeting No. 31, September 22, 1961, in *Lt. Col. Oleg Penkovsky: Western Spy in Soviet GRU*, http://www.foia.cia.gov/penkovsky.asp (April 21, 2004).

5 Cf. *Стратегическое ядерное вооружение России* [Strategic Nuclear Weapons of Russia] (Moscow: IzdAT, 1998), pp. 3–6; Mikhail Pervov, *Зенитное ракетное оружие противвоздушной обороны страны* [Anti-Aircraft Missile Weaponry of the Air Defence Forces of Russia] (Moscow: Aviarus-XXI, 2001), pp. 104–5; *Советская военная мощь от Сталина до Горбачева* [Soviet Military Power from Stalin to Gorbachev] (Moscow: Voennyi parad, 1999), pp. 150–61.

6 Cf. Jörg K. Hoensch, "The Warsaw Pact and the Northern Member States," in *The Warsaw Pact: Political Purpose and Military Means* (eds), Robert W. Clawson and Lawrence S. Kaplan (Wilmington: Scholarly Resources, 1982), pp. 33–8; V.A. Zolotarev (ed.), *История военной стратегии России* [History of the Military Strategy of Russia] (Moscow: Kuchkovo pole, 2000), p. 383; Andrej A. Gretschko, *Die Streitkräfte des Sowjetstaates* (Berlin: Militärverlag der DDR, 1975), pp. 98–101; Anatoli Gribkow, *Der Warschauer Pakt. Geheimnisse und Hintergründe des östlichen Militärbündnisses* (Berlin: Edition q, 1995), pp. 34–6.

7 Cf. *Die sowjetische Militärmacht. Geschichte, Technik, Strategie* (Bayreuth: Gondrom Verlag, 1979), pp. 202–6; *Военачальники ракетных войск стратегического назначения. Сборник очерков* [Military Leaders of the Strategic Missile Forces. Collection of Sketches] (Moscow: TsIPK RVSN, 1997), pp. 8–10; Raymond L. Garthoff, *Soviet Strategy in the Nuclear Age* (New York: Praeger, 1958), pp. 224–6.

8 Cf. *Ракетный щит отечества* [The Missile Shield of the Motherland] (Moscow: TsIPK RVSN, 1999), pp. 52–4; *Die Streitkräfte der UdSSR. Abriß ihrer Entwicklung von 1918 bis 1968* (Berlin: Militärverlag der DDR, 1974) pp. 658–60; J.I. Korabljow,

W.A. Anfilow, and W.A. Mazulenko, *Kurzer Abriß der Geschichte der Streitkräfte der UdSSR von 1917 bis 1972* (Berlin: Militärverlag der DDR, 1976), pp. 305–6.

9 *Zeittafel zur Militärgeschichte der Deutschen Demokratischen Republik 1949 bis 1968* (Berlin: Deutscher Militärverlag, 1969), p. 135. (The text and all German citations were translated by Phill Hill. All Russian citations were translated by the author.)

10 Cf. Speech of the Soviet Deputy Minister of Defense Marshal Andrei A. Grechko on the evaluation of a command post exercise by the GSFG and the EGA, May 1961, p. 2, DVW-1/5203, BA–MA; Speech of Soviet Minister of Defense Marshal Rodion Ia. Malinovskii on the evaluation of a command post exercise by the GSFG and the EGA, May 1961, p. 5, DVW-1/5203, BA–MA.

11 Speech of Nikita S. Khrushchev at the 4th Session of the Supreme Soviet. *Pravda*, January 14, 1960; Bernhard Bechler, "Der Raketen-Kernwaffenkrieg – eine neue Qualität des bewaffneten Kampfes," *Militärwesen*, no. 5 (1962): 658–60.

12 Cf. Letter from Aleksandr M. Vasilevskii and Vasilii D. Sokolovskii to Iosif V. Stalin, January 21, 1953, pp. 60–4, 682/164/17 (the archive number comprises the file numbers, record, and repository, separated by oblique strokes), Rossiiskii gosudarstvennyi arkhiv sotsialnoi i politicheskoi istorii (Russian State Archive of Socio-Political History – hereinafter referred to as: RGASPI); Elucidation on the Deployment of Airfields for Long-Distance Bombers, January 10, 1953, pp. 13–17, 697/164/17, RGASPI. Altogether, eleven operational air bases were to be built for the Tu-95 and M-4 strategic bombers in the Soviet-controlled area between 1953 and 1955, from which London, Madrid, New York, Washington, Chicago, Guam, Pearl Harbor, and other targets in the United States could be attacked. See also, I.V. Bystrova, *Военно-промышленный комплекс СССР в годы холодной войны* [The Military-Industrial Complex of the USSR in the Years of the Cold War] (Moscow: IRI RAN, 2000), pp. 85–91.

13 Cf. Andrei A. Kokoshin, *Армия и политика: Советская военнополическая и военно-стратегическая мысль 1918–1991 годы* [Army and Politics: Soviet Military–Political and Military-Strategic Thought, 1918–1991] (Moscow: Mezhdunarodnye otnosheniia, 1995), pp. 137–46; Zolotarev, *История военной стратегии России* pp. 399–401.

14 Cf. *Die Streitkräfte der UdSSR*, pp. 656–7; Kokoshin, *Армия и политика*, pp. 60–1; Steven J. Zaloga, *The Kremlin's Nuclear Sword: The Rise and Fall of Russia's Strategic Nuclear Forces 1945–2000* (Washington, DC: Smithsonian Institution Press, 2002), pp. 78–9; Arnold L. Horelick and Myron Rush, *Strategic Power and Soviet Foreign Policy* (Chicago, IL; London: University of Chicago Press, 1966), p. 29.

15 Cf. Vasilii D. Sokolovsky (ed.), *Military Strategy. Soviet Doctrine and Concepts* (New York; London: Praeger, 1963), pp. 14–15.

16 Cf. S.N. Kozlov, M.V. Smirnov, I.S. Baz', and P.A. Sidorov, *О советской военной науке* [About Soviet Military Science] (Moscow: Voenizdat, 1964), pp. 65–6.

17 Cf. Zolotarev, *История военной стратегии России*, pp. 399–401.

18 Cf. Sokolovsky, *Military Strategy*, pp. 285–8.

19 Cf. M.M. Kirian, *Военно-технический прогресс и вооруженные силы СССР. Анализ развития вооружения, организации и способов действий* [Military-Technical Progress and the Armed Forces of the USSR. The Analysis of Development of Arms, Organization and Ways of Actions] (Moscow: Voenizdat, 1982), pp. 239–44 and 314–18; V.A. Zolotarev, O.V. Saksonov, and S.A. Tiushkevich, *Военная история России* [Military History of Russia] (Moscow: Kuchkovo pole, 2001), p. 619.

20 Cf. Thomas W. Wolfe, *Soviet Power and Europe, 1945–1970* (Baltimore, MD; London: The Johns Hopkins Press, 1970), pp. 199–201; Speech of Colonel Michail G. Leshin, Russian Institute of Military History, on the Conference of the Institute of Contemporary History Munich/Berlin: The Armed Forces of the USSR, USA, West and East Germany during the Cuban-Missile Crisis 1962, October 15, 2002.

21 Cf. Rodion Malinovskii, *Die Strategie des Kernwaffenkrieges*, Moscow 1964, pp. 38, 238, DVL-3/29942, BA–MA (Unauthorized German translation of a Soviet top secret

handbook on nuclear warfare for the Chiefs of the Military Districts of the Soviet Union).

22 Cf. Speech of the Soviet Minister of Defense Marshal Rodion Ia. Malinovskii on the evaluation of a command post exercise by the GSFG and the EGA, October 1961, p. 52, DVW-1/5203, BA–MA; B.W. Panow (ed.), *Geschichte der Kriegskunst* (Berlin: Militärverlag der DDR, 1987), pp. 523–4.

23 Cf. Study material for the Chiefs of Staff of the EGA: *Offensive Operations of a Combined-Arms Army in the Initial Period of a War*, December 5, 1958, pp. 94–6, DVW-1/4358, BA–MA.

24 Cf. Steven J. Zaloga, *Soviet Air Defence Missiles: Design, Development and Tactics* (Coulsdon: Jane's Information Group, 1989), pp. 5–25; Wilfried Kopenhagen, *Deutsche Fla-Raketen (Wasserfall-Schmetterling-Taifun u.a.) und ihre sowjetischen Kinder* (Wölfersheim-Berstadt: Podzun-Pallas, 1998), pp. 11–21; Mikhail D. Evtif'ev, *Из истории создания зенитно-ракетного щита России* [From the History of the Creation of a Air Defense Missile Shield of Russia] (Moscow: Vuzovskaia kniga, 2000), pp. 54–80.

25 Cf. Pavel Podvig (ed.), *Russian Strategic Nuclear Forces* (Cambrigde: The MIT Press, 2001), pp. 412–4; Zaloga, *The Kremlin's Nuclear Sword*, pp. 98–9.

26 Cf. Ivan G. Pavlovskii, *Сухопутные войска СССР. Зарождение, развитие, современность.* [The Land Forces of the USSR. Origin, Development, Present] (Moscow: Voenizdat, 1985), p. 212.

27 Cf. Sergei G. Gorshkov, *Морская мощь государства* [The Sea Power of the State] (Moscow: Voenizdat, 1976), pp. 361–80.

28 Cf. *Zeittafel zur Militärgeschichte der Deutschen Demokratischen Republik 1949–1988* (Berlin: Militärverlag der DDR, 1989), p. 147; Thomas M. Forster, *NVA – Die Armee der Sowjetzone* (Cologne: Markus-Verlag, 1967), p. 224.

29 Cf. Hoffmann's lecture on the evaluation of the operational and strategic command post exercise *Buria*, undated, p. 138–40, DVW-1/6103, BA–MA.

30 Cf. Hoffmann's paper on the evaluation of the operational and strategic command post exercise *Buria*, undated, p. 152, DVW-01/6103, BA–MA.

31 Cf. Map of reports for the time between October 1, 1961, 10:00 and October 5, 1961, 22:00, undated, p. 305, DVW-1/6289-2, BA–MA; Hoffmann's lecture on the evaluation of the operational and strategic command post exercise *Buria*, undated, p. 137, DVW-1/6103, BA–MA; Report of General Gerhard Wessel (G 2) for the Military Command Council of the FRG, November 7, 1961, BW-2/2226, BA–MA.

32 Cf. Speech of Soviet Minister of Defense Marshal Rodion Ia. Malinovskii on the evaluation of a command post exercise by the GSFG and the EGA, October 1961, pp. 56–8, DVW-1/5203, BA–MA.

33 Ibid., pp. 56–63; Central Intelligence Agency – Memo for General Taylor, Annex: Soviet and Satellite Forces in Europe facing NATO, September 6, 1961, *The Berlin Crisis, 1958–1962* (Chadwyck-Healey, Inc., Alexandria, VA; Washington, DC: The National Security Archive, 1991), microfiche, document 02444.

34 Cf. Information about the mobilization possibilities of the Western European NATO states, July 1, 1962, pp. 6–13, DVW-1/25816, BA–MA.

35 Cf. Material related to the operational and strategic command post exercise *Buria*, undated, p. 13, DVW-1/6302, BA–MA.

36 Cf. Operational Directive for the command post exercise *Buria*, September 30, 1961, p. 28, DVW-1/6289, BA–MA.

37 Cf. Operational Directive No. 01/61 of the Minister of National Defence of the GDR September 29, 1961, pp. 57–8, DVW-1/6289, BA–MA; Material related to the operational and strategic command post exercise *Buria*, undated, p. 2, DVW-1/6302, BA–MA.

38 Cf. Letter from Hoffmann to Konev, October 1, 1961, p. 65, DVW-1/6289, BA–MA; Map of reports for the time between October 1, 1961, 10:00 and October 5, 1961, 22:00, undated, p. 305, DVW-1/6289-2, BA–MA.

39 Cf. Hoffmann's lecture on the evaluation of the operational and strategic command post exercise *Buria*, undated, pp. 138–9, DVW-1/6103, BA–MA.

40 Cf. Hoffman report to the National Defense Council on the command post exercise *Buria*, November 29, 1961, pp. 7–8, DVW-1/5173, BA–MA.

41 Hoffmann's lecture on the evaluation of the operational and strategic command post exercise *Buria*, undated, p. 138, DVW-1/6103, BA–MA.

42 Cf. Rodion Malinovskii, *Die Strategie des Kernwaffenkrieges*, pp. 86–7, DVL-3/29942, BA–MA [Unauthorized German translation of a Soviet top secret handbook on nuclear warfare for the Chiefs of the Military Districts of the Soviet Union].

43 Cf. Hoffmann's paper on the evaluation of the operational and strategic command post exercise *Buria*, undated, pp. 153–5, DVW-1/6103, BA–MA.

44 Cf. War picture – Case "A" of the Armed Forces Staff of the Bundeswehr (Fü B III 6), December 14, 1961, pp. 4–15, BW-2/2228, BA–MA.

45 Cf. Hoffmann's paper on the evaluation of the operational and strategic command post exercise *Buria*, undated, pp. 153–5, DVW-1/6103, BA–MA; Hoffmann's lecture on the evaluation of the operational and strategic command post exercise *Buria*, undated, pp. 139–40, DVW-1/6103, BA–MA.

46 Cf. Operative report of the East German Navy, October 8, 1961, p. 78, DVW-1/6289, BA–MA; Map of the command post exercise *Buria*, undated, p. 304, DVW-1/6289–2, BA–MA; "Dyrektywa Operacyjna Nr. 002, Sztab Frontu Nadmorskiego" [Operational Directive Nr. 002, Staff of the Coastal Front], October 4, 1961, http://www.isn.ethz.ch/php/documents/collection_12/docs/Operational Directive_041061.pdf (April 21, 2004). For more details see, Paweł Piotrowski, *A Landing Operation in Denmark*, http://www.isn.ethz.ch/php/collections/coll_12.htm (April 21, 2004).

47 Cf. Hoffmann's paper on the evaluation of the operational and strategic command post exercise *Buria*, undated, pp. 153–5, DVW-1/6103, BA–MA; Hoffmann's lecture on the evaluation of the operational and strategic command post exercise *Buria*, undated, pp. 139–40, DVW-1/6103, BA–MA; Map of the combat actions of the 40th Army and the 41th Army Corps of the EGA between October 6 and 10, 1961, undated, p. 25, DVW-1/6303, BA–MA; "Meldunek Dowódcy Frontu Nadmorskiego według sytuacji" [Situation Report by the Commander of the Coastal Front], October 10, 1961, http://www.isn.ethz.ch/php/documents/collection_12/docs/SituationReport_101061.pdf (April 21, 2004).

48 Cf. Rodion Malinovskii, *Die Strategie des Kernwaffenkrieges*, p. 131, DVL-3/29942, BA–MA [Unauthorized German translation of a Soviet top secret handbook on nuclear warfare for the Chiefs of the Military Districts of the Soviet Union].

49 Ibid., p. 26–219.

50 Cf. Letter from N. Vovgai to S.I. Semin, June 10, 1962, p. 20, 331/80/4372 (the archive number comprises the file number, record, and repository, separated by oblique strokes), Rossiiskii gosudarstvennyi arkhiv ekonomiki (Russian State Archive of the Economy – hereinafter referred to as: RGAE).

51 Cf. Joachim Schunke, "Feindbild und militärische Beurteilung des Gegners in der NVA," in *Im Gleichschritt? Zur Geschichte der NVA*, ed. Walter Jablonsky and Wolfgang Wünsche (Berlin: Das Neue Berlin, 2001), pp. 187–8; Speech of the commander-in-chief of the Joint High Command Marshal Andrei A. Grechko on the evaluation of a command post exercise by the GSFG and the EGA, October 14, 1961, pp. 69–71, DVW1/5191, BA–MA; Problems of the Command Post Exercise *Buria*, undated, pp. 20–2, DVW-1/6303, BA–MA; Hoffmann's paper on the evaluation of the operational and strategic command post exercise *Buria*, undated, p. 200, DVW-01/6103, BA–MA.

52 Cf. *Zur geschichtlichen Entwicklung und Rolle der Nationalen Volksarmee der Deutschen Demokratischen Republik* (Potsdam: Militärgeschichtliches Institut der DDR, 1974), pp. 185–6. Until the GDR ceased to exist, this outline of the history of the East German Army was classified.

53 Cf. Central Intelligence Agency, National Intelligence Estimate (NIE) 12–65, "Eastern Europe and the Warsaw Pact," August 26, 1965, http://www.isn.ethz.ch/php/documents/collection_7/docs/nbb36_1.pdf (April 21, 2004).

54 Cf. Draft resolution of the PCC of the Warsaw Pact (bearing the following handwritten note "confirmed 29 March 1961"), March 19, 1961, p. 96, 792/79/4372, RGAE; Ross A. Johnson, Robert W. Dean, and Alexander Alexiev, *Die Streitkräfte des Warschauer Pakts in Mitteleuropa: DDR, Polen und ČSSR* (Stuttgart: Seewald, 1982), pp. 31–2; Wolfe, *Soviet power and Europe*, pp. 150–2.

55 Cf. Vladislav M. Zubok and Hope M. Harrison, "The Nuclear Education of Nikita Khrushchev," in *Cold War Statesmen Confront the Bomb: Nuclear Diplomacy since 1945*, ed. John Lewis Gaddis, Philip H. Gordon, Ernest R. May, and Jonathan Rosenberg (Oxford: Oxford University Press, 1999), pp. 150–4.

56 Speech of Soviet Minister of Defense Marshal Rodion Ia. Malinovskii on the evaluation of a command post exercise by the GSFG and the EGA, May 1961, p. 7, DVW-1/5203, BA–MA.

57 For more details on these Soviet missiles see, A.B. Shirokorad, *Энциклопедия отечественного ракетного оружия 1817–2002 гг.* [Encyclopedia of Russia's Rocket and Missile Armament 1817–2002] (Moscow: AST, 2003).

58 Cf. Note on the fulfillment of requirements of the armies of the Warsaw Pact countries for military hardware from 1961 to 1965, March 1961, pp. 106–7, 792/79/4372, RGAE.

59 Cf. Report from GOSPLAN to the Central Committee of the CPSU on the expected fulfillment of production requirements for arms deliveries, December 20, 1961, p. 36, 759/79/4372, RGAE.

60 Cf. Draft text of speech by Deputy Chairman of GOSPLAN Mikhail V. Khrunichev for the meeting of the PCC "On Arms Production Specialization in the Warsaw Pact Countries and Mutual Supply of Military Hardware," March 27, 1961, pp. 84–5, 792/79/4372, RGAE; Draft resolution of the PCC of the Warsaw Pact (bearing the handwritten note "confirmed 29 March 1961"), March 19, 1961, pp. 96–8, 792/79/4372, RGAE.

61 Cf. Note on the fulfillment of the requirements of the armies of the Warsaw Pact countries for military hardware from 1961 to 1965, March 1961, pp. 106–7, 792/79/4372, RGAE; *Zur geschichtlichen Entwicklung und Rolle der Nationalen Volksarmee*, p. 200.

62 Cf. Appendix to the draft resolution of the PCC of the Warsaw Pact – lists of arms deliveries for the member states, 1962–1965, March 1961, pp. 24–65 – 792/79/4372, RGAE. For more detailed information on the R-11 and Luna nuclear weapon delivery systems, see Harald Nielsen, *Die DDR und die Kernwaffen: Die nukleare Rolle der Nationalen Volksarmee im Warschauer Pakt* (Baden-Baden: Nomos 1998).

63 Cf. Record of discussions of the Joint High Command on December 1–2, 1960, December 1960, pp. 59–71, AZN 32594, BA–MA; Martin Kunze, "Das nukleare Trägerpotential der Nationalen Volksarmee," in *Im Gleichschritt?* pp. 201–8.

64 According to the minutes of the Joint High Command meeting of March 31, 1961, the following combat troops of the EGA were under Warsaw Pact command in peacetime: 1 missile brigade (R-11), 4 motorized rifle divisions, 2 armored divisions, 3 training regiments, 2 artillery regiments, and 2 anti-aircraft regiments. The air force provided 2 air defense divisions, comprising a total of 5 anti-aircraft missile regiments and 6 fighter squadrons, and also 1 helicopter squadron, 1 signal regiment, and 8 ground support battalions. The entire combat naval resources of the Volksmarine [People's Navy], comprising 4 frigates, 18 corvettes, 12 missile patrol boats, 27 large torpedo boats, 45 small torpedo boats, 12 minelayers, 24 minesweepers, and 18 landing craft, plus 1 *Sopka* missile battery, were also under the command of the Joint High Command. Further security and supply units of the EGA were also included, such as reconnaissance, sapper, intelligence, signal, and transport troops. In total, already in peacetime there were 90,000 men under the command of the military leadership of the

Warsaw Pact. Only the Ministry of National Defense, the training facilities, and the military district (*Wehrbezirk* and *Wehrbereich*) commands remained under the command of the GDR. For a defense situation at the beginning of the 1960s, a further three (mobilization) divisions and newly formed troop formations were to be placed under the command of the Joint High Command. The combat strength of the East German forces was stated in the protocol in 1961 as at around 200,000 men. Another 40,000–50,000 men were to serve as territorial defense troops and would therefore have been under the command of the Ministry of National Defense rather than the Warsaw Pact. Cf. Breakdown of target strengths of the East German Army prepared for the chief of staff of the Joint High Command, Army General Aleksei Innokentevich Antonov, January 30, 1962, pp. 37–47, AZN 32871, BA–MA. See also Heinrich Engelhardt, "Das Mobilmachungssystem der NVA," in *NVA: Anspruch und Wirklichkeit; nach ausgewählten Dokumenten*, ed. Klaus Naumann (Hamburg; Berlin; Bonn: Mittler, 1996), pp. 301–16; Fritz Streletz, "Der Nationale Verteidigungsrat der DDR und das Vereinigte Oberkommando des Warschauer Vertrages," in *Rührt euch! Zur Geschichte der NVA*, ed. Wolfgang Wünsche (Berlin: Edition Ost, 1998), pp. 130–73.

65 Cf. Martin Kunze, "Das nukleare Trägerpotential der Nationalen Volksarmee," pp. 214–23. The reason for the prompt delivery of the missiles may have been an exchange of letters to this effect between Ulbricht and Khrushchev, in which the East German Head of State and Party Chairman, immediately after the meeting of the Armaments Committee of COMECON held on March 17, requested that priority should be given to the missile deliveries. See letter from the Minister of National Defense, Army General Heinz Hoffmann, to the commander-in-chief of the Joint High Command, Marshal Andrei A. Grechko, March 24, 1961, pp. 1–2, AZN 32598, BA–MA.

66 Cf. Letter from Malinovskii, Riabikov, and Arkhipov for the CC of the CPSU, July 6, 1962, p. 312, 298/80/4372/, RGAE.

67 Cf. Letter from Khrushchev to Kádár, January 1962, p. 18, 298/80/4372, RGAE.

68 Cf. Draft resolution of the USSR Council of Ministers on the delivery of an R-11 missile brigade to Hungary, January 1962, pp. 8–12, 298/80/4372, RGAE. The Soviet Union did not charge its alliance partners for any of the costs for the storage of warheads in the USSR. For details on the handing over and installation of nuclear warheads, see Nielsen, *Die DDR und die Kernwaffen*, pp. 115–35 and Martin Kunze, "Das nukleare Trägerpotential der Nationalen Volksarmee," pp. 228–30. Here, too, an exception applied in the case of East Germany. The atomic warheads allocated to the EGA under the command of the Group of Soviet Forces in Germany (GSFG) were already located on East German territory. In the mid-1960s, East Germany had built two nuclear warhead depots for this purpose, handed over for the use by the GSFG on completion. The facilities near Stolzenhain and Himmelpfort were each capable of housing up to 120 nuclear warheads. Himmelpfort was to supply the 3rd Army of the EGA (Military District III), to be formed in the event of war, with atomic warheads, and the Stolzenhain depot was designed to supply the requirements of the 5th Army (Military District V) for nuclear weapons. See Manfred van Heerde, *Stahltür 01–2001: Kernsprengkopflager 5001 der Sowjetischen Streitkräfte in Deutschland* (Frankfurt/Oder: Stahltür, 2001); *Geheimes Atomwaffenlager in Deutschland*, production of the Galileo unit of the Pro Sieben television channel, February 28, 2002.

69 Cf. Study material for the East German Chiefs of Staff: *Offensive Operations of a Combined-Arms Army in the Initial Period of a War*, December 5, 1958, p. 95, DVW-1/4358, BA–MA; Combat order for the 35th Army Corps of the EGA in the "Nordwind" exercise, June 28, 1962, pp. 338–41, DVW-1/5195, BA–MA.

70 Speech of the Deputy Soviet Minister of Defense Marshal Andrei A. Grechko on the evaluation of a command post exercise by the GSFG and the EGA, May 1961, p. 1, DVW-1/5203, BA–MA.

71 Speech of the Soviet Minister of Defense Marshal Rodion Ia. Malinovskii on the evaluation of a command post exercise by the GSFG and the EGA, October 1961, p. 52, DVW-1/5203, BA–MA.

72 Cf. Ibid., p. 52.
73 Cf. Ibid., pp. 58–9.
74 Speech of the Soviet Minister of Defense Marshal Rodion Ia. Malinovskii on the XXII Congress of the CPSU. *Neues Deutschland*, October 23, 1961, no. 294.
75 Cf. Paweł Piotrowski, *A Landing Operation in Denmark*, http://www.isn.ethz.ch/php/ collections/coll_12.htm (October 24, 2005); Map of command post exercise *Buria*, undated, p. 304, DVW-1/ 6289–2, BA–MA.
76 Cf. Vojtech Mastny, Petr Luňák, Anna Locher, and Christian Nünlist, *Taking Lyon on the Ninth Day? The 1964 Warsaw Pact Plan for Nuclear War in Europe and Related Documents*, http://www.isn.ethz.ch/php/collections/coll_1.htm (October 24, 2005). See also the article of Vojtech Mastny in this book.
77 Speech of the commander-in-chief of the Joint High Command Marshal Andrei A. Grechko on the evaluation of a command post exercise by the GSFG and the EGA, October 14, 1961, p. 59, DVW-1/5191, BA–MA.
78 Cf. Hans-Christian Pilster, "Vor zwanzig Jahren: Das erste große Warschauer-Pakt Manöver gegenüber Mitteleuropa," *Soldat und Technik*, no. 10 (1981): 545; USAREUR Intelligence Estimat 1962 (U), January 1, 1962, p. 21, http://www.isn.ethz. ch/php/collections/coll_7.htm (October 24, 2005).
79 Cf. Report of General Gerhard Wessel (G 2) for the Military Command Council of the FRG, November 7, 1961, BW-2/2226, BA–MA.
80 Cf. Joachim Schunke, "Feindbild und militärische Beurteilung des Gegners in der NVA," pp. 187–8; Letter from General Antonov to General Hoffmann, September 14, 1961, pp. 72–4, AZN 32595, BA–MA; Situation reports of the Armed Forces Staff of the Bundeswehr (Fü B II 3), October–November 1961, BW-2/2226, BA–MA.
81 Cf. Harald Kießlich-Köcher, "Kriegsbild und Militärstrategie der UdSSR," in *Rührt euch!* pp. 581–7.

3 War plans from Stalin to Brezhnev

The Czechoslovak pivot

Petr Luňák

In assessing the importance of Soviet military planning in Eastern Europe, the case of Czechoslovakia is special and critical for the understanding of the vicissitudes of that planning, its few strengths and many weaknesses. Situated on the frontline of a possible clash between the East and West although not on the main strategic direction, as were Poland and the German Democratic Republic (GDR), Czechoslovakia played throughout the entire Cold War a prominent role in the Soviet strategy for winning the next European war. Yet its armed forces, though numerous if measured against the size of the country, were hardly impressive in view of the challenges they were supposed to overcome. Following the transformation of the Soviet military theory and practice in the wake of Stalin's death, the untested Czechoslovak armed forces had been expected to bear the brunt of the first stages of an offensive war against the US forces stationed in the Federal Republic of Germany (FRG). This was to be done with the support but very little participation of the Soviet troops that were to be fully engaged on the strategic, northern direction. After 1968, even as the presence of Soviet troops on Czechoslovak soil reduced the significance of the Czechoslovak armed forces for the implementation of the Soviet strategy, the Czechoslovak troops were still expected to march deep into the West alongside the Soviet army.

As a result of the initiative of the Parallel History Project and the generous declassification policy of the Czech Ministry of Defense, we now have more information about Czechoslovakia's planning for war during the Cold War than we have about the plans of any other country within the Soviet bloc, particularly the Soviet Union itself. The Czechoslovak documents differ from similar documents released to date from other Eastern European archives in that they contain not only designs for Warsaw Pact maneuvers but also detailed plans as well as their summaries in the event of a military conflict in Europe.

However, although these documents offer significant insight into the Czechoslovak role in the war preparations of the East, they provide only a partial view of the overall eastern military planning. Based on Soviet instructions, the available plans rarely – beyond the routine invocation of inflicting the greatest damage possible on the imperialists – mention the way in which, according to the Soviet planners, the US–Soviet clash would develop or what would be the next stage of the conflict after the Czechoslovak armed forces had fulfilled their putative historical role in defeating the first echelons of the imperialist armies. Until we have access to Soviet military archives (still only a remote possibility) we can only speculate about the Soviet intentions.

Stalin's windfall and its pitfalls

Given that the country was not traditionally part of the Russian security perimeter and did not even share a border with the Soviet Union during the interwar period, Czechoslovakia's strategic importance for Stalin was not immediately obvious. Having acceded to the French–Czechoslovak alliance in 1935 for political rather than military purposes, Stalin had little reason to regret the demise of the alliance after the French defaulted on their obligation and the Czechoslovak elites did not find their nation worth defending. Accordingly, Stalin struck a deal with Hitler that seemed to provide for peace with Germany as well as a free hand in areas that he considered crucial to Soviet security.

Seeing the Soviet Union as the ultimate guarantor of a solution to the German question, the exiled president Edvard Beneš and his mostly Soviet-friendly entourage during the Second World War turned Czechoslovakia into the only willing Soviet ally in Eastern Europe. This happened at the insistence and with the encouragement of Czechoslovak Communists who were notoriously subservient to Mascow, rather than as a result of direct pressure from Moscow itself.

Nor did Czechoslovakia play a prominent role in Stalin's postwar strategic designs for Europe compared with Poland, Finland, Romania, or even Hungary. Moscow contented itself with the territorial acquisition of Transcarpathia and did not act upon the proposal of some overzealous Slovak Communists to break Slovakia away and turn it into a Soviet republic. It showed its readiness to tolerate some sort of pluralist system in Czechoslovakia dominated by the Communists, relying on the region's most Russophile or even Sovietophile populace outside of Bulgaria. Similar to the case in France, Italy, or Belgium but very different from that in other Central European countries, the Communists in Czechoslovakia won the largely free – although not entirely fair – elections in 1946.

Defeats of Communists in local elections in western occupation zones in Germany as well as the timely expulsion of subversive Italian and French Communists from their national governments in 1947 cast doubt on the realization of Stalin's vision of a weak, fragmented Europe susceptible to the influence of Communists although not necessarily under their direct rule. Having originally planned to participate in the Marshall Plan on its own terms, Moscow turned it down as a sign of political reversal, forcing Warsaw and Prague to do the same. With the Iron Curtain falling, Czechoslovakia, which had previously been of little strategic significance, acquired a strategic importance of the first order.

Having been served to Moscow on a silver platter, Czechoslovakia fell easy prey for Stalin once he decided to take it in 1948 – with virtually no resistance from the country's democratic elites or the quiescent population.

It is something of a paradox that the few combat traditions the country had were mostly connected to the exploits of the Czechoslovak legions who actively participated in the fight against the Bolsheviks and who were thus the only segment of Czechoslovak society – except for the Communists – to acquire first-hand experience of Soviet Russia. Under the leadership of Ludvík Svoboda, after the Communist putsch, these traditions were quickly disposed of, together with western-minded, although not necessarily anti-Soviet, members of the Czechoslovak Army Corps formed in the West. (Svoboda was a former legionary who was notorious for his subservience to Soviet marshals but masqueraded as a non-Communist Minister of Defense during 1945–48.) Accordingly, under the stewardship of the ubiquitous Soviet advisors, the Czechoslovak armed forces were purged – with Svoboda himself one of the victims in 1950. Under defense minister Alexej Čepička, who had no frontline experience but proved his credentials while presiding over the bolshevization of the Czechoslovak judiciary, the class-minded Czechoslovak command set about imagining a future conflict with the West, which was viewed as being intent on aggression.

The Czechoslovak plans drafted under Stalin, at the time when the risk of East–West confrontation was arguably most acute, remained unequivocally defensive. According to the *Orel* (Eagle) plan drafted by the Czechoslovak general staff in January 1951, the expected western attack could begin with an assault on Soviet forces in the GDR and the Soviet occupation zone in Austria. It would then continue against "the people's democracies in Czechoslovakia and Hungary, with the assistance of Yugoslavia," with the goal of creating a bridgehead for an attack against the Soviet Union. Nevertheless, as far as western preparedness to carry out such an offensive was concerned, the Czechoslovak document tended to take a somewhat longer-term perspective, for it supposed that "the imperialists do not intend to start the fight without German divisions." However, it would be necessary in any case to "expect American efforts to shorten the deadline for building a European army to include German divisions, and to increase the number of those divisions" (a reference to the process launched by the Pleven plan in fall 1950).

Czechoslovak planners estimated that the West was capable of fielding a maximum of 33 divisions on the first day of the conflict, 39 a week after mobilization, and 56 nine days after the beginning of the conflict. As to air forces, the Czechoslovak command came to the less reassuring conclusion that the West had an 11:1 superiority in the number of planes in the Central European theater. However, assuming that the adversary's ultimate goal was to occupy Soviet territory, the general conclusion was that "the western imperialists will not have sufficient forces in 1952 to begin a military conflict."[1]

The aim of the *Orel* plan was to not allow the enemy "to penetrate Czechoslovak territory." Thereafter, it was to "create advantageous conditions for an offensive," without specifying what that offensive would look like.

The *Pěst* (Fist) plan of March 1951 was a continuation of *Orel* after the completion of mobilization. Its objective was for the Czechoslovak army, after successfully defending its home territory, to launch an offensive and over four or five days "to reach the rivers Naab and Danube" and "control bridgeheads on the south side of the Danube River in the area of Regensburg – Straubing."[2]

These early plans aimed to anticipate alleged offensive preparations in the West. They were deemed necessary to counter a putative western surprise attack such as had brought the Soviet Union to the verge of defeat in the summer of 1941 – as Stalin knew better than anyone else. Preparations, of course, could not be concealed – just as in June 1941. Therefore, mobilization was to be announced "as soon as the concentration of enemy forces in the depth of the territory of West Germany becomes obvious... so as to precede the mobilization of the enemy even at the price of what seems to be a premature mobilization."[3]

In order to avoid a repetition of the Soviet 1941 experience, these plans emphasized early action. Whereas the Soviet generals were preparing to fight their previous war, the Czechoslovak plans attempted to avoid some of their past mistakes.

The plans assumed that the West would from the outset make use "especially of its air force for ruthless bombing of towns and villages, industrial enterprises and especially railroads, bridges, and all communications." The first objective of these attacks would be "to break the morale of our peoples, and cripple the mobilization and concentration of the Czechoslovak army." They would be followed by an invasion and occupation of the country by mechanized units. Although eastern strategists were not far off the mark in predicting the West's emphasis on bombing to destroy the ability of its adversary to wage war, their belief in an intended massive thrust eastward was mistaken, as Stalin was in a position to know. However, Stalin also knew how fragile his Communist-ruled dependencies still were, and he could not be certain what would happen if their resilience were to be tested, so the imagined scenario played to his primary fear. All he could do, for whatever it was worth, was prepare the Czechoslovak army for this dire eventuality, no matter how improbable.

The Czechoslovak plans of the period do not mention the role of the Soviet armed forces in repelling the enemy's onslaught. In extremis, would Stalin not have wanted them to get involved in fighting the Americans, just as he did not get them involved in Korea? Would he perhaps even let Czechoslovakia go, just as he was ready to let North Korea go when its regime was facing collapse under the pressure of the advancing US forces in October 1950?[4] Despite – or perhaps because of – his record of exercising options he later had reasons to regret, Stalin liked to keep his options open. And the despot did not trust the Czechoslovak army any more than he trusted any other Eastern European army.

In January 1951, at the historic Moscow meeting, Stalin startled East European Communist dignitaries by setting "a two to three year" deadline for completion of their war preparations, curiously noting that "it is abnormal that you [East Europeans] should have weak armies." As a result, the Czechoslovak armed forces rose from 170,000 men at the beginning of 1951 to 297,000 men two years later.[5]

Yet the plans *Sokol* (Falcon), and *Hvězda* (Star) worked out in the spring of 1953 by the Czechoslovak military command contained little by way of innovation. According to *Sokol* plan, the main mission of the Czechoslovak forces continued to be "to prevent the penetration of enemy... troops into Czechoslovak territory." This was to be accomplished not only by persistent defense but also through "concentrated strikes against the yet-unprepared enemy," thus undermining his ability to inflict major damage on own forces. The aim again was to create conditions for an offensive without laying out the specifics. Of four submitted variants of the *Hvězda* Plan, President Klement Gottwald, with the consent of his Soviet advisors, approved the scenario in which the Czechoslovak armed forces were to concentrate after mobilization in the vicinity of Prague and then determine on the basis of further developments whether to undertake offensive or defensive operations.[6] These hardly impressive Czechoslovak measures do not shed much light on possible Soviet intentions.

Stalin's death in March 1953 means we can only speculate as to what his intentions were in the long run. Given that we know so little about Soviet war planning at the time, the absence of documents in the Czechoslovak archives containing detailed offensive military planning – beyond vague references to creating advantageous conditions for an offensive – does not automatically confirm Stalin's stance as irreversibly defensive. As documents from other former Warsaw Pact countries suggest, despite the overall military superiority of the East on the ground, the condition of the eastern military machinery and the fragility of Communist regimes probably discouraged Stalin from entertaining more ambitious scenarios. It was perhaps just a matter of time before the increasing eastern military power and the consolidation of Eastern European Soviet dependencies would allow for a strategy that was worthy of true Bolsheviks.

Revision of Stalinist military thought

Stalin's theory of permanently operating factors conformed not only to the lesson he drew from his Second World War experience but also to the fact of US nuclear superiority, which he could not hope to alter in his lifetime. He could not hope to win in a nuclear war; at most, he could hope to deny the enemy a total victory.

Accordingly, after Stalin's death, a debate took place among Soviet marshals on the implications of nuclear weapons. The conclusion was that the moment of surprise in a nuclear conflict has a strategic significance that could determine the outcome of the war in its initial stages. Therefore, in order to prevail in a future conflict, the Soviets concluded that each side would have to aim to be able to launch a surprise attack if war appeared imminent.

Since the debate centered on the role of nuclear weapons in warfare it was not immediately relevant to Czechoslovakia, which did not have them. For several years after Stalin's death, Czechoslovakia's order of battle and the philosophy behind it remained more or less the same as when he was alive. Operational plans up to 1954, for example, mentioned the possibility of using chemical and biological weapons but left nuclear weapons out of the picture.

Only in 1956 did the Czechoslovak command work out its first military strategy that relied on the use of nuclear weapons. According to the plan, approved under the code name *Zástava* in 1957, the West might attack the territory of Czechoslovakia in pursuit of either of two objectives: to cut off Soviet units in the GDR by continuing the offensive into Poland or to move to take control of the uranium mines in Bohemia (Jáchymov and Příbram). However, it was felt that the imperialists would not launch the attack until the 12 German divisions available for NATO had been built. Thus, "the danger of attack on Czechoslovakia [would] be significantly increased" in 1959–60, when the FRG was to be fully integrated into NATO under the terms of Paris accords of 1954. Even so, they said, the present danger should not be underestimated, as the West could "launch an attack with a small number of divisions, relying on weapons of mass destruction to complete the initial surprise attack, and on a gradual increase in the power of the mobilized forces."[7]

The Czechoslovak command derived two possible scenarios. First, in the event of a surprise attack, the Czechoslovak People's Army would have to take up defensive positions and "prepare conditions for launching the offensive in cooperation with neighbors." Alternatively, an immediate attack might be considered if preparations for a western attack were discovered. In such an event, Czechoslovak troops should "strike in the direction of Pilsen-Nuremberg, with the use of nuclear weapons, and in coordination with our neighbors break the concentrated forces of the enemy that is preparing to attack our country." These, of course, would have had to be Soviet nuclear weapons as the Czechoslovak army had none.[8]

The Czechoslovak command was evidently kept in the dark about Soviet intentions beyond the initial stage of any conflict. The offensive component of the overall defensive *Zástava* plan was, according to the Soviet command, intended only to "prepare for the concentration of troops and their deployment for an attack." Czechoslovak strategists, presumably in line with the instructions of their Soviet masters, did not plan at the time for any deep advance into western territory. If any such planning was undertaken, it was entirely in Soviet hands.

The nuclear revolution in Soviet military thought, with its emphasis on the decisive importance of the initial stages of the war for the eventual outcome, was not easy to reconcile with Moscow's continued reluctance to equip satellite armies with nuclear weapons. The Czechoslovak command did not conceal its doubts as to whether it was capable of fulfilling the task assigned to it in the face of an increasing number of western troops armed with nuclear weapons. Its assessment of the *Zástava* plan concluded with a fatalistic observation:

> The Czechoslovak People's Army still has no prospect of receiving nuclear arms of either tactical or operational range; it is also still unknown what atomic resources will be acting in favor of the operations of Czechoslovak People's Army units; this causes problems in working out some of the calculations of the operational plan.[9]

This shows how misleading NATO's practice of counting the satellite armies as full-fledged assets in figuring Soviet military potential was.

There is no indication that Khrushchev himself had any interest in deploying nuclear weapons on the territory of his Eastern European dependencies. After all, even the famously subservient Czechoslovak leadership could not be trusted more than other leaderships. Moreover, deployment would have complicated Khrushchev's efforts toward demilitarization of the Cold War, as manifested in his reduction of the Soviet and East European armies. In October 1955, it was agreed that the Czechoslovak armed forces on active duty went down from 255,000 to 195,000 men. Nevertheless, in the event of war Czechoslovakia was still expected to field 850,000 men.[10]

The Soviet leader, serious in his attempts to create a demilitarized zone in Central Europe, was above all trying to bring about the departure of American troops from the territory of the FRG. He was, therefore, willing to consider withdrawing his troops from some of the Eastern European countries, as he did from Romania in 1958. When Khrushchev mentioned in 1959 the possibility of Soviet troops leaving Hungary, it came as an unpleasant surprise to the Hungarian leader János Kádár, who had been brought to power by Soviet tanks in 1956. Later Khrushchev also considered withdrawing Soviet troops from Poland, as he briefly mentioned during a meeting of the Political Consultative Committee of the Warsaw Pact in 1960.[11]

Eastern bloc exercises in the late 1950s ignored the growing divergence between Soviet plans and Czechoslovak reality. Plans postulated that a western attack would be met by massive nuclear retaliation using Soviet strategic weapons, followed by a Warsaw Pact ground offensive also using nuclear weapons, despite the fact that Eastern European armies did not have such weapons at their disposal. The Czechoslovak command's worries were soothed by an assumption that any military conflict would be preceded by a period of tension, during which there would be time for nuclear weapons to be deployed.[12] This was in apparent conflict with the repeated assertion of Soviet strategists of the importance of the first moments of the war.

The Soviet marshals were aware of the discrepancy and worked toward changing the plans in line with their preferences. In 1957 in East Berlin, Minister of Defense Marshal Georgii Zhukov spoke about the possibility of reaching the Channel in less than two days in the event of mounting a surprise attack against the West. A few months later in Prague he unwittingly confirmed his way of thinking by telling his audience that "we should not speak openly about.... the sudden pre-emptive attacks."[13] Despite Zhukov's dismissal, Supreme Commander of the Warsaw Pact Unified Command Ivan Konev, presiding over April 1959 maneuvers to simulate a massive ground thrust into Western Europe, criticized the Czechoslovaks for basing their counter-strike purely on defensive thinking and not on the goal of the "destruction of the adversary."[14]

Czechoslovak leaders had little choice other than to live with Moscow's vagaries, which stemmed from the growing divergence between the political conduct of the Cold War exemplified by Khrushchev and military planning for "hot war" conducted by Soviet marshals. Having been assigned the unenviable task of resisting western forces on their own during the initial stages of a war, the Czechoslovak command seems to have been kept in the dark as to the precise Soviet plans for the next stage. Could Moscow until the late 1950s have been considering a mere pushback of the enemy forces without a massive ground counter-offensive, followed by some sort of political settlement, as suggested by the Czechoslovak *Zástava* plan? An affirmative answer to this question would imply not only a less revolutionary departure from late Stalinist plans than is generally assumed to have taken place but also a glimpse of a sounder strategy than the absurd plans developed in the 1960s.

If Warsaw Pact strategists reckoned that a western attack was not imminent, this was because the other side was assumed not yet to have managed to put together the required number of ground forces. In April 1959, six months after Khrushchev's ultimatums sparked the Berlin Crisis, the Czechoslovak command had come to the conclusion that "the present status of ground forces thus far does not meet the requirements of NATO for launching war." However, this situation was deemed to be only temporary, for by 1963 twelve German divisions would finally be built, French forces would be freed up from Algeria, and the number of "atomic strike units" would also be increased. Likewise, American intercontinental nuclear missiles would be available in 1960. For now, the balance was more favorable to the West in regard to air forces, but these would not be enough to compensate for "the insufficiency of ground forces, which is thus far not offset by the required number of ground-based means of atomic attack, and does not allow for the development of larger-scale operations."[15]

Khrushchev's strategic innovations

The Czechoslovak documents lend support to the view that Khrushchev's emphasis on the all-out nuclear character of the next war was initially little more than posturing for political show, without much operational substance. They shed new light on how limited was the impact of Khrushchev's strategic innovations, stemming from the alleged successes of Soviet missile technology and epitomized by his early 1960 announcement of massive cuts in Soviet ground troops.

New operational plans for the Czechoslovak People's Army being drafted on Soviet instructions in 1960 may or may not have been an expression of opposition by the conservative military establishment to Khrushchev's pressure to reduce conventional forces and certain categories of conventional armaments. In any event, one could hardly read into them any hope of bringing the emerging Soviet strategy in line with Khrushchev's demilitarization rhetoric. According to these plans, if the West managed to carry out a first nuclear strike, Czechoslovak troops were immediately to start the counter-offensive and by the end of the fifth day they were to be operating 100–120 km inside the territory of the FRG. On the evening of the fifth day, Soviet reinforcements were to arrive and "from there go on to attack further in the western direction." According to the assessment of the Czechoslovak command, this was the maximum push the Czechoslovak armed forces could achieve on their own in the event of a surprise attack by the enemy.

If, on the other hand, "a massive rocket attack of an operational/strategic character by the Soviet Union" was successfully carried out, the Czechoslovak general staff planned on the fifth day already to be reaching the bridgehead on the Rhine, where Soviet forces would take up the initiative. All the offensive forces of the Czechoslovak army would be pitted against the FRG, as the plan included "assuring the neutrality of Austria by means of a quick advance by allied forces from Hungary" onto Austrian soil.[16] Despite Khrushchev's statements and perhaps intentions of early 1960, the role of ground forces was far from being reduced. According to Czechoslovak military documents, the Soviet leadership approved what were apparently Czechoslovak "arguments for the necessity of transferring military activity onto enemy territory as soon as possible, regardless of the arrival of allied [Warsaw Pact] armed forces."[17]

The reorganization of the Czechoslovak armed forces reflected the Soviet command's penchant for massive ground operations on the model of the Second World War. The proposed changes were focused – at least for the Czechoslovak People's Army (ČSLA) – not primarily on reducing the overall number of armed forces but instead on keeping the existing units "at nearly wartime strength levels during peacetime." This was to be achieved through reorganization and reducing planned wartime personnel rosters in the mechanized infantry and tank divisions while preserving "the instant preparedness of the main combined armed forces for combat activity with emphasis on offensive operations."[18] In other words, there should be a greater number of smaller but more mobile units, prepared to go on the march into enemy territory. Thus, planned reductions of Soviet ground forces were not accompanied by a similar downsizing of Eastern European armed forces.

The timing of these changes was as important as the changes themselves. Initial rounds of discussions between high-ranking Soviet and Czechoslovak officers were held in the spring of 1960. It seems, however, that the Soviet party leadership was not ready at that time to allow the Soviet Command to undertake anything that could impede what it considered to be the road toward the solution of the Berlin issue on Soviet terms. Thus, in April 1960, the Soviet command announced that whereas air-to-ground missiles would be supplied to the Czechoslovak armed forces, ground-to-ground missiles, which were more useful in offensive operations, were not to be provided "in view of the political situation."[19] Shortly before, Moscow had decided to withdraw the medium-range missiles recently issued to the Soviet troops on GDR territory.[20]

After the aborted May 1960 summit in Paris, hopes of arriving at a solution of the Berlin issue seemed all but dashed, and Moscow decided to speed up its preparations in view of NATO's alleged intention to have its armies "at the maximum level of combat readiness by 1963." In October 1960 the Soviet command confirmed that ground-to-ground missiles would be supplied to the Czechoslovak armed forces.[21] A further step toward an outright offensive posture was taken when Moscow announced in February 1961 that by 1964 ground-to-ground missiles for use at divisional level would also be supplied. Evidently, although it was ready to adopt a bolder strategy that would better reflect its deep-seated suspicions of western intentions, the military had to wait until the party leadership was ready to give its consent.[22]

The decision to provide East European allies with these arsenals was officially adopted at a session of the Political Consultative Committee of the Warsaw Pact in March 1961 in Moscow. However, for Czechoslovak generals the effect of these welcome measures was diminished by the fact that the nuclear warheads (use of which was to be decided exclusively by the Soviets) were to remain on Soviet soil until tensions began to escalate; only then would a special Soviet unit transfer them to the territory of the Eastern European satellites.

All of these measures were adopted before the Berlin Wall was erected in the summer of 1961. Shortly after the wall was built, Khrushchev cancelled the announced reduction of Soviet ground troops, thus putting an end to all hopes of a possible recasting of the Soviet strategic posture.

The 1964 war plan

When evidence about contemporary decision making began to filter out after the end of the Cold War it became clear that the Berlin crisis had been more serious than it had seemed. Having sparked the crisis in the belief that he would be able to wrest from the West a solution to the Berlin issue on his own terms, Khrushchev eventually mismanaged it. On the eve of his contentious June 1961 meeting with J.F. Kennedy in Vienna, he estimated at only 5 percent the probability that signing a peace treaty with East Germany and denying the West the right of access to Berlin would result in a war with the West.[23] In the wake of Kennedy's announcement of defensive measures in late July 1961, Khrushchev lost his 95 percent certainty. Nevertheless, after the construction of the Berlin Wall the following month, which was then seen as a deliberate measure to defuse the crisis, Moscow started high-visibility preparations in order to dissuade the West from going to war over Berlin or, in the worst case, in order to be ready to fight the war should it break out.

As the crisis mounted, with the prospect of Moscow's conclusion of a separate peace treaty with East Germany coming closer, the Czechoslovak armed forces were tasked with preparing the country's communications systems for the arrival of Soviet troops and nuclear ammunition.[24] Expecting an enemy attack on the dams on the Vltava River, which would result in devastating floods, in July 1961 the Czechoslovak government – apparently less sure than Khrushchev that war would not erupt – had already ordered pontoon bridges to be produced to enable the Czechoslovak army to cross the flooded river. The bridges were still not ready when the crisis peaked, so the government intended at least to reduce the water level in the dams.[25]

In order to convince the West that it was ready to start a war in Europe, in September–October 1961 the Warsaw Pact implemented a massive war game under the code name *Buria* (Storm). The scenario was that in the wake of a massive nuclear attack by NATO, the Polish army would pour into the northern part of West Germany and then take the Netherlands and Denmark. In a similarly ambitious exercise in December 1961, the Czechoslovak front, with 130 nuclear bombs at its disposal, was assigned the task of reaching the area of Besançon–Belfort in the shortest possible time.[26]

Although conflict was averted after Khrushchev's decision by the end of 1961 to shelve indefinitely the signing of the peace treaty with East Germany, the crisis had a more enduring impact than previously thought. To the great satisfaction of Soviet marshals, Khrushchev's unfortunate mismanagement of the Berlin crisis paved the way for the continuing militarization of the Cold War and intensified war planning. According to eastern military planners, the possibility of a military clash over Berlin remained one of the likeliest war scenarios in Europe, confirming the lasting effects of the Berlin crisis.

Even though the Cuban missile crisis took place in the western hemisphere, it had an impact on Soviet military planning for a possible conflict in Europe. According to participants in the Soviet operation, Moscow strategists concluded in the wake of the crisis, apparently on the assumption that the other side had drawn the same lesson, that a global nuclear conflict between the superpowers was difficult, if not impossible, to imagine. What was possible to imagine was a conflict in Europe fought with the superpowers' nuclear arsenals.[27] Hence, the superpower détente in the wake of the Cuban missile crisis was far from reassuring in terms of Soviet military planning as far as a European conflict was concerned.

In the summer of 1964, Moscow issued a direct order to modify previous plans, apparently in line with the experience of the recent crises. According to these instructions the Czechoslovak troops were to reach eastern France by the eighth day from the start of the offensive.[28] According to the new operational plan drafted on the basis of this instruction and approved by President Antonín Novotný on October 14, 1964, the Czechoslovak armed forces were to penetrate into the territory of the Federal Republic of Germany and then to continue westwards. The aim was reaching the line Langres-Besançon by the seventh or eighth day from the beginning of the offensive. The Czechoslovak front was then supposed to move on Lyon.

The plans drafted in 1960 assumed reaching the Rhine if a Soviet nuclear attack against military targets in Western Europe was launched, or alternatively a penetration of 100–120 km within four or five days without such an attack. The new plan meant that the Czechoslovak front would apparently have to move deep into enemy territory, regardless of whether or not the strategic/operational nuclear strike had been successfully launched.[29]

The Soviet explanation – that the time required for the second echelon of troops from Poland and the Soviet Union to reach Central Europe had been "recalculated" – was apt to convince only those who wanted to believe it. Some skeptical members of the Czechoslovak command believed that the Soviet failure to consider the effects of an all-out nuclear exchange meant that the Soviets had attempted to formulate a strategy for winning a war in Europe on the basis that they could avoid a direct clash with the United States.

Many of the usually loyal Czechoslovak generals had serious reservations about the implications of the plan. The Czechoslovak front was now expected to advance far into enemy territory against a strong adversary and bear the brunt of the combat for considerably longer than previously planned. The contemporary analysis of the adversary by the general staff was far from encouraging:

> NATO troops in the southeast of the FRG represent in all aspects a strong and well-prepared enemy that can in no way be underestimated. Today's balance of forces is not favorable to us, and if not redressed by a strong rocket attack

right at the outset of the war, there is no guarantee of quick success. . . . Also significant is the attainment of a nearly unified organization by the [NATO] armies that are to operate in the Central European theater. . . . A significant balance between the forces of the US, FRG, and France has been attained especially in rocket forces, artillery, mechanized infantry, communications, and military engineers and logistics . . . faith [in NATO's] own forces is being strengthened, standards of internal discipline are being increased . . . cohesion between all the armies of NATO is deepening.[30]

This unfavorable balance of forces for the Czechoslovak side was due not only to the greater number of delivery vehicles on the enemy side but also to the fact that the potential opponent "has, unlike us, nuclear warheads right with him." According to the Czechoslovak command, the only way to equalize this negative balance would be to undertake a preemptive strike without delay. However, this was complicated by the fact that the transfer of nuclear warheads to Czechoslovakia would take between 12 and 16 hours. As a result, the Czechoslovak general staff had doubts about its own ability to carry out the plan and avoid the territory of Czechoslovakia becoming a battlefield for ground operations, including the use of medium- and short-range nuclear weapons.[31]

The 1964 plan made no provision for an early phase of the war before the use of nuclear weapons, suggesting that in planning for a European conflict the Soviet command was not even entertaining the possibility of nonnuclear war in Europe. In a sense, then, the efforts of the United States to increase the number of available options did not have an immediate impact on eastern planning. The threshold between conventional and nuclear conflict was thus, perhaps, more an intellectual construct of Kennedy's strategists than a real factor in any potential conflict.

If the plan was a blueprint for a European-only war in which a direct clash between the United States and the Soviet Union would be avoided, as some in the Czechoslovak command assumed, it nevertheless did nothing to reduce the role of ground operations; on the contrary, their role was increased. The operations thus conceived reflected no reduction of the Moscow planners' inflated military ambitions, as they continued to rely on the occupation of a large part of Western Europe.

The Czechoslovak leadership faced a dilemma over the consequences of the possible future presence of nuclear warheads on their own territory in peacetime. The possibility of the rapid use of nuclear weapons was potentially one of the few equalizers against a stronger, nuclear-armed enemy facing the Czechoslovak armed forces. On the other hand, the permanent presence of Soviet weapons and troops on Czechoslovak soil, without the possibility of influencing decisions about their use, would only increase the risk of becoming the target of a Western strike. The dilemma was illustrated by the reaction of the Czechoslovak leadership to the proposal of the Polish Minister of Foreign Affairs Adam Rapacki that a nuclear-free zone be created in Central Europe. The Czechoslovak ministries of defense and foreign affairs were against the first phase of the proposal, which was to freeze the number of nuclear weapons in Central Europe, as it would rule out the possibility of deploying nuclear weapons on Czechoslovak territory in the future. Prague changed its mind only after it was ordered to do so by Moscow, which hoped in this way to block the western Multilateral Force project, whereby the United States would provide its allies – especially the FRG – with semi-independent nuclear capability.[32]

Overall, the Czechoslovak leadership hoped that despite uncertainties over Soviet intentions, Soviet nuclear weapons on Czechoslovak soil would influence the balance of forces on the Central European battlefield in its own favor. For the Soviet command, freed from Khrushchev's attempts to bring the Soviet military strategy into line with his efforts to demilitarize the Cold War, the presence of nuclear warheads on Czechoslovak territory would be another step toward realizing the ambitious – and, it should be noted, doubtful – plan to march deep into the West. The Soviet generals were unwilling, however, to explain to their Eastern European allies the rationale behind the war plans and, in a period of growing détente, instead argued for the deployment of nuclear weapons in Czechoslovakia on the basis that the possibility of a surprise attack by the West was increasing.

Unable to influence the formulation of Soviet war plans and subject to increasing Soviet pressure, the Czechoslovak leadership finally decided in the spring of 1965 to officially request that an agreement be signed for the deployment of nuclear warheads on Czechoslovak soil. The request came in the wake of Grechko's announcement at the Legnica war games in March 1965 to the effect that Moscow was ready to conclude an agreement as the West could mount a surprise attack at any time without "a period of tensions."[33] Such a conclusion was hardly justifiable in view of the continuing détente, but it reflected the dire reality that after Khrushchev's dismissal, imagining the next war was left entirely up to the generals, with the Brezhnev leadership giving them a free hand.

The agreement reached in December 1965 dealt with such minute details as security measures to be taken at the top-secret locations where the weapons were to be stored (military exercise sites Mimoň, Jince, and Bílina) but completely left out anything about the manner in which these weapons were to be used in combat, leaving the decision entirely to the Soviets.[34] Czechoslovakia and the other Eastern European countries could only dream about a double-key system on the western model, and unlike France and the United Kingdom, they had no possibility of having at least some influence on escalation by using nuclear weapons of their own.

The crisis of the Warsaw Pact and its nuclear strategy

The first serious discussion of reform in the Warsaw Pact came about both as an effort by the Soviet leadership to make the alliance more effective as an instrument for the planning and waging of war and as a means of dealing with the dissatisfaction of Eastern European satellites over the way the alliance worked. When, in January 1966, Moscow offered its allies some form of institutionalization of the alliance, it was plain that the main intent of the Soviet leadership was to improve the effectiveness of already-existing mechanisms for the allies' participation rather than to give them increased influence in drafting alliance plans. The allies, in turn, tried individually to increase that influence.

In the wake of the Cuban missile crisis, Romania increasingly distanced itself from the Soviet Union. In an attempt to avoid the worst consequences of Moscow's conduct of the Cold War, the Romanian leadership sought an assurance from the United States that Romania would be spared a nuclear attack if it remained neutral in a US–Soviet conflict.[35] Following the Soviet initiative to reform the Warsaw Pact, Bucharest ironically adopted Khrushchev's project of concurrently disbanding military alliances in Europe, but with the primary goal of diluting or even dissolving the Warsaw Pact.

Although they had similar grievances vis-à-vis the Soviet management of the alliance, the northern allies, Czechoslovakia and Poland, could not hope to be spared in a nuclear conflict. Their unenviable geostrategic location, rather than the minimal chance of Moscow loosening ties with its strategically important allies, was at the root of their subsequent policies to reform the Warsaw Pact. Rather than question the desirability of maintaining the Soviet-sponsored alliance, Poland attempted to prevent the possibility of a nuclear war by proposing nuclear-free zones in Central Europe, thus presenting a challenge to the Soviet doctrine.

Czechoslovakia had as strong an interest in reforming the Warsaw Pact as Poland, but for different reasons. Its concrete goal with respect to Soviet doctrine was not the denuclearization of Central Europe; instead, it was to gain assurances that in the event of conflict, nuclear weapons would be employed in accordance with existing plans. Czechoslovak officers, who could hardly be accused of insufficient loyalty to their Soviet counterparts, saw the core issue as being not only the necessity of precisely defining the planning responsibilities of the Pact's joint command in time of peace but above all the way the allied armed forces would work together during war.[36]

In the apparent hope that approved documents would make it more difficult for the Soviets to ignore agreed plans, the Czechoslovaks proposed the formulation of a strategic concept for waging war in Europe. Still unable to conceal their mixed feelings about the implications of the 1964 plan, they requested clarification "of the anticipated effect (in terms of time and space) of strategic strikes on the West European battlefield (during both the first massive strategic strike and during the entire period of assignment of Czechoslovak troops)."[37]

In May 1966, the Czechoslovak delegation to meetings on the reform of the Warsaw Pact expressed its satisfaction that it had been agreed that the supreme commander of the Warsaw Pact "would also be First Deputy Minister of Defense of the USSR, as this would provide direct influence on the use of the strategic forces and resources of the USSR on behalf of the Allied armed forces."[38] This would have been cold comfort, however, if a nuclear war had actually been started.

Warsaw Pact strategists rightly perceived that if the West was in all probability unable to defeat the eastern alliance in a conventional war, or faced defeat itself, then it would have no choice but to resort to using nuclear weapons. In June 1964, Warsaw Pact exercises code-named *Sputnik* assumed for the first time a European conflict that would begin not with a nuclear exchange but with a conventional attack by the West with the limited goal of "annexing" the GDR. If developments were unfavorable, the scenario asssumed that the West would be prepared to use weapons of mass destruction on the third day after the attack.[39] In the same vein, from 1965 on, the exercise instructions for the Czechoslovak army envisaged practicing the initial phases with the use of conventional weapons only, although the main scenario remained – in line with the 1964 plan – a nuclear conflict.

In the spring of 1965, the Czechoslovak command expressed the following opinion on the impossibility of limiting an escalation under the current circumstances:

> There is no way it can be expected even in theory that the side that is evidently weaker in classical [conventional] armaments, or perceives the ratio of forces to be disadvantageous, will not use weapons of mass destruction just because it means violating a few rules or scruples.... And it would become even more absurd if [the attacking side] were to expect such consideration from the defender, or expect that the defender would exacerbate his situation by waiting to use his own nuclear weapons until the moment when the aggressor uses his.[40]

Whatever the considerations in regard to the character of a future war, the existing Soviet plans presented the Eastern European countries with unpleasant prospects. Czechoslovak forces had instructions to march west, with only a fraction expected to survive the first days; meanwhile, as the more outspoken military representatives pointed out, the Czechoslovak leadership would be left without a single division for territorial defense.

The frequent re-equipping of the Eastern European armies to prepare for every kind of offensive war strained their economies.[41] To the Soviet command's annoyance, in 1964 in a rare moment of standing up to excessive Soviet demands, the Czechoslovak command suggested abolishing three air regiments in order to save resources. The Soviet command opposed the reduction, even though it agreed that the ČSLA would still be able to achieve its mission as set out in the 1964 plan. When the chief of the general staff, General Otakar Rytíř, opposed the Soviet requirements at the January 1966 meeting in Moscow, the Soviet command refused to approve the five-year plan for the buildup of the Czechoslovak armed forces. Only in April 1967 was the dispute resolved, when Brezhnev himself intervened in favor of the Czechoslovak arguments. The dispute was a vivid example not only of the insufficiency of the Warsaw Pact to solve this kind of problem but also of the fact that Prague's suggestion only mitigated the economic consequences of the Soviet strategy rather than offering a viable alternative.[42]

Overestimating the strategic foresight of the opponent, in 1968 General Rytíř went so far as declaring the doctrine of flexible response to be a clever ruse by the West to force the Eastern bloc into economically debilitating preparations for every possible type of conflict. However, unable to break from his past, the general suggested that a better option would be to plan a massive nuclear war as the main scenario for a next conflict.[43]

Although Soviet concepts of the conventional phase of a conflict were based on the assumption of the overall superiority of Warsaw Pact conventional forces, they ignored the rather important fact that along the planned Czechoslovak line of attack, the potential adversary had overall conventional superiority. In view of the absence of nuclear weapons on its own territory, the Czechoslovak command was concerned that in the event of a nuclear attack by the West, the Czechoslovak front would be wholly incapable of taking the offensive action required by the operational plan. Czechoslovak estimates were that the situation would steadily worsen for the first three or four days of a conflict, at the end of which the Czechoslovak troops would be able to undertake only limited offensive action in some places. By that time, according to the 1964 plan, the Czechoslovak front was supposed to be operating in central Germany. It was alleged that only "measures realized during the period of growing danger" (that is, issuing nuclear warheads to Czechoslovak units) could at least somewhat mitigate this generally disadvantageous situation. Otherwise, the West's superiority against the Czechoslovak front in terms of conventional forces, and its absolute superiority in terms of nuclear weapons, would make the plan of reaching eastern France within seven to eight days impossible.[44]

Frustrated by the Soviets, progressive Czechoslovak military experts took advantage of Israel's lightning victory against the Arab alliance in the Six-Day War of 1967 to raise a number of questions they considered relevant to the European theater as well. According to a contemporary report on the Middle East conflict, the Arab defeat was the result of an overall lack of preparedness, lack of coordination in operational planning, and poor intelligence work. Although some parts of the Czechoslovak evaluation could be interpreted as supporting Soviet efforts to streamline the Warsaw Pact, the positive conclusions drawn regarding the military rationale of the steps taken by Israel ran counter to the Soviet strategy. According to Czechoslovak military specialists, Israel had rightly concentrated on destroying selected targets from the air and not on an exhausting and difficult frontal attack on the enemy's entire force, as was envisioned in the plans of the Warsaw Pact to defeat NATO.[45]

Although Moscow brushed aside these conclusions, they resurfaced during the 1968 Prague Spring. Instructors at the Military Political Academy wrote a memorandum to the new party chief, Alexander Dubček, which recommended, among many daring revisions of the imposed Soviet wisdom, the formulation of a true Czechoslovak strategy that would try to prevent an outbreak of war in Europe. In view of the limited military capabilities of the country, political rather than military means should be employed. If nevertheless a war broke out, the Czechoslovak leadership should concentrate on key objectives such as limiting "its destructive consequences on [Czechoslovak territory] and against its population." This was a clear challenge to the plan for a frontal march to the west assigned by the Soviets.[46]

Although the agitation within the Czechoslovak military indicated that many of its more enlightened minds had long been having misgivings about where the

Soviet strategy was leading the country, few actually acted upon these misgivings. Dubček, in particular, never cast doubt upon the loyalty of his country to the Warsaw Pact. During a March 1968 Sofia meeting of the Political Consultative Committee, in an intervention against an open Romanian obstruction to reforming the Warsaw Pact, Dubček stated, "as far as we are concerned, our security is solved by the nuclear might of the Soviet Union."[47]

Nonetheless, the question remained of what might happen if the reform-minded Communist leadership lost control of the situation and a liberated society began to raise hitherto taboo issues, including the consequences of implementing the Soviet strategy for country's survival.

In another variation on the supposed military motivation of the August 1968 invasion, a recent study of "fraternal aggression" argues that the operation was largely intended to alter the military balance in Europe by moving the Soviet army to an advanced position in Czechoslovakia and installing Soviet nuclear weapons on its territory.[48] There is no indication, however, that these considerations played a significant role in the Soviet decision to invade the country in order to reverse its course toward democratization. The nuclear-equipped Soviet troops in the GDR and Poland provided enough of a counterbalance to the military inferiority on the Czechoslovak line of attack, which was to be partially redressed by storing nuclear weapons on Czechoslovakian soil, as agreed in 1965. Available sources indicate that Prague was always more worried than Moscow about the ability of the Czechoslovak forces to implement the strategy.

There is no evidence that Prague may have intentionally procrastinated with the agreed construction of the nuclear storage facilities, supposed to have been completed by mid-1967.[49] Although the deadline was not met, the Czechoslovak leadership never questioned the decision in earnest. When in May 1968 Defense Minister Bohumír Lomský recommended to Dubček that "in view of the current political situation" the prospective presence of the Soviet weapons and some 750 personnel should be reconsidered he added that their deployment is "fully justified by the defense needs of Czechoslovakia and the whole Socialist camp." Alternatively, he suggested training Czechoslovak troops to look after the facilities, presumably until the "political situation" has changed.[50] Clearly, the Czechoslovak command was worried the most about how the democratizing Czechoslovak society would accept foreign military presence on its soil.

Rather than questioning the basic assumptions of the Soviet strategy, Prague focused on easing its economic burdens. When in 1967 the Czechoslovak leadership mooted the possibility of changing the operational plan of the Czechoslovak armed forces, it again used economic arguments.[51] In the same vein, before the invasion the Czechoslovak leadership had already envisaged decreasing peace-time troop levels from 231,000 to 170,000–180,000 and lowering the number of reserves by about 50,000 draftees. Doubts on the part of the Czechoslovak command as to the Soviet concept of war were exacerbated by the fact that Moscow, despite the planned deployment of nuclear warheads on Czechoslovak territory, had no plans to deliver a replacement for the R-11/SCUD missiles, which was to be retired between 1970 and 1973.[52]

The aftermath of 1968

After 1968, the strategic importance of Czechoslovakia and its army was not the same as it had been before. Although the invasion itself did anything but demonstrate the ability of the East to pursue its ambitious strategy on the ground, from that point onward Moscow did not have to rely on the Czechoslovak armed forces in implementing it. In this respect, the completion between December 1968 and the spring of 1969 of three facilities to store nuclear weapons, to be made available to the Czechoslovak armed forces, was much less significant as the Czechoslovak front had been fully integrated into the Soviet army.[53]

Similarly, purges of the Czechoslovak officer corps coincided with the completion of the reform of the Warsaw Pact in 1969, which created a unified strategic culture. If, in the 1960s, Czechoslovak generals had complained that they were inadequately informed of Soviet strategic intentions, the reformed Warsaw Pact settled that problem to some extent by taking into Soviet confidence selected top brass, though not a significant number of Czechoslovak officers.

Just how seriously the Czechoslovak army, closely guided from Moscow, embraced the notion that a war could be waged and won without resort to nuclear weapons is very difficult to ascertain from the documents. It may not have been very clear in the planners' minds either.

The overall character of Moscow's intentions remained difficult for its allies to fathom. According to the operational plans in effect, the conflict on the Central European battlefield was expected to be nuclear from the beginning, yet maneuvers included scenarios beginning with attacks by the West, either using or not using nuclear weapons. From the standpoint of the Czechoslovak front, the main difference between the two scenarios was the speed of the scheduled advance to the West. For example, in the TARAN exercise, the Czechoslovak front was to control the territory as far as the German–French border within 11 days with the use of nuclear weapons and within 17 days without them.[54]

Either way, it was assumed that the conflict would sooner or later enter a nuclear phase. In the *Západ* (West) war games of 1969, it was assumed that the enemy would attack with conventional weapons and advance into Czechoslovakia and the GDR. After launching counter-offensives, the eastern forces were to take the offensive while the West, "after failing to reach the designated objective by conventional means," would employ tactical nuclear weapons. Reflecting Soviet views on the matter, former supreme Warsaw Pact commander and then the Soviet defense minister, Marshal Andrei Grechko, criticized participants playing the enemy side for having unrealistically "advanced to the depth of 600 kilometers [into Eastern bloc territory] without the use of nuclear weapons."[55]

The Czechoslovak evidence casts doubt on those contemporary western estimates which assumed that Soviet strategy had substantially changed. Although the Soviet command considered the possibility of an early stage of the conflict without the use of weapons of mass destruction, according to the plans the likeliest scenario for the conflict remained a surprise nuclear strike by the West. Operational plans from 1974 assumed a nuclear attack by the West, after which eastern armies were to advance by all possible means in the direction of Nuremberg–Stuttgart/Munich and "by the seventh and eighth day to reach the line Langres-Besançon" to "mount an attack on Lyon," suggesting hardly any change from the 1964 plan.[56] Thus, if Soviet exercises acknowledged the possibility of a conventional war, it was not as a substitute for, but as a prelude to, nuclear conflict.

The Israeli victory in the 1973 Yom Kippur War, which was regarded as a possible preview of a conflict in Europe, was not seen by the Warsaw Pact command as a challenge to its existing strategy but rather as a reminder of its own weakness in the area of modern communications technology. In the aftermath of the war, at a meeting of Warsaw Pact defense ministers, Marshal Grechko emphasized "the need to build and employ communications systems comprising a complex of cable, radio, radio relay, tropospheric, and cosmic (INTERSPUTNIK) assets" and pointed out that NATO allegedly was devoting 30 percent of its entire military budget to such assets.[57]

Curiously, according to the Czechoslovak operational plan of 1977, Czechoslovak units were to reach the French border by the eighth to ninth day, regardless of whether nuclear weapons were employed, suggesting that the planners "solved" the problems around their strategy by ignoring them.[58] However, the eastern strategists were more realistic during actual maneuvers, acknowledging implicitly that the ground forces of the enemy had significantly improved. For example, during the *Západ 77* exercises, the Warsaw Pact, attacked by NATO behind a façade of false maneuvers, was not able to go on the offensive until after the eighth day, with the arrival of the second echelon of troops; it was then unable to advance westward by more than 100–150 km in three to four days.[59]

Conclusions

Throughout the Cold War, Czechoslovakia had little choice but to follow Moscow's orders. During Stalin's time, there was less reason for concern as the plans remained defensive, even after in 1951 he called upon his Eastern European lieutenants to have their armies ready for war in a few years. If the Czechoslovak Communists had something to worry about other than being purged by Stalin, it was how their increasingly disillusioned population would behave in an East–West conflict, especially given that Stalin's intentions for such a scenario were far from clear. There may even have been suggestions that he might let the country go, just as he was apparently ready to do in the case of North Korea when military fortune turned against the Communist armies there.

This kind of ambiguity disappeared along with Stalin. Yet, this provided little comfort to the Czechoslovak rulers as the country's vulnerability became even more obvious after the Soviet doctrine changed into an offensive one and the Czechoslovak armed forces were assigned the ambitious task of marching far to the west in the wake of the Berlin crisis. The Czechoslovak command knew this was a tall order as it would involve defeating high-quality US forces deployed in the southern part of the FRG. However, as good soldiers and Communists, the Czechoslovak military spent a great deal of resources to make that strategy work.

The "temporary" deployment of Soviet troops in 1968, together with subsequent purges, silenced the discussions within the Czechoslovak command and brought the tall order closer to implementation.

There is little indication that the Czechoslovak party leadership, even during the Prague Spring, ever attempted to correct the way in which decisions were made and implemented in the Eastern bloc. Despite the ideas of some progressive elements within party and military circles, Prague never presented an alternative to the Soviet doctrine in the way Poland tried to implement nuclear-free zones. In the debate on the reform of the Warsaw Pact, Czechoslovak loyalists focused on creating effective mechanisms for implementing the plans rather than formulating them. The main reservations from the Czechoslovak side focused on the economic rather than political ramifications of the Soviet strategy.

The significance of Czechoslovak armed forces for Soviet plans decreased after the 1968 invasion, when the Soviet army took over responsibility for the strategic-operational direction. For the next 20 years, until Gorbachev's strategic revolution, the Warsaw Pact continued its bizarre planning for winning a nuclear war in Europe with the full support of the Moscow-appointed Czechoslovak leadership, who cared little that in such a scenario their country would serve as the battlefield for a nuclear inferno. Even in retrospect, this is, to say the least, unsettling.

Notes

1 Operační směrnice pro plán Kryt země [Operational directive for the plan "Protection of the Land"], č.j. 160, operační správa (sál), fond Varšavská smlouva (unsorted), Central Military Archive in Prague (VÚA).

2 Operační směrnice Pěst [Operational directive "Pěst"], č.j. 22674, operační správa (sál), fond Varšavská smlouva (unsorted), VÚA.

3 Ibid.

4 Vojtech Mastny, *The Cold War and Soviet Insecurity: The Stalin Years* (Oxford: Oxford University Press, 1996), pp. 104–6.

5 Figures can be found at www.vojenstvi.kvalitne.cz/armada/povalecna/cisla/2.htm

6 Informační zpráva o operačních přípravách (20.4.1953) [Informational report on operational preparations of the Czechoslovak armed forces for the general staff, April 20, 1953], č.j. 11428, operační správa (sál), fond Varšavská smlouva (unsorted), VÚA.

7 Informační zpráva o stavu příprav generálního štábu pro mimořádná opatření k 1.5.1957 [Informational report on the state of preparations of the general staff for extraordinary measures as of May 1, 1957], č.j. 21, operační správa (sál), fond Varšavská smlouva (unsorted), VÚA.

8 Ibid.

9 Ibid.

10 Протокол совещания по соголосованию изменений к плану развития Вооуженных сил Чехословакии [Agreed text on changes in the development plan of the Czechoslovak armed forces], č.j. 0035, operační správa (sál), fond Varšavská smlouva (unsorted), VÚA.

11 Zpráva o zasedání Politického poradního výboru Varšavské smlouvy v únoru 1960 [Report on a meeting of the Political Consultative Committee of the Warsaw Treaty Organization in February 1960], č.j. 4338/GŠ-OS-1966, operační správa (sál), fond Varšavská smlouva (unsorted), VÚA. See Aleksei Adzhubei, *Te desiat let* (Moskva: Sovetskaia Rossia), 1989, pp. 155–6.

12 Interview with Colonel Karel Štěpánek, former head of the operations room of the General Staff of the Czechoslovak People's Army. The interview took place in early 2000.

13 Sven Aage Christensen and Frede Jensen, "Superpower under Pressure: The Secret Speech of Minister of Defence Marshal Zhukov in East Berlin, March 1957," Web site of the Parallel History Project on NATO and the Warsaw Pact, December 2003, www.isn.ethz.ch/php; Записки из выступления маршала Жукова на научной конференции, май 1959 г [Notes from lecture by Marshal Zhukov at a scientific conference, May 1957], č.j. 0273, sig. 4/1-2, kart. 16, sekretariát ministra, 1957, fond Ministerstvo národní obrany (MNO), VÚA.

14 Доклад маршала И. С. Конева на разборе военной игры в марте-апреле 1959 г [Lecture by Marshal Konev at the Czechoslovak war game in March–April 1959], č.j. 12429, operační správa, Varšavská smlouva (unsorted), VÚA.

15 Informační zpráva o operačním plánu ČSLA pro Vojenskou komisi obrany ÚV KSČ k 27. dubnu 1959 [Informational report on operational plans of the ČSLA for the Military Defense Committee of the CC CPCz as of April 27, 1959], č.j. 7040, operační správa (sál), fond Varšavská smlouva (unsorted), VÚA.

16 Doklad náčelníka gen. štábu ČSLA pro Vojenskou komisi obrany 15. prosince 1960 [Report of the chief of the general staff of the Czechoslovak People's Army for the Military Defense Committee of the Central Committee of the CPCz of December 15, 1960], č.j. 12524, operační správa (sál), fond Varšavská smlouva (unsorted), VÚA.

17 Ibid.

18 Upřesnění perspektivního plánu výstavby a rozvinutí Čs. lidové armády v míru a ve válce v letech 1961–1965 [Precision of prospective plan for buildup and development of the Czechoslovak People's Army in peace and war for 1961–1965], č.j. 12516, operační správa (sál), fond Varšavská smlouva (unsorted), VÚA.

19 Zpráva o návrhu změn v plánu výstavby ČSLA na léta 1961–1965 [Report on proposals of changes in the plans for buildup of the Czechoslovak People's Army for 1961–1965], č.j. 39030/19, operační správa (sál), fond Varšavská smlouva (unsorted), VÚA.

20 Matthias Uhl and Vladimir I. Ivkin, "'Operation Atom': The Soviet Union's Stationing of Nuclear Missiles in the German Democratic Republic, 1959," *Cold War International History Project Bulletin* 12–13 (2001), pp. 299–307.

21 Průběh informace náčelníka generálního štábu o důsledcích konzultace, říjen 1960 [Information on consultation provided by the chief of the general staff, October 1960], č.j. 390030/22, operační správa, fond Varšavská smlouva, VÚA.

22 Zápis z porady konané 13. února 1961 v generálním štábu ČSLA [Minutes of meeting held on February 13, 1961, at the general staff of the Czechoslovak People's Army], č.j. 38635, operační správa (sál), fond Varšavská smlouva (unsorted), VÚA. See also Matthias Uhl, "Nuclear Warhead Delivery Systems for the Warsaw Pact, 1961–1965," www.isn.ethz.ch/php.

23 Zápis besedy N. S. Chruščova s vedoucími činiteli ÚV KSČ a vlády ČSSR ve Smolenici u Bratislavy 1. června 1961 [Minutes of the meeting of N. Khrushchev with Czechoslovak communists at Smolenice near Bratislava, June 1, 1961], in Michal Reiman and Petr Luňák, *Studená válka 1954–1964: sovětské dokumenty v českých archivech* [The Cold War, 1954–1964: Soviet documents in Czech archives] (Brno: Doplněk), 2000, pp. 193–210.

24 Schválení opatření nařízených Hlavním velitelem Spojených ozbrojených sil států-účastníků Varšavské smlouvy dne 8.9.1961 [Approval of measures of Enhanced Combat Readiness of the Warsaw Pact countries of September 8, 1961], September 14, sig. 17/4, Vojenská komise obrany, VÚA.

25 Karel Sieber, "Vltavská kaskáda, hospodářská krize Novotného režimu a hrozba jaderné války po druhé berlínské krizi," www.coldwar.cz.

26 Rozbor štábního cvičení provedeného ve dnech 12.–15.12.1961 [Analysis of the staff exercise held December 12–15, 1961], č.j. 004922, sig. 17/2–61, kart. 348, 1961, operační správa, fond MNO, VÚA.

27 See Chapter 1 by Vojtech Mastny.

28 Doklad po jednání omezeného kabinetu ministra dne 1. března 1965 na operačním sále [Presentation at the meeting of the defense minister's cabinet in operations room, March 1, 1965], č.j. 15016, operační správa (sál), fond Varšavská smlouva (unsorted), VÚA.

29 Petr Luňák, "Planning for Nuclear War: The Czechoslovak War Plan of 1964," *Cold War International History Bulletin* 12–13 (2001), pp. 289–99.

30 Doklad pro jednání omezeného kabinetu ministra dne 1. března 1965 na operačním sále [Report for restricted meeting of defense minister cabinet on March 1, 1965, in operations room], č.j. 15016, operační správa (sál), fond Varšavská smlouva (unsorted), VÚA.

31 Ibid.

32 Rapackého plán – stanovisko MNO [Rapacki plan – Position of the Czech Foreign Ministry], č.j. 011136, sig. 19/1-37/13, kart. 167, 1965, operační správa (sál), fond MNO, VÚA. Zpráva ministerstva zahraničí [Report of the Czech Foreign Ministry], č.j. 0010357, sig. 19/1-37/5, kart. 167, 1965, operační správa (sál), fond MNO, VÚA.

33 Doklad ministru národní obrany o zvláštních objektech – akce "JAVOR" [Information for the Defence Minister on special objects – operation "JAVOR"], č.j. 18008, 43/67, operační správa, Varšavská smlouva, VÚA

34 Соглашение между правительством СССР и правительством Чехословакии о мерах по повышению боевой готовности ракетных войск [Agreement between the governments of the Soviet Union and Czechoslovakia concerning measures to enhance combat readiness of Rocket forces, December 1965], č.j. 33167, operační správa, Varšavská smlouva, VÚA.

35 Raymond L. Garthoff, "When and Why Romania Distanced Itself from the Warsaw Pact," *Cold War International History Bulletin* 5 (1995), p. 111.

36 Materiály k otázce Spojeného velení (koncept) [Draft materials to the question of the Joint Command], č.j. 39042/1, operační správa (sál), fond Varšavská smlouva (neuspořádané), VÚA.

37 Materiály pro jednání v Moskvě 4. – 8. 2. 1966, bod 7 – Strategická koncepce vedení války [Material for the meetings in Moscow 4–8 February 1966, item 7 – Strategic Concept for Conduct of War], č.j. 39042/9, operační správa, Varšavská smlouva, VÚA.

38 Informace o zasedání ministrů obrany v Moskvě ve dnech 27.–28.5.1966 k otázkám Statutu Spojeného velení [Information about the meeting of defense ministers May 27–28, 1966, on questions related to the status of the joint command], č.j. 39042/56, operační správa (sál), fond Varšavská smlouva (unsorted), VÚA.

39 Rozbor cvičení Sputnik [Analysis of the exercise "Sputnik"], č.j. 0011500, sig. 17/2-3/177, kart. 271, 1964, operační správa (sál), fond MNO, VÚA.

40 Doklad pro jednání omezeného kabinetu ministra dne 1. března 1965 na operačním sále [Report for restricted meeting of defense minister's cabinet on March 1, 1965, in operations room], č.j. 15016, operační správa (sál), fond Varšavská smlouva (unsorted), VÚA.

41 K. Kaplan, *Kořeny československé reformy 1968* [The roots of the Czechoslovak reform] (Brno: Doplněk), 2000, pp. 37–41.

42 Informace ministra obrany B. Lomského prezidentu A. Novotnému z jednání s L. Brežněvem 14. dubna 1967 [Information from Defense Minister Lomský to President Novotný on meeting with L. Brezhnev April 14, 1967], in A. Benčík, J.Navrátil, and J. Paulík, *Vojenské otázky československé reformy 1967–1970: Vojenská varianta řešení čs. krize* [Military issues in the Czechoslovak reform, 1967–1970: The Military option in the solution of the Czechoslovak crisis] (Brno: Doplněk), 1996, pp. 326–7, 303–9.

43 Vystoupení náčelníka generálního štábu čsl armády generála Rytíře na mítinku pracovníků generálního štábu 13. března 1968 [Speech of chief of the general staff General Rytíř at a meeting of the general staff on March 13, 1968], in A. Benčík, J. Navrátil, and J. Paulík, op. cit. pp. 78–80.

44 Textová část 1. konceptu makrostruktury ČSLA, 1968 [Textual section of the first concept of the macrostructure of the ČSLA, 1968], č.j. 12033, operační správa (sál), Varšavská smlouva (unsorted), VÚA.

45 Vyhodnocení válečných zkušeností z Blízkého Východu a návrhy na opatření ČSLA [Evaluation of war experience from the Middle East and draft proposals for the Czechoslovak People's Army], č.j. 001845, sig. 2/2–5, kart. 44, 1968, operační správa, fond MNO, VÚA.

46 Memorandum třiceti vědeckých pracovníků Vojenské politické akademie a Vojenské technické akademie s návrhem československé vojenské doktríny, 4. červen 1968 [Memorandum by staff of the Military Political Academy and Military Technical Academy containing a proposal of Czechoslovak military doctrine, June 4, 1968], in A. Benčík, J. Navrátil, and J. Paulík, op. cit. pp. 137–44.

47 Výsledky porady PPV v Sofii ve dnech 6.–7. března 1968 [Results of the Sofia meeting of the Warsaw Pact PCC, March 6–7, 1968], č.j. 15296, operační správa (sál), fond Varšavská smlouva (unsorted), VÚA.

48 Jiří Fidler, *21.8.1968, Okupace Československa, bratrská agrese* [The occupation of Czechoslovakia: A fraternal aggression] (Praha: Havran), 2003.

49 As claimed by Col. Karel Štěpánek in an interview with the author in early 2000.

50 Informační zpráva pro 1. tajemníka ÚV KSČ, květen–červen 1968 [Information Report for the First Secretary of the Central Committee of the Communist Party of Czechoslovakia, May/June 1968], č.j6071/20-ZD-GŠ/OS, operační správa, Varšavská smlouva, VÚA

51 K. Kaplan, op. cit. p. 41

52 Textová část 1. konceptu makrostruktury ČSLA [Textual section of the first concept of the macrostructure of the ČSLA], č.j. 12033, operační správa (sál), Varšavská smlouva (unsorted), VÚA.

53 Doklad ministra národní obrany k otázkám makrostruktury ČSLA a struktuře MNO dne 17.2.1969 [Presentation of the defense minister on the macrostructure of the ČSLA and the structure of the defense ministry of February 17, 1969], č.j. 4016, operační správa (sál), fond Varšavská smlouva [unsorted], VÚA.

54 Doklad zámyslu armádního cvičení TARAN (srpen 1970) [Design of the exercise "TARAN," August 1970], č.j. 0022612/1, sig. 4-2/5-1, kart. 123, 1970, operační správa (sál), fond MNO, VÚA.

55 Материалы разбора игры Запад (říjen 1969) [Materials from the analysis of the war game Zapad, October 1969], č.j. 18004, operační správa (sál), fond Varšavská smlouva (unsorted), VÚA.

56 Plán týlového zabezpečení operace ČsF (1974) [Plan of the rear operation of the Czechoslovak front, 1974], č.j. 452, kart. 12, operační správa (sál), fond Varšavská smlouva (unsorted), VÚA.

57 Zápis ze 6. zasedání Výboru ministrů obrany členských států Varšavské smlouvy [Minutes from the 6th session of the Committee of Defense Ministers of the Warsaw Treaty Organisation], č.j. 39038/19, kart. 10, operační správa (sál), fond Varšavská smlouva (unsorted), VÚA.

58 Operační plán ČSLA [Operations Plan of the ČSLA], č.j. 22674, operační správa (sál), fond Varšavská smlouva (unsorted), VÚA.

59 Материалы разбора учения Запад-77 [Materials from the exercise "Zapad–77"], č.j. 22013, operační správa (sál), fond Varšavská smlouva (unsorted), VÚA.

4 The Warsaw Pact's special target
Planning the seizure of Denmark

Frede P. Jensen

Introduction

An attack on Denmark occupies a prominent place in the extensive East German and Polish files pertaining to Warsaw Pact military exercises. From 1961 until the 1980s, Soviet, Polish, and East German officers in Warsaw Pact commands staged numerous exercises in which they simulated breaking through the Danish Straits and capturing Danish territory, both land and sea. Because the exercises, the objectives of which were determined by the Soviet General Staff, were held for many years with the basic concept hardly changing, it may be assumed that the idea of capturing Denmark as part of a major offensive against Western Europe played a significant role in overall Soviet planning for a possible war between East and West.

The nature of documents on Warsaw Pact military exercises raises two general questions for research, one purely military, the other mainly political. The military question has to do with the relevance of these documents in discussing the Soviet Union's possible performance in a war situation and can be summarized as a question of the extent to which the exercise documents increase our knowledge about the still largely secret Soviet war plans of the Cold War. The second question, the mainly political one, concerns the Soviet political leadership's intentions. Does knowledge about Soviet war planning provide a basis for any conclusions about the Soviet leadership's longer-range intentions toward the West?

To begin, we will examine the connection between the command post exercises and plans drawn up for the actions of the Soviet Union and its allies in a war situation, which were hidden in the Soviet General Staff in Moscow. Is it possible to establish a direct link between the two? Were the operations against Denmark, which were simulated during command post exercises, copied from war plans that were operational at the time of the exercises (which, until the 1970s, existed mostly as staff exercises, without troop involvement)? First of all, under what circumstances would the Soviet Union and its allies consider using nuclear weapons, and would they use them to the extent indicated in the exercise documents? Or do these documents from staff exercises tell us less than we think? It is possible that there was only an indirect link between the exercises and actual Soviet war plans.

Initial interpretations of the East German documents assumed that the exercises were proof of the aggressive intentions of the Soviet leadership. These interpretations appeared in the international press in the early 1990s as well as in the German Defense Ministry's study *Warsaw Pact Military Planning in Central Europe: A Study* (1992). This remains the conventional perception, though it has since been rejected from several quarters. In one of the first proper analyses of the documents, Beatrice Heuser emphasized that, from a researcher's point of view, it was impossible to reach conclusions about foreign policy goals from the details of military planning. This point is specifically addressed in the section on War planning and political intentions. Moreover, Heuser stresses that military exercise plans cannot be viewed as evidence of how military strategists saw the possible details of the course of a war. As she sees it, the exercises defined and limited the options available to the military leadership in the event of war. It was likely that they rehearsed the capabilities and operations that the strategists regarded as the most important options. The exercises illuminated the situations that military planners anticipated and demonstrated how they wanted their forces to handle such situations.[1]

Carl-Axel Gemzell, the Nordic research pioneer in this area, saw this material in a discourse-analytical perspective. Warsaw Pact exercises consisted of "thought material" capable of contributing to structuring alternative forms of military action for the Soviet leadership. In his interpretation, they could therefore have played a disastrous role in a crisis situation. According to Gemzell, there was nothing to indicate that the idea of capturing Denmark had gained ground within the Soviet General Staff or had been used as a basis for politically sanctioned plans. Moreover, to a great extent Gemzell interpreted the planning dynamic in light of the maritime priorities of the Soviet naval commander, Sergei G. Gorshkov, during "the struggle for a maritime plan of operation" – the subtitle of Gemzell's 1996 article. This interpretation was based on the assumption that there was a sharp conflict between Soviet marshals and admirals, in which the fleet challenged the army's preeminent position and sought to win allies within the Warsaw Pact military leadership.[2]

Later, Gemzell seems to have moved closer to Heuser's point of view that the East German exercise documents indicate which plans and considerations the Soviet military leadership thought worth testing in practice.[3] In other words, this interpretation places the emphasis on accumulating practical experience: the exercises could be called a kind of military laboratory.

Warsaw Pact exercises were also a main theme of the investigations of the German officer and researcher Harald Nielsen into the subject of the German Democratic Republic (GDR) and nuclear weapons, this being one of the most comprehensive examinations of GDR documents so far. In a detailed point-by-point analysis of the Warsaw Pact exercise system and of Soviet nuclear weapons procedures at the front, Nielsen emphasized the difference between Soviet and US strategies for the use of nuclear weapons. As the Soviets never accepted the US and NATO philosophy of looking at nuclear weapons as "political weapons" and for decades threatened to react to even limited western use of nuclear weapons with massive nuclear strikes, in the final analysis Nielsen tended to look at Soviet nuclear strategy first of all as an exercise in deterrence with a very high degree of credibility.[4]

The present chapter will follow up Nielsen's work by stressing that during the Cold War, and independently of any exercises or considerations derived from military theory, prepared-military plans – here called "war plans" – existed for a general war between East and West. The Soviet General Staff had been ordered to prepare these plans and was responsible for updating them. The preparation of such plans is one of the main tasks of any general staff in peacetime. In my view, interest should focus on these plans to a greater extent than has been the case up until now. Therefore, a more precise question will be asked, namely, what relationships can be demonstrated or seen as plausible between the large-scale staff exercises that were held repeatedly by the Warsaw Pact countries, and the prepared but unpublicized Soviet war plans which undoubtedly consisted of a wide-ranging complex of plans?

The point of departure for the case made later will be that we now know elements of Polish and Czechoslovak operational plans from the 1960s, prepared according to directives from the Soviet General Staff. From them, we have gained a direct insight into actual operational documents and thinking, something we did not have earlier. First of all, it is possible to compare the Polish plan approved by Moscow in 1961 for an attack on Denmark in case of war with the plans for exercises drawn up at the same time as a consequence.

The agreement between the Polish plan of operation and the command post exercises discussed in this chapter indicates a quite extensive degree of structural congruity between the Warsaw Pact command post exercises at a high level and the Soviet plans for general war. This comes as no surprise. If war between East and West broke out, the dispositions of the war planning should not come as a surprise to the high-level commands, which already had a substantial degree of responsibility, and it was therefore natural for the exercises to contain elements and conditions of the war planning that could be recognized and had been the focus of training. To introduce commanding officers to totally unexpected planning tasks in case of war would be to invite chaos. This indicates that existing war plans had a heavy influence on the exercise scenarios, a relationship supported by the continuity that dominated the exercise picture until the second half of the 1980s, when the defense orientation of the party under Gorbachev took control of Soviet military planning, as indicated later.

But ideas should also flow in the opposite direction, from exercises to war plans, in the form of the experience gained by officers during the exercises and their creative input. This was another main rationale behind the numerous exercises. The extensive exercise evaluations and other theoretical and educational reviews point to the importance which, on the part of the Soviet military, was placed on this aspect. Stated more precisely, one of the functions of the exercises was their contribution to continued updating and refining within the agreed framework spelled out in the existing war plans.

This chapter offers arguments for the following points of view:

1   The large-scale Warsaw Pact command post exercises served important military and political functions, including practicing and refining the existing war plans.
2   There was a structural congruity between the command post exercises at a high level within the Warsaw Pact and the existing complex of war plans.
3   The offensive plans against Western Europe (and Denmark) did not reflect crisis management or contingency planning for a "limited war" but are to be regarded as a worst case scenario or plans for a "general war," that is, for a situation that contained the possibility of a major, final showdown between East and West.

Sources for Warsaw Pact war planning

Neither the Soviet Union nor Russia has been forthcoming with the publication of their war plans from the period after 1945. Even now, only a 1946 plan has been published, one which has limited value for the Cold War research.[5] However, after the GDR's demise, a singular research situation arose in which a state's entire military archives, or what was left of it, became accessible to historical investigation. Even though the most sensitive documents had been removed to the Soviet Union or destroyed, the East German military archives nevertheless contain a comprehensive and to some extent still unexamined material on the preparations of East German forces for war in terms of instructions for mobilization, material from Warsaw Pact and national exercises on various levels, Soviet instructions for military training, Soviet education material for general staff courses, articles on all aspects of military strategy and warfare (in the secret military publication *Militärwesen*), etc. All these documents have direct or indirect connections with existing war plans.[6] A growing body of material on war planning has also been brought to light in Poland, where, however, there continues to be limited and apparently arbitrarily controlled access to military archives.[7]

Poland's and Czechoslovakia's operational plans

Knowledge of Soviet war plans has grown over the past few years, as researchers have gained access to a limited but important body of operational material from the East. This material includes war plans for Poland and Czechoslovakia from the early 1960s, prepared under the close supervision of the Soviet General Staff. These operational plans were from the second highest level of the Soviet command hierarchy, the so-called fronts, which correspond to army groups in western military parlance. In the overall Soviet concept, "the Western war theater" envisioned the creation of five or six fronts in the event of a general war.[8] As for Poland, we know the origin and content of the operational plan. As for Czechoslovakia, the Russian text to a summary of the plan has been preserved, detailing a Czechoslovak army offensive into southern Germany.

The Polish historian Paweł Piotrowski has described the rationale behind the war plan prepared between 1961 and 1963 for the Polish forces, following a Polish approach to the Soviet Union. For reasons of national sovereignty, it was crucial for the Poles to lead their own front in any war, which included a Polish thrust against the Netherlands and Denmark, including a complicated landing operation on the coast of Zealand (Sjaelland). According to Piotrowski, Polish officers prepared their own plan of operation (OP-61) based on a handwritten directive signed by the Soviet defense minister, Marshal Rodion I. Malinovskii. This directive indicated the direction of the attack and the basic parameters of Polish operations.[9]

Piotrowski has only had direct access to part of the plan,[10] but his reconstruction is supported by a number of facts. There is also a clear coincidence between his description and the "Coastal Front" operations that are revealed in the East German and Polish exercise material. In addition, it should be noted that the Polish plan did not stand alone but reflected Soviet intentions, and it must be assumed to have been carefully connected to overall Soviet plans, since Soviet forces (from all branches) would play an important role in the entire operation.

Aside from the Polish plan, we now also have access to the content of a 1964 Czechoslovak war plan, or more precisely to "an authoritative summary of the 'sharp' war plan" (Vojtech Mastny). The document was published by the Parallel History Project (PHP) in 2000 as a "Plan of Action of the Czechoslovak People's Army for the War Period."[11] This is a summary of the operational plan for front operations through southern Germany toward France (Lyons), led by the Czechoslovaks. The plan is in Russian, and internal indications suggest that it was prepared in close cooperation with the Soviet General Staff, just as the Polish plan had been. This plan, dated October 11, 1964 and signed by Czechoslovak Defense Minister Bohumír Lomský as well as two leading generals, was later endorsed by the signature of Czechoslovak President Antonín Novotný in his capacity as commander-in-chief of the Czechoslovak armed forces. This text must be regarded as the most important eastern operational document available to the general public for research. The content of the plan is marked by the focus of the Khrushchev period on operations involving nuclear weapons, but its substance remained in effect through the 1960s if not longer. The extent to which this plan was later updated, possibly due to the shakeup of events in Czechoslovakia in 1968, is still not known.

Thus the picture today is such that we know of two eastern war plans – for the Second and Third Fronts (or in Soviet terminology "the Coastal Front" and "the Southwestern Front"). This new information about plans for front operations brings with it an important change in research conditions compared to the 1990s, because it is now possible to compare the main parameters of command post exercise materials with similar elements in real operational material. However, we only have limited knowledge based on eastern sources about the main eastern attack that was to have been carried out by the Soviet armies in the GDR, aimed at central West Germany (the "First West Front" or "Central Front," and, in the second echelon, the "Fourth Front"). What is known is based mostly on teaching materials from East German general staff courses as well as comments from Soviet officers. Soviet Marshal Pavel Rotmistrov, in a conversation with an American officer in June 1965, said that the Soviet Union would maintain the capacity to overrun Europe within 60–90 days in either a nuclear or conventional war.[12]

The earlier belief, based on sources available in the early and mid-1990s, that it was not known whether the idea of capturing Denmark had gained support within the Soviet General Staff or had been made the basis of politically sanctioned plans, can no longer be maintained. Comments by Polish officers have provided ample documentation of the 1961 Moscow meeting at which the Russians accepted Poland's proposal for a more independent role in a war situation.[13] There is also no reason to doubt that the directive that Defense Minister Malinovskii signed for the Polish generals at that same 1961 meeting in Moscow, spelling out the division of military roles, was endorsed by the Soviet leadership. This new arrangement was a matter of Polish sovereignty, based on overall political considerations and decisions that the generals were not competent to make independently.

Following the experience of the Soviet leadership with Defense Minister Marshal Georgii K. Zhukov's "bonapartism," which led to his fall in the autumn of 1957,[14] relations between the party and the military were changed to the benefit of the party. For the remainder of the Cold War the party's primacy remained unchallenged, and no important military decisions could be made without it. There can therefore be no doubt that the Soviet leadership was informed about, and ultimately responsible for, both political and military cooperation within the Warsaw Pact. It has also been correctly noted that Soviet party leaders were "party functionaries with a strong military background."[15] The authoritative and major military work, *Military Strategy* (first published under Marshal Sokolovskii's name in 1962), emphasized the subordinate role of military strategies in relation to politics.[16] It can therefore be concluded that military planning regarding Denmark was sanctioned by the Soviet leadership, its details being developed in line with directives from the Soviet General Staff.

Command post exercises: elements of war planning in the exercise material

The theory that exercise scenarios and war planning were closely connected is supported by the fact that, in general, Warsaw Pact command post exercises simulated an approximation to a war situation. By contrast with eastern propaganda claims, the exercises were usually based on the real military strength of NATO forces as well as on western operational and tactical doctrines (gathered by intelligence services). As regards Warsaw Pact forces, the point of departure was real own-force levels, as well as the various agreements that Warsaw Pact countries had entered into with each other about cooperation in a war situation. The agreements specified the conditions under which the respective operations should be initiated, including a growing number of specific military procedures and command arrangements.

Command post exercises that included the Soviet Union, Poland, and the GDR normally started by establishing the lines of command and assigning combat units for operations against the Danish straits and northern Germany, that is the Coastal Front and "The Unified Baltic Sea Fleets," the former headed by the Polish commander-in-chief, the latter by the commander-in-chief of the Soviet Baltic Fleet. In the Soviet view, the activities of the eastern fleets in the Baltic constituted a front operation. As a typical example, at the beginning of the command post exercise "VAL-77," the Coastal Front and The Unified Baltic Sea Fleets, the latter consisting of the "First Fleet" (the Soviet Baltic Sea Fleet), the "Second Fleet" (the Polish Navy), and the "Third Fleet" (the GDR *Volksmarine*), were created "by the commander-in-chief's decision" of June 26, 1977.[17] While there is no doubt that this was similar to the subordinate relationship that the Russians would demand in a war situation, it is nonetheless peculiar that it was only in the 1980s, following efforts by Marshal Nikolai Ogarkov to strengthen Warsaw Pact command structures, that member states set up a real wartime supreme command within the Warsaw Pact. Until then, there seemed to be no clarity about the wartime command structure. Only after 1984 were the Unified Fleets formally defined as the operational wartime formation of the three fleets.[18]

Naval cooperation during command post exercises was regulated by a body of documents with the name *Baltika*, to which there are multiple references in the exercise material. This was a Soviet-prepared and often revised set of instructions for stages of readiness, coordination of cooperation and intelligence activities aimed at NATO (and other) countries. *Baltika* was also used as a basis for national planning.[19] This body of documents is mentioned in the final assessment of the "VAL-77" exercise, and a new clarification of the contents is suggested, since it is said: "The joint documents 'Baltika' for the co-operation of the Unified Fleets have again stood the test. It is necessary, however, to clarify and perfect the documents on the basis of the latest knowledge."[20]

Command post exercises: main parameters of the exercises

The present section focuses on what could be called the *main elements* or the *main parameters* of exercise sequences performed during Warsaw Pact command post exercises that specifically targeted Denmark and northern Germany. By "main elements" is understood the military objectives mentioned in the exercise material, the military strategy, the area of operation, and the major operations conducted by Warsaw Pact forces in the area. Most major Warsaw Pact exercises contain explicit references to these elements. In tactical exercises dealing only with a part of the Coastal Front operation or the operations of The Unified Baltic Sea Fleets, the main elements are introduced as a general framework or are presupposed.

Objectives

During the entire period of détente, these included the complete annihilation of Danish and allied forces in the area, and capture of Danish land and sea territory as a subordinate goal under the Eastern forces' major offensive toward the West and the neutralization of NATO forces in Western Europe.

The military strategy

The military strategy is consistent with the Soviet military theory of *attack* or *offense*, although defensive operations were not excluded at the tactical or operational level. Throughout the period of détente, East German divisions had the task of carrying out delaying operations against the attacking (!) German and Danish forces (Jutland Division) in the north German area during the first few days of a war, then giving way to the arriving Polish divisions which were supposed to carry out the main attack. This division of responsibilities seems to have been retained to the end of the 1970s, when a reinforced GDR army was given the task of attacking Lower Saxony and later Schleswig-Holstein (from 1987–88).[21] From the beginning of the 1980s defensive operations played a greater role, but the offensive orientation was only given up in the final years of the Warsaw Pact.

Area of operation

The area of operation included all of Denmark and northern Germany, stretching from the island of Bornholm to the Deutsche Bucht. Contrary to what the Danes expected, Bornholm was to be captured at the beginning of the war (day 2). The only real extension of the area of operation came in the 1970s, when a landing operation in southern Norway was added as an immediate extension of the capture of Denmark. During the "VAL-77" exercise, this second landing operation was ordered from day 13 or day 14, with eight amphibious ships moving toward southern Norway.[22]

It is obvious that Sweden does not feature as an objective in the exercise material. On the contrary, the desire to maintain Sweden's neutrality was stressed during the exercises. During the evaluation of "VAL-74," the commander of the East German fleet, Admiral Wilhelm Ehm, highlighted the importance of capturing Denmark early in order to keep Sweden neutral.[23] In NATO's threat assessments, an attempt by Warsaw Pact forces to capture the Swedish coast of the Sound in connection with the breakthrough of the Straits was not ruled out.

Main operations

The major operations in the exercise scenarios between 1961 and the 1980s were (1) an extensive landing on the east coast of Zealand by Polish and Soviet troops, carried out with flanking support from the Unified Fleets, and combined with air drops on Zealand by Polish paratroopers. In connection with this, an East German infantry regiment would land on the island of Falster, while Polish forces would occupy the island of Bornholm. (2) In the west, Schleswig-Holstein and Jutland would be attacked and occupied by a Polish army which, in a side operation, would capture the island of Funen and surrounding islands, possibly with assistance from the East German fleet.

For the Warsaw Pact navies, the main operational goal was the elimination of NATO forces in the western part of the Baltic and breaking through the Danish straits, which was planned as a battle of attrition carried out by Soviet naval forces in the Sound and East German naval forces in the Belts. Extensive minesweeping operations were aimed at creating a small passage through the minefields blocking the Belts and the Sound, while Warsaw Pact battle groups would attack Danish and other NATO forces protecting the minefields. This would be closely linked to achieving control of the Kattegat, with operations reaching to the North Sea. In the North Sea, Soviet nuclear-armed submarines deployed in a number of lines would engage an expected US carrier group and other NATO units. Extensive air operations were anticipated during all phases, carried out by Soviet, Polish, and East German aircraft.

The aforementioned parameters remained unchanged to the 1980s, even though the scenarios might vary from exercise to exercise, depending on the size (strategic or tactical exercises) and chosen objective of the exercise. This continuity is striking and provides evidence that the exercises had deep roots in the corresponding war plans. From the late 1980s, the new military thinking introduced by Gorbachev and the people around him begins to show through.

War planning and political intentions

Based on the relationships described between war plans and military exercises, I shall now discuss the second overall issue of the chapter: the relationship between war planning and political objectives. In other words, did the clearly offensive character of the military planning reveal the Soviet leadership's aggressive foreign policy intentions, as has often been claimed? Or, more cautiously, what type of war was the Soviet leadership preparing for? Under what conditions would it mobilize and deploy the large military apparatus amassed by the Warsaw Pact countries?

Historians and military planners have stressed that it is essential to differentiate between foreign policy objectives and military planning for war. Criticizing what she perceived to be journalistic misuse of the source material from the East German military archives in the German press, Beatrice Heuser wrote: "The existence of exercises and military planning alone, of whatever nature, cannot permit the conclusion that there was any intention to realize these plans in the absence of concrete provocation."[24] This observation is also relevant for various interpretations in the Danish debate.

In reality, ongoing military planning in itself does not tell us anything decisive about a state's foreign-policy objectives. An offensive military posture is not incompatible with a defensive or status-quo-oriented political system. Perhaps for geopolitical reasons, a number of great military powers have prepared offensive military plans, even though their general foreign policy was aimed at preserving the status quo, as was true of France and Russia, for example, in the years leading up to 1914.[25] The Czechoslovak and Polish war plans mentioned earlier, as well as command post exercises staged within the Warsaw Pact, therefore cannot be taken as proof of Soviet intentions to initiate war at a suitable point in time. Such far-reaching assessments cannot be based on the types of source material presented here. Statements about foreign-policy intentions must be based on information about the political leadership's thinking and foreign policy conduct over a period of time.

As already mentioned, the major Warsaw Pact command post exercises can be seen as a concrete product, as well as evidence, of Soviet planning for a major war with the West. However, the available evidence suggests that the post-Stalin Soviet leadership had no intention of waging such a war, which would have implied incalculable risks because of the proliferation of nuclear weapons. Still, the leadership could not rule out the possibility that since at some point a major war might become unavoidable, it was prudent to be prepared.[26] Despite a notable relaxation of relations between East and West after the Cuban missile crisis – a relaxation that, despite some ups and downs, lasted until the late 1970s – the major political systems were in global competition, and every so often stood facing each other menacingly.

The possibility of a decisive war did not go away. In other words, preparations had to be made for the worst-case scenario or – as a Polish general put it in the PHP interview – "the dark hour."[27] By worst-case, the communist camp probably understood a US-led assault on the Soviet Union aiming at the liberation of Eastern Europe and the elimination of communism in the Soviet Union.

Already by 1955, any idea of liberating Eastern Europe by coercive measures had been abandoned by US strategists because it was too dangerous.[28] Furthermore, this notion had become even less likely by the 1970s, as the Soviet Union achieved nuclear parity, as well as a certain kind of conventional superiority in the European theater. But the balance of power between East and West was a dynamic one consisting of many elements, not the least important of which was continuous research and development in virtually all fields of arms production especially in nuclear weapons (e.g. the introduction of independently targetable nuclear warheads in missiles equipped with MIRV, or Multiple Independently Targetable Reentry Vehicles). This meant that a decisive technical breakthrough by one party was always a possibility, with strategic consequences for the balance of power. Both West and East were aware, too, that war could start because of a misunderstanding, a possibility they tried to minimize in the early 1970s by strengthening institutionalized crisis management tools (1971: The "Accidents Agreement" and The "Revised Hot Line Agreement").

It is no surprise that the Soviet Union envisaged various possibilities of how a major war might break out. This is evident in the outline of the Warsaw Pact command post exercise of September 30 to October 10, 1961, where it is specifically mentioned that the idea of the exercise was built on one of the possible variants for the start of war in the European theater.[29] We may assume that the Soviet Union operated with a war plan containing various opening gambits, depending on the structural character of the western forces and the West's possible attack positions. To judge from Soviet nuclear preparedness during the détente period (which was typically lower than in the West), major war was probably a relatively distant possibility for the East – as it was for western intelligence services[30] – but a possibility for which, for a number of reasons, they wanted to ensure that they were not caught unprepared.

In its threat perceptions, Danish military intelligence operated with two war scenarios, (1) a general war and (2) a limited war against Denmark, both eventualities being caused first of all by a breakdown of NATO's will and cohesion. In the latter scenario Soviet forces or proxy forces from Poland or the GDR would invade Zealand (this was only considered a risk up to 1974), Bornholm, and the southern Danish islands of Lolland, Falster, and Møn.[31] However, during the Warsaw Pact exercises which had an operation against Denmark as a theme, no attention was apparently given to either real crisis management nor contingency planning for a crisis of a more local character, that is, for "limited war." It can be assumed that the Soviet Union prepared contingency plans for a possible clash with western powers during the Berlin Crisis of the late 1950s and the beginning of the 1960s. But judging from the available information, an attack on Denmark or parts of the country was only part of the plan for a general war. This meant that, during détente, the possibility that Denmark would be involved in a war was as hypothetical as all-out war itself.

Use of nuclear weapons

As with similar western plans, the Soviet plans for general war were based on highly hypothetical crisis scenarios, the kinds of extreme cases that fortunately never materialized. This comes through most clearly in the place given to nuclear weapons in exercises, the aspect that attracted the most attention when details of the exercise material were presented to the European public in the early 1990s.

Up until the mid-1960s, the prevailing Soviet perception was that a war between East and West would inevitably develop into a general nuclear war involving the territory of the superpowers. This perception can be understood as a rewriting of the then-current American nuclear strategy ("massive retaliation"). In reality this meant that, because of American superiority in strategic bombers, the communist countries would be subjected to massive nuclear strikes, to which the Soviet Union could seek to retaliate with a nuclear attack on the United States' European allies.

The year 1965 saw the first indications of a Soviet change of military doctrine on nuclear war, and by the late 1960s the Soviets apparently felt that their improved ability to reach targets in the United States made a nuclear war unacceptable for that country. Therefore, a new phase began about that time, in which the Soviet leadership – partly in response to NATO's introduction of its "flexible response" strategy in 1967 – envisaged the possibility of a nuclear war limited to Europe, including an opening phase containing either a small or a large conventional element. The tendency in a number of feelers and proposals to the United States in the 1970s, which culminated with the production of a Warsaw Pact draft treaty

(November 1976) to be submitted to the participants of the Helsinki process banning first use of nuclear weapons – the proposal being reaffirmed in Brezhnev's often-quoted Tula speech in 1977 – has been interpreted by many as an attempt to reject the use of nuclear weapons and limit a major war to the conventional area.[32] To summarize, there are indications of repeated attempts by the Soviet Union to make a deal with the United States on banning the use of nuclear weapons, thus changing NATO's nuclear plans for the defense of Western Europe, at the same time as the Soviet Union was increasing and modernizing its nuclear (and conventional) arsenal and improving its ability to wage war at different levels with new types of nuclear missiles such as the SS-20.

Whatever motives the Soviets had for launching the idea of the non-first use of nuclear weapons, the offer was not acceptable to the majority of western political leaders and strategists in the 1970s. In their view new Soviet arms developments, both conventional and nuclear, were strengthening existing Soviet conventional options in Europe. In this situation, Western decision makers felt unable to deter the Soviets from possible future adventurism without the element of uncertainty created by nuclear weapons.

How do the exercise scenarios compare with the above picture of Soviet military doctrine? Do they confirm or refute established interpretations?

In the Warsaw Pact exercises of the Coastal Front, the change in the Soviet military doctrine on nuclear war can be demonstrated from the summer of 1966. No Warsaw Pact naval exercises were held in 1965. In a short Warsaw Pact signal exercise held between March 16 and 18, 1966, which was defined as an "operational staff exercise" leading to a landing on the islands of the Danish Sound and Belt zone, hostilities were deemed to have started with a nuclear missile attack from the side of "West" on objectives on the side of "East." This exercise therefore points back to the exercise pattern of the early 1960s. There is no mention of a Warsaw Pact nuclear reply in this exercise, which dealt principally with signals and intelligence.[33] When, after the hiatus of several years mentioned earlier, landing exercises against Zealand were resumed with the "Brise" exercise (June 27–July 2, 1966) led by Polish Vice-Admiral Zdzisław Studziński, followed immediately by the "Baikal" fleet exercises (July 21–27, 1966) chaired by the Warsaw Pact Supreme Commander, Marshal Andrei A. Grechko, they were implemented as conventional exercises, keeping open the nuclear option only as a reply to a western use of nuclear weapons.[34]

This appears already in the introduction of the theme for the exercise "Brise," which, in accordance with Soviet military practice, is carefully worded: "The organization and command of landing operations under the conditions of the threat of use of weapons of mass destruction in the beginning of the war." On the landing operation in particular, it states that, "in case of a nuclear war," ten nuclear strikes would be made against enemy objectives in the landing area if the enemy were to use nuclear weapons against the attacking fleet.

In the command post exercise "Rügen" (April 15–22, 1968), instructions call for the mission to be accomplished by conventional means unless the West introduces nuclear weapons.[35] From that time on, the typical sequence in these exercises does not envisage any first use of nuclear weapons by the East. In the "VAL-74" command post exercise, there are two variants, one conventional, the other nuclear.[36] The exercises therefore seem to confirm the version of Soviet thinking on nuclear war that we encounter in part of the research, especially in the work of Raymond L. Garthoff. He pointed to a "transitional phase" in Soviet doctrine from the mid- to late 1960s to the 1970s, in which decade the Soviets sought to prevent any use of nuclear weapons in war while at the same time preparing themselves for the possibility of nuclear war on all levels. Independently, Harald Nielsen also identified a doctrinal dividing line in the mid-1960s and, in material from East German general staff courses, uncovered another important development starting in 1966, namely the introduction of a distinct "nuclear front operation" ("First nuclear strike of the front") which differed from the strategic nuclear strikes.[37]

As we know from the Cuban missile crisis, the choice of using nuclear weapons was a political decision to be made by the Soviet leader in his capacity as commander-in-chief.[38] At the front level, the initial use of nuclear weapons accordingly required a signal from above. This was also necessary because the Soviets planned strikes with strategic nuclear weapons against many targets in Europe for reasons related to the composition of their nuclear forces. Coordination of "the first nuclear weapons strike" therefore had to come from the top. The exercise material for the Coastal Front indicates a significant element of strategic nuclear strikes against targets in Denmark if the war went nuclear.

Guidelines existed for determining the scope of the use of nuclear weapons. Harald Nielsen, using East German general staff material, determined in his investigation that as many as 50 percent of warheads would be used in the first nuclear strike and 20–30 percent in the next, the remainder constituting a reserve. Since the number of available warheads was steadily increasing throughout the détente period, that would explain the ever-growing number of nuclear weapons incorporated into exercise scenarios. Nielsen also indicated that the Polish and Czechoslovak fronts were probably provided with fewer nuclear weapons than the Soviet First Front (which had been provided with approximately 250 weapons for its first nuclear strike).[39] In a way, this is confirmed by the exercise material from the Coastal Front. In the exercise "VAL-77," for example, one precondition was that the Coastal Front had no more than 157 nuclear weapons at its disposal, the assumption being that the West was able to strike with up to more than 150–160 nuclear weapons including the carrier-based ones against targets in the Coastal Front area.[40]

What were the implications of these exercise scenarios for Soviet behavior in a real war? The use of nuclear weapons envisaged in the exercise scenarios for the Coastal Front was based on the worst-case scenario of the Soviet General Staff and presupposed a US-led attack on the Warsaw Pact countries that would soon turn into a nuclear war. This scenario and its presuppositions was in Western eyes a hypothetical and malicious construction accusing the United States and NATO of harboring aggressive intentions, but less hypothetical was the possibility of a nuclear war triggered by miscalculation of the other side's intentions during an East–West crisis. Since the 1950s, both superpowers had been prepared for nuclear preemption in a war situation, hoping to limit the number of nuclear weapons at the opponent's disposal through a surprise attack. Whether targets in Denmark were included in Soviet preemptive calculations is unknown, but it can be supposed that nuclear installations in other NATO countries, especially in West Germany, would be the primary targets in such an operation.

According to texts used in East German general staff courses, the Soviets reckoned with the possibility of a period in a nuclear war with a "limited" use of operational tactical nuclear weapons, and under certain conditions part of their strategic weapons too. Unfortunately our knowledge of these plans is very limited, and the possibility that the words available to us contain a veiled reference to preemption cannot be ruled out. According to one interpretation, the stated limitation referred only to geography, not to numbers, and it was clear that the Soviets had no intention of copying US and NATO ideas of limited nuclear war. So it was possible that, at the beginning of a nuclear war, the Soviets would limit their use of nuclear weapons to the Western war theater (which included Denmark) and use conventional weapons in more peripheral theaters.[41]

The quantities of nuclear weapons envisaged in Warsaw Pact exercise scenarios most probably reflect the size of the nuclear arsenal at the Warsaw Pact's disposal, then or in the near future. However, the quantity of nuclear weapons delivered against targets in Denmark in a real war would be different and would depend on many different circumstances, among other things the progress of Warsaw Pact front operations against Danish territory (the range of the front nuclear weapons was about 250 kilometers) and on the USA's and NATO's ability to destroy Warsaw Pact nuclear missiles and nuclear aircraft. Presumably the number of nuclear weapons available for targets in Denmark would be lower, though Doomsday-like enough, than those described in the exercise scenarios, which were usually based on there being optimal conditions for Warsaw Pact forces to operate.

The planned operations against denmark

Offensive operations against Danish territory became part of Polish exercise scenarios as early as 1950.[42] In an exercise that year, a Polish army was sent against Denmark, which was "liberated" within approximately three weeks. The main operation included a thrust up through Jutland, while the islands and Copenhagen were to be occupied by forces that would go ashore on Falster. The exercises, presided over by Stalin's close associate and Polish Minister of Defence Marshal Konstantin K. Rokossovskii, took place in May and June 1950 and should possibly be seen in connection with the increase of international tension up to the outbreak of the Korean War (June 25, 1950). Later in the same decade Denmark still appears in Polish exercises, but it is still uncertain whether these exercises reflect concrete war planning.[43]

In the naval area, Soviet planning was defensive until well into the 1950s. A more offensive orientation against the Danish straits appears in 1958. To judge by the exercises, the goal from now on was to block the southern entrance to the Straits in case of war thus seeking to prevent significant Western naval forces from entering the Baltic Sea.[44]

In the summer of 1961, significant changes took place in both the content of the Warsaw Pact command post exercises and the language they used. For the first time the exercise theme became the "Occupation of the Sound and Straits zone."[45] Beginning in autumn 1961, the operational exercise framework is provided by the "Coastal Front" led by the Poles, in which Soviet and East German land and naval military forces participated, along with "The Unified Baltic Sea Fleets" led by a Soviet admiral.[46]

This revised exercise scheme was introduced at the same time as the Polish approach to the Soviet Union mentioned earlier, and it probably reflects the fact that the Polish–Soviet agreement regarding war plans had an immediate effect on the exercise plan. The Moscow meeting also had immediate consequences for the East Germans, who were given an important maritime role in the new operational plan, in which they would secure the western flank for a large-scale landing force, neutralize the West German fleet, and assist in breaking through the Great Belt.

There is, however, the question of how far the Soviet Union progressed in the years immediately after 1961 in preparing new war plans. It is known that the new Polish operational plan was in preparation from 1961 to 1963. As already mentioned, the Czechoslovak plan is dated October 1964. Moreover, a conspicuous halt to large-scale Warsaw Pact exercises appears to have occurred in 1964–65, probably connected to General Secretary Khrushchev's overthrow, but also possibly the result of deliberations during the drafting of a new military strategy with a revised approach to the use of nuclear weapons. In 1966, exercises dealing with a landing operation against Zealand were resumed and were to be repeated for the next twenty years. The resumption of these exercises on the basis of a new war scenario starting with a conventional phase may indicate that a revised war plan had been established by that point.

Under all circumstances, the exercise scheme for the Coastal Front and the Unified Fleets was based on a comprehensive air, land, and sea operation against Schleswig-Holstein, the western part of the Baltic, Denmark, and the Danish straits aimed at eliminating all resistance and subjugating Denmark within a short period of less than fourteen days. As expected, the focus changes from exercise to exercise during the period described, depending among other things on which tactical or operational elements the Soviet side wanted to practice. At their core, however, all the operations take place within the same general scenario.

The following sections examine the larger sub-operations, included in the occupation of Denmark, with the focus on land operations. A distinction is made between "The Zealand Operation" and "The Jutland Operation." In this connection, the emphasis is not on tactical details but on identifying jumps or new tendencies that point to changes in the underlying plans.

The Zealand operation

The main element of this operation was the Polish Coastal Front's landing and establishment of two bridgeheads on the east coast of Zealand (in Køge Bay near Copenhagen and in Faxe Bay), which, combined with drops of airborne troops at various sites, would ensure control of the island, including Denmark's capital, after two to three days spent subduing Zealand's defense forces.

The continued expansion of the Warsaw Pact's landing capacity, especially throughout the 1960s, as well as its adherence to a seemingly fixed pattern of landing exercises reflect the unquestioned place of landing operations in Soviet war plans during the entire period. The importance of capturing the Danish strait area was also repeatedly highlighted during exercise evaluations.[47]

Although all Warsaw Pact naval exercises were suspended in 1964 and 1965 (with the exception of a small staff exercise from March 23 to 26, 1964), national exercises were not, and the East Germans did rehearse an amphibious operation for their own forces, first in a preliminary command post exercise (August 1964) and later in a naval exercise with a landing on the island of Usedom. In both cases the landing was presumed to take place on the island of Falster.[48] When the major Warsaw Pact exercises were resumed in the summer of 1966 with the exercise code-named "Baikal," in which a "real" landing was carried out, the East Germans expressed displeasure over the pause in the exercises, which seems to have been a decision of the Soviets. A number of deficiencies were apparently uncovered. Admiral Gorshkov, second-in-command during the "Baikal" exercise (July 21–27, 1966), was highly critical of the tactical implementation of the landing operation.[49] It is worth mentioning that, from the Warsaw Pact command post exercise "Rügen" (April 15–22, 1968), the time for the landing in Zealand was postponed from day 2 until the morning of day 4, a timing that subsequently remained unchanged throughout the period.

If we now examine the size of the forces that were chosen for the Zealand operation, they seem to have remained unchanged from the late 1960s. The impression given was that the sixth Polish airborne division would be dropped at various places on Zealand before the landing operation began, in order to create confusion in the Danish defense, while the landing itself was to be carried out by the seventh Polish marine division, a Polish motorized infantry division, and a Soviet marine infantry regiment. On balance, three reduced divisions of less than 20,000 Warsaw Pact soldiers seem to have been tasked for the Zealand operation.[50] The critical point during the war was no doubt that the existing fleet of Warsaw Pact landing craft was only capable of carrying perhaps half the landing forces to Zealand in a single movement. The consolidation of the bridgehead and the widening of the operation therefore required the landing boats being followed by a large fleet of merchant ships bringing in soldiers, vehicles, fuel, etc.[51] This massing of ships would be filled with risks in all phases of the operation. The invading Polish and Soviet forces would be confronted on the ground by Zealand's two mobilized brigades and local defense forces (up to 40,000 men, including the Home Guard).

The real change in the operations appears only in the 1970s, when the landing operation in Køge Bay disappears from the exercises, leaving only a Faxe Bay landing. A landing with a Soviet marine infantry brigade seems to have been practiced in Køge Bay for the last time during the exercise "Rügen" in 1968. The possibility that the landing in Køge Bay, close to Denmark's capital, had been designed as a decoy maneuver – a routine element in Soviet tactical and operational planning – cannot be excluded.

The task of seizing the islands to the south of Zealand went to the East German forces which on day 2 (from 1968, day 4) were to carry out a landing operation on the east coast of Falster with their 29th infantry regiment as well as transferring tanks and heavy materiel to the ferry port of Gedser.[52] The occupation of Lolland is mentioned from time to time up to the mid-1960s, but from then on only the seizure of Falster and Møn feature constantly in the exercises.

The Coastal Front landing operation against Zealand was to be carried out against an increasingly improved Danish (and West German) anti-invasion defense, consisting of several lines of defense (submarines, mines, air attack, ground forces), and in the East's calculations, also equipped with nuclear weapons (bombs as well as American nuclear-armed anti-ship mines) for use against the invading fleet.[53] Moreover, Warsaw Pact countries had only a limited ability to prevent the formation of an anti-invasion defense by the other side during a period of tension without provoking a war. In the exercise scenarios, the typical point of departure is that the Danish navy has succeeded in laying mines off the beaches chosen for the invasion.

Although during the 1970s the East acquired additional capability in the form of a larger number of helicopters (and a promise of hovercrafts), NATO forces also increased in strength (including, among other things, the introduction of Harpoon missiles). The landing operations involved great and increasing risk, which the East made no effort to hide in its internal assessments. The difficulty of the operation is repeatedly mentioned in exercise to exercise. In the 1974 evaluation of command post exercise "VAL-74," Marshal Ivan I. Iakubovskii noted that troop landings had always been, and always would be, the most complicated joint operations of an army with a fleet.[54] This is probably the closest one comes to a recognition of how risky the planned operation was.

The picture is clouded by the fact that, as mentioned, the East in the late 1960s fixed the landing for day 4. This was probably because the launching of the invasion depended on general developments along the entire front, especially on establishing control of the sea and air sectors. With full control over the Baltic Sea, minesweeping of the straits could be launched and the risk to the invading force minimized. But the choice of day 4 may also have been based on the possible use of nuclear weapons. The East expected a western use of nuclear weapons after 3–4 days of conventional warfare. By postponing the landing operation, the decision to launch the invasion could be based on crucial information about whether the West had crossed the nuclear threshold or was on the brink of doing so. Once the operations moved into the nuclear phase, the landing operation would be a completely different matter, one where the course of developments had to be regarded as very uncertain.

In Danish defense circles, repelling an invasion was not regarded as impossible. It was expected that an operation against Zealand would fail if one-third of the invasion force could be eliminated.[55] This was, of course, not an unforeseen eventuality in the eastern commands. If the landing operation, for whatever reasons, were to be given up or failed, the commander-in-chief of the Coastal Front could change the emphasis to the simultaneous East German operation against Falster and try to take Zealand from a secure base on the occupied southern islands at a later stage, since these were less well-defended than Zealand. In this scenario, a rather complicated war picture could emerge, with a front line running south of Zealand and through the Danish straits.

The Jutland operation

The task of seizing Jutland was given to the Fourth Polish Army through a long overland sweep. They would move out from their base near Warsaw, pass through the East German forces defending the internal German border at Mecklenburg, then defeat the West German and Danish defenders of Schleswig-Holstein and Jutland. This operation was calculated using short time frames. In 1962, it was predicted that the German–Danish border would be crossed by day 2, a time frame that was changed in the late 1960s to at least day 4. One of the goals of this rapid advance, aside from the capture of the Kiel Canal with as little damage as possible, was to gain control of German airfields and maritime facilities in Schleswig-Holstein, thus weakening the defense of Denmark, including the anti-invasion defense of Zealand.

The prevailing assumption in western intelligence services until well into the 1970s, namely that Soviet troops (helped by Polish and East German troops) would move ahead to the Kiel Canal and take up a position there,[56] can now be seen to have been false. It is obvious in all versions of the exercise material that the northward operation was to be carried out in a single movement and that the capture of Jutland was to be accomplished quickly. In retrospect, the time line for this advance must be viewed as highly optimistic. In the late 1960s by day 3 the Polish army was to be at the Kiel Canal, by day 6 at the Esbjerg-Kolding line, while all of Jutland was to have been seized by day 9. Assuming no weapons of mass destruction were used, the Poles would be given a few days more to conquer Jutland. For instance, in the exercise "Waffenbrüderschaft" (October 1970) the Poles would reach the German–Danish border at day 6 and occupy all of Jutland by day 11.[57]

The sources strongly suggest that control over the Kiel Canal was regarded from the beginning as very important for establishing a naval base in the Deutsche Bucht (the southern part of the North Sea). Considerable specialized equipment was kept on standby to make the canal usable as soon as possible after it had been captured. In 1963, during the "Priliv" naval exercise led by Admiral Gorshkov, canal-clearing operations were envisaged as beginning on day 2, and air defense was to be in place by day 5 for points of support in the Deutsche Bucht.[58] The various implications of the canal's destruction were carefully considered. The establishment of a naval base in the Deutsche Bucht was probably regarded as decisively important for operations in the southern part of the North Sea, especially to prevent NATO forces from landing on Jutland's west coast.

It is hard to understand how a Polish army, not particularly strong, could carry out the assault on Jutland within the time frame indicated, with just four divisions (two armored divisions and two mechanized divisions). The fact is that the Poles planned to send their best divisions toward the west. According to the available information, the Fourth Army consisted of weaker units, in terms of both personnel and equipment.[59] With their forces, the Poles would not have the 3:1 strength advantage normally considered a condition for a successful offensive. As indicated earlier, the East assumed that the West was not inferior in nuclear weapons in the Coastal Front area. Unless the Soviet military leadership had a second echelon at its disposal – which is not mentioned in the exercise material – it can be assumed that, throughout the whole period, implementation of the Jutland operation rested on rather optimistic and hypothetical calculations.

These calculations may have been based on the widely accepted and apparently unrevised notion in the East that the Danish armed forces were weak and could be easily overrun. Only on such a basis, it is possible to understand the various exercise scenarios and time frames, all assuming very limited Danish resistance, and expecting the capture of Jutland to be little more than a parade-ground march. This picture seems to have been retained without taking account of the possibility that the war might develop a nuclear phase, with both sides using nuclear weapons.

The capture of Funen and the islands to its south remained part of the Jutland operation. The troop movements to Funen were to take place across the Little Belt bridge, and if that were destroyed, then with support from the East German navy. The seizure of the fort on the island of Langeland was given a high priority and was tasked to East German special forces. If the war entered the nuclear phase, the fort – along with other major Danish military installations – would become a target for nuclear strikes.

Conclusion

The years of détente in the 1960s and the 1970s witnessed a certain easing of tensions between East and West. The United States and the Soviet Union started negotiations on arms control and began limited cooperation in some areas. At the same time, however, they continued to compete for worldwide influence and to pursue a relentless arms race. Thus, even if the fear of a war between East and West diminished and was considered unlikely in NATO threat assessments of the period, both sides continued to draw up comprehensive plans for the eventuality of a general war. This chapter discusses the Warsaw Pact's war plans in terms of their relevance for the territory of Denmark.

The chapter argues that there was a structural congruity between Soviet planning for a general war and the scenarios used in the Warsaw Pact command post exercises involving the Polish-led "Coastal Front" and the Soviet-led "Unified Baltic Sea Fleets." This interpretation is based mainly on the close affinity between the now known front operational plan prepared for the Polish forces by the Soviet General Staff in the 1960s and the comprehensive Warsaw Pact exercise material found in the East German military archives. It is also shown that the major command post exercises followed doctrinal developments in Soviet military strategy using basically simulated force levels, tactics, and command structures in respect of the anticipated war situation. The chapter further points to the fact that the major parameters of the exercises (objectives, strategy, area of operation and main operations) remained unaltered to the 1980s, thus demonstrating a continuity which provides evidence of the influence of the underlying war plans.

It is further stressed that the offensive war scenarios found in both the Warsaw Pact command post exercises and in the front operational plans cannot by itself be taken as evidence of aggressive intentions on the part of the Soviet leadership. They had little to do with the day-to-day foreign policy of the Soviet Union and should rather be interpreted as reflections of war plans drawn up by the Soviet General Staff, based on a Soviet worst-case scenario of a possible general war between East and West. As Warsaw Pact exercises assumed aggression by the United States, the foundation of the war plans was probably a hypothetical situation in which Warsaw Pact countries would be subject to a US-led attack to liberate Eastern Europe and destroy Soviet communism.

Warsaw Pact command post exercises from 1961 and Polish operational plans from 1963 envisage large-scale offensive operations against Danish territory and surrounding waters as part of the large Warsaw Pact operation into West Germany. This lasted till the 1980s, when Soviet military doctrine was changed under Gorbachev. Central to the planning for the Coastal Front were the occupation of Denmark by an airborne/landing operation against Zealand and the capture of Jutland by a Polish army. The entire campaign was to be terminated within a fortnight, if necessary with the help of chemical weapons and tactical and strategic nuclear weapons. At the same time, Soviet and East German naval forces would try to force the Danish straits with a view to establishing a strong position in the North Sea and – in plans in the 1970s – to carry out a landing in the south of Norway.

However, Warsaw Pact ground and naval operations seem to have been based on optimistic assessments rather than reflecting critical estimates of the existing ratio of forces. Warsaw Pact operations had to be carried out against an increasingly improved and confident NATO defense in the area of the Danish straits, including possible use of weapons of mass destruction. In any case the landing operation on Zealand remained a considerable gamble.

Notes

1 Beatrice Heuser, "Warsaw Pact Military Doctrines in the 1970s and 1980s: Findings in the East German Archives," *Comparative Strategy* 12 (1993): 43.
2 Carl-Axel Gemzell, "Warszawapagten, DDR och Danmark. Kampen for en maritim operationsplan" [The Warsaw Pact, the GDR, and Denmark. The Struggle for a Maritime Strategy], *(Dansk) Historisk Tidsskrift* 96:1 (Copenhagen: Den danske historiske Forening: 1996): 32–84.

3 Carl-Axel Gemzell, "'Doorkeeper' – Kontinentalmakten och Danmark" ["'The Doorkeeper' – the Continental Power and Denmark"], in *Fra mellemkrigstid til efterkrigstid. Festskrift til Hans Kirchhoff and Henrik S. Nissen på 65-årsdagen oktober 1998*, ed. Henrik Dethlefsen and Henrik Lunbak (Copenhagen: Museum Tusculanums, 1998), pp. 782ff.

4 Harald Nielsen, *Die DDR und die Kernwaffen. Die nukleare Rolle der Nationalen Volksarmee im Warschauer Pakt* (Baden-Baden: Nomos, 1998).

5 M.A. Garelov, "Otkuda ugroza" [From where comes the threat), *Voienno-istoricheskii zhurnal*, no. 2 (1989): 24ff.

6 For the East German military archives, see in particular *Findbücher zu Beständen des Bundesarchivs, Vol. 58. Kommando der Volksmarine. Teil 1*, and *Vol. 61. Kommando der Landstreitkräfte der Nationalen Volksarmee. Bestand DVH* (Koblenz: Bundesarchiv, 1997).

7 Cf. the article in the Polish daily newspaper *Rzeczpospolita* on July 25, 2003, published in translation on the PHP Web site, http://www.isn.ethz.ch/php/news/MediaDesk/Rzeczpospolita_030725_engl.htm

8 Cf. Harald Nielsen, *Die DDR und die Kernwaffen*, pp. 27ff.

9 Cf. Paweł Piotrowski, "Desant na Danię" [Landing in Denmark], *Wprost*, no. 25 (June 23, 2002): 82–4. The article is available on PHP's Web site in an English translation, http://www.isn.ethz.ch/php/documents/collection_12/piotrowski.htm (May 28, 2003).

10 Personal communication to author, June 14, 2003.

11 "Supreme Commander of the Armed Forces of the ČSSR Antonín Novotný 1964," *Plan of Actions of the Czechoslovak People's Army for War Period*, published on the PHP Web site, http://www.isn.ethz.ch/php/documents/collection_1/docs/warplan1-engl.htm (May 28, 2003). The text is introduced and analyzed on the PHP Web site by Vojtech Mastny (Introduction: "Planning for the Unplannable") and Petr Luňák ("The Warsaw Pact War Plan of 1964"). For the discussion see ibid. Peter Veleff and Hans Werner Deim ("The Operational Plan of the Czechoslovak People's Army for the War Phase of 1964 – Was it a Real Operational Plan?") and Vojtech Mastny ("Comment on the Critique of the 1964 Plan by Peter Velef and Hans Werner Deim").

12 Marshal Rotmistrov's comment has been published by Raymond L. Garthoff in *Deterrence and the Revolution in Soviet Military Doctrine* (Washington, DC: The Brookings Institution, 1990), p. 18, note 13.

13 Vojtech Mastny, *Warsaw Pact Generals in Polish Uniforms: Oral History Interviews*, published on the PHP Web site, http://www.isn.ethz.ch/php/collections/coll_9.htm (May 28, 2003).

14 For Zhukov's fall, see Otto Preston Chaney, *Zhukov* (Norman and London: University of Oklahoma Press, revised edition, 1996), p. 442.

15 Joseph D. Douglass, Jr and Amorettea M. Hoeber, *Soviet Strategy for Nuclear War* (Stanford, CA: Hoover Institution Press, 1979), p. 90.

16 Andrei Kokoshin, *Soviet Strategic Thought, 1917–91* (Cambridge, MA: The MIT Press, 1998), p. 50.

17 Bundesarchiv-Militärarchiv in Freiburg (in the following abbreviated "BA–MA"): "Evaluation carried out by East German fleet commander." DVM 10/36851, p. 26.

18 Friedrich Elchlepp, Walter Jablonsky, Fritz Minow, Manfred Röseberg, eds, *Volksmarine der DDR. Deutsche Seestreitkräfte im Kalten Krieg* (Hamburg, Berlin, Bonn: Mittler & Sohn, 2nd edition, 2000), pp. 107ff.

19 For the document collection *Baltika*, which in the 1980s consisted of more than forty documents, see Friedrich Elchlepp *et al.*, *Volksmarine der DDR*, pp. 103ff.

20 BA–MA: DVM 10/36852, p. 96.

21 Dieter Farwick, ed., *Ein Staat – Eine Armee. Von der NVA zur Bundeswehr* (Frankfurt am Main: Report, 1992), pp. 60ff.

22 Exercise evaluation of "VAL-77" by the commander-in-chief of the East German navy. BA–MA: DVM 10/36851, p. 28.

23 Exercise evaluation. BA–MA: DVM 10/33860, p. 64.
24 Beatrice Heuser, "Warsaw Pact Military Doctrines in the 1970s and 1980s," p. 438 and note 4.
25 Terence Zuber, *Inventing the Schlieffen Plan* (Oxford: Oxford University Press, 2002), pp. 254ff.
26 Michael MccGwire, *Military Objectives in Soviet Foreign Policy* (Washington DC: The Brookings Institution, 1987); Vladislav Zubok and Constantine Pleshakov, *Inside the Kremlin's Cold War. From Stalin to Krushchev* (Cambridge, MA; London: Harvard University Press, 1996).
27 According to Mastny, *Warsaw Pact Generals.*
28 The US and British policies of covert action and "psychological warfare" against the Soviet Union in the 1940s and 1950s are covered in extensive detail in Richard J. Aldrich, *The Hidden Hand. Britain, America and Cold War secret Intelligence* (London: Murray, 2001), pp. 269ff.
29 The chosen variant of the exercises is a Western attack on the Warsaw Pact countries with the weight of the action in the North Atlantic, the North Sea, and the Danish Straits. BA–MA: DVM 10/14974, pp. 000073–000100 ("Bericht").
30 The Danish Defence Intelligence Service (DDIS) assessment of the probability of war remained unchanged between 1974 and the end of the 1970s: "The probability of an armed conflict between NATO and Warsaw Pact countries can be assessed as limited, although it exists." Archive of DDIS: "Truslen mod Danmark" [The Threat against Denmark], varying editions (1974, 1976, 1978). There is every probability that the Danish assessment reflected the common NATO assessment. The Danish assessment was contained in a section of the threat analysis classified "Secret" and thus known to very few.
31 Archive of DDIS: "The Threat against Denmark," 1978: N-2.
32 For the development of the Soviet nuclear strategy, see Raymond Garthoff, *Deterrence and the Revolution in Soviet Military Doctrine*, pp. 49ff.
33 BA–MA: DVM 10/19686. Petr Lunák has shown (see note 11, "The Warsaw Pact War Plan of 1964," note 16) that the Czechoslovak People's Army had already sent out guidelines in 1965 – no doubt following Soviet guidelines – for training for operations without the use of nuclear weapons.
34 BA–MA: Forschungsstudie zum Thema "Kommandostabs- und Truppenübungen der Seestreitkräfte/Volksmarine 1956–1970," MS by Volker Seibt, No year, pp. 134–40 (exercise "Brise"), pp. 141–48 (exercise "Baikal").
35 Ibid., pp. 164–70.
36 BA–MA: Forschungsstudie zum Thema "Kommandostabs- und Truppenübungen der Volksmarine 1971 bis 1987," MS by Peter Köhnen, pp. 42–3.
37 Raymond L. Garthoff, *Deterrence and Revolution in Soviet Military Doctrine*, p. 71; Harald Nielsen, *Die DDR und die Kernwaffen*, pp. 70ff. The first nuclear strike of the front appear in exercises in 1967.
38 Cf. Harald Nielsen, *Die DDR und die Kernwaffen*, p. 133, citing Anatolii I. Gribkov, *Im Dienste der Sowjetunion* (Berlin: edition q, 1992), p. 251.
39 Harald Nielsen, *Die DDR und die Kernwaffen*, p. 104f.
40 BA–MA: DVM 10/36852, pp. 47–8, 63. According to the East German exercise evaluation the "West" made 181 nuclear strikes while the "East" made 108.
41 Harald Nielsen, *Die DDR und die Kernwaffen*, p. 80f.
42 Paweł Piotrowski, "Desant na Danię" [Landing in Denmark], note 9 as well as his manuscript "Front Polski (Nadmorski) po II Wojnie Światowej" [The Polish Front – Coastal Front – after the Second World War]. See also Henry Andreasen, "Denmark, Sweden and Polish Military Planning During the Early Cold War," *STUDIA SCANDINAVICA* 19 (Gdansk 2003): 78f.
43 In interviews with Polish generals published by Vojtech Mastny, there are conflicting details about this (see note 13).

44 In the command post exercise of May 12–17, 1958, Soviet units were placed in the western part of the Baltic Sea to destroy NATO units trying to break through. The Danish straits were to be mined by the East. BA–MA: Forschungsstudie zum Thema "Kommandostabs- und Truppenübungen der Seestreitkräfte/Volksmarine 1956–1970," MS by Volker Seibt, pp. 28–9.

45 This appears in the East Germans' own fleet exercise from July 31 to August 12, 1961. BA–MA: Forschungsstudie zum Thema "Kommandostabs- und Truppenübungen der Seestreitkräfte/Volksmarine 1956–1970," p. 70. The exercise was halted because of the Berlin crisis in August 1961.

46 The exercise from September 30 to October 10, 1961 is defined as "Operativ-strategische Kommandostabsübung des Vereinten Oberkommandos." BA–MA: Forschungsstudie zum Thema "Kommandostabs- und Truppenübungen der Seestreitkräfte/Volksmarine 1956–1970," p. 79.

47 In connection with the exercise "Soiuz-72," the commander-in-chief of the Warsaw Pact, Marshal Iakubovskii, characterized the capture of the Danish Strait area as "one of the most important, maybe the most important, operation within our theater of war," see Elchlepp *et al.*, *Volksmarine der DDR*, p. 254. "The theater of war" was a precise concept in Soviet military terminology. "The Western Theater of War," which we are referring to here, stretched from Leningrad to Iceland and consisted of Central Europe and Western Europe, including Britain.

48 BA–MA: Forschungsstudie zum Thema "Kommandostabs- und Truppenübungen der Seestreitkräfte/Volksmarine 1956–1970," pp. 117–22, 123–8 (exercise "Woge"). Only East German forces participated in these exercises.

49 BA–MA: Forschungsstudie zum Thema "Kommandostabs- und Truppenübungen der Seestreitkräfte/Volksmarine 1956–1970," pp. 146–8.

50 This was the case in the exercise "Rügen" from 1968. BA–MA: Forschungsstudie zum Thema "Kommandostabs- und Truppenübungen der Seestreitkräfte/Volksmarine 1956–1970," pp. 164–70.

51 In the Warsaw Pact command staff exercise "Brise" (June 27–July 2, 1966) the landing fleet, called *Baltika*, numbered 350 ships, including 110 landing ships and landing boats and 48 transporters. BA–MA: Forschungsstudie zum Thema "Kommandostabs- und Truppenübungen der Seestreitkräfte/Volksmarine 1956–1970," p. 137.

52 For an example, see the previously mentioned Warsaw Pact command post exercise September 30–October 10, 1961. BA–MA: Forschungsstudie zum Thema "Kommandostabs- und Truppenübungen der Seestreitkräfte/Volksmarine 1956–1970," pp. 84–5.

53 BA–MA: DVM 10/36834. A number of the documents derives from a meeting in Baltiisk, September 27–30, 1976, about the problems arising from western developments in the area of mines. The focus was on the threat from improved western types of mine from the mid-1980s. American mines with nuclear warheads are mentioned in the document, "Die Vorbereitung der dänischen Seestreitkräfte auf den Einssatz der Minenwaffe in der Sund-Beltzone."

54 Exercise evaluation. BA–MA: DVM 10/33860, p. 40.

55 Information given to author by a high-ranking Danish naval officer in March 2003.

56 Archive of the Danish Defence Intelligence Service (DDIS): "The Threat against Denmark," 1978, p. M-2.

57 BA–MA: Forschungsstudie zum Thema "Kommandostabs- und Truppenübungen der Seestreitkräfte/Volksmarine 1956–1970," p. 221.

58 The exercise ran from 10–16 August 1963, and had as a specific theme–aside from capturing the Danish straits, "The transfer of heavy forces to the North Sea, as support for the land front." BA–MA: Forschungsstudie zum Thema "Kommandostabs- und Truppenübungen der Seestreitkräfte/Volksmarine 1956–1970," pp. 104–10.

59 Paweł Piotrowski, "Desant na Danię," see note 9.

5 "Is this the best they can do?"

Henry Kissinger and the US quest for limited nuclear options, 1969–75

William Burr

During the middle decades of the Cold War, American national security planners worried that a US–Soviet crisis could lead to a nuclear catastrophe and cognizant that threats of massive nuclear use had diminishing credibility, searched for ways to make nuclear threats politically useful and believable. National security adviser Henry Kissinger believed that the massive destructiveness inhering in the US nuclear war plan, the Single Integrated Operational Plan (SIOP), made it irrational and incredible. While powerful taboos[1] dissuaded policymakers from actual nuclear use, Nixon and Kissinger sought plans and capabilities for limited nuclear attacks to control escalation, discourage conflict, and reduce the danger and destructiveness of nuclear use. Wishfully believing that nuclear war might be controllable, Kissinger remarked in June 1972 that the US government faced the "risk of our being paralyzed in a crisis because of the lack of plans short of an all-out SIOP response."[2]

The Nixon administration's efforts to refine nuclear strategy by changing top-level guidance on nuclear targeting has been explored in significant studies by historians and social scientists, including Fred Kaplan, Jan Nolan, David Rosenberg, Scott Sagan, Desmond Ball, and Terry Terriff.[3] This earlier work appeared before the more or less steady declassification of primary source material on nuclear planning during the 1970s made it possible to look at this subject in greater depth and detail. Drawing on new sources, this chapter will focus on the policymaking process that the Nixon administration initiated to provide the president with a wider range of nuclear options during an East–West crisis. Although security guarantees based on the threat of nuclear use underlay the US role in NATO, Nixon and Kissinger believed that the catastrophically huge SIOP attack options made those guarantees implausible. While Kissinger sought ostensibly more credible nuclear options, he encountered bureaucratic resistance. Not only was Secretary of Defense Melvin Laird skeptical about limited options, defense officials cast doubts on the possibility of controlled escalation and CIA analysts claimed that the Soviets did not accept the possibility of limited nuclear war.

Kissinger practically "gave up" on SIOP reform,[4] but three years into Nixon's first term, Laird became responsive to White House interests by requesting a study of nuclear targeting. Shaping this initiative was the need to accommodate nuclear targeting plans to the growing supply of Multiple Independently Targetable Reentry Vehicles (MIRVs). By mid-1972, the Pentagon's Foster Panel had produced a report recommending a policy of controlled escalation based on choices ranging from SIOP-like options for major attacks to successively smaller selective, regional, and limited attack options. In January 1974, Nixon had signed National Security Decision Memorandum (NSDM) 242 instructing the Pentagon to update nuclear targeting plans so that the president would have options in a crisis. While skeptics continued to question the possibility of controlled escalation and suggested that the new policy could weaken NATO, Kissinger was committed to the view that limited options could make nuclear threats more credible and prevent a larger conflagration.

NSDM 242 instructed the Pentagon to produce a range of options, military officials, including the Joint Strategic Target Planning Staff (JSTPS) raised obstacles, even questioning whether civilians should be involved in such sensitive issues as nuclear targeting or if limited nuclear options even made sense. Within two years, the JSTPS had created a new SIOP but it was far from what Kissinger had sought; the options remained large and massively devastating. Indeed, new research suggests that nuclear planning consistently underestimated the destructiveness of nuclear weapons.[5] Nevertheless, as long as top US officials defined Soviet foreign policy as inherently threatening, successive presidential administrations would seek limited nuclear options as an alternative to a nuclear holocaust.

The SIOP briefing and the search for alternatives

When they came to power, the first priority for Nixon and Kissinger was ending the Vietnam War, while preserving a central role for the United States in world affairs. So that adversaries understood that challenges would be met, Nixon and Kissinger believed it critically important to preserve the credibility of American power, even to the point of threatening irrationally disproportionate uses of military force – the "madman" strategy – to coerce adversaries. Nixon's inaugural address suggested the importance of the credibility doctrine when he observed, "to all those who would be tempted by weakness, let us leave no doubt that we will be as strong as we need to be for as long as we need to be."[6]

White House concerns about the credibility of American power dovetailed easily with a concern about the credibility of threats. Henry Kissinger had made his name as an academic nuclear weapons expert and had been thinking about the problem of nuclear deterrence, including the "graduated use of force," since the mid-1950s. While supporting "flexible response" notions of building up conventional forces to strengthen nuclear deterrence, he was critical of the concept of "assured destruction" that sought to deter threatening Soviet military moves with the possibility of massive attacks on urban-industrial centers.[7] Since the 1950s, he believed that such threats, especially with respect to the security of NATO Europe, had little credibility to adversaries or allies. Indeed, a year before he joined the Nixon admiration, Kissinger argued that military power in the nuclear age had become "abstract, intangible, elusive" and difficult to "translate into a plausible threat." Policymakers had to know how to manipulate their adversaries so that a nuclear threat would be taken "seriously," even if it was not made earnestly. Kissinger remained deeply interested in the problem of using military force to signal political intentions and create "politically meaningful threats," but he did not find solutions readily available.[8]

The difficulty of creating "meaningful threats" may have become even more evident when Nixon and Kissinger received a SIOP briefing at the Pentagon on January 27, 1969.[9] They would learn that the war plan's starting point was the National Strategic Targeting and Attack Policy (NSTAP) which set three priorities for destruction: (1) nuclear threat targets (task ALPHA) which were always the chief concern, (2) other military targets (task BRAVO), and (3) urban-industrial resources (task CHARLIE). The NSTAP priorities provided the basis for the SIOP which consisted of five basic attack plans. If decision makers had strategic warning that the Soviets or, less likely, the Chinese were gearing up to attack the United States, the SIOP had three options for preemptive nuclear strikes: (1) against nuclear threat targets, (2) against nuclear threat and other military targets, and (3) against nuclear, other military, and urban-industrial targets. If the Soviets struck first, SIOP-4 provided for two retaliatory options: (1) against remaining nuclear and other military targets, or (2) against nuclear, other military, and urban-industrial complexes. Each of these attack options involved the launching of thousands of nuclear weapons; by 1972, when MIRVs were being deployed, the "minimum" strategic attack employed over 2,000 warheads. According to contemporary estimates, US strategic forces had the capability to "inflict 40 percent Soviet fatalities (90 million)" with the Soviets having about the same capability, 40 percent US fatalities or 80 million.[10]

The briefing that Nixon and Kissinger heard may have mentioned the SIOP's damage expectancy (DE) requirements. In keeping with the practices of the Strategic Air Command (SAC), the JSTPS required extreme damage to targets. For hard targets such as missile silos, damage expectancy was 98 percent. With such requirements in mind, planners assigned several bombs or warheads to a designated ground zero (DGZ). Significantly, DE numbers drew on calculations of blast damage but overlooked an equally important nuclear effect – mass fire – which led to a significant underestimation of the destructiveness of nuclear weapons. Heavy weapons requirements and underestimation of destruction were sources of the "overkill" concept that has been routinely associated with the SIOP.[11]

The existence of several major SIOP options was the legacy of Secretary of Defense Robert S. McNamara who had pushed for "no cities" counterforce strategies so that presidents would have more choices. It was difficult, however, for civilian officials to change the nuclear planning system. Former Secretary of Defense James R. Schlesinger, a critic of massive attack strategies during the 1960s, retrospectively observed that the SIOP embodied the JSTPS's "tendency" to put organizational effort into planning a "perfect attack" that would destroy all targets. Using the latest intelligence and weapons technology, the JSTPS constantly updated the massive strikes that constituted the plan so they would more effectively meet the criteria spelled out in the NSTAP.[12]

Nixon or Kissinger's reactions to the briefing suggested deep misgivings. Some years later, Kissinger remembered calling McNamara and asking "Is this the best they can do?" During a meeting of the National Security Council Verification Panel in August 1973, Kissinger obliquely observed that the briefing "didn't fill him [Nixon] with enthusiasm." Another comment was stronger, that "if that's all there is [Nixon] won't do it," possibly implying that the president was reluctant to order the execution of the war plan.[13]

Nixon's doubts about nuclear war plans, with all their implications for NATO strategy, were evident during a February 1969 National Security Council (NSC) discussion on military strategy. When the conversation suggested that US first strikes and launch on warning decisions would invite massive Soviet strikes causing immense devastation at home, Nixon implied that a president might not automatically order nuclear strikes in response to Soviet military moves: the Soviets "used to know [how an] American president might react. But not now." As a veteran of Eisenhower administration nuclear policy debates, Nixon was familiar with concerns about the credibility of massive retaliation; he understood that in an age of nuclear parity, Soviet leaders would assume that a US president might hesitate to launch a massive nuclear strike to defend allies. Kissinger observed that Western Europeans did not realize that US nuclear guarantees for Europe "depended on a first strike" in response to Soviet military moves. But that was "no longer true" because of the dangers to the United States. As Nixon added, in a statement that would have appalled a NATO audience, the "nuclear umbrella is no longer there."[14]

Not wanting the president committed to massive nuclear threats to back security guarantees, Kissinger observed, "It's difficult to believe either side will launch everything." Nuclear war "is more likely to be limited" and "smaller packages will be used to avoid going to larger one[s]." Several months later when Kissinger suggested the possibility of smaller options, senior CIA and Defense officials expressed skepticism whether the Soviets would launch a "discriminating attack." After Kissinger "wondered how one rationally could make a decision to kill 80 million people," CIA Deputy Director for Intelligence R. Jack Smith countered that a Soviet limited strike "was the least likely contingency" because Moscow's strategic doctrine assumed all-out use. Kissinger kept wondering, however, "whether if we make limited use of nuclear weapons, the Soviets would make an all out response." Smith believed he knew the answer; once a few nuclear weapons are used, "the response is likely to be irrational."[15]

Not persuaded by skeptical views, Kissinger remained interested in the availability of more "discriminating options" than massive SIOP attacks in the event that the Soviets launched a smaller attack on US strategic forces. With Nixon's approval, Kissinger signed National Security Study Memorandum (NSSM) 64 which asked Laird to evaluate US strategic forces and their "capability to deter and respond to less than all-out or disarming Soviet attacks" as well as to study a range of possible nuclear war outcomes. The Pentagon was also to take into account "actual and required capabilities of the US command and control system" and to make recommendations for improvement in that area.[16]

Deputy Secretary of Defense David Packard supported Kissinger's interest in strategic options but suggested that the issue was not simply getting a better set of plans. He believed that it was important to "place greater emphasis on improving our command, control, decision making, and other war-fighting capabilities" so that command authorities had choices other than the massive SIOP options. Like senior Defense officials before him, Packard worried that the vulnerabilities of the command-control-communications system could make it difficult for command authorities to execute a complex nuclear option in the middle of a crisis. This would be a recurring theme in the discussion of prospective nuclear options. For example, the NSSM 64 study on "less than all-out strikes" concluded that US "Command Centers do not possess the combination of survivability and capability which is required for the conduct of limited strategic nuclear war."[17]

Some elements of the military bureaucracy had a positive interest in the feasibility of limited nuclear options. During the late 1960s and early 1970s, the RAND Corporation worked closely with Air Force General Richard Yudkin on the "NU-OPTS" (Nuclear Options) project that had as its premise the notion that "limited nuclear warfare is a possibility inherent in the logic of the nuclear environment." Believing that top officials needed to have "selective nuclear options" that could be used to control escalation and minimize collateral damage, Yudkin and his Air Force colleagues developed concepts of nuclear targeting involving dozens instead of thousands of weapons. While Yudkin briefed officials at Los Alamos, the State Department, and the Defense Department, and the text of one of his speeches attracted the attention of Kissinger's military assistant Colonel Alexander Haig, NU-OPTS appears never to have gotten a hearing at the White House or the highest levels of the Pentagon. Nevertheless, it had a positive impact on some Pentagon officials who would play a significant role in later developments.[18]

Apparently unaware of NU-OPTS, Kissinger wanted the national security bureaucracy to look into the possibility of limited nuclear options. To signal White House interest in policy changes, Kissinger included language in Nixon's first annual foreign policy report that questioned the rigidity of nuclear options. The onset of strategic parity posed

> new and disturbing problems. Should a President, in the event of a nuclear attack, be left with the single option of ordering the mass destruction of enemy civilians, in the face of certainty that it would be followed by the mass slaughter of Americans?[19]

Perhaps to put some direct pressure on the war planners and to dig more deeply into the SIOP, on March 6, 1970, Kissinger received briefings from the JSTPS on the strategic threat as well on military options "both within and outside of the SIOP." JSTPS director and SAC commander-in-chief Bruce Holloway reported that Kissinger "expressed special interest in the flexibility of force application."

Kissinger may not have known what the right questions were because Holloway observed, "certain aspects of the SIOP...were deliberately not gone into." Characteristically, the keepers of the SIOP did not want civilian officials, even the president's chief security adviser, investigating its most sensitive inner workings.[20]

That Holloway could feel that he misinform Kissinger and even report it to the Joint Chiefs of Staff (JCS) Chairman suggests that the military had little interest in working with him in rethinking the SIOP. That was no less true of Secretary of Defense Laird who had not made flexible strategic options a priority for nuclear planning, not least because Laird found the concept of limited nuclear use to be impractical. The Pentagon's "Strategy Guidance Memorandum" of January 1970 discussed nuclear strategy and deterrence in terms that resonated with concepts of assured destruction, for example by arguing that the threat of "unacceptable" consequences that underlay deterrence "may require the capability and the clear will to inflict an unacceptable level of damage on any aggressor." While the guidance suggested that the possibility of "less than-SIOP options" was under review, State Department officials who read the document were troubled by the lack of interest in "realistic SIOP targeting options" that would allow more discriminating attacks. Nevertheless, Nixon's annual foreign policy report published in the same month made it evident that the White House continued to seek "appropriate responses without having to resort to mass destruction."[21]

The Foster panel

By the close of 1971, Laird was becoming responsive to White House interest in alternatives to massive attacks and took steps to initiate a targeting policy review. An important consideration was the prospective SALT I agreements which would include a treaty severely restricting, if not completely banning, ABM deployments. An ABM Treaty would undercut a widely touted reason for the deployment of MIRVs on Minuteman III: more reentry vehicles were needed to evade Soviet anti-missile defenses. Chief SALT negotiator Gerard C. Smith already believed "we are going to have trouble finding appropriate targets for the more than 7,000–9,000 reentry vehicles that we will soon have." When Assistant Secretary of Defense for Systems Analysis Gardiner Tucker heard a SAC briefing on targeting, he realized that the ABM treaty would mean that the war plan would have to be adjusted to meet missile warhead availabilities.[22]

In January 1972 Laird authorized a special committee, chaired by Director of Defense Research and Engineering John Foster, to devise a "National Nuclear Target and Attack Policy" to provide guidance to the JCS. With the DOD Strategic Target Policy Committee, or the Foster Panel as it became generally known, a group of top Pentagon civilian and military officials was going to begin the review of the SIOP that Kissinger had been seeking.[23]

When the panel completed its initial report in June 1972, NSC staffer Philip Odeen reported to Kissinger that it was a "radical departure" from the NSTAP in substance and in format. The "difference is that the current policy is to win the war through the destruction of the enemy's forces and military capability" whereas the "new, proposed policy aims at trying to stop the war quickly and at a low level of destruction." In contrast to the NSTAP, the Defense proposal sought to control escalation by providing limited options and make it possible to "demonstrate our resolve in a crisis and punish the enemy, but to refrain from striking cities so as to provide an incentive for terminating the conflict." Moreover, unlike the NSTAP which was predicated on the least likely scenario of a massive Soviet attack, the new policy proposal recognized the "great uncertainty that exists as to how a war might begin."[24]

The panel proposed to strengthen deterrence by developing procedures for controlling escalation. One was to establish "boundaries" for escalation, for example, by limiting destructiveness of weapons and also by striking targets that minimized civilian losses. US forces would also seek to maintain a survivable reserve or "swing force," for example of missile-launching submarines (SSBNs), that could discourage escalation by threatening urban-industrial targets. Moreover, targeting would initially avoid command and control facilities so that the adversary could "control escalation and not resort to 'automatic' responses."

If limited options failed and major war broke out, the Foster Panel proposed using nuclear forces to destroy those military, political, and economic assets that would be "essential" to the enemy's "postwar recovery." To the extent that such targets were destroyed, the US's "postwar power and influence" would be enhanced relative to the adversary. Tacitly providing more targets for the large supply of MIRVs, "recovery" was defined broadly; for example, conventional forces would be a significant target category because of their importance to exercising "internal control over post-attack recovery, [securing] external resources for the enemy's post-attack recovery, and [continuing] to threaten the United States and its allies." While destroying population as such was not an objective, political leaders, armies, and industrial facilities were targets because of their importance to recovery. Tacitly the concept of "recovery capability" was replacing the notion of "assured destruction," but the difference was more semantic than real.[25]

The Foster Panel proposed four categories of attack options. "Major attacks," the first category, were essentially the same as the existing SIOP attack options. According to one of Kissinger's aides, they would "still essentially destroy all of the Soviet Union and China."[26] The three other categories were selected, regional, and limited attack options. "Selected options" amounted to "smaller packages," drawn from the major attack plans, to cover targets that potentially threatened the United States or allies. Among the targets of selected attack options (SAOs) were Soviet nuclear threat to the US or to NATO, naval threat to NATO, Soviet air defenses, conventional threat to US allies and forces in Asia, and the Chinese nuclear threat. Some of the selected options were based on existing alliance war plans, for example, NATO's General Strike Plan targeting Warsaw Pact forces. To control escalation and to help the adversary understand the limited nature of the attack, each of those categories would come with withholds, for example national capitals or targets collocated in urban areas would not be automatically attacked.

When policymakers wanted to constrain the scale of violence, the Foster Panel envisaged "limited" and "regional" options. Using either strategic or theater nuclear forces, the former could be used for several purposes: "signaling" (to demonstrate the great risk of combat), "response in kind," or to gain "local advantage" (if, for example, US forces were under an onslaught of enemy conventional forces). So that the president had a variety of military choices, the panel recommended that the JCS establish a special staff to develop "preplanned limited options and design ad hoc options as required." "Regional options" would be used to counter "threats to any region" – for example, East Asia, Southwest Asia, Western Europe – from Soviet nuclear strikes, prolonged conventional war, or even a short conflict. Nuclear strikes in regional conflicts would be possible under three conditions: in the event of Soviet nuclear attacks, a "prolonged conventional war" (presumably to break a deadlock), or "after a short war" (perhaps to avert escalation). Top commanders would prepare detailed plans although the National Command Authority – the President and the Secretary of Defense – would closely control any use of nuclear weapons, with high priority placed on minimizing civilian losses.

To limit civilian fatalities, the panel proposed changes in the degree of destructiveness of nuclear attacks by lowering DE requirements. While the SIOP had set DE as high as 98 percent, the panel proposed no more than 90 percent, permissive enough to assure a substantial nuclear attack against a given DGZ. The panel also proposed that damage calculations take into account fatalities caused by radiation (instead of using blast damage calculations only) as a way to provide a "yardstick... for avoiding collateral nuclear damage in Limited Options." Although heading in the direction of a more realistic assessment of the destructiveness of nuclear weapons, the panel apparently paid no attention to nuclear firestorms, a likely cause of devastation.[27]

The work of the Foster Panel represented the kind of challenge to the standard JSTPS war planning that was Kissinger's objective. Appraisals of the Foster Panel's work were generally favorable. At the end of the August, the Joint Chiefs weighed in with their support; they found the proposal "acceptable and in the US interest." Nevertheless, they believed that because of all the complexities, it would "take approximately two years to fully develop and integrated into US planning and capabilities."[28]

Wanting to move forward, Laird wrote to Nixon that the Foster Panel's work provided a "sounder basis" for nuclear planning while preserving the threat of massive destruction that he saw as essential for deterrence. When he was leaving government, Laird presented the final report to Nixon in December, asking the NSC to give it "prompt attention." Odeen, however, believed that the regional and limited nuclear options need more work, so did the matter of policy coordination with NATO. The problem was that some European allies saw the concept of flexible response as "a synonym for limited nuclear war in Europe and [the] decoupling of U.S. strategic forces" from US security guarantees. Washington had to decide whether it wanted to "precipitate a strategic debate" within the alliance.[29]

NSSM 169

To build upon the Pentagon's momentum and to review the Foster Panel's thinking, on February 13, 1973, Kissinger signed NSSM 169 and ordered an ad hoc group to review "existing nuclear policy" and evaluate "alternative changes to current policies." The review would "take into account" the work of the Foster Panel and complete its work by April 15.[30] Not surprisingly, John S. Foster chaired the NSSM 169 ad hoc group.[31]

Running well past its deadline, the ad hoc group produced a seventy-four page "summary report" in June 1973, not long before the Brezhnev–Nixon summit in Washington and the signing of the Agreement on the Prevention of Nuclear war. The study gave interagency blessings to Foster's earlier efforts, including the findings on controlled escalation and the proposed range of attack options. Moreover, the group gave priority to political, economic, and military targets "critical to the enemy's postwar power and recovery," and measures to establish "a relatively small, specified reserve force" that, after US retaliation, could "deter postwar coercion" of the United States and its allies.[32]

While the NSSM 169 group endorsed the Foster Panel's basic approach, the analysis pointed to uncertainties – the possibility that limited options could weaken deterrence, impair NATO relations, and weaken the effectiveness of US nuclear forces (e.g. withholding command and control targets could "facilitate enemy retaliation").[33] Yet, there was "no guarantee that escalation can be controlled," whether, for example, an adversary would read a limited attack as a signal to stop fighting or to escalate. Yet, with all of the risks, the group concluded that trying to control escalation to encourage an early termination of conflict provided the "most promising means" of limiting damage. Moreover, the panel speculated that various evidence, including Warsaw Pact planning documents (presumably acquired through espionage) and Soviet command and control exercises, suggested that the Soviets, despite their public dismissal of limited nuclear war, might be developing their own strategies for fighting limited nuclear war. But the language on Soviet options was carefully hedged – no one could be sure how the Soviets would respond.[34]

The report indicated internal debate over the impact of the new policy on deterrence. Some argued that if an adversary believed that Washington would not "employ its central strategic systems…in response to local aggression" that could make conflict more likely by weakening deterrence. Others argued that the focus on postwar recovery targets would enhance deterrence by establishing a "direct threat to each of the three main power blocs within the Soviet Union and the People's Republic of China (PRC), namely, the political regime, the technocrats, and the military." A weakness of the recovery target emphasis was that political leaders or war-supporting industry, much less conventional forces, could not be targeted without damaging population centers. That made the new policy not much different from "assured destruction"; critics could see it as a "cynical attempt to rationalize what we would actually do in a massive attack."[35]

The NSSM 169 group saw reasons why the Europeans could support the new approach, for example, because it targeted Warsaw Pact conventional forces.

Nevertheless, limited options could trouble NATO Europe; for example, it could be possible to interpret the term "escalation boundaries" to mean that Washington wanted to limit the fighting to Western Europe. Moreover, some believed that the whole concept of regional attack options should be scrapped because it would raise concerns about "decoupling."[36]

When confronted with such arguments, Kissinger complained, "Some Europeans...believe it is necessary that we guarantee our own destruction" by giving them "assurances" about massive responses to an attack on NATO. The Europeans should not "ask us to commit suicide" and they could not expect the United States to remain paralyzed in a crisis, owing to a lack of nuclear options. Nonetheless, Kissinger had little choice but to be concerned about European responses.[37]

Unlike earlier studies, the ad hoc group did not treat command and control problems as barriers to further work on limited options. Nevertheless, it acknowledged that direct attacks on communications links posed threats to their survivability. Moreover, executing limited options during regional conflicts could create "acute" problems. It would be impossible to assure command authorities that the current command-control-communication system could meet their needs "in all cases."

In keeping with Kissinger's interest in "out-of-area" scenarios for US–Soviet confrontations, the NSSM 69 group prepared a set of contingency plans designed to test the adequacy of the proposed nuclear policy and of US nuclear capabilities in a series of several specific scenarios involving Central Europe, Korea, China and the Soviet Union, and Iran–Iraq.[38] The Arab–Israeli conflict that soon broke out was not among the contingencies, perhaps reflecting widely held assumptions that a Middle East war was unlikely to occur. Kissinger, however, had been concerned about a Soviet preventive strike against the Chinese nuclear program and the Beijing–Moscow scenario reflected that apprehension; it posited strikes on Soviet targets by US B-52 bombers and Polaris missiles after Beijing had asked Washington for help. Odeen saw these studies as unrealistic; they did not discuss the Soviet response, gave "no real feeling that nuclear weapons provide a useful military capability," and seemed "little related to the proposed policy."[39]

Whatever Kissinger may have thought about the first cut of contingency plans, he wanted to go forward. After securing agreement from Secretary of Defense James Schlesinger and JCS Chairman Thomas Moorer that the Chiefs would prepare "operations plans" for discussion with the president in November, Kissinger met with the NSC Verification Panel. As he explained, the new policy approach was important not least because if "the only option [is] killing 80 million people [that] is the height of immorality." Apparently persuaded that limited options and fewer casualties were more ethical, Kissinger was more interested in solving two basic problems: how to get the new policy implemented and what to say publicly about it. While happy with the report and a draft presidential directive, he believed that having an "impeccable document" was less important than action by the Joint Chiefs to "put together some options" to help the president better understand what it meant to order the limited use of nuclear weapons. He wanted the Chiefs to "start planning as though the directive were approved."[40]

What to say publicly about limited nuclear options posed a daunting problem. DCI William Colby argued that it was "vital" that Soviet leaders "know we have limited options"; otherwise they might react "automatically" and cause a nuclear catastrophe. Yet, Kissinger was not sure how much the Soviets should know; he wanted some ambiguity as a deterrent: make the Soviets worry but also make them want to prevent a military crisis, "we want the Soviets to think that the situation might get out of hand, while on the other hand we want to persuade them not to let it get out of hand." Kissinger was skeptical of CIA views that the Soviets had "unlimited urge to escalate. I think they will be looking for excuses not to escalate." Nevertheless, a credible nuclear posture was essential because of his "nightmare" that in light of growing Soviet strength and "with our domestic problems, someone might decide to take a run at us." What exactly would be said to the Soviets and the Chinese, Kissinger believed, would be determined after the president and the cabinet had received a briefing on the first set of options.

Toward NSDM 242

In September 1973, Kissinger became Secretary of State and the Nixon administration soon became preoccupied with the Arab–Israeli war and the ensuing negotiations. Although the October War involved a low level nuclear alert, it was the one contingency that the NSC staff had not considered in their scenarios of limited nuclear options. Work on nuclear planning generally slowed and the November deadline for a set of limited nuclear options slipped by. That the earlier report linked targeting and acquisition policy also tended to delay a decision until Kissinger decided that nuclear targeting should be treated separately. By late 1973, it became possible to finalize a NSDM for Nixon's signature.[41]

In the final stages of preparing the NSDM, Kissinger encountered dissenting views. Winston Lord, director of the State Department's Policy Planning Council and one of Kissinger's closest assistants, expressed reservations about the concept of "controlled nuclear escalation." The concept of constraining nuclear war had not been sufficiently thought through while the idea of controlled escalation itself might suggest to Moscow that the US's "will" to escalate to all-out war was weakening. Lord worried about lowering the nuclear threshold: the production of more and more plans for limited nuclear use implied an "over-reliance on nuclear forces"; indeed, the NSSM 169 study "comes very close to regarding the use of nuclear weapons as routine." Yet, the limited use of strategic weapons against Soviet targets posed "incalculable risks" of escalation. Finally, the new strategy could produce US "overconfidence in the applicability of nuclear escalation," a problem that could have unpredictable consequences. If the Soviets accepted the new US approach "might not [they] have some advantages in playing a tit-for-tat nuclear game?" Then, the danger was that Washington could be "more exploitable."[42]

Kissinger thought Lord had written a "good paper," but he was not persuaded. On January 7, 1974, he sent Nixon a memorandum enclosing NSDM 242, on

"Policy for Planning the Employment of Nuclear Weapons." Revisiting the case for a new approach to targeting policy, but without mentioning any of the uncertainties, Kissinger observed that the concept of "win[ning]" a nuclear war had become "increasingly irrational" and the United States needed a more credible strategy based on controlled response and limited options. The new approach "maintains the major SIOP-type options" for general war, but, Kissinger strained to argue, they were different and implicitly more humane: no longer aiming at "wholesale destruction of Soviet... forces, people, and industry," they targeted instead "Soviet military, economic, and political structures." To avoid acknowledging the likelihood that limited options could involve mass death, Kissinger elided the problem that people create and inhabit "structures."[43]

Nixon signed NSDM 242 on January 17, 1974. To begin making the creation of a variety of nuclear options a routine government operation, Nixon set a series of deadlines. He instructed the Secretary of Defense to produce guidance for the "revision of operational plans" and the creation of regularly updated sets of attack options. Nixon also ordered a review of command and control and crisis management procedure as well as the creation of a special staff to advise the president on nuclear use decisions in a crisis. Finally, the agencies would prepare studies on what to tell allies and adversaries about the new strategy and how the Soviets and the Chinese might react to it.[44]

While NSDM 242 was secret, an unexpected development made the limited options issue public. On January 10, only a few days after Kissinger sent his memo to Nixon, Schlesinger publicly broached elements of the new strategy without consulting the White House. His comments during a session with foreign correspondents were improvised and "miscalculated" by giving more of an emphasis on counterforce than was in the NSDM or the earlier studies. He tried to correct this impression a few weeks later by giving a more measured presentation on flexible response and controlled escalation. These public statements enraged Kissinger, whose relationship with Schlesinger was deteriorating (it had already been competitive), because he may have expected to announce the thinking behind NSDM 242. Despite Kissinger's prolonged effort on behalf of flexible nuclear options, the new approach would become known as the "Schlesinger Doctrine."[45]

Reactions to the new strategy

Foreign government reactions to the new policy were mixed. While the Soviets publicly criticized the "Schlesinger doctrine," in informal discussions some responses were relatively composed, as was the NATO's private reaction. That the policy announcement had not significantly impaired East–West relations would make Schlesinger confident enough to discuss it in some detail in publicly released annual reports.

The State Department found it relatively easy to accommodate NATO allies to the new strategy. Ambassador Donald Rumsfeld, the US representative to the North Atlantic Council in Brussels, briefed NATO's Nuclear Planning Group (NPG) on

February 4, 1974. He emphasized the concepts of strengthening deterrence with a broad and flexible range of nuclear options, which could be used to control escalation if deterrence failed. The "options to be developed should provide for a level, scope, and duration of violence which are limited in a manner which can be clearly and credibly communicated to the enemy." Rumsfeld assured his audience that the new approach "enhance[s] credibility, rather than decoupling the US strategic forces from the Alliance." Following his instructions, Rumsfeld avoided the most sensitive issues, such as escalation boundaries, the variety of attack options, as well as the plans to target Soviet recovery capabilities. While some in the NATO audience wondered (as had some State Department officials) whether the new policy lowered the threshold for nuclear weapons use, no one questioned his arguments. Rumsfeld reported that the briefing had been "very well received."[46]

The drafters of the NSSM 169 study correctly anticipated an "adverse" Soviet reaction to any US announcement of a new targeting policy. The unfavorable response to the Schlesinger doctrine could not be missed. With no-first nuclear use the Kremlin's policy since 1973 and military strategy focused on capabilities to wage nonnuclear war, Soviet leaders treated the concept of limited nuclear conflict as intrinsically dangerous. Not only was the risk of escalation too great, they believed that Washington favored concepts of nuclear options to coerce Moscow while avoiding general war.[47]

A study led by Fritz Ermarth at CIA corroborated the hostile reaction but suggested that the Soviets were developing capabilities for waging limited nuclear war even if military doctrine posited massive strikes. The CIA analysts believed that the Soviets might even countenance limited nuclear options in conflicts on the European and Asian periphery; besides the traditional emphasis on a "theater-wide nuclear strike," Soviet military planning might become open to concepts of selective battlefield use or demonstrative use. Nevertheless, "exchanges involving the central territory of the two superpowers are least likely to remain limited." Soviet planning would continue to emphasize massive nuclear strikes in a US–Soviet conflict. However the Soviets assessed the practicability of limited options, "likely qualitative improvements in future Soviet forces will likely enhance their inherent capabilities for limited nuclear operations in theater or intercontinental war."[48]

Conferences sponsored and cosponsored by the USA Institute involving US military officers and Soviet arms control specialists showed a mixed Soviet reaction to the new strategy. During a spring 1974 meeting, the Soviets showed "anxiety and discontent" over Schlesinger's statements because they implied "lowering of the nuclear threshold," "abandonment of assured destruction," and a "first strike posture." At another conference, more adverse reactions surfaced, although comments made in private were "temperate." One expert, O.N. Bykov, acknowledged that Schlesinger "may have intended his targeting to increase deterrence," although he was "skeptical" that this was the best way to do it. Bykov also granted that the Soviets probably had their own "mirror image" Schlesinger Doctrine, while another expert conceded that Soviet targeting policy did "not greatly differ from the US." The "problem" was that Washington, unlike Moscow, "talks about it." With Soviet policy trying to downplay nuclear use, the implication was that the public US discussion of limited nuclear options was bad for international relations.[49]

Despite Soviet misgivings, Washington kept "talking about it," hoping to reassure Moscow that deterrence, not domination, was the main objective. After Schlesinger had made his public statements in January 1974, successive annual reports from his office spelled out why he believed that capabilities to control nuclear escalation were essential to strengthen deterrence. Thus, in March, Schlesinger stated that the United States needed a "series of measured responses which bear some relation to the provocation [and] have prospects of terminating hostilities before general nuclear war breaks out." Moreover, he declared a year later, it was necessary for the Soviets to understand that "no opponent should believe that he could attack ... U.S. targets of military or economic value without finding similar or other appropriate targets in his own homeland under attack." Right or wrong, Schlesinger believed that Moscow "clearly" understood why the United States had developed a flexible targeting strategy; he also saw no evidence that Moscow perceived the new US strategy as "destabilizing." Nevertheless, Schlesinger's public statements about nuclear strategy, as well as comments suggesting the possible first use of nuclear weapons, incensed Brezhnev who informed President Ford that "your Defense Secretary is speaking day after day precisely about laying down rules for the conduct of nuclear war, not about preventing such a war."[50]

Toward SIOP-5

During the two years that followed the signing of NSDM 242, the Pentagon approved new guidance based on the Foster reports. Moreover, the JSTPS prepared a new war plan, SIOP-5.

The Joint Chiefs moved relatively quickly to create a "small nuclear operations element" within the Joint Staff to plan regional and limited nuclear options (RNOs/LNOs) in peacetime and manage them during war. Schlesinger's nuclear policy assistant Donald Cotter[51] instructed the Joint Chiefs to carry out the NSDM, beginning with an initial set of limited nuclear options by late April. In addition, he established a Pentagon working group to analyze the target structures that would "markedly reduce the power and influence" of China and the Soviet Union after a US attack.[52]

The initial set of LNOs that Cotter requested appear to have dovetailed with the contingency planning that had begun in 1973. Plans under way at the Pentagon in 1974 related to "concepts" involving crises in six countries. Like the preliminary scenarios developed in 1973, some stipulated military responses to a "a fairly specific Soviet attack" stemming from crises in Iran (an "Iran–Iraq confrontation"), West Germany, Turkey, the Korean peninsula, and China. In addition, the Pentagon was looking at crises in Norway and Turkey. Each contingency would have about 4 or 5 attack options, ranging from "blocking operations" with atomic demolition munitions (ADMs) to "fairly extensive battlefield nuclear attacks."[53]

US planning on nuclear options reached a decisive moment in early April when Schlesinger approved the "Policy Guidance for the Employment of Nuclear Weapons" (also known as "Nuclear Weapons Employment Policy" or NUWEP).[54] Serving as the basis for implementing guidance that the Chiefs would send to top commanders, NUWEP stipulated targeting priorities "fundamental to securing the relative power and influence of the United States and its allies." Among them were the following: destroying the enemy's "national political controls," destroying those urban-industrial and economic resources needed for post-nuclear war "national and military recovery," and destroying or neutralizing "those enemy military forces" needed to "exercise internal control" after the attack and which could threaten the United Sates and its allies.

To ensure that the National Command Authority had "preplanned" options offering the greatest flexibility in a crisis, Schlesinger requested the Chiefs to prepare major attack, selected, regional, and limited nuclear options. Like previous versions of the SIOP, the Major Attack Options (MAO) had the objective of destroying nuclear threat targets; a new objective, or at least a new formulation, was the destruction of postwar recovery targets. The most comprehensive retaliatory or preemptive attack could include both of those categories, while a preemptive attack could include nuclear and conventional threat targets. In order to control escalation, policymakers would have the option of withholding a variety of target systems such as urban areas (for the preemptive attack against nuclear targets), specific countries, national political leadership, and "national military control."

NUWEP included eleven Selected Attack Options (SAO) targeting Soviet or Chinese nuclear threats to the United States, or Soviet nuclear, naval, or ground-based threats to NATO Europe. The guidelines were relatively specific; for example, one SAO sought to "neutralize the Soviet nuclear threat to the United States," by attacking such "representative target categories" as ICBM bases, homeports and bases for missile-launching submarines, bomber bases, nuclear storage facilities, sensors needed for executing "timely launches" of Soviet strategic forces, and Soviet civilian and military controls. Another option aimed to "neutralize the ground-based military threats to NATO" by attacking such targets as military controls and major military headquarters, transportation and logistic facilities. To maintain communications with the adversary as well as to allow it to control escalation, guidance for SAOs included "prohibited target categories" mainly, although not entirely, urban areas as well as Moscow (or Beijing), national-level military controls, and facilities for evaluating nuclear attacks.

Abjuring the targeting of "civilian populations" NUWEP stipulated that "objective targets" not include "residential structures." Thus, SAOs prohibited attacks on urban targets meaning targets that were in, or "colocated" with, areas having a population of 100,000 or more. A target was considered colocated if an attack would cause "moderate damage to 10 percent or more of the residential floor space."

Even if civilian population was not targeted, the guidance acknowledged that "substantial damage to residential structures and population may nevertheless result." Indeed, everything in the guidance suggested that civilian fatalities were an inevitable consequence of the attack options. Following the recommendations of the Foster Panel, the DE for any DGZ would not "normally exceed 90 percent," which would ensure a major effort to destroy a target. To include more realism in calculating DE, planners were to forecast the collateral damage on a given DGZ that attacks on nearby targets could cause. Further, for limited nuclear options, planners were to take into account fatalities caused by fallout (nothing was said about fire effects). Nevertheless DE could exceed 90 percent if, for example, extra effort was necessary to destroy air defenses or if eliminate targets "critical to theater commanders."

The major attack options were certain to produce massive civilian fatalities. In the event of a preemptive attack on Soviet strategic forces, each nuclear target – missile site, bomber base, or SSBN base – would be attacked by "not less than one warhead," potentially exposing any nearby town or village downwind to fallout and other nuclear effects. This contradicted the DE limitations but may have reflected a compromise with target planners who chaffed at restraints on counterforce attacks. Targeting plans for a retaliatory attack against the Soviets or the Chinese were to assure the following: (1) "moderate damage on facilities comprising approximately 70% of [the] war-supporting economic base," (2) the delivery of at least one weapon on an industrial facility in the top 250 Soviet and top 125 Chinese urban areas (ranked by economic value), (3) the delivery of least one weapon on major government centers, and (4) the neutralization of "other targets" such as military installations "critical to post-attack recovery." Most of these targets were inevitably close to, or embedded in, heavily populated areas, which made the prohibition of population as an "objective target" little more than a formality.[55]

Despite presidential backing, the Pentagon's progress in developing LNOs was slow. By mid-November 1974, Donald Cotter found that the senior military officials who were responsible for implementing the NSDM were out of sympathy with it. They did not believe that "significant staff time" should go into planning LNOs because they were "unlikely to be executed." That was because "any limited attacks on Soviet territory will trigger an all-out attack nuclear exchange." Moreover, the military leadership believed that nuclear planning was the business of the military and "should not involve the national civilian leadership." The deep-seated view in the high command and JSTPS planners was that the SIOP was their affair only – a view that was plainly hard to override.[56]

Cotter recommended that Schlesinger hold "tutorial" sessions with the Joint Chiefs to rebuild a consensus for limited nuclear options. Progress was slow, however, and before Schlesinger could see SIOP-5 through, President Ford fired him for reasons unrelated to nuclear planning. By then, Schlesinger was not satisfied with the follow-up work on NSDM 242; as he saw it, the planners at JSTPS were only "shaving down" the MAOs, in effect creating "mini-SIOPs." The supposedly limited options involved such large strikes, Schlesinger believed, that if SAC had executed them, they would have failed to convince Soviet leaders that Washington was trying to avoid a major nuclear exchange.[57]

Schlesinger's successor, Donald Rumsfeld, would give final approval to the new SIOP in early 1976. Little has been declassified about SIOP-5; according to secondary sources, it embodied NUWEP provisions for attacking Soviet nuclear threat, conventional forces, and Soviet "recovery capabilities" (including political and economic resources) as well as a reserve ("swing") force that could be used to coerce an adversary by holding urban targets hostage. It included both MAOs (no doubt with preemptive and retaliatory alternatives) and SAOs, the options for which Schlesinger's guidelines had provided the most detail. Apparently, limited and regional options were not integral to the SIOP although ongoing nuclear planning was creating them. Targeting "recovery" greatly expanded the target list to over 25,000 DGZs, which meant that even with MIRVs there was a significant gap between the number of targets and the 15,000 plus weapons in the strategic nuclear stockpile.[58]

Whatever was new in SIOP-5, both Kissinger and his successor Zbigniew Brzezinski found it highly unsatisfactory. In April 1976, Kissinger observed,

> the largest option in 1969 is only half the size of the smallest option today. If you look at it, it offers a form of warfare with 100 million dead as a lower limit, even if we attack first.

Plainly, he did not find the preplanned options that he believed were essential for controlling escalation.[59] After Carter and Brzezinski received a SIOP briefing, the latter made the same criticisms of the war plans that Nixon and Kissinger had made:

> I was struck by the relative rigidity of the SIOP options and by the limited choice that they leave you in the event of a major conflict. You are, in effect, left with the option of initiating a response which, irrespective of the version, amounts to at least the first phase of a massive central war.[60]

Faced with this problem, the Carter administration initiated new efforts to make the SIOP more responsive to presidential control, although it would encounter skepticism about the credibility of limited options.[61]

Conclusion

During the Nixon administration, the president and his national security adviser worried about the credibility of nuclear war plans, wanted military options that would give the White House an alternative to a catastrophic nuclear exchange in a confrontation with Moscow. By 1974, Henry Kissinger had achieved a presidential directive, NSDM 242, which mandated the flexible nuclear options that he believed were necessary to make deterrence work and even constrain nuclear war. It took several years before the Pentagon became willing to initiate the detailed planning that Kissinger sought. With the Foster Panel, the NSSM 169 study, NSDM 242, and NUWEP, the Pentagon developed concepts of, and guidance for, a wider range of nuclear attacks. Nuclear planning, however, was a contested realm and the organizations responsible for it were initially reluctant to change standard procedures. Kissinger and Schlesinger were challenging deep-seated organizational routines that were difficult to change. Moreover, military and civilian officials were talking past each other. What would make Kissinger and Schlesinger comfortable – diverse nuclear options to improve deterrence and reduce the risk of war and escalation – troubled military planners and even some of Kissinger's advisers, who worried about the new policy's plausibility as well as its implications for US–European relations. Despite Kissinger's and Schlesinger's support for a SIOP with diverse attack options, the initial result of their reform effort was a war plan whose central features were the massive nuclear strikes that they saw as incredible and irrational.

The Nixon administration laid the groundwork for an approach to nuclear targeting policy that successive Cold War presidents would sustain to varying degrees. Fortunately, no crisis emerged that required policymakers to test theories of controlled escalation. The inherent danger of nuclear deterrence created efforts to refine it, but the new strategy was just as problematic as the older threat of massive strikes. Uncertainties about the Soviet military response in a crisis and the extreme danger posed by nuclear use could only raise questions whether limited strategic strikes would be any less dangerous than massive retaliation. Henry Kissinger was no less interested in avoiding nuclear war but, at the same time, he found it essential to have credible military options that would validate the ultimate threat of nuclear punishment. Thus, he dismissed arguments against controlled escalation and pressed for contingency plans that would give the president and his advisors alternatives to the SIOP options. The interest in limited nuclear planning was an understandable one in a world where the superpowers were armed to the teeth, but it was unknowable whether it could mitigate the grave danger of a nuclear-based military posture.

Acknowledgments

The author thanks Raymond L. Garthoff, Jeffrey Kimball, Vojtech Mastny, Jeffrey Richelson, James R. Schlesinger, Gardiner L. Tucker, and Robert Wampler for helpful comments and suggestions. He also thanks the National Security Archive for its support.

Notes

1 For discussion of the notion of a "nuclear taboo," see Thomas Schelling, "The Role of Nuclear Weapons," in L. Benjamin Ederington and Michael J. Mazar, eds, *Turning Point: The Gulf War and U.S. Military Strategy* (Boulder, CO: Westview Press, 1994), pp. 105–15; Peter Gizewski, "From Winning Weapon to Destroyer of Worlds: The Nuclear Taboo in International Politics," *International Journal* LI (Summer 1996): 397–418; and Nina Tannenwald's major study, *The Nuclear Taboo: The United States and the Nonuse of Nuclear Weapons Since 1945* (Cambridge, UK: Cambridge University Press, 2006).

2 Ambassador Johnson to Acting Secretary, "DPRC Meeting – June 27, 1972," June 29, 1972, National Archives (NA), Record Group 59 (RG 59), Records of State Department, Subject-Numeric Files (SN) 1970–73, DEF 1 US.

3 Fred Kaplan, *The Wizards of Armageddon* (Stanford, CA: Stanford University Press, 1991); Janne Nolan, *Guardians of the Arsenal: the Politics of Nuclear Strategy* (New York: Basic Books, 1989); David A. Rosenberg, "Nuclear War Planning," in Michael Howard, George J. Andreopoulos, and Mark R. Shulman, eds, *The Laws of War: Constraints on Warfare in the Western World* (New Haven, CT: Yale University Press, 1994); Desmond Ball and Jeffrey Richelson, eds, *Strategic Nuclear Targeting* (Ithaca, NY: Cornell University Press, 1986); and Terry Terriff, *The Nixon Administration and the Making of U.S. Nuclear Strategy* (Ithaca, NY: Cornell University Press, 1995).

4 For "gave up," see memorandum of conversation, "SALT, Soviet–US Relations, Angola, Cuba, Africa, PRC, TTBT, PNE," April 1, 1976, RG 59, Records of the Counselor 1955–77, box 4.

5 See Lynn Eden, *Whole World on Fire: Organizations, Knowledge, and Nuclear Weapons Devastation* (Ithaca, NY: Cornell University Press, 2004).

6 For credibility and the madman theory in Nixon–Kissinger Vietnam policy, see Jeffrey Kimball, *Nixon's Vietnam War* (Lawrence, KS: University Press of Kansas, 1998). For "tempted by weakness," see "Inaugural Address," January 20, 1969, *Public Papers of the President of the United States, Richard Nixon, Containing the Public Messages, Speeches, and Statements of the President, 1969* (Washington, DC: Government Printing Office, 1971), p. 3.

7 Kissinger, *American Foreign Policy: Three Essays* (New York: W.W. Norton, 1969), pp. 67, 87, and 90. For Kissinger's study of nuclear weapons during the 1950s, see Walter Isaacson, *Kissinger: A Biography* (New York: Simon & Schuster, 1992), pp. 82–90. See also Lawrence Freedman, *The Evolution of Nuclear Strategy* (New York: St Martin's Press, 1989), pp. 106–9, 117, 375–6, Terriff, *The Nixon Administration*, pp. 53–60, and Kimball, *Nixon's Vietnam War*, pp. 68–70.

8 Kissinger, *American Foreign Policy: Three Essays*, pp. 45, 59–61, and 69.

9 For details on the briefing and Nixon's reaction, see William Burr, "The Nixon Administration, the 'Horror Strategy,' and the Search for Limited Nuclear Options, 1969–72: Prelude to the Schlesinger Doctrine,' *Journal of Cold War Studies* 7 (Summer 2005): 34–78. For structural rigidity of the SIOP during the 1960s and early 1970s, see Rosenberg, "Nuclear War Planning," pp. 175–82.

10 Leonard Wainstein, C.D. Cremeans, J.K. Moriarty, and J. Ponturo, *The Evolution of U.S. Strategic Command and Control and Warning, 1945–1972*, Institute for Defense Analyses, Study S-467, June 1975, pp. 346–7; Desmond Ball, "The Development of the SIOP, 1960–1983," in Desmond Ball and Jeffrey Richelson, eds, *Strategic Nuclear Targeting* (Ithaca, NY: Cornell University Press, 1986), p. 63; "Strategic Policy Issues," February 1969, NPMP, NSCF, HAK Office Files, box 3, Strategic Policy Issues. For over 2,000 warheads, see Phil Odeen to Kissinger, "NSSM 169 – Nuclear Policy," June 8, 1973, Freedom of Information Act (FOIA) release, copy at the National Security Archive, Washington, DC.

11 See David A. Rosenberg, "The Origins of Overkill: Nuclear Weapons and American Strategy, 1945–1960," *International Security* 7 (Spring 1983): 3–71. For 98 percent, see Phillip Odeen to Kissinger, "Secretary Laird's Memo to the President Dated December 26, 1972 Proposing Changes in U.S. Strategic Policy," January 5, 1973, FOIA release, copy at the National Security Archive. For SAC's search for extreme damage, see Eden, *Whole World on Fire*, p. 181.

12 Telephone interview with James R. Schlesinger, April 18, 2003. For Schlesinger's role at the RAND Corporation, where he supported studies of nuclear options, see Kaplan, *The Wizards of Armageddon*, pp. 357–8

13 Memorandum of conversation, "SALT, Soviet-US Relations, Angola, Cuba, Africa, PRC, TTBT, PNE," April 1, 1976, RG 59; Jeanne W. Davis to Kissinger, "Minutes of

the Verification Panel held August 9, 1973," August 15, 1973, with transcript attached, NPMP, NSC Institutional Files (hereafter NSCIF), H-108, Verification Panel Minutes, 2-15-72 to 6-4-74 (3 of 5). See also James G. Blight and David A. Welch, *On the Brink: Americans and Soviets Reexamine the Cuban Missile Crisis* (New York: Hill and Wang, 1989), p. 63.

14 "Notes on NSC Meeting 14 February 1969", NPMP, NSCIF, H-020, NSC Meeting, Biafra, Strategic Policy Issues, 2/14/69 (1 of 2). A few days later, Nixon observed that the "nuclear umbrella in NATO [is] a lot of crap." See "NSC Meeting – February 19, 1969," NPMP, NSCIF, H-109, NSC Minutes Originals 1969 (1 of 5).

15 "Notes on NSC Meeting 14 February 1969", NPMP, NSCIF, H-020, "NSC Meeting, 2/14/69." Winston Lord to Kissinger, June 6, 1969, enclosing minutes of NSC Review Group Meeting, "Review of U.S. Strategic Posture," June 29, 1969, NPMP, H-111, SRG Minutes Originals 1969 (3 of 3).

16 Kissinger to Nixon, "Additional Studies of the U.S. Strategic Posture," July 1, 1969, NPMP, NSCIF, H-156, NSSM-64 (1 of 3); NSSM 64, Kissinger to Secretary of Defense, "U.S. Strategic Capabilities," July 8, 1969, FOIA release, copy at the National Security Archive.

17 Wainstein *et al.*, *The Evolution of U.S. Strategic Command and Control and Warning, 1945–1972*, pp. 430–2.

18 For more detail on NU OPTs, see Burr, "The Nixon Administration, the 'Horror Strategy,' and the Search for Limited Nuclear Options." For the impact of NU OPTs on mid-level Pentagon officials, see Terriff, *The Nixon Administration*, p. 100.

19 Terriff, *The Nixon Administration*, pp. 67–8; "First Annual Report to the Congress on United States Foreign Policy for the 1970s," February 18, 1970, *Public Papers of the President of the United States, Richard Nixon, Containing the Public Messages, Speeches, and Statements of the President, 1970* (Washington, DC, Government Printing Office, 1971), p. 173.

20 SAC message to JCS/CJCS, "Visit of Dr. Henry A. Kissinger to HQ SAC," March 10, 1970, NA, RG 218, Records of Joint Chiefs of Staff, Records of JCS Chairman Earle Wheeler, box 10, 031.1 President (March 1, 1969). For secrecy of SIOP information, see Peter Feaver, *Guarding the Guardians: Civilian Control of Nuclear Weapons in the United States* (Ithaca, NY: Cornell University Press, 1992), pp. 56–60.

21 U. Alexis Johnson to David Packard, April 2, 1970, enclosing "Strategy Guidance Memorandum," SN 70–73, DEF 1 US; "Second Annual Report to the Congress on United States Foreign Policy," February 25, 1971, *Public Papers of the President of the United States, Richard Nixon, Containing the Public Messages, Speeches, and Statements of the President, 1971* (Washington, DC, Government Printing Office, 1972), p. 312. During a telephone interview Melvin Laird said that the idea of improving credibility through limited options "sounds greats but the idea of dropping a few nuclear weapons somewhere was not practical." Interview, July 11, 2003.

22 Gerard C. Smith to Kissinger, November 5, 1971, FOIA release to the National Security Archive; Gardiner L. Tucker to Terry Terriff, February 12, 1990, copy provided by Gardner Tucker to author; Terriff, *The Nixon Administration*, pp. 100–2. For exact numbers of MIRVs coming on line during the 1970s, see Natural Resources Defense Council, "Table of U.S. Nuclear Warheads," at http://www.nrdc.org/nuclear/nudb/datab9.asp.

23 Tucker to Terriff, February 12, 1990. Members included Gardiner Tucker, Assistant Secretary of Defense for International Security Affairs Warren Nutter, JCS Chairman Thomas Moorer, Joint Staff Director Air Force General John Vogt, and Admiral John Weinel (who took over the Joint Staff when Vogt left). Air Force General Jasper Welch, Foster's deputy, chaired the working group that prepared the draft reports. For the membership, see Seymour Weiss, "National Target and Attack Policy," October 2, 1972, FOIA release, copy at the National Security Archive; and Terriff, *The Nixon Administration*, pp. 103–5.

24 The following discussion draws on Odeen to Kissinger, "DPRC Meeting, June 27 on Strategic Policy," June 24, 1972; "HAK Talking Points DOD Strategic Targeting Study Briefing, Thursday, July 27, 1972"; and Odeen to Kissinger, "Secretary Laird's Memo to the President Dated December 26, 1972", January 5, 1973, enclosing "Analytical DoD Targeting Study Results and Proposals," both FOIA releases, copies at the National Security Archive.

25 Terriff, *The Nixon Administration*, pp. 177–8. Targeting population as such was in violation of international law (Fourth Geneva Convention). Rosenberg, "Nuclear War Planning," p. 165.

26 Jan M. Lodal to Secretary Kissinger, "DOD Follow-Up on New Nuclear Employment Policy (NSDM 242)," February 9, 1974, FOIA release, copy at the National Security Archive.

27 Odeen to Kissinger, "Secretary Laird's Memo to the President Dated December 26, 1972," January 5, 1973, enclosing "Analytical Summary DOD Targeting Study Results and Proposals."

28 Ambassador Johnson to Acting Secretary, "DPRC Meeting – June 27, 1972," June 29, 1972, SN 1970–73, DEF 1 US; Weiss, "National Target and Attack Policy," October 2, 1972, FOIA release, copy at the National Security Archive.

29 Odeen to Kissinger, "Secretary Laird's Memo to the President Dated December 26, 1972," January 5, 1973.

30 Ibid.; Jeanne M. Davis, "Memorandum for Recipients of NSSM 1969," February 13, 1973, FOIA release, copy at the National Security Archive.

31 Ibid. The ad hoc group included Odeen, Gardiner Tucker, Weiss, and Ronald Spiers from the State Department, Lieutenant General Louis Seith, director of Plans and Policy at the Joint Staff, and David Brandwein, director of the CIA's Foreign Missile and Space Analysis Center. See Odeen to Kissinger, "NSM 169 – Nuclear Policy," June 8, 1973, FOIA release, copy at the National Security Archive.

32 "NSSM 169 Summary Report," June 8, 1973, p. 1, enclosed with Secretary of Defense Schlesinger memorandum to Kissinger, July 13, 1973, FOIA release, copy at the National Security Archive.

33 If the group discussed the Foster Panel recommendations on DE, no trace of the discussion shows up in its report.

34 Ibid., pp. 17, 44–6.

35 Ibid., pp. 15, 48–9.

36 Ibid., pp. 22, 56–60.

37 Davis to Kissinger, "Minutes of the Verification Panel held August 9, 1973," August 15, 1973.

38 During 1972–75, Iran–Iraq tensions were high, in part because the Shah of Iran, with assistance from the CIA, was covertly assisting a Kurdish insurgency in Iraq, then considered a Soviet client in light of a recent friendship and cooperation treaty with Moscow. See Raymond L. Garthoff, *Détente and Confrontation: American-Soviet Relations from Nixon to Reagan* (Washington, DC: Brookings Institution, 1994), p. 357.

39 Odeen to Kissinger, "NSSM 169 – Nuclear Policy," June 8, 1973; William P. Quandt, *Peace Process: American Diplomacy and the Arab-Israeli Conflict Since 1967* (Washington, DC; Berkeley, CA: Brookings Institution; University of California Press, 1993), pp. 150–1. Only weeks before, when meeting with Brezhnev, Kissinger found the latter's tough talk on China worrisome. Brezhnev "claimed China was the only threat to the USSR and in effect, probed the possibility of taking joint action against Chinese nuclear facilities, or at least having the US remain passive while the Soviets did so." Kissinger to the President, "Report on Meetings with Brezhnev," May 11, 1973, NPMP, President's Personal Files, Alpha/Name Subject, box 14, Russia-RN-Eyes Only.

40 For Schlesinger's instructions, see J.R. Schlesinger to Chairman, Joint Chiefs of Staff, "Operational Plans for Nuclear Forces," August 11, 1973, FOIA release, copy at the

National Security Archive. For a transcript of the Verification Panel meeting, see Jeanne W. Davis to Kissinger, "Minutes of the Verification Panel held August 9, 1973," August 15, 1973, with transcript attached, NPMP, NSC Institutional Files, H-108, Verification Panel Minutes, 2-15-72 to 6-4-74 (3 of 5). For more details, see William Porter to Secretary of State Rogers, "NSSM 169, U.S. Nuclear Policy," August 13, 1959, SN 70–73 DEF 1 US (document incomplete in file).

41 Jan Lodal to Secretary Kissinger, "DOD Follow-Up on New Nuclear Employment Policy (NSDM 242)," February 9, 1974, and Lodal to Kissinger, "Nuclear Weapons Policy – NSSM 169," December 29, 1973, FOIA releases, copies at the National Security Archive.

42 Lord to Kissinger, "NSSM 169 – Nuclear Weapons Policy," December 3, 1973, excised FOIA release, copy at the National Security Archive. For doubts in the NSC staff, see also Terriff, *The Nixon Administration*, pp. 185–6.

43 Kissinger to the President, "Nuclear Policy," January 7, 1974, and Secretary of Defense, Director of Central Intelligence, and Director, Arms Control and Disarmament Agency, President Nixon to Secretary of State, "Policy for Planning for Employment of Nuclear Weapons," January 17, 1974, FOIA releases, copies at National Security Archive.

44 Ibid.

45 Terriff, *The Nixon Administration*, pp. 186–9; Kaplan, *The Wizards of Armageddon*, p. 373. For the Kissinger–Schlesinger rivalry, see Isaacson, *Kissinger*, pp. 521–2 and 622–4. For "miscalculated," telephone conversation with James Schlesinger, April 25, 2003.

46 US Mission NATO cables 568 and 574 to State Department, "Modification to U.S. Strategic Policy," February 4, 1974, enclosed with Acting Secretary of State to Assistant to President for the National Security Affairs; Chairman, Joint Chiefs of Staff; Director of Central Intelligence; Deputy Secretary of Defense; and Director, Arms Control and Disarmament Agency, "NSDM 242 Declaratory Policy Report," May 10, 1974, FOIA release, copy at the National Security Archive. Holding back the concept of striking postwar recovery targets raised problems for deterrence: "what effect will this threat have if no one knows about it?" Disclosing it, however, could trigger a debate over "what difference exists between this policy and Assured Destruction." May 10, 1974, FOIA release, Copy at National Security Archive.

47 Garthoff, *Détente and Confrontation*, pp. 466–7; Garthoff, *Deterrence and the Revolution in Soviet Military Doctrine* (Washington, DC: Brookings Institution, 1990), pp. 14, 60–4, 74, 83, and 176; Michael MccGwire, *Perestroika and Soviet National Security* (Washington, DC: Brookings Institution, 1991), pp. 24–6.

48 W.E. Colby to Recipients, "Soviet and PRC Reactions to US Nuclear Weapons Employment Policy," August 1, 1974, with enclosure, FOIA release, copy at National Security Archive.

49 "NSDM 242 Declaratory Policy Report," May 10, 1974; US Embassy, Soviet Union Airgram 385 to State Department, "U.S.–Soviet Symposium Discusses Strategic Issues," October 10, 1974, FOIA release, copy at National Security Archive.

50 *Report of the Secretary of Defense James R. Schlesinger to the Congress on the FY 1975 Defense Budget and FY 1975–1979 Defense Program* (Washington, DC: Government Printing Office, 1974), pp. 35–41; *Report of the Secretary of Defense James R. Schlesinger to the Congress on the FY 1976 and Transition Budgets, FY 1977 Authorization Request and FY 1976 Defense Programs* (Washington, DC: Department of Defense, 1975), section I, p. 13, and section II, pp. 2–7; Message from Brezhnev to Ford, July 11, 1975, enclosed with Kissinger to President, "Talking Points: Brezhnev's Further Complaints About Secretary Schlesinger," n.d., RG 59, Office of the Counselor, 1955–77, box 7, Soviet Union June–July 1975; *New York Times*, July 2, 1975.

51 For a highly useful interview with Cotter, see Nuclear History Program Oral History Transcript No. 2, "An NHP Interview with Donald R. Cotter," December 18, 1990,

Center for International Security Studies at Maryland, School of Public Affairs, University of Maryland.
52 D.R. Cotter to Dr Hall, Dr Marshall, Mr Shearer, Mr Aldridge, Mr Walsh, Vice Admiral King, Lt. General Seith, and Vice Admiral De Poix, "Analysis of Political, Economic, and Military Targets," March 15, 1974; Joint Chiefs of Staff to Secretary of Defense, "Crisis Management," March 18, 1974; D.R. Cotter to Chairman, Joint Chiefs of Staff, "NSDM 242 Tasks," March 21, 1974, FOIA releases, copies at the National Security Archive.

53 Jan Lodal to Secretary Kissinger, "DOD Follow-Up on New Nuclear Employment Policy (NSDM 242)," February 9, 1974.

54 J.R. Schlesinger to Chairman, JCS, "Nuclear Weapons Employment Policy," April 4, 1974, FOIA release, copy at the National Security Archive; General John A. Wickham to General Scowcroft, "Nuclear Weapons Employment Policy," April 10, 1974, enclosing "Policy Guidance for the Employment of Nuclear Weapons," April 3, 1974, NPMP, NSC Institutional Files, box H-243, NSDM 242 [2 of 2].

55 While Schlesinger intended the destruction of 70 percent of total Soviet industrial capacity *as a whole*, it was discovered sometime in the early 1980s that JSTPS planners had interpreted the guidance to mean destroying 70 percent of *every* industrial facility, which led to a significant increase in the number of targets. Later on, for a variety of reasons, the counter-recovery mission was eliminated from SIOP planning. See Desmond Ball and Robert C. Toth, "Revising the SIOP: Taking War-Fighting to Dangerous Extremes," *International Security* 14 (Spring 1990): 71.

56 D.R. Cotter to Secretary of Defense, "NSDM Implementation – Action Memorandum," August 13, 1974, and D.R. Cotter to Secretary of Defense, "Implementation Status of Revised Nuclear Weapon Employment Guidance – Action Memorandum." November 18, 1974, excised copies, FOIA release, copies at the National Security Archive.

57 Telephone conversations with James Schlesinger, April 18 and 25, 2003.

58 Terriff, *The Nixon Administration*, pp. 207–9; Nolan, *Guardians of the Arsenal*, pp. 117 and 125. During most of the 1970s, after MIRVs were deployed, the number of strategic warheads was relatively flat, over 15,000. See Natural Resources Defense Council, "Table of U.S. Nuclear Warheads," at http://www.nrdc.org/nuclear/nudb/datab9.asp#fortyfive. Terriff, in *The Nixon Administration*, pp. 205–7, notes the JSTPS's doubts but implies that the planning staff was ultimately responsive to civilian guidance.

59 Memorandum of conversation, "SALT, Soviet–US Relations, Angola, Cuba, Africa, PRC, TTBT, PNE," April 1, 1976, RG 59, Records of the Counselor 1955–77, box 4.

60 Zbigniew Brzezinski to the President, "JCS Briefings: NSC Action Implications," *c.* February 1, 1977, excised copy, Jimmy Carter Library, Zbigniew Brzezinski Collection, box 21, Carter, Jimmy Sensitive (1/77–9/78).

61 For developments during the Carter administration, see Desmond Ball, "Development of the SIOP, 1960–1983," in Ball and Richelson, eds, *Strategic Nuclear Targeting*, pp. 75–9. During Senate hearings, John Glenn (Democrat, Ohio) questioned the value of limited nuclear options arguing that massive attacks had the "best deterrence." Not impressed by arguments about credibility he observed, "I get lost in what is credible and not credible. The whole thing get so incredible when you consider wiping out whole nations, it is difficult to establish credibility." Stephen Schwartz, ed., *Atomic Audit: The Cost and Consequences of U.S. Nuclear Weapons Since 1945* (Washington, DC: Brookings Institution, 1998), pp. 492–3.

6 Silent allies and hostile neutrals

Nonaligned states in the Cold War

Wilhelm Agrell

During the Cold War, the nonaligned countries sometimes were described as representing a third way in a Europe dominated by the two opposing blocks. The nonaligned countries, especially from their own perspective, were by their very existence assumed to diffuse tension and occasionally tried to act as bridge-builders between east and west. In the military history of the Cold War, the role of the nonaligned was more complex, introducing an element of uncertainty in strategic calculations and war planning. This chapter briefly outlines the role of the nonaligned in US, NATO, and to some extent Warsaw Pact planning. How this interacted with the policy and planning of a nonaligned country is illustrated with the case of Sweden, based on official investigations into Swedish military contacts with the west during the Cold War and declassified documents on Swedish war plans into the 1970s.

Neutrals and nonbelligerents

It is not possible to deal with the role of the nonaligned countries in NATO and Warsaw Pact policy and planning after 1949 without first paying attention to the background during the Second World War. In the war, all belligerents and their allies were faced with the problem of those not participating in the war as well as those sliding off and changing side. Nations, political leaders, and military establishments that would dominate the first decades of the Cold War learned these lessons.

In the years preceding the war, the small European states found that there was no credible collective security system or guarantee available. The Abyssinian war destroyed the credibility of the League of Nations, the Munich crisis dissolved the "Little Entente," and British–French guarantees to Poland were insufficient to deter Germany and the Soviet Union from war. The small states had few if any choices and in the end only a handful managed to avoid war or occupation (Ireland, Sweden, Switzerland along with Portugal, Spain, and Turkey).

The German minister of propaganda Joseph Goebbels declared that the neutrals should be terrorized into submission, a policy that with varying degree of success was conducted against the encircled Sweden and Switzerland until the war turned and the German arms were defeated. The German policy was neither ideological nor legalistic, the main element was to pursue vital German security interests and counteract those of the opponents. The adjustment of neutral countries' policy toward concessions to the Allies during the later period of the war led to remarkably little opposition from the German side, even when taking into account their fading military capability.

The Soviet view of the formally nonaligned countries of the "cordon sanitaire" was never based on any trust in their reliability and ultimate intentions. Soviet naval planning in the Baltic in the 1930s was based on the assumption that the "hostile neutrals" (Finland, the Baltic states, Sweden, and Denmark) would not hesitate to let British naval forces into the Baltic and support a war of aggression from the capitalist powers against the Soviet Union.[1]

The Soviet Union thus encompassed a more ideological attitude than was the traditional legalistic or pragmatic attitude toward nonallied countries in the 1920s and 1930s. Its view was based on the conviction that the economic system of a country was the major determining factor in foreign policy and military aspirations. The deep suspicion against "hostile neutrals" was displayed in the secret annexes to the Molotov-Ribbentrop treaty, the annexation of the Baltic States and the demands and subsequent attack on Finland (and continuing pressure during the bilateral inter-war period 1940–41). After the German attack, Soviet concern with neutrals was limited for obvious geopolitical reasons. The only neutrals close to the Soviet Union were Sweden and Turkey. Given the military development in the east, the Soviet attitude had to be defensive and restrained until Stalingrad. However, Soviet clandestine operations and submarine attacks against iron-ore shipping along the Swedish Baltic coast were carried out from the outbreak of the war. Soviet political pressure mounted as the war drew to an end and Soviet forces reoccupied the Baltic States.

The British attitude toward neutrality was dressed in proper diplomacy but contained a considerable pragmatic element. Typical is a remark by the British minister to Stockholm Victor Mallet to foreign minister Christian Günther in 1943 that Britain did not regard Sweden as neutral but nonbelligerent in favor of the Axis powers. As the fortunes of war had shifted, Sweden was expected to adopt a similar policy in favor of the Allies. British bombers regularly used Swedish airspace for raids against Germany in the late part of the war (as was also the case with Swiss airspace). Toward Ireland, Britain adopted a similar pragmatic policy; the Irish had not been forced to concessions to Germany and the Axis, but were nevertheless put under increasing pressure to terminate German presence in the country and allow the Allies access to vital facilities.[2]

The United States was less pragmatic than the British in its approach to the European neutrals. To some degree this could probably be understood against the background of the drastic change of status from nonbelligerent to a leading allied power after Pearl Harbor. The Americans tended to regard the neutrals as free riders, unhelpful when it came to defeating the Axis powers. The US note delivered to the Irish government in 1944, demanding the expulsion of German and Japanese diplomats, was an example of this attitude.[3]

The Second World War thus produced not only a set of lessons learned by small states trying with a variety of strategies and outcomes to avoid being drawn into the conflict. The Soviet Union as well as the western powers had acquired a corresponding experience of dealing with the neutrals and nonbelligerents. While the literature on small-state security during the Cold War has dealt in depth with these lessons from the prewar and war years, less attention – if any – has been devoted to lessons or rather attitudes and patterns of behavior among the major powers toward the nonaligned.

The politics of alliance versus non-alliance

The nonaligned states of Cold War Europe did by definition not constitute a homogenous group, just as little as nonsocialist states or nondemocratic states. The concept of European nonalignment was a gradual product of the political and diplomatic agendas of the Cold War. The nonaligned countries in Cold War Europe were a mixed, changing group of states with very little in common and it would thus be a mistake to regard nonalignment as some kind of distinct "third way."

It is easily overlooked that, until the creation of the Brussels Pact in March 1948, Europe consisted exclusively of occupied or nonaligned countries. The Soviet Union was introducing a set of friendship treaties with countries within the Soviet sphere of influence, but the significance of these treaties remained unclear. The considerable uncertainty on the course of action of the countries of Western Europe is reflected in the first American postwar contingency plans for a possible war with the Soviet Union. In the first of a series of studies known as the *Pincer* plans, issued in March 1946, the United States itself was presumed to remain neutral or nonbelligerent in case of a Soviet aggression initially directed against the British positions in the Middle East. The main Soviet war aim was assumed to be the control of the eastern Mediterranean and the Persian Gulf oil resources, although the Soviet Union would be forced to initiate hostilities in Western Europe as well. The United States would, according to this study, supply Britain with lend-lease, but not enter the war until after six months. How the occupation forces in Germany could fight a Soviet onslaught while the US remained formally neutral was not explained in the plan.[4]

In a new version of the plan issued in May 1947, the US role in a war with the Soviet Union was more clear-cut. But the assumed roles of the European states varied; East Germany (the Soviet Zone) would follow the Soviet Union along with a number of reluctant satellites. Austria, Czechoslovakia, and Finland would not resist a Soviet attack, while France, Poland, and West Germany would react according to the circumstances. Only Belgium, the Netherlands, Luxembourg, Denmark, and Norway would, according to the US estimate, resist a Soviet attack. Sweden and Switzerland would remain neutral but defend themselves if attacked.[5] What kind of response was expected from the nonexisting West German state remains unclear.

This pattern of uncertainty and ambiguity was to a considerable extent clarified in the period of 1948–49. The Brussels Treaty and the creation of NATO decided the matter for the majority of the Western European countries, whereas the Soviet Union established and consolidated a firm grip over the countries controlled by the Soviet armed forces, the main exception being Austria and in a limited sense Finland, where the Porkkala base was unexpectedly returned in 1956.

Finland remained in a precarious position after the termination of hostilities with the Soviet Union in September 1944. Although spared occupation, Finland was forced to adjust to Soviet demands enforced by an Allied Control Commission. With the peace treaty signed in 1947, the Control Commission was withdrawn and the Treaty of Friendship, Cooperation, and Mutual Assistance of April 1948 formalized the position of Finland *vis-à-vis* Soviet security demands. On the domestic level, Finland however was consolidated as a western democratic state, and the Soviet Union accepted that the Communist Party from 1948 lost its seats in the government.[6]

The formation of the Atlantic Pact was a more complex process, since it relied on a voluntary choice by individual countries, determined not only by foreign policy and security concerns but also by historical factors, public sentiments, and the opinion of key policymakers. This was perhaps most clearly displayed in the case of Ireland, invited by the US and Britain to join the alliance in 1949. The Irish government declared itself willing to accept the offer – as long as Ireland could join the alliance as a united country, including the six counties of Northern Ireland. This displayed the bottom line of Irish neutrality; with the Eastern Rising still in fresh memory, the British were not to receive any favors from the republic until the issue of the six counties in the north was settled. The NATO issue thus threatened to reactivate old bilateral ghosts, and the proposal was quickly dropped without any further attempts to push it.[7]

The continued existence of nonaligned countries constituted a complicating factor both in terms of strategy and foreign policy for the major powers. Some countries vital to NATO's strategic interests remained outside the alliance, while the case of Yugoslavia was a more clear-cut loss from the Soviet perspective. Yugoslavia was a case of ideological dissent of the first order but also a considerable strategic disadvantage for the Soviet Union in southeastern Europe.

The creation of NATO coincided with and was a key element in the first high tide of the ideological confrontation of the Cold War. From a US perspective, the lack of will to join the alliance could therefore be interpreted as lack of will to side with the "Free World" against the Communist bloc. The US ambassador to Stockholm H. Freeman Matthews pursued this line and advised the government to place Sweden out in the cold; there was no place for neutrality in a confrontation between democracy and dictatorship.[8] Sweden remained under US pressure until 1952, when secret negotiations led to an agreement where Sweden accepted to follow the Coordinating Committee for export to Communist areas (COCOM) list regarding export to the Soviet bloc in return for an agreement on access to US military export.[9]

Switzerland, although of significance for NATO-planning, was as permanent neutral not put under pressure to join the alliance. The same was the case with Ireland, but as noted earlier for quite different reasons (the issue or nonissue of Northern Ireland being more important than Irish NATO membership for both Ireland and Britain). Austria did not reappear as an independent security policy actor until 1955 and was bound by the neutrality clause of the State Treaty. The Austrian neutrality of 1955 thus was a kind of addendum to the post-Yalta partition of the European continent; the formal status of Austria determined the extent and limitations of the zones of interests but did hardly have any significance for the strategy and war planning of the two blocs. The role or fate of Austria was a matter of politics and geography, as was the case with Belgium in 1914 and 1940. For a small country, the worst thinkable mistake was still to be located in the wrong place.

Spain represents the other side of the coin. Due to the perceived strategic importance of Spain in the late 1940s and early 1950s, the US was eager to push for a Spanish NATO membership. The Franco regime, the prewar ally of fascist Italy and Nazi Germany, however, was too unpleasant a partner for most politicians in Western Europe, and Spanish membership in NATO thus became politically impossible as long as the Franco regime remained in power.[10] For basically the same geostrategic reasons, the US was eager, and more successful, in pursuing the issue of NATO membership for Greece and Turkey, both joining the alliance in 1952.

Yugoslavia and Albania represent a fundamentally different pattern compared to the rest of the nonaligned. They were breakaway states, perceived by Moscow as parts of a communist bloc. Albania's termination of Soviet military presence in 1961 was also a breach in the formal pact structure. Yugoslavia's significance for both alliances was however far greater than Albania's, and the political impact of the breakaway became considerable, with Yugoslavia as a key member of the nonaligned movement.

The ideological perspective initially dominated the Soviet attitude toward the concept of nonalignment in Eastern Europe; the introduction of socialism in a country was, according to the dogmatic interpretation of Marxism, an irreversible development. Equally dogmatic was the principle of the superiority of the Soviet Communist Party and in reality the Soviet state. Nonalignment of socialist states was therefore a contradiction in terms. This, together with power politics dressed in ideological terms, was displayed in the fierce reaction to and difficulties in coping with Yugoslavia and Titoism. Soviet suppression of breakaway attempts by Hungary, Czechoslovakia, and Poland can be explained in terms of power politics and the growing Soviet use of the Warsaw Pact as an instrument for controlling disintegration in the empire.[11]

From a Soviet political perspective, nonalignment was quite another matter when it came to countries defined as capitalist. The Soviet Union quickly grasped the potential of neutralization and exploited this in the post-Stalinist years as well as through the 1960s and 1970s. Promoting nonalignment among western countries was perceived as a political strategy to block further expansion of NATO (this was the case with Sweden from the mid-1950s) and to distance individual members from NATO cooperation (a recurring pattern in the policy toward Norway and Denmark).

From the early 1950s, the security policy patterns of the alliances versus the nonaligned were in most respects settled. The breakaway of Albania in 1961 certainly did not alter this picture; neither did the recurring cases of dissidence within the alliances. The nonaligned, far from a homogenous group, comprised a number of European countries that for a variety of reasons remained outside the two blocs (although not necessarily without links to them).

Strategic uncertainty: the non-aligned of southern Europe

The utterly pessimistic US studies and war plans of the late 1940s foresaw no realistic defensive alternative in Western Europe. The best the United States could hope for in the plans called *Pincer* (1946–47), *Halfmoon* (1948), and *Dropshot* (1949) was to hold the British Isles until reinforcements could reach Europe.[12] However, a possibility was to retain a foothold in the most remote part of the continent, the Iberian Peninsula. In the *Pincher* plans, Soviet and satellite forces were estimated to reach the border between France and Spain on day $D + 50 - D + 60$.[13] A year later, this estimate was revised to between day $D + 35$ and $D + 45$, depending on the level of French resistance.[14] But to mount a major offensive against Spain, the Soviet Union would have to concentrate considerable ground forces and air support.

Spain was not regarded as a suitable allied bridgehead or base for strategic air operations (later this would change drastically). But the peninsula did have vital strategic importance for the west in terms of naval control of the Mediterranean. The relatively large, although outdated, Spanish army constituted a capability that could be reinforced with the relatively limited resources available from the United States.[15] If Spain, however, would try to remain neutral, there were a number of options, among them a forced landing in Spanish Morocco or an open violation of Spanish neutrality, with forces being sent directly to continental Spain.[16]

The resistance from European NATO members blocked the issue of Spanish membership, although the United States for some time continued to work for this during the 1950s. The major strategic issues were however solved on a bilateral basis through the US–Spanish agreement of 1953, granting the United States considerable base rights in Spain in return for economic aid. Although not formally a member of the alliance, Spain was with this agreement integrated in the military cooperation through a back door.

In early NATO planning, the pessimistic perspective of the US war plans prevailed. Spain is mentioned as a possible foothold, and the degree of Spanish resistance would depend on "developments before the outbreak of war."[17] With the signing of the bilateral US–Spanish agreement and the NATO membership of Greece and Turkey, the center of attention shifted to the eastern Mediterranean. On a broader level, NATO strategy started to change toward defense of key regions, a strategy no longer based on the assumption that Europe would be almost completely overrun. In a NATO strategy document from 1957, the defense of Spain or the significance of the Iberian Peninsula was not mentioned among the strategic objectives of the alliance. With a shift toward the defense of the Italian Alps, the Po Valley, northern Greece, and the Dardanelles, Spain became a strategic backwater.[18]

Further to the east, the strategic situation of NATO looked even gloomier in the late 1940s. Soviet forces from the occupation zone in Austria, spearheaded by the battle-hardened Yugoslav partisan army, were assumed to overrun the weak defense that could be organized in Italy. In December 1946, the US Joint War Planning Committee (JWPC) estimated that the Yugoslavs, even without Soviet reinforcement, would be able to reach La Spezia-Florence-Ancona by day D + 20. With Soviet support, the offensive would reach Rome on day D + 60 and the Straits of Messina by day D + 75.[19] If Spain was regarded as an asset, although uncertain, to the western powers, communist Yugoslavia constituted a major military menace against the west's positions on the Soviet southern flank.

All this changed with the break between Moscow and Belgrade in 1948, although it is worth noting that western planners did not at once grasp the strategic significance of this break. In November 1949, the US Joint Chiefs of Staff (JCS) assumed in the *Offtackle* plan that the Soviet forces on the southern front would invade Italy, but without elaborating what role Yugoslav forces and Yugoslav territory would play in this operation.[20] As the impact of the rift between Belgrade and Moscow became apparent, Yugoslavia was transferred into the non-aligned category. Here the key strategic issue for both alliances in case of war was, if the territories of these countries should be regarded as a buffer zone, a vacuum or an accessible asset.

In the case of Yugoslavia, NATO planners in March 1950 concluded that it was impossible to forecast the alignment of the country in the event of war. But it was assumed that the Soviet Union probably had to employ force to use Yugoslav territory if the present regime was not overthrown.[21] The recommended NATO strategy toward Yugoslavia was to support local resistance against the Soviets "so as to withhold the Soviet forces as far as possible to the east."[22] In 1952, however, NATO assessment of the Yugoslav course of action had shifted further; Yugoslavia was now assumed to probably participate in hostilities against the Soviet bloc in case of Soviet aggression in Europe, even if the country would not be attacked.[23] Yugoslavia was described as the only *lapsed satellite* and its participation in the war would, according to the NATO planners, "afford the Allies considerable psychological advantage as well as some military aid."[24]

In 1956, a new aspect of the nonaligned status had entered the NATO planning, the risk of an isolated Soviet attack against peripheral non-NATO countries. The premise was that such an attack could be carried out below the nuclear threshold and without substantial countermeasures from NATO. The Soviet Union could also employ force or threat of force to gain influence over nonaligned countries.[25] In general and noncommitting terms, the planners now pointed at the need for the forces of certain NATO nations to retain flexibility to meet military situations outside the NATO area.

The strategic situation in southern Europe also concerned two other nonallied countries, Switzerland and Austria. Switzerland's neutrality was taken for granted by the western powers, but it was also assumed that the country would resist if attacked by Soviet forces.[26] If Soviet forces could gain access to Switzerland, they could pose a serious threat to the United States and allied positions in northern Italy.[27] The same was valid for Austria, both prior and after the signing of the State Agreement. In a comment in 1957 on the State Agreement of 1955, the NATO Military Committee noted that Austrian neutrality had created the advantage of the withdrawal of Soviet forces from Austria, but at the price of the disadvantage of exposing the flanks of southern Germany and northern Italy.[28] Austria thus was a case of a perceived vacuum and accessible transit area for Soviet forces. Against this strategic background, unofficial military contacts became an option both for Austria and the western powers.

The lack of access to Warsaw Pact or Soviet documents corresponding to the strategic assessments and guidelines of the NATO Military Committee make any direct comparison impossible. However, from what is known from documents of Warsaw Pact military planning regarding the forces in Czechoslovakia and Hungary, Austria was regarded in a corresponding way as a potentially hostile power and area for offensive operation against the positions of the western powers. The documents from 1964–65 also represent the change in Soviet doctrine toward offensive operations under the conditions of full-scale nuclear war.

A plan for a staff war game at the Soviet Southern Army Group in Hungary in 1965 describes a scenario where war is initiated by the mutual exchanges of nuclear strikes. Among the targets attacked by the "easterners" were a number of Austrian cities and military facilities. On the second day of the operations, the "easterners," according to the scenario, would decide to destroy the enemy "south of Munich" and to employ the 25th Hungarian army to destroy "the Klagenfurt grouping of the enemy," thus opening the route for offensive operations through Austria into northern Italy.[29]

The published war plan of the Czechoslovak People's Army from 1964 deals with offensive operations toward southern Germany and northern France. Although the plan does not deal with operations south of Munich it gives some indirect insight into calculations on Austria. If Austria were to remain neutral on the third day of war, one Soviet mechanized rifle division from the Southern Group of Forces deployed in Czechoslovakia opposite to Lenz would be transferred to the Czechoslovak front (see Chapter 3 by Petr Luňák in this book).[30] This indicates that Warsaw Pact planning *vis-à-vis* Austria was drawn up according to several alternatives of which continued neutrality was one.

Dealing with the gray zone: the non-aligned of northern Europe

If the geostrategic factors were the key element in the role of the nonaligned in the strategic calculations in southern Europe, the same was true for the situation in the north. The pessimistic approach of the early American war plans led to the conclusion that Scandinavia, although valuable both for the defense of the west and an assumed target of a Soviet offensive, could not be supported and hence not defended.

In May 1947, the US JWPC estimated that it was unlikely that Scandinavia could be defended. Three Soviet divisions were assumed to overrun Denmark in ten days, 7 divisions would be allocated for Norway. Like Switzerland, Sweden was assumed to remain neutral but would resist if attacked. Finland, with the Soviet base at Porkkala and the Soviet-dominated control commission still in place, was not thought to resist a Soviet attack.[31] In the planning documents from 1947, the United States evaluated the alternatives of holding Scandinavia or to leave Norway and Sweden to their own devices, concentrating instead on other theaters. The United States would limit operations in the north to the occupation of the North Atlantic islands, first of all Greenland, for defensive purposes and due to its value for the Soviets as a base for attack against North America. Greenland was therefore to be occupied regardless of the views of the Danish government. Spitsbergen and Jan Mayen, although marginally useful to the Allies, were too close to the Soviet mainland to be seized and held. Iceland was however an important air and naval base.[32]

In 1949, this theme was further elaborated in the plan *Dropshot*, a strategic study of a possible war eight years later, in 1957. Norway and Sweden were regarded as strategically important to the Allies, both from an offensive and a defensive standpoint. However, the forces assumed available in 1957 by Norway and Sweden were estimated to be about two-thirds of the minimum level required to withstand a full-scale Soviet onslaught at day D + 1, 5 months. Since allied pre-D-day reinforcements to the Nordic countries were assumed politically unacceptable, the only alternative was a major prewar reinforcement program of the national defenses.[33] This would however risk draining other more vital regions in Central Europe. Scandinavia was not *that* important.[34]

In the NATO Medium Term Defence Plan of 1950 a similar view of the Soviet threat prevailed:

> A campaign against Scandinavia would have the objectives of securing complete control of the Baltic to provide naval and air bases for operations against trade routes and Allied bases in the North Atlantic, to add depth to the air defense of the Soviet Union, and to deny the use of air and naval bases to the Allied powers.[35]

To reach this goal, the Soviets could either bypass Sweden in order to try to ensure initial Swedish neutrality or attack Scandinavia as a whole. This choice was not simple, especially as the Soviets could not be sure that Sweden would remain inactive and passively await encirclement. The conclusion of the Military Committee was therefore that the more Denmark and Norway gathered strength, the more the Soviet side would consider it unlikely that Sweden could be lured into passively accepting encirclement and thus the probability for a simultaneous attack against all three Scandinavian countries increased.[36] Such an attack would be launched in the far north, through Finland and from the south, where the main thrust was foreseen.[37]

There are some similarities as well as some important differences with the situation of Spain. In both cases the western planners, on the one hand, saw a considerable strategic demand for coordination and cooperation, on the other hand, while Spain wanted to join NATO and escape international isolation, Sweden had rejected the option of joining the alliance. NATO simply had to conclude that Sweden was of considerable importance in any regional defense planning and that the full cooperation of Sweden at some later date would greatly enhance the defensive strength of the Alliance.[38]

In December 1952, the shift to a more optimistic assessment and thus a more ambitious defensive strategy was visible also regarding northern Europe. It was now obvious that the Finnish–Soviet pact of 1948 had not made Finland a satellite or semi-satellite. Now the NATO planners assumed that Finland initially would try to remain neutral, not willingly giving the Soviets any military assistance, and try to avoid giving permission to Soviet troops to move into Finland. Under some circumstances, she could even be expected to fight Soviet forces entering Finnish territory without permission (cf. the assumption on Yugoslav intentions and possible courses of action in the same document).[39] The NATO strategy was now to defend Scandinavia as a whole: "Plans for the defence of Norway and Denmark, and also of Sweden should this be possible, must therefore be integrated."[40]

Sweden and the dilemmas of non-alignment and neutrality

The single most important factor in determining the Swedish security policy in the Cold War was the fact that the country had survived the armed clashes in northern Europe 1939–45 virtually unscratched. From a Swedish perspective the country had survived three major security threats; the Soviet attempt to occupy Finland in the Winter War 1939–40, the German "Operation Weserübung" resulting in the conquest of Denmark and Norway in 1940, and the German encirclement 1940–43 with political pressure and a number of crises when Germany seemed to prepare an attack. In the closing weeks of the war, Sweden was put under allied pressure to prepare for an intervention in occupied Denmark and Norway, but such an intervention was not necessary thanks to the swift and unconditional surrender of the German forces throughout Scandinavia. So, Swedish neutrality had been a winning concept, at least things looked that way from the perspective of most Swedish citizens and politicians. Anyone trying to make a plea for a different concept thus had to come up with very convincing arguments. As the years passed, the consensus on neutrality in itself became the most fundamental argument. From the late 1950s onwards, to question or even discuss the concept of neutrality became almost an offence, something that presumably would create uncertainty in the eyes of foreign powers and thus harm national security. These unwritten rules had to be respected by leading politicians, diplomats, and officers, and later during the Cold War the system of imposed self-censorship even extended to researchers and journalists.[41] But this set of rules for public policy and public debate was one thing; the security dilemma of a small nonaligned country in a strategic gray zone was something quite different.

Before the Second World War, Swedish operational defense planning had been based on three assumed alternatives:

Case I: War with Germany
Case II: War with the Soviet Union
Case III: War with the western powers

In 1945, it was obvious to the Swedish Supreme command that the only valid threat came from case II, and this remained the single concept for all operational planning throughout the Cold War, contrary to recurring declarations that Swedish neutrality should be defended in all directions and against anyone trying to violate it. However, case II was more than enough for the limited domestic defense resources of Sweden. With the outcome of the war, the Soviet positions had been pushed westwards and made Sweden far more exposed than in the mid-war years. Soviet forces could reach southern Sweden from Poland and occupy eastern Germany and central Sweden from the Soviet Baltic republic. And with Finland linked to the Soviet security system by the 1948 treaty, Sweden no longer could count on Finland as a buffer zone in the north.

The first postwar military contingency planning reflected this increased geostrategic threat. In 1946, the Supreme Command assumed that the aim of a Soviet attack on Sweden would be to secure bases in Sweden for a further attack on Denmark and Norway, from where air and sea operations could be conducted against Britain.[42] While the Swedish forces were estimated to be able to repulse an attack against southern Sweden, due to the Soviet lack of vessels suitable for an amphibious attack, a major onslaught against northern Sweden had to be met with delaying actions where the Swedish forces were assumed to fall back toward the south and along the iron-ore railway toward Narvik in northern Norway.

The assumed Soviet numerical superiority was overwhelming; the Swedish intelligence estimated that the Soviet forces in northern Europe in May 1945 consisted of 175 infantry divisions and 65 armored brigades deployed between Lübeck and Leningrad, supported by more than 10,000 combat aircrafts.[43] Against the massive supremacy the Soviet Union was assumed to be capable of deploying against Sweden, the Swedish army could mobilize the equivalent of twelve infantry divisions with limited armored support. The over-all Swedish defense strategy was, given this numerical inferiority, to delay a Soviet attack, to avoid an early devastating defeat, and to gain time for "help from the outside."[44]

In 1944, the conservative and pro-German supreme commander general Olof Thörnell had been succeeded by the pro-allied general Helge Jung. After the war Jung, along with the air force commander general Bengt Nordenskiöld, saw an orientation toward the western powers as necessary to balance the Soviet supremacy in the Baltic and the high north. Another necessity was the coordination of the defense efforts of the Scandinavian countries; in a future war the whole area was assumed to constitute one single theater of operations and the countries could not be defended independently.

This was the strategic rationale behind a Swedish initiative for a Scandinavian defense union in 1948–49, including mutual security guarantees. After long negotiations the initiative finally fell, mainly due to US unwillingness to supply an independent regional alliance with weapons. The formation of the Atlantic alliance, with the explicit US and British security guarantees, fundamentally changed the situation for Norway and initially to somewhat lesser extent for Denmark.

From the Swedish side the Scandinavian initiative had been launched with somewhat contradictory goals. While the foreign minister Östen Undén saw it as a possible "neutrality pact," allowing the three countries to stay out of the looming east–west conflict, the Swedish military saw the pact as an indirect link to the western powers. Given the strategic situation at the beginning of the Cold War, this goal was not abandoned as Denmark and Norway joined the Atlantic Pact in 1949, but was pursued through new channels, thus creating a double-layer security policy dominating Swedish security and defense planning in the Cold War.[45]

Officially Sweden declared a policy of "nonalignment in peace aiming at neutrality in war." This was interpreted to mean that Sweden had to avoid such binding cooperation in the domain of foreign and defense policy that might compromise the credibility of neutrality. For the same reason no operational military cooperation or coordination of defense planning could take place, the main exemption being planning and preparations for UN-peacekeeping forces.

The strategic rationale behind the Scandinavian defense initiative did however remain; in a major war Scandinavia would inevitably become one single theater of operations and Norwegian and Swedish defense efforts would, with or without any alliance, be mutually dependent. As a result of the joint staff planning during the negotiations, a detailed plan for the most imminent coordination existed. In place in 1949 were therefore both an agenda and a network of contacts for discrete coordination behind the officially declared policies.

In the autumn of 1949, both the Norwegian and the Swedish governments gave their approval to secret military contacts for possible cooperation in case of war.[46] The contacts established between Sweden and Norway as well as Sweden and Denmark were focused on coordination of high-level communication systems, air defense, supply routes, and naval minefields. The coordination was most extensive concerning air operations, while considerably less was done in the field of ground operations.[47] The most extensive peacetime cooperation and coordination concerned intelligence.[48]

For the Swedish side, the development of the joint command structure within NATO following the outbreak of the Korean War initially became a considerable obstacle. The Scandinavian links had been established between the national defense commands in Sweden, Denmark, and Norway, and now the latter two had, with the introduction of the joint command, been deprived the task of operational planning. From the government perspective, it was vital that Sweden only maintained contact with individual countries not with NATO as an organization.[49] From 1952–53, this was sorted out with Norway in the role of go-between in the coordination of Swedish and NATO planning in the earlier-mentioned fields, an arrangement known by and approved by the United States.[50]

The supreme commander general Nils Swedlund, when leaving his post after 10 years in office in 1961, summarized the position of the armed forces in a personal memo to his successor, the air force general Torsten Rapp: The official Swedish policy of nonalignment was to be respected, but should be abandoned immediately if Sweden was drawn into hostilities. Preparations for this contingency had to be carried out, but Swedlund warned against placing any segment of the Swedish forces under NATO command and integrating them with the forces of NATO's command for northern Europe, AFNORTH. Even as a cobelligerent, the Swedish government and the High Command should retain both political and operational control over the Swedish armed forces.[51]

In 1966, the Swedish defense planning was thoroughly revised and new operational directives were distributed from the Supreme Command to subordinate commands.[52] With only minor changes added in 1973, the operational directives remained in effect up to the late 1970s, when the security environment and the general conditions for the Swedish defense began to change more profoundly. The 1966 directives represented a shift to a more forwardly defense strategy where the explicit goal was to absorb and repulse a Soviet attack in the coastal area or close to the land border to Finland.[53] Air and naval forces were to be deployed in an anti-invasion role with an area of operations extending to the Soviet Baltic military district and to Finland, in case Soviet forces entered the country.[54] Help from the western powers continued to play an important role in the plan; one of the aims of the defensive Swedish operations was to secure areas crucial for supply and to ensure that "military assistance from abroad can become effective."[55] The directives to the regional military commands leave no doubt that this meant areas close to southern and mid Norway.

There are no indications in Swedish material that offensive combined-arms operations from NATO forces over Swedish territory were ever contemplated in Swedish planning, neither as joint Swedish–NATO operations nor as independent NATO operations with Swedish consent. Probably such contingencies seemed highly unlikely, given the correlation of forces in the northern theater of operations during the first decades of the Cold War. Two important exceptions should however be noted. The first is offensive submarine operations in the Baltic where some kind of "division of labor" was secretly established between the Swedish, Danish, and West German navies.[56] The other exception concerned air operations.

Offensive NATO air operations passing through Swedish airspace was an expected but more complex contingency (as it was during the Second World War), and available evidence indicates that there was no intention and planning to interfere with these operations – instead the Swedish air force secretly made certain adjustment of the technical facilities to make it possible to serve NATO aircrafts in case of emergency.[57] While most of this was covert preparation, there was also an overt side, the air-rescue agreement between Denmark, Norway, and Sweden. According to this agreement communication links were established between the air surveillance systems, later the Sector Operation Centers in the NADGE-system and the corresponding Swedish STRIL-60 system. Danish, Norwegian, and Swedish combat aircraft also regularly landed on each other's military air bases, officially for the crews to accommodate themselves with procedures in case of emergency landings.

A number of runways on Swedish airbases, mainly along the Baltic coast, were rebuilt and extended in the 1950s and 1960s, although the reason for this was never explicitly mentioned even in secret documents. The official commission investigating Swedish preparations for western assistance in the early Cold War arrived at the conclusion that these runways had been constructed with the dual purpose of serving the Swedish air force and – should such a contingency arise – NATO tactical aircrafts as well as strategic bombers from Britain and the United States. In the latter case the bases would most likely have served as emergency rescue landing facilities.[58]

In 2002, the governmental investigator ambassador Rolf Ekéus in his report concerning Swedish security policy in the 1970s and 1980s argued that it was highly unlikely that the improvement of runways would have been a preparation for deployment of NATO aircrafts on Swedish airbases. Instead the improvement could be seen as an adjustment to serve purely Swedish purposes.[59] The issue is however somewhat clarified by a lengthy entry in Prime Minister Tage Erlander's diary for 1953. The diary was made accessible in 2003. On May 13 that year, the Supreme Command briefed the leaders of the social democratic party and the non-socialist parties. The leader of the conservative party Jarl Hjalmarson, according to Erlander's account, strongly argued in favor of making preparations for NATO assistance. General Swedlund took a somewhat more cautious line, explaining that the Supreme Command, including the Chief of the air force general Bengt Nordenskiöld (well known for his pro-NATO stance) had agreed that the most important help would be air attacks against enemy forces carried out from bases abroad. It would, in Swedlund's opinion, be difficult to improvise cooperation between Swedish and foreign aircrafts on a joint airbase. An alternative however was a swift evacuation of certain airbases "that entirely could be utilized by the helpers."[60]

It is also evident from Erlander's diary that the Swedes were well-informed about NATO strategic assessments. In January 1953, Erlander commented the utter pessimism of what he called "the NATO protocols," obviously referring to the strategic assessment drawn up by the NATO Military Committee on December 9, 1952 (see earlier discussion).[61] These protocols were made available to the Swedish ambassador at the Organization for European Economic Cooperation (OEEC) in Paris, who supplied his government with a summary.

The secret Swedish military cooperation with the west during the Cold War does on the whole not appear to have been a case of "politicizing generals" or the segmentization of bureaucratic politics. The parallel diary accounts of Erlander and Swedlund confirms a system based on considerable mutual understanding, where the politicians generally were the ones who defined the limitations of the contacts and the key officers, likewise generally accepted these limitations even when disliked or deemed over-cautious.[62] This is not surprising, given the specific character of Swedish decision making in the first postwar decades, dominated by networks built on personal trust, mutual interests, and shared national goals.

There was a common awareness among the handful of persons fully informed that for small countries outside the blocs the threat to their independence and survival came both from the peace-time struggle in the ongoing Cold War and from the armed confrontation that might escalate from this struggle. The double-layer Swedish security policy should be interpreted against this background. Especially Erlander's diary is informative about the high awareness of the key players (Erlander himself, the defense minister and to somewhat less extent the foreign minister), of the overt and covert aspects of the security policy, and the absolute need for secrecy on the latter.

Silent ally, hostile neutral?

The covert links between Sweden and the NATO-countries thus had two sides. On the one hand, there was the Swedish goal to secure vital and realistic military assistance in case of war while at the same time not compromising the policy of nonalignment in the eyes of the Soviet Union or the domestic public opinion. On the other hand, there were the goals of individual NATO-countries, of NATO's joint northern European command and of the United States as a global power.

The strategic goals in northern Europe elaborated in the NATO-plans explain the various initiatives to unofficially integrate the Swedish defense, first of all with the defenses of Denmark and Norway. But in the longer run, integrating Sweden into NATO-plans and strategies also concerned the United States and the crucial aspects of reinforcement and support in time of war. Between the Scandinavian countries this cooperation was facilitated by a curious loophole in the Swedish concept of non-alignment; political and military contacts with the Scandinavian countries were regarded as less sensitive than contacts with UK or US officials, although the practical difference might be hard to establish. The US State Department, becoming aware of these contacts, saw their potential and encouraged their NATO partners to pursue a policy of gradual, case-by-case oriented cooperation and coordination.[63] This solved some problems of the perceived necessity of a common Scandinavian defense strategy. Both the political structure of NATO and the declared Swedish policy of nonalignment did however impose certain limitations as to how far an unofficial coordination could be developed.

In April 1960, the US National Security Council (NSC) issued a policy document concerning Denmark, Norway, and Sweden. The strategic assessment contained the same elements as earlier NATO-plans. The Scandinavian area was of vital importance to the alliance, although the NSC adds that the value of the region as a base for western retaliatory operations is limited by Swedish neutrality and the unwillingness of Denmark and Norway to permit such use.[64] Sweden's membership in NATO was however not regarded as necessary to western defense. The reason for this was not a negative attitude to Swedish neutrality or doubts on the strategic significance of Sweden for the defense of Scandinavia. On the contrary, the United States should be prepared to come to the assistance of Sweden in the event of a general war "without prejudice to US commitments to

NATO." And in case of an isolated Soviet attack, the kind of unspecified contingency mentioned in the NATO-planning documents, the United States should be prepared to come to the assistance of Sweden as part of a NATO or UN response. In a footnote this was clarified to relate only to unilateral US planning and not to planning within NATO.[65]

The policy toward Sweden was confirmed and further elaborated by the Kennedy administration in a Department of State Guideline in June 1962. Since the Swedish position in case of a general war could not be predetermined, it was regarded as important to secure Sweden's position in a war as "a friendly neutral." In case of an attack on Sweden alone, the United States should be prepared to come to assistance:

> Planning and preparations for this contingency must be conducted only on a unilateral US basis, since some NATO powers may be sensitive to a preferential assistance guarantee to a neutral non-member, and the Swedish government has scrupulously avoided any identification with NATO. It would, however, be highly important to inform our NATO allies in advance of any such actions we proposed to take.[66]

This US policy of bilateral or rather unilateral security guarantees most likely played an important role for US–Swedish security cooperation throughout the Cold War period, including the years of "deep-frozen" diplomatic relations during the later part of the Vietnam War.

No corresponding Soviet or Warsaw Pact documents are available for the Scandinavian area. Polish documents on defensive planning and the establishment of the "Maritime Front" in the 1960s however give some indirect guidance as to the general outline of Soviet and Warsaw Pact planning and preparations for operations in the Baltic and toward Scandinavia. The available operational plan for the Polish 1st and 2nd Armies from 1951 indicates a predominately defensive planning against raids and amphibious operations along the Baltic coastline. Remarkable is however a passage on the military capability and intentions of the Scandinavian countries:

> The states neighboring directly with us in the Baltic – Sweden, Norway and Denmark – have relatively small quantities of forces for starting operation right on the day of a war breakout. But after initiating mobilization (M-2–M-4) they may be ready for operations, creating a threat to Poland's sea coast.[67]

The real threat was however identified as the Anglo-American forces as well as the German army under reconstruction in West Germany, "part of which can be transferred to the Scandinavian states to initiate direct operations along the seacoast of Poland."[68] It is obvious from this document that Sweden in this context is regarded as a hostile neutral, belonging to the same category as the NATO members (Denmark and Norway). The perceived threat from German operations through Scandinavia indicates an expected repetition of the patterns of the Second World War.

In the 1960s, the Polish "Maritime Front" was organized with the task of conducting deep offensive operations against the northern Federal Republic of Germany (FRG) and Denmark with the goal of seizing the Baltic Straits within 10–13 days in case of nuclear war and 14–18 days of conventional war.[69] Although no firm conclusion could be drawn from the goals of the Maritime Front, it seems highly unlikely that Soviet planning for the Baltic Fleet, the Northern Fleet, and the Baltic and Leningrad military districts would have departed drastically from the planning in Central Europe and along the southern coastline of the Baltic.

Some concluding remarks

The nonaligned countries in Cold War Europe did not constitute a distinctive or homogenous group. There were the old neutrals like Switzerland and Sweden, the more recent Ireland, the reestablished Austria, and the aspiring neutral Finland. To this came breakaway Yugoslavia and later Albania as well as the denied NATO-member Spain. There were nearly as many reasons for staying out of the alliances, as there were nonaligned.

From the perspective of the alliances and the emerging superpowers things looked different. The nonaligned, whatever the reason, constituted a specific form of strategic uncertainty, less important in some cases, a major cause for concern in other. Nonalignment as such could be regarded as a problem, as was the case when NATO was established, or as an advantage, as was the case with numerous Soviet proposals to dissolve the alliances, neutralize Germany, or extract Denmark and Norway from NATO. In principle the same applied to the Warsaw Pact countries but was never exploited by NATO for fear of destabilizing the heritage of the Yalta agreement and thus the perceived fundament for stability and peace in Europe.

Unofficial arrangements, understandings, and contacts could make up for some of the discrepancies between strategic necessity and political realities. Few nonaligned, if any, lacked altogether some links with an alliance. There is a considerable NATO–US overweight in this respect – very little is known of any unofficial contacts between the nonaligned countries and the Soviet Union or other Warsaw Pact countries.[70]

To conclude, on the level of military strategy and planning, the nonaligned on the whole represented a secondary issue during the Cold War from the perspective of the two superpowers and their alliances. There are, as described above, some exceptions, but they are indeed exceptions. It is fair to say that the nonaligned introduced an element of uncertainty into the military planning of the alliances. The extent of this uncertainty cannot yet be determined from the limited insight we have into the planning procedure and its outcome. However, it should be kept in mind that some allied countries represented considerable uncertainties which perhaps were of far greater significance than the uncertainties about the non-aligned.

Notes

1 See Andrei A. Kokoshin, *Soviet Strategic Thought, 1917–91* (Cambridge: MIT Press, 1998), pp. 80–5.
2 For Irish security policy during the Second World War, see Trevor C. Salmon, *Unneutral Ireland. An Ambivalent and Unique Security Policy* (Oxford: Clarendon Press, 1989). Thomas E. Hachey claims in "The Rhetoric and Reality of Irish Neutrality," *New Hibernian Review* 2 (2002): 26–43, that the sole reason for the United States and Britain to tolerate Irish neutrality was the strategic significance of Northern Ireland.
3 T. Ryle Dwyer, *Strained Relations: Ireland at Peace and the USA at War, 1941–45* (Dublin: Gill and Macmillan, 1988).
4 Steven T. Ross, *American War Plans 1945–1950. Strategies for Defeating the Soviet Union* (London: Frank Cass, 1996).
5 Ross, *American War Plans 1945–1950*, p. 40.
6 Kimmo Rentola, "From Half-Adversary to Half-Ally: Finland in Soviet Policy, 1953–58," *Cold War History* 1 (2000): 75–102.
7 Hachey, "The Rhetoric and Reality of Irish Neutrality."
8 Paul M. Cole, *Neutralité du jour: The Conduct of Swedish Security Police since 1945* (Ann Arbor, MI: University Microfilms International, 1992).
9 There has been a considerable debate on the nature of the Swedish–US agreement. Although it did not constitute a secret alliance agreement, the security implications were far greater than officially admitted during the Cold War. The agreement is discussed in the 1994 report from the Commission investigating the Swedish policy of neutrality up to the end of the 1960s, *Om kriget kommit ... Förberedelser för mottagning av militärt bistånd 1949–1969. Betänkande av Neutralitetspolitikkommissionen* [Had there been a war ... Preparations for the reception of military assistance 1949–1969] (Stockholm: Fritzes, SOU 1994: 11). An important background to the agreement is given in the document *A Report to the National Security Council by the Executive Secretary on the Position of United States with Respect to Scandinavia and Finland, January 8, 1952*, NSC 121 (Reprinted in facsimile in the report of the commission).
10 The Spanish issue and the political resistance from among others the Danish government is discussed in Poul Villaume, *Alliert med forbehold, Danmark, NATO og den kolde krig. En studie i dansk sikkerhedspolitik 1949–1961* [Allied with limitations, Denmark NATO, and the Cold War. A study of Danish security policy 1949–1961] (Copenhagen: Eierne 1995), pp. 676–86.
11 Vojtech Mastny, "The New History of Cold War Alliances," *Journal of Cold War Studies*, 2 (2002): 55–84.
12 Ross and Anthony Cave Brown, *Operation: World War III. The Secret American Plan "Dropshot" for War with the Soviet Union, 1957* (London: Arms and Armour, 1978).
13 Ross, *American War Plans 1945–1950*, p. 22.
14 Ibid., p. 42.
15 Early 1948 the US Joint War Plan Committee estimated that 12 British or US divisions would be needed along with air support from 9 aircraft carriers and over 700 land-based aircraft.
16 Ross, *American War Plans 1945–1950*, pp. 42–3.
17 *North Atlantic Military Committee, Decision on M.C. 14/1, 9 December 1952*, p. 8, NATO Archives.
18 *Overall Strategic Concept for the Defence of the North Atlantic Treaty Organization Area, MC 14/2 (Revised) 21 February 1957*, p. 24, NATO Archives. Spain is also absent in a declassified strategic document from 1969, *Measures to implement the Strategic Concept for the Defence of the NATO-Area, MC 48/3, 6 May 1969*, pp. 371–82, NATO Archives.

19 Ross, *American War Plans 1945–1950*, p. 39.
20 Ibid., pp. 113–14.
21 *North Atlantic Military Committee, Decision on M.C. 14, 28 March 1950*, pp. 7 and 37, NATO Archives.
22 Ibid., p. 46.
23 *North Atlantic Military Committee, Decision on M.C. 14/1, 9 December 1952*, p. 8, NATO Archives. The Italian representative did include a dissenting view in a footnote, stating that in the Italian opinion Yugoslavia would try to remain neutral, at least initially in the event of general war.
24 Ibid., p. 22. Further on in the document the advantages for the allies are specified; the support from Yugoslav forces was assumed to have a marked effect on the situation both on the Italian and Greek Front, whether appreciable enemy forces would be drawn off and the depth of the allied position would be increased (p. 25).
25 *Directive to the NATO Military Authorities from the North Atlantic Council, 13 December 1956*, p. 5; *A Report by the Military Committee to the North Atlantic Council on Overall Strategic Concept for the Defence of the North Atlantic Treaty Organization Area, MC 14/2 (Revised), 21 February 1957*, p. 12; and *Military Decision on MC 14/3. A Report by the Military Committee to the Defence Planning Committee on the Overall Strategic Concept for the Defence of the North Atlantic Treaty Organization Area, MC 14/3 (Military Decision), 22 September 1967*, p. 6, NATO Archives.
26 The NATO planning document of 1950 mentions the importance of western reliance on the support of Switzerland to hold the alpine areas. This indicates an interest in military cooperation and coordination. *North Atlantic Military Committee, Decision on M.C. 14, 28 March 1950*, p. 46, NATO Archives.
27 Ross, *American War Plans 1945–1950*, p. 91, referring to the US plan *Halfmoon* of May 1948.
28 *A Report by the Military Committee to the North Atlantic Council on Overall Strategic Concept for the Defence of the North Atlantic Treaty Organization Area, MC 14/2 (Revised), 21 February 1957*, p. 17, NATO Archives.
29 *Plan of the Two-Stage Front Command War Game to be Conducted on Map in the Southern Army Group, 12 June 1965*, document available from World Wide Web on the homepage of the Parallel History Project, http://www.isn.ethz.ch/php/documents/collection.
30 *Plan of Action of the Czechoslovak People's Army for War Period*, document available from World Wide Web on the homepage of the Parallel History Project, http://www.isn.ethz.ch/php/documents/collection.
31 Ross, American War Plans 1945–1950, p. 40.
32 Ibid., p. 47. The significance of Iceland was regarded as so great that it either should be seized as early as possible or, if the Soviets got there first, to retake the island with an amphibious operation.
33 Brown, *Operation: World War III*, pp. 151–3, from the reprint of the text of the *Dropshot*-plan. Denmark, although important because of its control over the Baltic approaches, was regarded as indefensible, due to overwhelming Soviet forces and lack of suitable topographical features.
34 Brown, *Operation: World War III*, p. 180.
35 *North Atlantic Military Committee, Decision on M.C. 14, 28 March 1950*, p. 42, NATO Archives.
36 Ibid., p. 38.
37 Ibid., p. 38a.
38 Ibid., p. 48.
39 *North Atlantic Military Committee, Decision on M.C. 14/1, 9 December 1952*, p. 8, NATO Archives.
40 Ibid., pp. 20–1. This goal was repeated in the strategic concept 1957.

41 In October 1983, at the height of the Soviet–Swedish diplomatic conflict over alleged submarine intrusions into Swedish territorial waters, the Swedish Minister of Defense Anders Thunborg in a widely referred speech warned against "gloomy prophesies" on the forthcoming collapse of the Swedish neutrality. This was generally interpreted as a warning directed against among others the professor in political science Kjell Goldmann who in a newspaper article had suggested tentative contacts with the NATO powers for a contingency where the Soviet Union would not respect Swedish neutrality in an armed conflict. *Dagens Nyheter*, October 28, 1983.

42 Bengt Wallerfelt, *Si vis pacem – para bellum. Svensk säkerhetspolitik och krigs-planering 1945–1975* [Swedish security policy and war planning 1945–1975] (Stockholm: Probus, 1999), pp. 41–3.

43 Ibid., pp. 46–7.

44 The explicit reference to outside help was not only made in the secret operations plans but also in lengthy declassified study published prior to a major parliamentary long-term defense decision in 1948, *Vårt framtida försvar – Överbefälhavarens förslag* [Our future defense – the proposal of the supreme commander] (Stockholm: Centralförbundet Folk och Försvar, 1947).

45 For a discussion of the estimates behind the Scandinavian defense initiative see Erik Noreen, *Brobygge eller blockbilding? De norska och svenska utrikesledningarnas föreställningar 1945–48* [Bridge-building or bloc-building? The security policy concep-tions of the Norwegian and Swedish foreign policy elites] (Stockholm: Carlsson, 1994).

46 Magnus Peterson, *"Brödrafolkens väl." Svensk-norska säkerhetspolitiska relationer 1949–1969* ["The well-being of the brother-peoples." Swedish–Norwegian security–political relations 1949–1969] (Stockholm: Santérus, 2003), p. 234. This PhD dissertation in history is the first comprehensive analysis of the Swedish–Norwegian military relations in the first half of the Cold War based on documents released since the early 1990s.

47 Peterson, *"Brödrafolkens väl." Svensk-norska säkerhetspolitiska relationer 1949–1969*, pp. 289–90.

48 Norway–Swedish intelligence cooperation is dealt with in Olav Riste and Arnfinn Moland, *"Strengt hemmelig." Norsk etterretningstenste 1945–1970* [Top Secret, Norwegian intelligence service 1945–1970] (Universitetsforlaget, Oslo, 1997); and in Magnus Peterson, "Man lär sig…'vem man kan hålla i hand när leken blir allvar': Svensk militär underrättelsetjänst och Norge under första delen av det kalla kriget" [You find out…"whose hand to hold in time of trouble": Swedish–Norwegian military intelligence cooperation in the first part of the Cold War], in Sven G. Holtsmark, Helge Ø. Pharo and Rolf Tamnes (eds), *Motstrøms. Olav Riste og norsk internasjonal historieskrivning* (Oslo: Cappelen, 2003).

49 The Swedish Prime minister Tage Erlander noted in his diary on January 16, 1953 that the supreme commander general Swedlund had asked the government to intervene against the plans to put the Norwegian forces under a joint NATO command. Erlander was doubtful since, as he wrote "I don't consider the cooperation being of any consid-erable value." Erlander also suspected that the Norwegian military wanted their Swedish counterpart to intervene on their behalf to retain some independence. *Tage Erlander: Dagböcker 1953* [Tage Erlander: diaries 1953] (Hedemora: Gidlunds förlag, 2003), p. 15. Further suspicion is aired in the entry for October 21. Swedlund now could inform Erlander that the NATO commanders had decided that all contacts with Sweden should be channeled through Norway: "That will probably be good. But worse was that the Norwegians had been told to give us all information without any limita-tions. I asked Swedlund 'Without any service in return?' – '– Yes, without any service in return.'" *Erlander: Dagböcker 1953*, p. 179.

50 Wilhelm Agrell, *Den stora lögnen. Ett säkerhetspolitisk dubbelspel i alltför många akter* [The big lie. A security–political double-play in too many acts] (Stockholm: Ordfront 1991); and Peterson, *"Brödrafolkens väl." Svensk-norska säkerhetspolitiska relationer 1949–1969*.

51 *Personlig avlämnings PM* [Personal memorandum for successor], Nils Swedlunds dagbok [Nils Swedlund diary], personarkiven, Krigsarkivet (KRA) [Royal War Archive].

52 In 1961 the Supreme Command was reorganized and the joint defense staff (*Försvarsstaben*) became responsible for all operational planning previously carried out by the air and naval commands. In 1966 this was followed by a major reorganization at the regional level; all air ground and naval forces where assigned to six new Military Districts (*Militärområden*), the only unit remaining directly under the Supreme Command was the Strike Group of the air force (*Första* Attackeskadern).

53 *ÖB operationsorder (ÖB Opo) 1967 för krigsfall II* [Supreme commanders operational directives for war-case II] Fst/Opl (Defence Staff Operations Branch)6/6 1966 nr H 310 and *ÖB operationsorder*, Fst/Opl 2 1973–10–15 KH 310, both documents in Fst KH-arkiv, Högkvarteret (Defence Staff Archive of Top Secret documents, Headquarters of the Swedish Armed Forces). As all operational war planning, these two documents were originally top secret (kvalificerat hemliga). They are in considerable detail referred in Wallerfelt, *Si vis pacem – para bellum*. On my request the documents were declassified by the Ministry of Defense in 2003, although the sections dealing with military coordination with Denmark and Norway were deleted.

54 The role of Finland in Swedish threat perception and military planning after 1944 is dealt with in Kent Zetterberg, *I skuggan av Stalin. En säkerhetspolitisk balansgång. Svensk bevakning av Finlands öde 1944–49* [In the shadow of Stalin. A security–political balancing act] (Stockholm: Probus, 1995); Wilhelm Agrell, "Finis Finlandiae: Finland I svensk militär planläggning under det kalla kriget" [Finland in Swedish military planning during the cold war], in Tapani Suominen (ed.), *Sverige i fred: Statsmannakonst eller opportunism?* [Sweden in peace: statesman craft or opportunism?] (Stockholm: Atlantis, 2002); and Olof Kronvall, "Finland in Swedish Security Policy, 1948–1962," in Karl L. Kleve (ed.), *The Cold War, Military Power* and Civilian Society (Bodø: Norwegian Aviation Museum, 2003).

55 *ÖB operationsorder (ÖB Opo) 1967 för krigsfall II*, p. 10.

56 *Fred och säkerhet. Svensk säkerhetspolitik 1969–89. Del 1–2* [Peace and security. Swedish security policy 1969–89, part 1–2] (Stockholm: Fritzes, SOU 2002: 108), pp. 728–31.

57 *Om kriget kommit...* (SOU 1994: 11).

58 Ibid., pp. 253–8.

59 *Fred och säkerhet. Svensk säkerhetspolitik 1969–89. Del 1–2* (SOU 2002: 108), pp. 732–3.

60 *Tage Erlander: Dagböcker 1953*, p. 98.

61 Ibid., p. 14. Erlander noted, "What else is there to be but Spain, England and Scandinavia?" He was also very critical against the idea of West German rearmament and "the horrible risks" this would pose for Germany's old enemies.

62 There are of course instances when this was not the case, especially when it came to intelligence and some of the details of joint military planning. The head of the Swedish secret intelligence service (*T-kontoret*) Dr. Thede Palm wrote in his posthumously published memoirs that his policy when it came to government approval was to avoid requesting it, thereby taking the entire responsibility on himself and ensuring full deniability for the government. See Thede Palm *Några studier till T-kontorets historia* [Sketches to the history of the T-kontoret] (Stockholm: Kungl. Samfundet för utgivande av handskrifter rörande Skandinaviens historia, 1999).

63 For the US attitude to unofficial inter-Scandinavian defense cooperation in the 1950s, see Wilhelm Agrell, *Fred och fruktan, Sveriges säkerhetspolitiska historia 1918–2000* [Peace and fear, the history of Swedish security policy 1918–2000] (Lund: Historiska Media, 2000); Rolf Tamnes, *The United States and the Cold War in the High North* (Oslo: ad Notam, 1991); and Villaume, *Alliert med forbehold*.

64 *U.S. Policy Towards Scandinavia (Denmark, Norway and Sweden)*, NSC 6006/1, April 6, 1960 (Reproduced in facsimile in the Report of the Swedish Commission on the Policy of Neutrality 1994).

65 Ibid., p. 8.
66 *Guidelines for Policy and Operations, Sweden*, Department of State, June 1962 (Reproduced in Facsimile in *Fred och säkerhet. Svensk säkerhetspolitik 1969–1989, Bilagedel, Slutbetänkande av Säkerhetspolitiska utredningen* (Stockholm: Fritzes, 2002).
67 *Operational Plan for the Dislocation of the 1st and 2nd Polish Armies in Case of War Operations in 1951*, document available from World Wide Web on the Homepage of the Parallel History Project, http://www.isn.ethz.ch/php/documents/collection. The document also refers to the threat posed by the numerically large commercial and fishing fleets of the Scandinavian states and the remaining Western European states of the Atlantic bloc.
68 Ibid.
69 *Excerpt from the Operational Directive No 2 of the Maritime Front, 31 May 1967*, document available from World Wide Web on the homepage of the Parallel History Project, http://www.isn.ethz.ch/php/documents/collection. Swedish military intelligence received fairly accurate information on the planning of the operations of the Maritime front. Swedish air force also made some preparations for strikes against possible landing beaches on the Danish islands.
70 The main exception are Soviet attempts to establish military cooperation with Finland in the 1960s and 1970s with reference to the 1948 Friendship, Cooperation, and Mutual Assistance Agreement between Finland and the Soviet Union. For Finland, coordinated planning and joint exercises would have severely undercut Finnish attempt to pursue a policy of neutrality. Thus for Finland, de-linking was a key security–political object during the Cold War and the detènte. Material on the Finnish–Soviet military contacts appear in abstract from papers of the Parliamentary Defence Committee 1958 and 1970–71, YLE Internet archives, http://194.252.88.3/motweb.nsf/sivut/arkisto

Part II

The politics of alliance management

7   The politics of military planning
Evolution of NATO's strategy

Andreas Wenger

Introduction

The development of NATO's strategic thinking in the 1950s and 1960s was driven by changing threat perceptions, the quest for a balance between deterrence and defense, and the search for an equilibrium between the strategic interests and the power positions of key member states. The key challenge the allies faced was how to reconcile what they believed were Soviet capabilities with what they perceived to be the Soviets' intentions and how to act on their overall perception of the Soviet threat. When it came to defining the means to counter the perceived threat, there was much debate within the Alliance about how NATO should link deterrence and defense and whether it should focus on terminating or on fighting a potential war. Most important, however, was the question whether NATO would be able to integrate the disparate political interests of its member states.[1]

NATO's strategic dependence on nuclear weapons evolved in a debate about the political usefulness of nuclear force at a time of rapidly changing nuclear balance between the superpowers. The credibility of the US nuclear guarantee was gradually discredited during the 1950s, as the Soviet potential to damage the American homeland slowly increased. At the time, Europeans feared that the evolving mutual vulnerability would lead either to a stalemate between the superpowers or, worse, to risk-taking by one of the superpowers before a stalemate could be reached, if that superpower perceived itself as temporarily at a military–technological advantage. A stalemate might lead to political decoupling, whereas risk-taking could destroy Europe completely. Consequently, increasingly fierce debates about burden sharing and political control marked the end of NATO's first decade.[2]

For much of the 1950s, NATO strategy and force planning focused on Soviet capabilities and worst-case scenarios. Yet by the late 1960s, deterrence increasingly depended on political tactics and the perception of Soviet intentions, and ambiguous concepts such as political warning, flexibility, and escalation had moved to the center of NATO's strategic debate. The Alliance had learned that deterrence in the age of mutual vulnerability depended on a combination of political will with regard to aims and uncertainty with regard to means. Moreover, political leadership could no longer be based on the crude logic that he who pays and controls the means decides on when and how to act.

By the end of the 1960s, NATO members built the new strategic concept on leadership by persuasion rather than by control, on institutional flexibility rather than on a clear chain of command, and on political consultation rather than on agreement about operational details. This chapter shows how NATO's security came to depend on nuclear weapons between 1949 and 1967 and why the nuclearization of NATO caused a precarious political balance among the allies. NATO's strategic thinking shifted between 1958 and 1963 from a doctrine of massive retaliation to a more flexible strategic posture. During this period, the allies, and especially Washington and Paris, had different political visions of Europe's future that clashed throughout their debate about military strategy. After France had left all integrated military commands, the 14 remaining NATO allies successfully transformed the organizational structure of the Alliance to accommodate the extensive political, strategic, and technological changes of the previous two decades. Once the allies had agreed that NATO should now have a political role in the interest of peace, a compromise on strategy became possible in late 1967.

The nuclearization of NATO: a delicate balance, 1949–57

Originally conceived to prevent the expansion of Soviet political influence in Europe, NATO served to contain fears of a new war in Europe. Article V of the Alliance treaty committed NATO members to mutual defense in only a limited way. Article IX, however, committed them to creating the organizational structures needed to eventually achieve collective self-defense.[3] Among the structures that were subsequently created, the Standing Group of senior military representatives from the United States, Britain, and France was tasked with the development of an overall strategic concept for the Alliance.

The Standing Group recognized that, given the military and economic realities, the defense of the North Atlantic area depended on "the ability to deliver the atomic bomb promptly."[4] Whereas the Soviet Union was believed to maintain its military capabilities at Second World War levels, the allies would take many years to reach such levels.[5] The success of NATO's strategic offensive in case of war depended on "the ability to carry out strategic bombing promptly by all means possible with all types of weapons, without exception."[6] Early strategic thinking in NATO reflected two beliefs: for the time being, the threat was as much political and economic as military. Should this change, however, NATO's military defense and deterrent depended on US nuclear power.

MC 14/1: the Korean War and the militarization of NATO

Western threat perceptions changed dramatically as a result of the detonation of the first Soviet atomic bomb in August 1949 and the outbreak of the Korean War in June 1950. The early demise of the US nuclear monopoly came as surprise and undermined Western confidence in US military strength. North Korea's aggression was perceived as proof of communist expansionism by means of military force. Western observers wondered whether military aggression could be expected along the German border. The challenges of the Cold War seemed to move away from the political to the military arena. This led the United States and its NATO allies to review their strategies, accelerate the build-up of their forces, to expand and integrate NATO's military and political structures, and accept West Germany's rearmament.

The first Soviet atomic explosion triggered a re-examination of US national security policies. The resulting NSC 68 report called for a rapid and sustained build-up of the political, economic, and military strength of the free world. Although President Harry S. Truman authorized the construction of the hydrogen bomb, the goal of his administration was to avoid "dependence on the strategic use of atomic weapons in the event of general war."[7] NSC 68 called for the strengthening of both conventional and nuclear weapons. It left the incoming Eisenhower administration with serious concerns about the huge cost of collective security and a concomitant danger of isolationism.

The fear that Western Europe might be the next target of communist aggression led to the establishment of an integrated military force under centralized command in late 1950. Within two years, Greece and Turkey joined the Alliance.[8] The Lisbon force goals, adopted in February 1952, called for the establishment of 96 NATO divisions by 1954, echoing the Truman administration's conviction that exclusive reliance on US strategic forces had to be overcome.

Between 1950 and 1952, NATO perceived a shift in the balance of power "from extreme [NATO] weakness toward strength." If the Lisbon forces were provided by 1954, "then the danger point can and will be passed."[9] In the meantime, however, war could not be discounted, given Soviet capabilities and Soviet intent, believed to be "the establishment of communism, directed from Moscow, throughout the world."[10] The Soviet Union enjoyed "a marked predominance in Armed Forces and conventional weapons over the free nations of the West." It was believed that the Soviets would pursue their goals "by a policy of political and ideological aggression, backed by the threat of overwhelming armed force."[11]

So far, the British military suggested, the Soviets had preferred "armed aggression by proxy,"[12] and they would understand that major military action against NATO countries would entail ever-greater risks as time progressed. However, unless the Western powers were "strong enough to neutralize each Communist move at the point where it occurs," a miscalculation by the Soviet leaders could lead to a war that was not intended by either side. In addition, the possibility could not be discounted that the Soviet government would decide to precipitate a general war before their present predominance in military power had been threatened by Western rearmament.[13] If war broke out, NATO's DC 13 conjectured, the Soviets would attempt to defeat NATO forces and reach the Atlantic, the Mediterranean, and the Middle East. Moreover, the Soviet Union might initiate air attacks in Europe and the Western hemisphere, using all types of weapons without exception.[14]

The Standing Group's report on strategic guidance, MC 14/1, approved on December 9, 1952, stated that NATO's deterrence and defense at the time was based on US nuclear superiority, while insisting that a conventional build-up be undertaken simultaneously. The strategic aim of NATO was "to ensure the defense of the NATO area and to destroy the will and capability of the USSR and her satellites to wage war, initially by means of an air offensive, while at the same time conducting air, ground and sea operations designed to preserve the integrity of the NATO area." In case of a USSR offensive, the report said, allied strategic air attacks would use "all types of weapons," and the land defense would "arrest and counter as soon as practicable the enemy offensive." The report concluded that, in the meantime, the conventional NATO forces fell "far short of requirements," and no relaxation of their planned expansion could be allowed.[15]

MC 48: the British and US push for massive retaliation

The British believed that US and NATO strategy overemphasized conventional weapons at the expense of nuclear weapons. Their 1952 global strategy paper called for increasing nuclear deterrence.[16] The Soviets had not risked an invasion of Western Europe because they knew that their aggression would be met by an immediate nuclear response. Moreover, the Lisbon force goals were politically and financially unattainable.

In British view, unless NATO used the atomic weapon, it could not hold the Russians on the Rhine but could only hold the Italian–Austrian bridgehead on the Continent.[17] London recommended to Eisenhower's successor as Supreme Allied Commander Europe (SACEUR), General Matthew B. Ridgway, to define NATO's force goals by relying on nuclear weapons. It came as something of a surprise that his subsequent report called for even bigger conventional forces than the Lisbon force goals, as a result of anticipated personnel shortages in the case of a nuclear attack.[18] The British hoped for better results from the incoming Eisenhower administration.

The British have often been credited for the American NATO strategy based primarily on nuclear power.[19] In fact, the Eisenhower administration integrated nuclear weapons into US security policy for a complex set of reasons, some of which did not coincide with the British view. The overhaul of basic national security policy resulted in NSC 162/2 stating that "in the event of hostilities, the United States will consider nuclear weapons to be as available for use as other munitions."[20] This made good sense both economically and strategically. Nuclear weapons made the cost of the Cold War tolerable, allowing Eisenhower to plan like his British counterparts – for the "long pull."[21] He was convinced that excessive military spending would endanger US democratic institutions and lead to a garrison state. Eisenhower's New Look made strategic sense since the Korean War had led to overextension of US armed forces and the first Soviet test of a hydrogen bomb on August 12, 1953 highlighted the growing vulnerability of the American homeland.

The Americans expected deterrence to work. Unlike the British, however, they also believed that should it fail, the United States would prevail in a general war. At the same time, anxiety about the increasing Soviet nuclear ability to strike the

American homeland led Washington to consider preventive war.[22] British Prime Minister Winston Churchill took exception to "any idea of the automatic use of atomic weapons, even in the case of a Communist renewal of hostilities in Korea."[23] British Foreign Secretary Anthony Eden suspected that the Americans would use intervention on behalf of the French in Indochina to launch war against China.[24] From a European standpoint, basing Europe's security on the US strategic deterrent was one thing; threatening massive retaliation to relatively minor conflicts in Asia was quite another. For Europe, the time when it could survive a general war with only limited damage had passed.

In April 1954, US Secretary of State John Foster Dulles urged NATO to agree to the use of "atomic weapons as conventional weapons against the military assets of the enemy whenever and wherever it would be of advantage to do so."[25] But the Eisenhower administration realized the political problems inherent in a nuclear concept for NATO and was prepared to accept a compromise. Dulles told the president to inform allies that the United States would not wage preventive war and would "be prepared to explore reasonable bona fide disarmament proposals."[26] NSC 5501 subsequently ruled out "the concept of preventive war or acts intended to provoke war."[27]

The British and French were reluctant to surrender the authority to implement NATO plans in the event of hostilities and so were the Americans.[28] Dulles therefore suggested that the guiding document, MC 48, be approved only "as a basis for planning and preparation of forces,"[29] thus leaving the authority to declare war when there was not time for consultation to the nation that controlled the weapons. If this was the carrot offered to the Europeans, the stick was the threat of a fundamental reappraisal of US foreign policy should they reject MC 48. Moreover, disunity on strategy within NATO would seriously jeopardize its deterrent value.

Anticipating a future in which atomic weapons would be plentiful, MC 48 committed NATO to a strategy of massive retaliation. It noted that nuclear superiority and strategic surprise would be the defining factors of modern war. Since, however, the initiation of war was contrary to "the fundamental principles of the Alliance," war could come only "as a result of Communist aggression." In that case, the Soviet's only hope of winning "would rest upon their sudden destruction of NATO's ability to counter-attack immediately and decisively with atomic weapons."[30]

MC 48 stated that "the primary aim of NATO must more than ever before, be to prevent war." With the planned increase of NATO nuclear forces, NATO would be able to "provide an effective deterrent in Europe and, should war come despite the deterrent, to prevent a rapid overrunning of Europe." The ability to use immediately atomic weapons, along with a German contribution to NATO, would "for the first time enable NATO to adopt a real forward strategy with a main line of defense well to the East of the Rhine-Ijssel ... on the assumption that atomic and thermo-nuclear weapons [would] be used in defense from the outset."[31]

MC 48 was a compromise driven by strategic, economic, and political factors. The nuclearization of NATO was essential to maintain confidence in the Alliance in the face of a rapidly changing balance of power. However, there remained considerable unease regarding the massive retaliation strategy, whose credibility decreased with the growing Soviet nuclear capability. The British Joint Planning Staff warned that, if deterrence failed, massive retaliation "might cause such destruction as to make the operation of large land forces impracticable."[32] In any case, the line between prevention and preemption in the nuclear age was very thin indeed. For the Europeans, security would depend solely on the good judgment of the US president.

MC 14/2: buying time with tactical nuclear weapons

The emphasis on nuclear power devalued NATO's conventional armament programs, particularly West Germany's rearmament. Its delays meant that a forward defense would not be feasible until 1959 at the earliest.[33] In the meantime, Western threat perceptions changed after Khrushchev's February 1956 announcement of unilateral troop cuts of one million men. British Foreign Secretary John Selwyn Lloyd told the North Atlantic Council (NAC) that the Soviets did not want war and would no longer risk it. Instead they would rely on massive penetration of the underdeveloped world by economic, technical, and cultural means.[34]

The threat to NATO was shifting from the military field to the political field, prompting NAC to set up a committee of "Three Wise Men" to investigate what could be done to strengthen economic and political ties among the allies.[35] In November, the divisive Suez Crisis reminded them how events outside NATO could have an important political impact on it. Moscow's nuclear threats to Paris and London encouraged those people in the two countries who thought that an independent nuclear force was a precondition for a truly sovereign foreign policy.

Already in April 1955, London had proposed to reduce NATO shield forces in Germany, limiting their function to dealing with "local infiltration, to prevent external intimidation and to enable aggression to be identified as such."[36] Eden was quick to add that Washington seemed to be considering major troop cuts as well, and he demanded a new directive to NATO military authorities to review NATO strategy.

Washington faced the prospect of increased defense budgets for the period 1957–60. For political reasons there had been no redeployments. Moreover, missiles had to be developed in addition to bombers. Savings could only be achieved by planning to use tactical nuclear weapons in any small war. Eisenhower's decision in the summer of 1956 to fully integrate these weapons into US security policy was based on financial rather than military and strategic considerations.[37] He decided not to take any US divisions out of Europe for the time being, however, since ground forces were essential to preserving flexibility. In Dulles's opinion, it was "one thing for us to rely on the new look, not being subject to insurrectionary or conventional attack as the Europeans are, and it is something else to propose it for the Europeans."[38]

In Paris, the Americans uncharacteristically argued in favor of conventional forces whereas the British having overcome their earlier skepticism about tactical nuclear weapons now argued for the integration down to the divisional level. The new NATO directive, focusing on Soviet intentions rather than on Soviet capabilities, produced a new strategic compromise. Since the Soviets were not likely to deliberately launch a major attack, even with conventional weapons, the Western shield forces should have the ability to deal with "infiltrations, incursions or hostile local action...without necessarily having recourse to nuclear weapons."[39]

MC 14/2, approved on May 9, 1957, perpetuated, with minor revisions, NATO's emphasis on strategic nuclear weapons as the main deterrent. Unlike MC 48, it took account of both Soviet capabilities and Soviet intentions. It presumed that the Soviets "could not count on achieving a profitable military and political victory." Therefore, the Soviets might conclude that "the only way in which they could profitably further their aim would be to initiate operations with limited objectives." NATO must therefore "be prepared to deal immediately with such situations without necessarily having recourse to nuclear weapons." Yet if the Soviets "sought to broaden the scope of such an incident or to prolong it, the situation would call for the utilization of all weapons and forces at NATO's disposal, since in no case is there a NATO concept of limited war with the Soviets."[40]

NATO's nuclearization resulted from a delicate balance of national, particularly British and American, strategic, economic, and political interests. NATO went nuclear at a point when the US nuclear guarantee of European security was increasingly in doubt because of rising Soviet nuclear capabilities. Changing threat perceptions and the changing balance of power required a revision of NATO strategic thinking. It would be much more difficult to achieve agreement about Soviet intentions, about how to fight a war in the nuclear age, and about the balance of political power within the Alliance.

A transition phase: the politics of military strategy, 1958–63

The launching, on October 4, 1957, of the first Soviet satellite, the Sputnik, meant that the United States had been overtaken in the field of long-range missile technology. It exposed the Eisenhower administration to domestic criticism that it had allowed a supposedly growing missile gap between the United States and the Soviet Union.[41] The US defense establishment debated whether relative military strength still mattered in the missile age. The Gaither Panel's report "Deterrence and Survival in the Nuclear Age" perceived an "extremely unstable equilibrium" for the foreseeable future, urging a build-up of US offensive capabilities at the cost of US$19 billion over the subsequent five years.[42] In view of the mutual vulnerability with the prospect of inflicting "50% casualties on a enemy,"[43] Eisenhower and Dulles were becoming confident that the Soviets would be deterred.

Although Eisenhower saw no military need for supplementing the defense budget, domestic pressures led him to set it at a level that would create confidence and stabilize public opinion. Criticized for inadequate public explanation of the impact of a nuclear stalemate,[44] he was limited by the need to maintain nuclear superiority to reassure the allies and uphold NATO's credibility. He had learned how important military superiority was for the allies psychologically and politically. The problem was, "how to inform our own people in a logical way of our military capabilities, without at the same time scaring our allies to death."[45] The resulting uncertainty among the public could be used by pressure groups to argue for bigger nuclear forces – the background of Eisenhower's warning against the military-industrial complex in his farewell address to the nation.[46]

Eisenhower's legacy: NATO strategy in the wake of Sputnik and the Berlin Crisis

Sputnik challenged the credibility of the US nuclear guarantee to Europe, resulting in pressure for control over nuclear forces not only from London and Paris, but also – causing particular concern in Moscow – from Bonn.

To mitigate fears of US isolationism, Washington adopted the policy of nuclear sharing. It offered to establish additional stockpiles of tactical nuclear warheads in Europe that could be made available to the allies in the event of war. NATO members agreed to accept US intermediate-range ballistic missiles (IRBMs), provided they could choose their location and control them. Rejecting the proposal by SACEUR General Lauris Norstad for a missile force under direct NATO control, the Eisenhower administration favored bilateral control. Eventually, Norstad secured placements in Italy and Turkey under SACEUR's direct control and in Britain under dual control thus providing NATO with limited influence over nuclear weapons with targets beyond the battlefield.[47]

The 1958 amendment to the Atomic Energy Act permitted a more liberal exchange of information with Britain on nuclear weapons, including their design, development, and production. President Charles de Gaulle of France saw this as discriminatory against his nation and consequently refused to accept nuclear warheads unless they were put under French control. He proposed that NATO be run by a trilateral directorate, which should decide on strategic plans and the use of nuclear weapons. When his demand was rejected, as he himself had expected, de Gaulle began a step-by-step withdrawal of France's naval and air forces from NATO's integrated commands in the Mediterranean and the Atlantic.[48] By the 1960s, the consensus among NATO members on US leadership of NATO had dissolved.

In August 1961 – against the background of the Berlin Crisis – Norstad informed NATO that its present forces could not defend the Alliance even with the use of nuclear weapons: "It would not be [a] question of choice since [the] mission assigned to SACEUR to defend [the] peoples and territories simply could not be carried out with [the] forces and all weapons presently available."[49] MC 14/2 simply did not adequately define the necessary size of conventional and nuclear NATO forces. The reason, according to the British Chiefs of Staff, was that the agreed policy was a compromise that submerged "fundamental international and inter-service differences of opinion."[50] Washington wanted the US contribution to be primarily nuclear and the European contribution primarily conventional. What the Americans labeled a "fair share" concept was degrading and unacceptable to the Europeans because of their merely having to supply troops. Wanting to expand its nuclear capabilities, Britain informed Washington that it planned to reduce its forces from 750,000 troops in 1957 to 400,000 troops in 1962.

In 1958, the outbreak of the Berlin Crisis transformed the question of how to deter limited aggression in Europe from the realm of strategic theory to the realm of daily politics. Both Eisenhower and Dulles deprecated Khrushchev's nuclear boasts as bluff on the grounds that he "does not desire war more than we,"[51] but feared that the Western position could be "nibbled away."[52] They believed that if the West accepted the risk of nuclear war as laid down in NATO's strategy and kept its unity the Soviets would withdraw their ultimatum.

Once the United States, Britain, and France started to discuss contingency plans for a Soviet challenge to Western access to Berlin the Europeans opposed an automatic nuclear response. According to British Ambassador in Washington Sir Harold Caccia "the British people will never be atomized for the sake of Berlin."[53] Chancellor Konrad Adenauer of Germany seemed to have developed "almost a psychopathic fear of what he considers to be 'British weakness'."[54] In 1960, Eisenhower insisted that "we must be ready to throw the book at the Russians should they jump us."[55] The unity of the Alliance depended not so much on the military value of its military preparations as on how these preparations were perceived by the allies.

Eisenhower was convinced that the United States could not fight a ground battle around Berlin. If the Soviets took Berlin by force, he believed "we have to then face up to the big decision but in the meanwhile we would do everything feasible to negotiate."[56] In public, Eisenhower held fast to a firm deterrence posture, but if a war broke out, he expected a period of hard conventional warfare while the politicians talked.[57] The focus then would be on alternative strategies to terminate war without completely destroying both sides' civil societies. Such alternatives were never considered by his administration, however. Instead, the Strategic Air Command (SAC) transformed the nuclear deterrent into a single integrated operational plan (SIOP-62) that provided for a massive, simultaneous nuclear offensive against the full set of military and urban-industrial targets in the Soviet Union, China, and Eastern Europe.[58]

Kennedy, the Berlin Crisis, and the politics of military planning

President John F. Kennedy brought a group of people into government who shared his campaign criticism of Eisenhower's defense policies and were convinced that the US military posture had to be strengthened and made more flexible. He approached the strategic dilemma of the decreasing credibility of the US security guarantee for Europe differently from his predecessor.

Alarmed by the dangerous inflexibility of the nation's nuclear war plan, National Security Advisor McGeorge Bundy informed the president that the plan "may leave you very little choice as to how you face the moment of thermonuclear truth."[59] In response to a small Soviet action in Central Europe, massive retaliation left the choice of "all or nothing at all, world devastation or submission."[60] According to Secretary of Defense Robert S. McNamara "the West cannot make a credible deterrent out of a incredible action, i.e., the inevitable destruction of Central Europe, the US and the Soviet Union."[61]

The new administration feared that local use of tactical nuclear weapons would rapidly escalate into general nuclear war. The Acheson report found NATO's tactical nuclear shield forces obsolete because the Soviets had acquired similar capabilities.[62] Kennedy's policy on tactical nuclear weapons was inconsistent: on the one hand, his administration made every effort to install electro-mechanical locks on all short-range nuclear weapons in Europe; on the other hand, for political reasons it continued delivering thousands of those weapons to allied territories throughout the 1960s.

To discourage national nuclear forces the administration emphasized central nuclear control. It agreed with the Acheson report that, in the long run, "it would be desirable if the British decided to phase out of the nuclear deterrent business. . . . The U.S. should not assist the French to attain a nuclear weapons capability." For foreign policy reasons, however, Kennedy did not terminate the multilateral nuclear force (MLF) project, hoping that this might eventually bring together all European weapons.

In Washington, the focus had shifted from deterrence to defense and from preemption to war termination – not least due to the Berlin Crisis. Kennedy called for increased conventional forces to deter limited aggression in Europe. They were to enhance the credibility of the nuclear deterrent by providing "a non-nuclear capability to impose a pause in the event of quite large attacks by the Soviet non-nuclear ready forces."[63] The pause was to give the adversary time to consider the grave consequences of escalation. SACEUR Norstad had reservations about a pause that might leave much of Germany destroyed and the rest of Europe doubtful about US willingness to escalate to a nuclear level. The Kennedy administration decided to raise the nuclear threshold without demanding a formal change of NATO's existing political guidelines.[64]

Norstad's successor as SACEUR General Lyman Lemnitzer wondered "how the US could politically square itself arguing for increased conventional capabilities for NATO on the one hand and sponsoring a force reduction on the other."[65] For NATO, the most important preconditions for flexibility were invulnerable nuclear weapons systems and a secure command and control system. Kennedy's multiple options strategy, however, reflected the view of his civilian strategists that uncertainty and ambiguity made threats work in a situation marked by potential mutual vulnerability.

In 1961, the Berlin Crisis provided the Kennedy administration with an opportunity to advance its new strategic ideas within NATO parallel with the overhaul of Berlin contingency planning. Reversing the earlier British approach, the Kennedy administration proceeded bottom-up from the level of operational planning. It accepted the key premise of Acheson's Berlin report of June 28, 1961 that the Soviet fears that interference with Western rights in Berlin would lead to nuclear war had diminished along with Soviet nuclear gains. Insisting that the Soviet perception had to be reversed, the report portrayed the Berlin issue as a test of will between Washington and Moscow over the US resolve to defend Europe. Acheson proposed a strategy of risk manipulation to signal the resolve even at the cost of nuclear war.[66]

Mutual nuclear vulnerability had weakened the link between the military capabilities and the political behavior of states. In conventional warfare, a country's political behavior was directly related to its actual military capabilities. In the nuclear age, however, vulnerability to atomic bombs had created a conceptual gap between the military capability and the political resolve. The credibility of a state had become elusive and highly dependent on subjective factors. At issue in the Berlin Crisis was influencing the beliefs of both adversaries and allies about one's resolve to use nuclear weapons. The different views of Washington, Bonn, London, and Paris about how best to manipulate nuclear risk perception depended on different strategic and political interests, geographic location, and economic considerations.[67]

Unlike Eisenhower's low-key approach to Berlin contingency planning, Kennedy's strategy of risk manipulation entailed a highly visible conventional build-up to signal to the Soviets that escalation would mean the use of nuclear weapons. Kennedy thus attempted to shift the responsibility for crossing the nuclear threshold to them. He counted on the deterrent value of announcing the military build-up. Marc Trachtenberg has suggested that contingency planning may have had a comparable function. Washington assumed that Moscow's understanding of Western plans through espionage enhanced the credibility of the deterrent.[68]

Norstad warned, however, that "the credibility of the deterrent can be destroyed by emphasizing a policy that could be construed by the Soviets as permitting them to become involved, and then, if they decide the risks are too great, to disengage."[69] From a German perspective, a conventional pause would lead to terrible losses in both territory and life. Therefore, even limited aggression should be countered with the immediate employment of battlefield nuclear weapons, for only this would force the Soviets to decide whether or not they would escalate. The Germans thought it "extremely unlikely" that they would.[70] Instead, the Western use of tactical nuclear weapons would make them realize "they [had] misjudged the situation and would cause them to stop their aggression."[71] If not, it would be impossible to avoid an all-out nuclear exchange.

The concept of a pause brought about by the use of nuclear weapons on the battlefield reflected Germany's political interests but from a military point of view it was highly questionable. General Maxwell Taylor, Military Representative to the US president, noted that "tactical nuclear weapons do not reduce force requirements; they impose many casualties and cause substantial physical damage; they also carry with them a risk of escalation."[72] The German approach relied primarily on the political signals their deterrence concept sent to both the Eastern bloc and Germany's Alliance partners. If deterrence failed, Germany could hardly hope to benefit from a nuclear war being limited to Europe.[73]

The British covered the middle ground. Like the Germans, they rejected the large conventional option suggested by the United States. Like the Americans, they doubted the possibility of limiting a tactical nuclear war to continental Europe. Like the Germans and the Americans, they sought ways to extend deterrence into the process of war. They wanted the decision to use a nuclear weapon to be a political one and called for the discriminate or selective use of nuclear weapons.[74] This was also what strategist Thomas Schelling proposed in early 1961 suggesting that the US develop a plan to use nuclear weapons selectively as part of a bargaining strategy designed to convey to the Soviets the message that a war might get out of hand.[75]

After the Berlin wall went up, Kennedy sped up the Berlin contingency planning. He intended the October 1961 National Security Action Memorandum No. 109 to ensure "a sequence of graduated responses to Soviet/German Democratic Republic actions in denial of our rights of access." These would range from diplomatic and economic initiatives to military measures including small probes of Soviet intentions, non-nuclear air action, non-nuclear ground operations in German Democratic Republic (GDR) territories in division and greater strength and supplementary naval blockade, selective attacks as a demonstration of the will to use nuclear weapons, limited tactical use of nuclear weapons, and, as a last resort, general nuclear war. Kennedy emphasized that non-nuclear operations were politically oriented, "aiming to display to the Soviets the approaching danger of possibly irreversible escalation."[76]

Norstad doubted that NATO could sustain an extended conventional defense and enforce a gradual and controlled escalation. In particular, he doubted the feasibility of firebreaks below the nuclear threshold. Like the Europeans, he believed that the West had to prepare for an explosive escalation.[77] Yet Kennedy enforced Washington's views.[78] By August 1962 there was considerable agreement on the Berlin contingency plans among the United States, Britain, France, and Germany.[79] The plans aimed at firebreaks to permit negotiations before a crisis situation could escalate into an all-out war. Unable to agree on strategic guidance and force planning NATO members nevertheless continued to argue about whether a conventional option was militarily feasible and politically acceptable.

McNamara's efforts at persuasion and the French veto

In the fall of 1961, the Kennedy administration faced the dilemma of how to sell the conventional option to the Europeans without destroying their already shaky trust in the American nuclear guarantee. Over the summer of 1962, Kennedy decided to focus on the "three fundamentals of freedom for Berlin, free access, and a western presence" while shifting "substantially toward acceptance of the GDR, the Oder-Neisse line, a non-aggression pact, and even the idea of two peace treaties."[80] The US stance was anathema to Bonn and Paris and made the Europeans wonder whether the Soviet nuclear strength had inspired the sudden US interest in Berlin negotiations and the conventional option.

Although Kennedy had known since February 1961 that the missile gap was in favor of the West rather than the USSR, he had to convince the allies of this. On October 21, 1961, Deputy Secretary of Defense Roswell Gilpatric reassured them that "we have a second strike capability which is at least as extensive as what the Soviets can deliver by striking first."[81] McNamara and Secretary of State Dean Rusk described dramatically superior US nuclear forces in speeches at the December 1961 NAC meeting that succeeded in reassuring the Europeans.[82]

In December 1961, Kennedy proposed to Congress a huge build-up of strategic forces, even though these were already vastly superior to the Soviet ones. Besides considerable bureaucratic and political pressures, perceived need to signal US resolve was behind these decisions.[83] As the Acheson report had emphasized, it was the act of building up forces, rather than the result of the build-up that mattered politically. However, Henry Kissinger had warned that the Acheson approach neglected the European obsession with nuclear weapons that could only be overcome "by a strategic concept in which both nuclear and conventional weapons have their place."[84] Reassuring the Europeans thus demanded bigger strategic forces than seemed justified in military terms.

The Berlin Crisis promoted a far-reaching reappraisal of NATO strategy. McNamara told the December 1961 NAC meeting: "We believe...that since military strategy for Berlin is a function of basic NATO strategy, the U.S. is under the strongest obligation to its allies not only to share its latest findings, but to indicate as frankly and candidly as it can what appears to it to be their inescapable implications for facing the Berlin crisis."[85] He proceeded doing so in his famous speech to NATO's foreign and defense ministers in Athens in May 1962 where he discussed nuclear retaliation in the case of a general nuclear war in terms of a no-cities counterforce strategy. He said that "military strategy in general nuclear war should be approached in much the same way that more conventional military operations have been regarded in the past. That is to say, our principal military objective, in the event of a nuclear war stemming from a major attack on the Alliance, should be the destruction of the enemy's military forces while attempting to preserve the fabric as well as the integrity of allied society."[86]

McNamara did not believe that the Soviets would reciprocate by refusing to attack US cities.[87] As long as the Europeans believed that the USSR would reciprocate, however, their fears that the United States might be forced to risk New York for Paris would be allayed. He made his statement to a European audience to send the right political messages. The strategy he described signaled confidence in the ability of US forces to destroy the Soviet forces. It also allowed him to argue that the Soviets would not initiate the use of nuclear force in case of a limited conventional engagement in Europe. Finally, the strategy emphasized central control. He warned that "weak nuclear capabilities, operating independently, are expensive, prone to obsolescence, and lacking in credibility as a deterrent."[88]

McNamara was skeptical about the tactical and demonstrative use of nuclear weapons in dealing with limited aggression: "Local engagement would do grave damage to Europe, be militarily ineffective, and would probably expand very rapidly into general nuclear war."[89] McNamara's most important conclusion was that the only credible deterrent to minor Soviet aggression was conventional. He urged meeting the goal of 30 divisions for NATO's central region, as outlined in MC 26/4. He cited Pentagon studies that suggested that the Warsaw Pact did not have overwhelming conventional superiority and that a conventional defense of Europe was indeed possible.[90]

Ironically, McNamara's attempt to make a political statement by describing a military strategy he believed had limited operational feasibility turned out to be a foreign policy disaster. Paris interpreted McNamara's speech as a direct attack on France's national nuclear weapons program. The issue of centralized nuclear control touched a nerve in London, which feared its sovereignty and prestige being undermined. McNamara's correcting himself that he had not been referring to the thoroughly coordinated British bomber force added fuel to the fire of outrage in Paris. If de Gaulle needed confirmation that the United States would never share nuclear control, McNamara had just provided it.

Since it was obvious that his strategy would not save Europe from destruction by late 1963 McNamara began to stress an assured destruction capability.[91] The new emphasis was primarily a product of political considerations. It showed mutual vulnerability as the basis of global stability. Assured destruction, compared with a counterforce strategy, also provided a better answer to the question of how much military power was enough for a credible deterrent. By then, however, it was too late to win de Gaulle over for a compromise on NATO's integrated military structure.

France perceived NATO as "the creature of US invention," which, in an era of mutual vulnerability, could no longer serve France's national interests.[92] In times of crisis, France believed it would be informed retrospectively of US decisions, rather than consulted in advance – as proved during the Cuban missile crisis in October 1962. De Gaulle became convinced that France would have to take full responsibility for its own security sooner rather than later.

In January 1963, Stikker began work on NATO force planning. However, the Military Committee was unable to reach a compromise on a basic strategy that would serve as the basis for NATO force goals. The allies could not agree on the duration of the conventional phase, the role of tactical nuclear weapons, and the definition of the nuclear threshold.[93] Washington, London, and Bonn were prepared to compromise, but Paris refused to move away from the "trip-wire" approach that had marked NATO's strategy since early 1961. In November 1963, Paris threatened to veto the further development of MC 100/1 and boycott the force planning exercise.[94]

By 1964, the exercise and revision of strategic guidance had come to a halt.[95] No compromise on strategy could be found before a solution of the fundamental political differences regarding the credibility of NATO's integrated military structure and its legitimacy as a forum of political consultation. France would have to leave the integrated commands before the remaining 14 allies could transform NATO into a less hierarchical Alliance at 14 and a more political Alliance at 15.

Successful transformation: military security and a policy of détente, 1963–68

In March 1966, de Gaulle announced that France would withdraw its remaining forces from NATO's integrated commands and would no longer place its forces at

NATO's disposal.[96] He opposed military integration and central control for political rather than military reasons. He believed that at a time of evolving détente, NATO could no longer serve as a legitimate forum for political consultation. US forces in Europe as a symbol of US hegemony had to go before détente could proceed. On the one hand, de Gaulle argued, Soviet threats "no longer [presented] the immediate and menacing character that they [had] presented formerly."[97] On the other hand, Europe had regained its economic strength while Washington had been drawn into the Vietnam War it could not win. All this suggested to de Gaulle that the Europeans had to assume Europe's political leadership.

France did not object to NATO in principle but to the dominant US role in its military structures. State Department analysts found the French view "reflective of a wider European feeling."[98] The Germans also believed it was "timely to take a look at the NATO organization" and that the Standing Group in particular needed "revamping."[99] The ultimate danger of de Gaulle's challenge was that Germany might shift to a more unilateral policy to concentrate on reunification and détente with the East.[100]

President Lyndon B. Johnson approached the task of re-evaluating US policy on Europe very carefully.[101] Against State Department hardliners, he opted for a quiet but firm policy while reserving an empty chair for France.[102] He realized that NATO's organizational structure had to accommodate the changed political circumstances. There had to be more political consultation between the 14 remaining allies, many of whom worried about an increased role of Germany in a trilateral leadership. Consequently, the military structures of the Alliance were reorganized less hierarchically. The Standing Group was abolished, and the new International Military Staff (IMS) at NATO headquarters, now in Brussels, was open to all member countries. Germany's special interests with regard to nuclear planning and decision-making were taken into account through the establishment of the Nuclear Defense Affairs Committee (NDAC) and its seven-member Nuclear Planning Group (NPG).[103]

There was a consensus in Washington that NATO had to expand its political role as an instrument of peace during the evolving détente. Acheson called for a strengthening of the political functions of the Alliance, in particular with regard to "the collective management of the German–Soviet relationship in the unsettled Central European setting that emerged from World War II."[104] Finally, Johnson and his administration recognized that only trilateral leadership by the United States, Britain, and Germany would resolve NATO's political and military crisis.[105]

Trilateral negotiations: compromise on strategy and burden sharing

The trilateral talks between Washington, Bonn, and London from September 1966 to April 1967 marked a turning point in the development of NATO's new strategic concept. The issues of strategy, force levels, deployments, and burden sharing were all closely linked. The Alliance's defense needs had to take into account the political interests, the military strengths, and the geographical locations of the big three. For domestic reasons, any solution had to strike a balance between economic and military security. NATO had to widen its definition of security and allow for the financial and budgetary priorities of its member states, together with their political and military priorities.[106]

McNamara's September 21, 1966 memorandum to Johnson stressed the importance of political factors in NATO strategy: "Our political objectives in maintaining a U.S. military presence in Europe have been and remain as important as our military objectives." These included the prevention of Soviet political pressure against Western Europe, the maintenance of NATO's cohesion, and the integration of German power in the multilateral structure of the West. Further, NATO should move "away from the emphasis mainly on massive attacks mounted with minimum warning and toward less extreme and far more likely nonnuclear contingencies."[107]

McNamara concluded that NATO had adequate nuclear forces, but pointed to qualitative deficiencies and major imbalances in its non-nuclear forces. "The real problem has been to define precisely the objectives for non-nuclear capabilities in a way which is military and economically feasible, and politically acceptable."[108] His September 1966 memorandum dealt with the dilemma of how US forces in Europe should be reduced whereas NATO's non-nuclear forces would "help deter and, if necessary, defeat larger-scale aggressions which the Soviet Union might initiate in the belief that we would not resist or would not initiate the use of nuclear weapons."[109]

The US devised "political warning and strategic mobility as a rationale for removing forces from Europe without reducing NATO military capabilities."[110] The US military rejected such diffuse concepts as a basis for force planning and force optimization. But these ambiguities were successful in allowing Washington, London, and Bonn to agree on NATO's new strategy. On November 9, 1966, in the first major breakthrough of the trilateral negotiations, the three countries signed the Agreed Minute on Strategy and Force[111] and concluded that "existing NATO conventional forces for the Central region are adequate in size to support a flexible response strategy."[112]

After de Gaulle's withdrawal from NATO's integrated commands had freed up the strategy debate, the negotiations of the big three forced their consensus on financial and defense priorities. After several rounds of tough negotiations, Washington, London, and Bonn eventually signed a compromise on force levels and burden sharing in April 1967. The compromise could fulfill its purpose only if it were integrated into the ongoing multilateral review of the military situation in Europe. The December 1966 NAC meeting therefore had to be used to inform and consult the other members of the Alliance.[113]

Harmel report: the nature of the threat and NATO's political role

On December 15, 1966, the NATO ministerial at fourteen was briefed about the results of the trilateral talks. It shifted final decision on political guidance for

NATO's military bodies onto the May 1967 ministerial. In the debate, marked by disagreement about the nature of the Soviet threat, two distinct viewpoints emerged. Harland Cleveland, US ambassador to NATO, reported that a majority of countries including Britain, Belgium, the Netherlands, Norway, and the United States, agreed on the need for "new substantive guidance around the theme of flexibility and a strategic concept which would give a realistic role to nuclear weapons and take into account the Soviet intentions and probable warning time." A second group, including Italy, Greece, and Turkey, stressed "the traditional elements of enemy capabilities rather than intentions, and maintaining maximum nuclear strength and deterrence so as to influence Warsaw Pact intentions."[114]

The key issue was whether or not the United States would be able to bridge the gap between Britain's optimism on détente and Germany's cautious stance. British Secretary of Defense Denis Healey stressed that the political guidance to NATO military planners should be "in a total political context in which the military are the servant and not the master of policy." He urged considering "enemy intentions as well as capabilities in the interest of realism" and believed "there would be at least months of warning" in view of Sino-Soviet tension. Bonn, however, feared that the Soviets would relax tensions selectively and isolate Germany. German Foreign Minister Willy Brandt said the Soviets might change their attitude during a period of tension. Since they could at any time use military power for political pressure the risk of Western escalation had to be preserved in the enemy's mind.

McNamara thought that the political and military warning aspects required more study.[115] This task was referred to the working groups studying the future of the Alliance as suggested by Belgian Foreign Minister Pierre Harmel.[116] This "Harmel exercise" led to a convergence of NATO members' views on the nature of the Soviet threat and the political role of the Alliance at a time of détente. Discussions on threat perceptions led to the conclusion that détente was a fluctuating process that had to be comprehensive and include the United States, Canada, and the Western European states as well as the Soviet Union and the Eastern European states.[117] Contrary to de Gaulle's view, NATO and détente were not incompatible: "While our principal objective remains the security of the North Atlantic area, this now involves, to a greater extent, questions of political tactics and actions as well as military issues."[118]

The Harmel discussions led to widespread consensus about NATO's roles in the interest of peace. It was agreed that US presence was vital to a peaceful order even beyond a European settlement while multilateral political and military consultation and cooperation within NATO remained a precondition for Western unity. Moreover, NATO members recognized that the Soviet Union could effectively block any European settlement; instead of driving a wedge between the Soviet Union and its Eastern European bloc partners, the West should therefore aim at involving all of them in constructive forms of economic, military, and political cooperation to support the development of the East. In particular, NATO should promote mutual force reductions as means to reduce the costs of the Cold War. Finally, multilateral and bilateral approaches to détente should be tested in such a way that selective détente could be avoided. NATO offered an excellent forum for establishing "harmonization on our side, and for maintaining a necessary degree of coordination in our bilateral and multilateral dealings with the East."[119] NATO played a key role in monitoring the domestic defense budget debates, the discussions within the Grand Coalition on progress of Germany's *Ostpolitik*, and the discussions between the United States and the Soviet Union on the Treaty on the Non-Proliferation of Nuclear Weapons (NPT), signed in 1968.

MC 14/3: politics and strategy

By late 1967, the Alliance had recovered its credibility as an integrated military structure and its legitimacy as the multilateral forum for political consultation in Europe. The Harmel report established a two-pillar strategy of military security and détente.[120] The Harmel report integrated the new compromise on strategy, force levels, nuclear planning, and crisis consultation that had been reached by the Defense Planning Committee (DPC) and the NPG within the broader context of a multilateral political dialogue about the future of East–West relations in Europe.

On December 12, 1967, the DPC adopted MC 14/3 as NATO's new strategic concept and agreed upon force commitments for 1968 and a five-year force plan. Rusk reported back to Washington that "the Fourteen now have in being a set of institutional arrangements enabling them realistically to tie together nuclear and conventional strategy, force planning and available resources."[121]

The new strategic concept integrated politics and strategy into a comprehensive deterrent concept consisting of the three factors – intention, capability, and uncertainty. It called for *manifest determination* to act jointly and defend the North Atlantic Treaty area against aggression, recognizable capability to respond effectively at any level of aggression, and flexibility in not allowing the aggressor to predict with confidence NATO's specific response, thus leading him to conclude that any attack involved unacceptable risk. Should deterrence fail, the concept foresaw three types of military responses: *direct defense* to "defeat the aggression on the level at which the enemy chooses to fight," *deliberate escalation* by steps to "defeat aggression by raising but where possible controlling, the scope and intensity of combat" while making the threat of a nuclear response progressively more imminent, thus weakening the enemy's "will to continue the conflict," and, finally, *general nuclear response* as "both the ultimate deterrent and, if used, the ultimate military response."[122]

There had been considerable last-minute disagreement about the document. Whereas most Europeans emphasized a deterrent strategy, the United States also valued a defensive strategy. Depending on their political interests, military power, geographic location, and economic considerations, various countries interpreted political warning, flexibility, and escalation differently. For the United States, flexibility meant that "NATO be in a position to defend European territory against a limited nonnuclear Soviet attack without resort to nuclear weapons."[123] Since, however, both the United States and Britain had to reduce at least some of their forces in Europe for domestic reasons, McNamara acknowledged that NATO's conventional option stopped short of "providing for a capability to deal successfully with any kind of nonnuclear attack without using nuclear weapons ourselves."[124]

With their emphasis on escalation the Europeans signaled that they were not prepared to accept risks greater than the United States did. They were "still inclined toward a public posture which emphasizes the risks of escalation rather than avoidance of escalation."[125] The NPG discussion, however, had made it difficult for them, in particular for the Germans, to imagine circumstances in which NATO's use of tactical nuclear weapons would be feasible.[126] In April 1967, the ministers endorsed political "guidelines" for the tactical use of nuclear weapons that involved Europeans and eased German concerns about the NPT by deciding that the "selective release of nuclear weapons employed from or on German soil" would be subject to confirmation by the German government.[127] However, the decision to use nuclear weapons remained solely with the US president.

Conclusion

NATO's flexible response strategy was a political compromise, as all strategic concepts had been since the foundation of the Alliance. Over the years, however, the compromise evolved considerably as a result of changing threat perceptions, a shifting military and economic balance of power, and the postures of member states. The political significance of the new strategy was decisive in 1967: the allies agreed on a common strategic concept after France left NATO's integrated military structures. The fourteen were determined to preserve the Alliance beyond its twentieth anniversary and into a period of East–West détente. The transformation into a less hierarchical Alliance of fourteen and a more political Alliance of fifteen was the answer to the Gaullist challenge. When the political interests of NATO member states could be merged into a political program for European security, the door was opened for a compromise on strategy.

The operational implications of MC 14/3 were less clear. The allies had agreed on the concepts of flexibility and escalation for varying and sometimes contradictory political reasons. There was never any agreement about how long the conventional phase of a war was likely to be. Further, the role of nuclear weapons was never precisely defined. The ambiguous wording of the new strategic document reflected NATO's nuclear learning: uncertainty made nuclear threats work in a situation of mutual vulnerability. Therefore, NATO's deterrent depended on determination and flexibility as much as on its military capability. At the same time, ambiguity of strategic terminology and operational war planning was a precondition for a political compromise on nuclear control and burden sharing.

Political leadership during a phase of mutual vulnerability and stirrings of détente in Eastern Europe depended on soft power rather than on hard power, on the flexibility and adaptability of NATO's institutions, and on common norms and values of its members. Political rhetoric, not military–technical considerations, drove NATO strategic thinking by the late 1960s. The military and technical feasibility of a strategy would likely never be tested. The political signals the strategy sent, however, had a direct and immediate effect on the adversary's and the other allies' perceptions.

During much of the 1950s, NATO strategic thinking had been dominated by the notion that the military capability of states was closely linked to their political behavior. For example, after the Korean War, NATO members naturally assumed that the Soviet Union would expand its political and ideological influence on the basis of its preponderant military power. In fact, NATO's threat perceptions shifted from the political field to the military field and back to the political field between 1949 and 1957. However, NATO never considered the gap between Soviet capabilities and intentions as significant enough for a fundamental reappraisal of NATO policies. NATO's dependence on nuclear weapons resulted from the belief that deterrence had to be based on a plausible defense concept. Forward defense was credible only if NATO compensated for its numerical inferiority in relation to the Soviets by including into its concept the technical superiority of US nuclear power. A commitment to massive retaliation in the case of war made it easier for the United States and for its European partners to compromise on burden sharing. At the same time, given US quantitative and qualitative nuclear superiority, massive retaliation – at least from a US perspective – made more strategic sense in the early 1950s than any other option.

In the 1950s there had not been a clear decision on how nuclear crisis consultation should proceed. MC 48 was approved as a basis for planning and preparing forces. The Europeans had accepted the political leadership of the United States in exchange for the US agreement to back down on preventive war. Yet in essence, NATO's nuclearization resulted from a very delicate and short-lived balance of the various allies' political interests: first, the launch of the Sputnik challenged the credibility of the US nuclear guarantee for Europe. As a result, US political leadership was being questioned more and more by the end of the 1950s. Second, the Berlin Crisis alerted the allies to the very real possibility that the Soviets might employ limited aggression. Consequently, the wisdom of NATO's massive retaliation strategy was increasingly questioned.

The United States and its allies perceived the Berlin Crisis as a test of the US's readiness to defend its allies in the event of a nuclear risk. As a consequence of the Berlin Crisis, the focus of the strategic debate within NATO shifted from deterrence to defense and from preempting war to terminating a possible war. The United States demanded a conventional build-up as a means of enhancing the nuclear deterrent. But for the Europeans and, in particular, for the Germans, a conventional pause as foreseen by the US's proposal was unacceptable, both militarily (with Europe as the battlefield) and politically (with the risk of decoupling). The Germans suggested as an alternative a tactical nuclear weapons pause as a means of preventing a loss of territory. The United States, in turn, rejected this option for military reasons (the risk of escalation and battlefield damage) and political reasons (a US loss of central control). Britain covered the middle ground and suggested a selective use of nuclear weapons as a political tool for stopping a war. The notions of flexibility, escalation, and uncertainty had entered the strategic debate with the aim of expanding the process of deterrence into war.

From a military point of view, the value of firebreaks along the Iron Curtain was questionable. However, more important from a political point of view was that the US emphasis on a conventional option coincided with growing US interest in Berlin negotiations and in the stabilization of the central European status quo. In addition, the debate about central nuclear control touched upon the sensitive issues of sovereignty and prestige. From a European perspective, Washington seemed to be tightening its control over NATO's integrated military command at the very moment when the political interests of the allies were diverging. De Gaulle was not prepared to accept US control. Military integration, in his view, had to go, and the political leadership in Europe was first and foremost the responsibility of the Europeans themselves.

With de Gaulle's withdrawal from all integrated military commands, the remaining allies were much better positioned to transform NATO into an Alliance that was more participatory and political. Washington realized that there had to be more political consultation among the 14 on nuclear planning and on decision-making, in particular. Further, NATO had to adopt a wider concept of security that would allow for a better balance between the members' military and defense priorities and their financial and economic priorities. Once a basic consensus on the nature of détente and on the fact that NATO should have a political role beyond a European settlement had been reached during the Harmel exercise, a new compromise on strategy, force levels, nuclear planning, and crisis consultation emerged.

Notes

1 On the evolution of NATO strategy in the 1950s and 1960s, see Jane E. Stromseth, *The Origins of Flexible Response: NATO's Debate over Strategy in the 1960s* (New York: St. Martin's Press, 1988); Beatrice Heuser, *NATO, Britain, France and the FRG: Nuclear Strategies and Forces for Europe, 1949–2000* (London: Macmillan, 1997); Helga Haftendorn, *NATO and the Nuclear Revolution: A Crisis of Credibility* (Oxford: Clarendon Press, 1996); Catherine McArdle Kelleher, *Germany and the Politics of Nuclear Weapons* (New York: Columbia University Press, 1975).

2 On the debate over nuclear strategy, see McGeorge Bundy, *Danger and Survival: Choices about the Bomb in the First Fifty Years* (New York: Vintage Books, 1988); Marc Trachtenberg, *History and Strategy* (Princeton, NJ: Princeton University Press, 1991); Andreas Wenger, *Living with Peril: Eisenhower, Kennedy, and Nuclear Weapons* (Lanham, MD: Rowman & Littlefield, 1997).

3 On the foundation of NATO, see Lawrence S. Kaplan, NATO *and the United States: The Enduring Alliance* (Boston, MA: Twayne Publishers, 1988); Dean Acheson, *Present at the Creation: My Years in the State Department* (New York: W.W. Norton & Company, 1969); George F. Kennan, *George F. Kennan: Memoirs 1925–1950* (New York: Pantheon Books, 1983).

4 Strategic Concept for the Defense of the North Atlantic Area, October 19, 1949, MC 3, in *NATO Strategy Documents 1949–1969*, ed. Gregory W. Pedlow (Brussels: SHAPE, 1997), pp. 3–8, 6.

5 Strategic Guidance for North Atlantic Regional Planning, March 28, 1950, MC 14, in *NATO Strategy Documents 1949–1969*, pp. 90, 91–100.

6 NATO Medium Term Defense Plan: Part I – Defense Policy and Concept of Operations, July 1, 1954, DC 13, in *NATO Strategy Documents 1949–1969*, pp. 117–24, 121.

7 Memorandum, Paul H. Nitze to the Secretary of State, January 12, 1953, Foreign Relations of the United States (FRUS), 1952–54, 2 (part 1), pp. 202–5.

8 Gregory W. Pedlow, ed., "The Evolution of NATO Strategy 1949–1969," in *NATO Strategy Documents 1949–1969*, pp. ix–xxv.

9 Note, "Estimate of the Relative Strength and Capabilities of NATO and Soviet Bloc Forces at Present and in the Immediate Future," November 10, 1951, MC 33, Parallel History Project (PHP), www.isn.ethz.ch/php/collections/coll_7.htm (accessed November 2003), pp. 1–19.

10 NATO Medium Term Defense Plan: Part I – Defense Policy and Concept of Operations, July 1, 1954, DC 13, in *NATO Strategy Documents 1949–1969*, pp. 117–24, 140.

11 Note, "Estimate of the Relative Strength and Capabilities of NATO and Soviet Bloc Forces at Present and in the Immediate Future," November 10, 1951, MC 33, PHP, www.isn.ethz.ch/php/collections/coll_7.htm (accessed November 2003), pp. 1–19.

12 Ibid.

13 Ibid.

14 NATO Medium Term Defense Plan: Part I – Defense Policy and Concept of Operations, July 1, 1954, DC 13, in *NATO Strategy Documents 1949–1969*, pp. 117–24, 118–19.

15 NATO Strategic Guidance, December 9, 1952, MC 14/1, in *NATO Strategy Documents 1949–1969*, pp. 197–228, 206–9.

16 On the Global Strategy paper, see Stephen Twigge and Alan Macmillan, "Britain, the United States, and the Development of NATO Strategy, 1950–1964," *Journal of Strategic Studies* 19, No. 2 (1996): 260–82, 261–2; Heuser, *NATO, Britain, France and the FRG*, pp. 30–6; Robert A. Wampler, *Ambiguous Legacy: The United States, Great Britain and the Foundations of NATO Strategy, 1948–1957*, PhD dissertation (Ann Arbor, MI: University Microfilms, 1991), pp. 389–414.

17 Report, "Defense of Europe in the Short Term," May 31, 1951, COS (51) 322, PHP, www.isn.ethz.ch/php/collections/coll_7.htm (accessed November 2003).

18 Wampler, *Ambiguous Legacy*, pp. 452–506.

19 Heuser, *NATO, Britain, France and the FRG*; Wampler, *Ambiguous Legacy*.

20 National Security Council (NSC) 162/2, "Basic National Security Policy," October 30, 1953, FRUS, 1952–54, 2, pp. 577–97, 593.

21 Eisenhower, Annual Message to the Congress on the State of the Union, February 2, 1953, Eisenhower Public Papers of the Presidents of the United States (PPS), 1953, pp. 12–34.

22 On preventive war thinking, see Trachtenberg, *History and Strategy*, pp. 100–15.

23 Memorandum of NSC meeting, December 10, 1953, FRUS, 1952–54, 15 (part 2), pp. 1653–5.

24 Memorandum, McCardle to the Secretary of State, April 30, 1954, FRUS, 1952–54, 16, pp. 629–30.

25 John Foster Dulles, "Talking Paper" for NATO Meeting in Paris on April 23, April 22, 1954, SS, "Disarmament – Atomic Weapons and Proposal, 1953, 1954, 1955 [2]," John Foster Dulles Papers, 1951–59, Seeley G. Mudd Library, Princeton, NJ.

26 Memorandum by the Secretary of State and the Secretary of Defense to the President, November 2, 1954, FRUS, 1952–54, 5 (part 1), pp. 531.

27 NSC 5501, "Basic National Security Policy," January 7, 1955, FRUS, 1955–57, 19, pp. 24–38.

28 Report, "Capabilities Study Allied Command Europe," September 2, 1954, JP (54) 76 (Final), PHP, www.isn.ethz.ch/php/collections/coll_7.htm (accessed November 2003); Report, "The Most Effective Pattern of NATO Military Strength," September 3, 1954, JP (54) 77 (Final), PHP, www.in.ethz.ch/php/collections/coll_7.htm (accessed November 2003).

29 Memorandum of Conversation, by the Director of the Policy Planning Staff, December 16, 1954, FRUS, 1952–54, 5 (part 1), pp. 548; Memorandum of Conversation, by the Assistant Secretary of State for European Affairs, December 19, 1954, FRUS, 1952–54, 5 (part 1), pp. 560.
30 Report by the Military Committee to the North Atlantic Council on the Most Effective Pattern of NATO Military Strength for the Next Few Years, November 18, 1954, MC 48, in *NATO Strategy Documents 1949–1969*, pp. 231–48.
31 Ibid.
32 Report, "Capabilities Study Allied Command Europe," September 2, 1954, JP (54) 76 (Final), PHP, www.isn.ethz.ch/php/collections/coll_7.htm (accessed November 2003).
33 Report by the Military Committee to the North Atlantic Council on the Most Effective Pattern of NATO Military Strength for the Next Few Years, November 18, 1954, MC 48, in *NATO Strategy Documents 1949–1969*, pp. 231–48.
34 Telegram from the US Delegation at the NAC Ministerial Meeting to the Department of State, May 5, 1956, FRUS, 1955–57, 4, pp. 57–62.
35 Telegram from the US Delegation at the NAC Ministerial Meeting to the Department of State, May 5, 1956, FRUS, 1955–57, 4, pp. 66–70; Telegram from the US Delegation at the NAC Ministerial Meeting to the Department of State, May 5, 1956, FRUS, 1955–57, pp. 70–1; Message, Secretary of State to the President, May 5, 1956, FRUS, 1955–57, p. 75; Message, Secretary of State to the President, May 6, 1956, FRUS, 1955–57, pp. 76–7.
36 Letter, Eden to Eisenhower, July 18, 1956, FRUS, 1955–57, 4, pp. 90–2.
37 Conference with the President, May 24, 1956, FRUS, 1955–57, 19, pp. 311–15.
38 Memorandum of Conference with the President, October 2, 1956, FRUS, 1955–57, 4, pp. 99–102.
39 Directive to the NATO Military Authorities from the North Atlantic Council, December 13, 1956, C-M (56) 138 (Final), in *NATO Strategy Documents 1949–1969*, pp. 269–76.
40 A Report by the Military Committee to the North Atlantic Council on Overall Strategic Concept for the Defense of the NATO Area, February 1957, MC 14/2, 21, in *NATO Strategy Documents 1949–1969*, pp. 279–313; Report, "Allied Command Channel Forces Study 1958–1965," November 6, 1957, JP (57) 128 (Final), PHP, www.isn.ethz.ch/php/collections/coll_7.htm (accessed November 2003).
41 Andreas Wenger, "Eisenhower, Kennedy, and the Missile Gap: Determinants of US Military Expenditure in the Wake of the Sputnik Shock," *Defence and Peace Economics*, 8, no. 1 (1997): 77–100.
42 NSC 5724, "Deterrence and Survival in the Nuclear Age: Report to the President by the Security Resources Panel of the Science Advisory Committee," November 7, 1957, Office of the Special Assistant for National Secutiry Affairs (OSANSA), NSC, Box 22, Dwight D. Eisenhower Library (DDEL) Abilene, KS. The report is in part reprinted in FRUS, 1955–57, 19, pp. 638–61.
43 Memorandum of a Conference with the President, November 4, 1957, FRUS, 1955–57, 19, pp. 621.
44 Bundy, *Danger and Survival*, pp. 334–50.
45 Memorandum of NSC meeting, December 12, 1957, FRUS, 1955–57, 19, pp. 704–9.
46 Eisenhower, Farewell Radio and Television Address to the American People, January 17, 1961, Eisenhower PPS, 1960–61, pp. 1035–9.
47 Heuser, *NATO, Britain, France and the FRG*, pp. 41–3; Twigge and Macmillan, "Britain, the United States, and the Development of NATO Strategy, 1950–1964," pp. 268–70.
48 Frédéric Bozo, *Deux stratégies pour l'Europe: de Gaulle, les Etats-Unis et l'Alliance atlantique, 1958–1969* (Paris: Plon et Fondation Charles de Gaulle, 1996).
49 Telegram to Department of State (August 24, 1961), "SACEUR Presentation to NAC Meeting," August 23, 1961, PHP, www.isn.ethz.ch/php/collections/coll_7.htm (accessed November 2003).

50 Report, "NATO Minimum Force Studies," November 14, 1957, COS (57) 244, PHP, www.isn.ethz.ch/php/collections/coll_7.htm (accessed November 2003).
51 Memorandum of Conference With the President, March 6, 1959, Berlin Crisis 1958–62, no. 907, National Security Archive (NSA) Washington, DC.
52 Memorandum of Conversation with the French Ambassador and his staff, February 3, 1959, Berlin Crisis 1958–62, no. 705, NSA.
53 Memorandum of Telephone Conversation with Secretary Dulles, March 6, 1959, Berlin Crisis 1958–62, no. 899, NSA.
54 Conversation with Chancellor Adenauer, May 27, 1959, Berlin Crisis 1958–62, no. 1309, NSA.
55 Memorandum of Conference with the President, August 19, 1960, Berlin Crisis 1958–62, no. 1944, NSA.
56 Memorandum of Telephone Conversation with Secretary Dulles, 6 March 1959, Berlin Crisis 1958–62, no. 899, NSA.
57 John Millar to Russell Fessenden, "NATO Military Concept," May 4, 1960, PHP, www.isn.ethz.ch/php/collections/coll_7.htm (accessed November 2003).
58 Rosenberg, "The Origins of Overkill," pp. 3–71.
59 Covering Note on Henry Kissinger's Memo on Berlin, McGeorge Bundy, July 7, 1961, "July 1961 Folder," Nuclear History Box 13, NSA.
60 John F. Kennedy, *The Strategy of Peace*, ed. Allan Nevins (New York: Harper & Brothers, 1960), p. 184.
61 Memorandum, "McNamara Meeting with von Hassel," November 13, 1964, RG 200, Robert McNamara Papers, Box 133, Memcons with Germany, Vol. 1, Sec. 1, National Archives and Records Administration (NARA), PHP, www.isn.ethz.ch/php/collections/coll_7.htm (accessed November 2003).
62 National Security Memorandum No. 40, see "A Review of North Atlantic Problems for the Future," March 1961, "NATO Acheson Report 3/61 Folder," Box 220, National Security File (NSF), John F. Kennedy Library (JFKL), Boston, MA; "To Members of the NSC from McGeorge Bundy," April 24, 1961, National Security Action Memorandum (NSAM) No. 40, "Vice Presidential Security File," Box 4, NSC-1961, Lyndon B. Johnson Library (LBJL), Austin, TX; Robert S. McNamara, Draft Memorandum for the President, "The Role of Tactical Nuclear Forces in NATO Strategy," January 15, 1965, Office of the Secretary of Defense, the pentagon, Washington, DC/Freedom of Information Act (DOD/FOIA).
63 "A Review of North Atlantic Problems for the Future," March 1961, "NATO Acheson Report 3/61 Folder," Box 220, NSF, JFKL, p. 51.
64 Letter, Arleigh Burke to Dean Acheson, March 20, 1961, CCS 9050/3070, "NATO (10 March 1961) Sec. 2," Joint Chiefs of Staff (JCS), National Archives and Records Service (NARS); Memorandum, Nitze to the Secretary of Defense, "General Norstad's Comments on NATO Policy," April 6, 1961, CCS 9050/3070, "NATO (10 March 1961) Sec. 2," JCS, NARS; Memorandum, Chairman of the JCS to the Secretary of Defense, March 7, 1961, CCS 9050/3070, "NATO (February 11, 1961) Sec. 1," JCS, NARS.
65 Memorandum Weiss to Johnson, "Meetings with Bohlen, Finletter, Lemnitzer, McConnell," May 27, 1964, RG 59, PHP, www.isn.ethz.ch/php/collections/coll_7.htm (accessed/November 2003).
66 Report by Dean Acheson, June 28, 1961, FRUS, 1961–63, 14, pp. 138–59.
67 Wenger, *Living with Peril*, pp. 197–272.
68 Trachtenberg, *History and Strategy*, pp. 223–4.
69 Memorandum, McNamara to Kennedy, "Military Build-up and Possible Action in Europe," Appendix A, September 18, 1961, Berlin Crisis 1958–62, no. 2484, NSA.
70 Memorandum, "McNamara Meeting with von Hassel on Strategic Objects," July 31, 1963, PHP, www.isn.ethz.ch/php/collections/coll_7.htm (accessed/November 2003).

71 Memorandum, "McNamara Meeting with von Hassel," November 13, 1964, PHP, www.isn.ethz.ch/php/collections/coll_7.htm (accessed/November 2003).
72 Taylor and Speidel, see Robert S. McNamara, Draft Memorandum for the President, "The Role of Tactical Nuclear Forces in NATO Strategy," January 15, 1965, PHP, www.isn.ethz.ch/php/collections/coll_7.htm (accessed/November 2003).
73 Memorandum Weiss to Johnson, "Meetings with Bohlen, Finletter, Lemnitzer, McConnell," May 27, 1964, PHP, www.isn.ethz.ch/php/collections/coll_7.htm (accessed/November 2003).
74 Heuser, *NATO, Britain, France and the FRG*, 47–52; Twigge and Macmillan, "Britain, the United States, and the Development of NATO Strategy, 1950–1964," pp. 270–3.
75 Thomas C. Schelling, "Nuclear Strategy in the Berlin Crisis," July 5, 1961, FRUS, 1961–63, 14, pp. 170–2.
76 Letter, Kennedy to Norstad, including NSAM 109, "U.S. Policy on Military Actions in a Berlin Conflict," October 20, 1961, FRUS, 1961–63, 14, pp. 520–3.
77 Memorandum of Meeting, October 20, 1961, FRUS, 1961–63, 14, pp. 517–19.
78 Memorandum for the Record by Legere, December 5, 1961, Berlin Crisis 1958–62, no. 2643, NSA.
79 John C. Ausland, "Briefing for President Kennedy on Berlin," August 2, 1962, Berlin Crisis 1958–62, no. 2842, NSA.
80 Memorandum, Bundy to the President, "Issues to be Settled with General Clay," August 28, 1961, Berlin Crisis 1958–62, no. 2415, NSA; see also Andreas Wenger, "Kennedy, Chruschtschow und das gemeinsame Interesse der Supermächte am Status quo in Europa," *Vierteljahrshefte für Zeitgeschichte*, 46, 1 (1998): 69–99; Marc Trachtenberg, *A Constructed Peace: The Making of the European Settlement, 1945–1963* (Princeton, NJ: Princeton University Press, 1999); Christof Münger, *Die Berliner Mauer, Kennedy und die Kubakrise: Die westliche Allianz in der Zerreissprobe, 1961–1963* (Paderborn: Schöningh, 2003).
81 Memorandum, Yarmolinsky to Sorensen, "Missile Gap Controversy," May 3, 1962, "May 1962 Folder," Nuclear History Box 14, NSA.
82 Minutes of National Security Council Meeting, December 19, 1961, "December 1961 Folder," Nuclear History Box 13, NSA.
83 See Desmond Ball, *Politics and Force Levels: The Strategic Missile Program of the Kennedy Administration* (Berkeley, CA: University of California Press, 1980). For the 1963–67 defense program, see McNamara, Draft Memorandum for the President, "Recommended Long Range Nuclear Delivery Force 1963–1967," September 23, 1961, DOD/FOIA, p. 4.
84 Memorandum, Kissinger to Bundy, October 3, 1961, Berlin Crisis 1958–62, no. 2523, NSA.
85 Airgram, "McNamara Remarks to NAC Meeting," December 15, 1961, PHP, www.isn.ethz.ch/php/collections/coll_7.htm (accessed/November 2003].
86 Remarks by McNamara, NATO Ministerial Meeting, May 5, 1962, Restricted Session, "May 1962 Folder," Nuclear History Box 14, NSA.
87 McNamara, January 19, 1962, Senate Armed Services Committee, Military Procurement Authorization, Fiscal Year 1963 p. 16; McNamara, January 25, 1962, House Appropriations Committee, Department of Defense Appropriations, Fiscal Year 1963, pp. 249–50; McNamara, DOD Press Conference, Pentagon, November 17, 1961, Public Statements of Robert S. McNamara, Vol. 3, 1961, Historical Office of the Secretary of Defense (HOSD), Pentagon, p. 1470; McNamara, Address to the Fellows of the American Bar Foundation, Chicago, February 17, 1962, "February 1962 Folder," Nuclear History Box 14, NSA, p. 5.
88 Remarks by McNamara, NATO Ministerial Meeting, May 5, 1962, Restricted Session, "May 1962 Folder," Nuclear History Box 14, NSA.
89 Ibid.

90 See Stromseth, *The Origins of Flexible Response*, p. 46.
91 Robert McNamara, Memorandum for the President, "Recommended Fiscal Year 1966–1970 Programs for Strategic Offensive Forces, Continental Air and Missile Defense Forces, and Civil Defense," December 3, 1964, DOD/FOIA, p. 4.
92 Memorandum from Weiss to Johnson, "Meetings with Bohlen, Finletter, Lemnitzer, McConnell," May 27, 1964, PHP, www.isn.ethz.ch/php/collections/coll_7.htm (accessed/November 2003).
93 Haftendorn, *NATO and the Nuclear Revolution*, p. 40.
94 Stromseth, *The Origins of Flexible Response*, pp. 51–7.
95 On the development of NATO's force planning exercise, see Haftendorn, *NATO and the Nuclear Revolution*, pp. 200–95.
96 Letter From President de Gaulle to President Johnson, March 7, 1966, FRUS, 1964–68, 13, p. 325; for de Gaulle's 1966 decisions, see Georges-Henri Soutou, "La décision française de quitter le commandement intègre de l'OTAN," in *Von Truman bis Harmel: Die Bundesrepublik Deutschland im Spannungsfeld von NATO und europäischer Integration*, ed. Hans-Joachim Harder (München: Oldenbourg, 2000), pp. 185–208; Frédéric Bozo, "De Gaulle, l'amérique et l'alliance atlantique: une relecture de la crise de 1966," *Vingtième Siècle* 43, Juillet–Septembre (1994): 55–68; Maurice Vaïsse, *Le Grandeur: Politique Etrangère du Général de Gaulle, 1958–1969* (Paris: Fayard, 1998).
97 Aide-Mémoire from the French Government to the US Government, March 11, 1966, FRUS, 1964–68, 13, p. 333.
98 Memorandum Weiss to Johnson, "Meetings with Bohlen, Finletter, Lemnitzer, McConnell," May 27, 1964, PHP, www.isn.ethz.ch/php/collections/coll_7.htm (accessed/November 2003).
99 Memorandum, "McNamara Meeting with von Hassel," July 31, 1963, PHP, www.isn.ethz.ch/php/collections/coll_7.htm (accessed/November 2003).
100 Memorandum, "Possible Effects of the NATO Crisis on German Foreign and Domestic Politics," Undated, No-Proliferation Policy (NNP), no. 713, NSA.
101 See Thomas A. Schwartz, "NATO, Europe, and the Johnson Administration: Alliance Politics, Political Economy, and the Beginning of Détente, 1963–1969," NATO Research Fellowships Programme, 1997–1999, www.nato.int/acad/fellow/97–99/schwartz.pdf (accessed/November 2003); Thomas A. Schwartz, "Lyndon Johnson and Europe: Alliance Politics, Political Economy, and 'Growing out of the Cold War'," in *The Foreign Policies of Lyndon Johnson: Beyond Vietnam*, ed. H.W. Brands (College Station, TX: Texas A&M University, Press 1999), pp. 37–60.
102 Diary Entry the Ambassador to the United Kingdom (Bruce), May 19, 1966, FRUS, 1964–68, 13, pp. 391f. On the importance of Johnson's leadership for his administration's foreign policies towards Europe, see Thomas A. Schwartz, "NATO, Europe, and the Johnson Administration: Alliance Politics, Political Economy, and the Beginning of Détente, 1963–1969."
103 NATO Ministerial Meeting, Scope and Strategy Paper, June 6–8, 1966, National Security Files, Conference Files 49–63, Box 409, LBJL; see Lawrence S. Kaplan, "The U.S. and NATO in the Johnson Years," in *The Johnson Years, Volume Three, LBJ at Home and Abroad*, ed. Robert A. Divine (Lawrence, KS: University Press of Kansas, 1994), pp. 119–49.
104 Memorandum by the Acheson Group, Undated, FRUS, 1964–68, 11, p. 407.
105 Memorandum From Secretary of Defense McNamara and Secretary of State Rusk to President Johnson, May 28, 1966, FRUS, 1964–68, 13, p. 402.
106 On the issue of burden sharing, see Harald Rosenbach, "Die deutsch-amerikanischen Verhandlungen über den Devisenausgleich, 1961–1967," *Vierteljahrshefte für Zeitgeschichte*, 46, 4 (Oktober 1998): 709–46; Hubert Zimmermann, "Der Konflikt um die Kosten des Kalten Krieges: Besatzungskosten, Stationierungskosten, Devisenausgleich," in *Die USA und Deutschland im Zeitalter des Kalten Krieges*

1945–1990: Ein Handbuch, Band I, 1945–1968, ed. Detlef Junker (Stuttgart: Deutsche Verlags-Anstalt, 2001), pp. 514–24.

107 Robert S. McNamara, Draft Memorandum for the President, "NATO Strategy and Force Structure," September 21, 1966, DOD/FOIA. Stromseth, *The Origins of Flexible Response*, p. 64; Haftendorn, *NATO and the Nuclear Revolution*, p. 53.

108 Draft Memorandum for the President, "NATO Strategy and Force Structure," January 16, 1968, PHP, www.isn.ethz.ch/php/collections/coll_7.htm (accessed/November 2003).

109 Robert S. McNamara, Draft Memorandum for the President, "NATO Strategy and Force Structure," September 21, 1966, DOD/FOIA.

110 Memorandum Fairley to Kohler, "NATO Strategy," December 1, 1967, PHP, www.isn.ethz.ch/php/collections/coll_7.htm (accessed/November 2003).

111 Agreed Minute on Strategy and Forces, November 9, 1966, FRUS, 1964–68, 13, p. 563.

112 Letter from John J. McCloy to President Johnson, November 21, 1966, FRUS, 1964–68, 13, p. 497.

113 Haftendorn, *NATO and the Nuclear Revolution*, pp. 200–319.

114 Cable (No. 24489) to the Department of State, "NATO Ministerial Meeting – Defense Planning," November 26, 1966, PHP, www.isn.ethz.ch/php/collections/coll_7.htm (accessed November 2003); see also Anna Locher and Christiann Nuenlist, "Reinventing NATO: Canada and the Multilateralization of Détente, 1962–1966," *International Journal* [Toronto], 58, 2 (Spring 2003): 283–302.

115 Cables (No. 012967 and 12968) to the Department of State, "NATO Ministerial Meeting – Defense Planning," December 15, 1966, RG 59, SN 64–66, NATO 3 FR (PA), PHP, www.isn.ethz.ch/php/collections/coll_7.htm (accessed/November 2003).

116 For an excellent study of the Harmel report, see Helga Haftendorn, "Entstehung und Bedeutung des Harmel-Berichts der NATO von 1967," *Vierteljahrshefte für Zeitgeschichte*, 40, 2 (April 1992): 169–220; Helga Haftendorn "The Adaptation of the NATO Alliance to a Period of Détente: The 1967 Harmel Report," in *Crises and Promises: The European Project, 1963–1969*, ed. Wilfried Loth (Baden-Baden: Nomos, 2001), pp. 285–322. For further assessments, see Pierre Harmel, "Forty Years of East–West Relations: Hopes, Fears, and Challenges," *The Atlantic Quarterly*, 25, 3 (Fall 1987): 259–69; Eugene V. Rostow, "Ein praktisches Friedensprogramm: Der 20. Jahrestag des Harmel-Berichtes," *NATO Brief*, 4 (Juli/August 1987): 11–17; Joachim Brockpähler, "Die Harmel-Philosophie: Ausdruck einer kreativen Friedensstrategie der NATO," *NATO Brief*, 6 (November Dezember 1990): 20–24.

117 Sub-Group I Draft Report, Subject of Discussion on September 18/19, 1967, NATO Archives, NISCA 4/10/4/1, Item 27; Final Harmel Report, East–West Relations Détente and a European Settlement, NATO Archives, www.nato.int/archives/harmel/harmel01.htm, 2 (accessed November 2003).

118 Memorandum for Rapporteurs, Future of the Alliance Study, July 18, 1967, NATO Archives, NISCA 4/10/5, Item 33, p. 6.

119 Sub-Group I Draft Report, Subject of Discussion on September 18/19, 1967, NATO Archives, NISCA 4/10/4/1, Item 27, p. 13.

120 Report of the Rapporteur Sub-Group 3, Mr Foy D. Kohler, USA, The Future Security Policy of the Alliance, NATO Archives, www.nato.int/archives/harmel/harmel03.htm. Final Harmel Report, East–West Relations Détente and a European Settlement, NATO Archives, www.nato.int/archives/harmel/harmel01.htm (accessed November 2003), p. 3.

121 Telegram from Secretary of State Rusk to the Department of State, December 14, 1967, FRUS, 1964–68, 13, p. 651.

122 Final Decision on MC 14/3: A Report by the Military Committee to the Defence Planning Committee on Overall Strategic Concept for the Defense of the NATO Area, January 16, 1968, MC 14/3 (Final), in *NATO Strategy Documents 1949–1969*, pp. 345–46.

123 Ibid.

124 Draft Memorandum for the President, "NATO Strategy and Force Structure," January 16, 1968, RG 200, Robert McNamara Papers, Box 77, Draft Memo to the President Vol. I, NARA, PHP, www.isn.ethz.ch/php/collections/coll_7.htm (accessed November 2003).
125 Memorandum Fairley to Kohler, "NATO Strategy," December 1, 1967, FOIA/Department of State, PHP, www.isn.ethz.ch/php/collections/coll_7.htm (accessed November 2003).
126 Telegram from the Mission to the NATO and European Regional Organizations to the Department of State, December 10, 1966, FRUS, 1964–68, 13, p. 510; Research Memorandum No. REU-35, June 11, 1968, FRUS, 1964–68, 13, p. 711.
127 Memorandum From Secretary of State Rusk and Secretary of Defense Clifford to President Johnson, FRUS, 1964–68, 13, p. 679; Research Memorandum No. REU-35, Undated, FRUS, 1964–68, 13, p. 711.

8 Alliance of democracies and nuclear deterrence

Beatrice Heuser

Much writing on International Relations has pondered the implications of a very unequal distribution of power in the relations between states. There is a tradition in the West going back in part to decision-making mechanisms within the Holy Roman Empire and to practices of peace negotiations that gives each represented state-like entity a formally equal right to be heard, a custom that precedes the intra-state principle of one-citizen-one-vote that was to become the essential hallmark of democracy. This has culminated in the formal equality of all members of the United Nations (UN) in the General Assembly, a practice reflected also for decades in decision-making in the European Communities/European Union. Nevertheless, this theoretic equality of all states, the large and the small, stands in blatant contradiction of the differences in size, wealth, military and economic strength, or at least historic standing, reflected in the UN in the distribution of permanent seats of the Security Council or in membership of the Group of Seven/Eight. Diplomatic practice has always aimed to find a middle way between these conflicting considerations.

International Relations theorists of the so-called Realist persuasion have strongly emphasized the importance of differences in power and have largely denied the differences of ideology and political culture in the way great powers have wielded their assets in relation to smaller powers. International Relations as an area of research "took off" after the Second World War, when the Cold War dominated European security. Even in that context, unbelievable though it may seem in view of the deeply ideological nature of the Cold War, there is plenty of evidence to sustain "Realist" theories about the treatment of allies by the two opposing superpowers. As we shall see in the following, it took America's Allies almost two decades of intermittent and often dead-ended negotiations to bring the successive Washington administrations around to taking their NATO Allies' concerns into consideration in their deterrence posture. And even after 1967, when MC 14/3 was adopted and the Nuclear Planning Group (NPG) was set up, the Americans sprang many unilateralist surprises of considerable consequence on their Allies in contravention of previous agreements.

In the following we shall reflect upon the influence of Western traditions of state equality and of consultation on NATO's deterrence posture. The assumption, resulting from my culturalist or *mentalité* approach which argues that political culture, ideals, and mentality not only influence strategy but also the decision-making apparatus and procedures through which strategy is formulated, is that NATO, as an alliance of democracies, must have been different in quality, in the strategies it adopted and the way in which it adopted them, from an alliance of communist party dictatorships. I therefore shall use the admittedly patchy knowledge I have about the workings of the Warsaw Treaty Organization (WTO) – as it is referred to in official documents emanating from this organization and its member states – as a point of comparison and contrast to evaluate the extent to which democratic values influenced NATO's nuclear deterrence stance.

Privileged partner: the United Kingdom

At the time of the signing of the Washington Treaty in April 1949, three members of the newly formed Alliance had the habit of close joint military planning, which was still being carried on, in part as a legacy of the Second World War. These were the United States, Britain, and Canada. At the same time, the Brussels Treaty Organization (BTO), also known as the Western Union Defense Organization (WUDO), established in 1948 for the members of the Western Union (Britain, France, and the Benelux countries) conducted a limited amount of military coordination of defense planning under the chairmanship of the British Field Marshal, Lord Montgomery of Alamein. Britain was thus in the position of being involved in two sets of military planning that contained many contradictions known primarily to the British.[1]

Moreover, for this period the United States was the only nuclear power in NATO, as Britain only held her first nuclear test in October 1952, and Britain's own nuclear bombs were first ready to be dropped from British aircraft in the late 1950s. (Before that, from late 1956 – the time of the Suez Crisis – British bombers were able to carry American free-fall bombs, doubtless a factor explaining the exaggerated feeling of strength which led the Eden Government to intervene militarily in Egypt.)

Montgomery, through his position in the BTO and, subsequently, as second in command to the newly established Supreme Allied Commander in Europe (SACEUR), was keenly aware of the fears of abandonment by the "Anglo-Saxons" (rightly) entertained by his French, Belgian, and Dutch colleagues in the Western Union. At the same time, he believed that these countries, and even Italy, if properly organized and inspired by the commitment to their defense of the United States and Britain, could make a considerable contribution to mutual defense. In the early 1950s, he played, perhaps, the key role in changing the US and British strategy to serve the interests of the European Allies to a greater extent, persuading them to agree to an Alliance strategy that would henceforth seek to defend, not merely stage a fighting withdrawal in, Norway, the Benelux countries (at least up to the Rhine-IJssel line), France, and Italy, with some hope perhaps even of having Greece and Turkey fend off total occupation.[2]

Realists would find it difficult to understand why Montgomery and the successive Attlee and Churchill governments backing him used all their influence to improve the defenses of their continental Allies. The explanation is simple, however, in that Realism fails to take into account the benefit to all deriving from Alliance solidarity, collective defense, and a pooling of effort.

The British were, and remain to this day, the initiates into America's most highly guarded secrets, the targeting plans for its strategic nuclear force. Other than (successfully) the British and (unsuccessfully) Charles de Gaulle in the late 1950s and early 1960s, the Europeans did very little until the 1980s to demand that the United States account for its general nuclear strike plan, in case of an escalation to greater and finally all-out nuclear exchanges. Just as the 1969 "Provisional Political Guidelines for the Initial Use of Nuclear Weapons by NATO" (PPGs) had concentrated on initial nuclear use by NATO, NATO strategy until the adoption of the "General Political Guidelines for the Employment of Nuclear Weapons in the Defense of NATO" (GPGs) in 1986 concentrated almost exclusively on this area and gave much less attention to questions of follow-on use or the whole series of options further up the escalation ladder. NATO's General Strike Plan (GSP), later renamed the Nuclear Operations Plan (NOP) of NATO, was not at the center of NPG deliberation, it seems, while most time and effort was devoted to pondering first and follow-on use options. In turn, the strategy of the WTO, including its nuclear use options, according to a former head of the Nuclear Activities Branch in the Supreme Head quarters of the Allied Powers in Europe (SHAPE), were "largely ignored" by NATO planners, who gave "most attention...to other matters."[3] This means that NATO's nuclear use guidelines were drawn up almost exclusively as a function of what planners from NATO member states, especially the United States, Britain, and the Federal Republic of Germany (FRG), thought reasonable and morally defensible, not as a function of the adversary's observable principles for nuclear use.

Before the establishment of the NPG in NATO, only Britain managed to obtain some consistent influence on US nuclear planning, bought clearly with Britain's own possession of nuclear weapons. Even in the late 1950s, British planners were allowed into joint targeting planning talks with the United States, and the enduring result of this are the British officers permanently stationed at the US strategic command in Omaha, Nebraska, dual-hatted as NATO's European liaison officers.[4]

America's military might, nuclear control, and unilateralism

The imbalance between the United States and its NATO Allies is of course both geographic (where only Canada shares the advantageous position of the United States) and military. North America's greater distance from potentially invading WTO forces does not need commenting upon, and it suffices to list the military advantages of the United States by pointing briefly at their size and state-of-the-art equipment (both functions of US economic might). America's nuclear arsenal, unparalleled in the world until the late 1960s, and then only by the USSR, in the last resort did and does of course give the United States an enduring ability to decide unilaterally whether, when, and how to use its strategic weapons without cooperation from, or the agreement of, its Allies. Basically, the argument can be made that the United States could discard any promises made to the Allies and proceed as it saw fit in case of a crisis or war. Indeed, there were many instances of US unilateralism.

These conform to any Realist's interpretation of the world where instances of American unilateralism, with Washington following policies or making decisions without consulting its Allies, would be seen as normal. Such instances include the US's flirtations in the mid-1970s with a "nuclear war-fighting" strategy. As US Secretary of Defense James R. Schlesinger said, "Our nuclear weapons in Europe are present for deterrence, and deterrence is made credible by a credible war-fighting capacity."[5] Schlesinger's successor, Donald Rumsfeld, later serving again in the George W. Bush administration, in the mid-1970s told the US Congress that his administration "plans its theater nuclear forces on the basis of war-fighting missions."[6] There is every sign that these ideas, elaborated in limited forms of "selective options" and "limited responses" and in quite extensive nuclear use options associated with the term "countervailing strategy" were taken very seriously by Allied governments and defense experts on both sides of the Atlantic.[7] But as we shall see, America's Allies managed to block any translation of this into NATO strategy.

Another outstanding instance of American unilateralism came on April 7, 1978, when US President Jimmy Carter took the Allies by surprise when, suddenly and without warning, announcing publicly that the US program for neutron bomb development and deployment would be postponed (indefinitely). As the enhanced radiation weapons (ERW) would have been deployed on European NATO territory for use in battle areas, European NATO governments would have needed to agree to this. There had thus been a long period of intra-NATO negotiations in which the United States had persuaded their Allied governments to "educate" their publics about the good sides of ERW, a campaign with massive resistance on the part of the peace movements which in 1977 regained their early 1960s strength over this issue. Having antagonized a vocal sector of their own electorates in this matter, and in the case of France, having decided to develop neutron bombs herself, European leaders were none too pleased to find that all their efforts had been in vain, and that in the case of the FRG, the Netherlands, Belgium, and others, governments were nonetheless left with well-organized, vocal anti-nuclear movements, which would give them much grief in the following years.

The last peak of the Cold War with its Euro-missile Crisis, 1979–85 included further remarkable instances of US unilateralism. A less prominent one was the US decision to set up a command center in High Wycombe in England as a fall-back HQ for wartime use. The better-known US initiative was President Reagan's "Star Wars" scheme, announced in 1983, at the height of the Euro-missile Crisis. Neither had been discussed in NATO in advance of US public proclamation. Then, according to Marco Carnovale, an Italian nuclear historian who later joined the International Staff at NATO, "in February 1985 a leaked secret Pentagon document revealed that, under certain circumstances, the US planned to station nuclear weapons" on the territory of some NATO members including Canada,

Spain, and Iceland "without their permission, even though it is a fundamental condition consensually agreed upon for US nuclear deployments."[8] Two years later, the Europeans had practically no influence on US President Ronald Reagan's decision jointly with Soviet leader Mikhail Gorbachev in Reykjavik to withdraw their Intermediate-Range Nuclear Forces (INF) from Europe. This decision came as a shock to many European *initiati*, as it had only been one year earlier that NATO had agreed on their GPGs, which relied especially on the cruise and *Pershing II* missiles eliminated by the INF agreement. Not even the leading US officer in Europe had been consulted in advance and was barely kept up to date with the evolution of US policy. SACEUR General Bernard Rogers remembered:

> Those of us who have been assigned the mission of making our contribution to the deterrence of war within NATO have not been consulted on the intermediate-range nuclear force proposals... What happens is that when the United States negotiators come to brief – quote "consult" – the allies on its proposals, I have not been invited to those meetings, although I've had a representative who sits in. He informs me of what the proposal is or, in my US role, I may have been able to receive from the United States at my SHAPE headquarters the national message traffic so that I could read what the political authorities were briefed on by the negotiators. But sometimes that consultation was held the day before the proposal was tabled in Geneva. Once we caught up with the proposals, I would then exercise the initiative to make my position [known] by messages to the United States when I felt it was necessary.[9]

General Rogers articulated the European governments' opinion that after INF NATO was worse off strategically than it had been in 1979 before the Montebello decision and the deployment of INF.[10] Again, this is a blatant example of US unilateralism, but fortunately one which paid off in view of Gorbachev's readiness to make all sacrifices necessary to ban the specter of the Third World War. Had the United States tried to consult its Allied governments in advance, most of them would have argued against the INF Treaty.

Overall, however, the United States soon learnt that in its (and its Allies') pursuit of deterrence, Alliance solidarity counted for very much, as did the support for the Alliance among the governments and indeed populations of the member states. American unilateralism only served to undermine this solidarity and was thus repeatedly recognized by US leaders as not being fully in the United States's interest. This is borne out by the very conciliatory stance the United States chose to adopt, time and again, *vis-à-vis* the wishes of its Allies, singly and collectively, as we discuss later.

The deployment of US nuclear forces in other NATO countries

Due to the US's nuclear monopoly within NATO – or after the achievement of nuclear power status by Britain and France, its nuclear preponderance – for the entire Cold War and after, nuclear warheads available to NATO countries, deployed in countries other than their owners', have always been US property, and in US custody.[11]

Nevertheless, the United States had to tolerate an impressive degree of anti-hegemonic behavior on the part of its Allies. Very early on, Norway and Denmark with their recent experience of German occupation decided not to allow the United States to station any nuclear weapons on their territory. Even before the signing of the Washington Treaty, on February 1, 1949, the Norwegian government decided that it would not allow foreign forces to be stationed in Norway as long as Norway was not under attack.[12] The Soviet Union had put pressure on the Norwegian government not to sign the North Atlantic Treaty; Oslo sought to appease Moscow by promising not to allow the establishment of foreign military bases unless it felt aggression was being threatened.[13] At least (and unlike Sweden which anyway was outside the Alliance), the Norwegian government was prepared to engage in formal negotiations about how foreign forces would be deployed to Norway in case of war, and, in 1952, at the Lisbon North Atlantic Council (NAC) meeting, Norwegian Foreign Minister Halvard M. Lange conceded that his government was prepared to host "visiting airplanes for short periods of time."[14] But in the summer of 1957, after the United States had decided to offer its European Allies nuclear weapons for deployment on their soil, the Norwegian Labor Party, then in government, decided at a party convention that no nuclear weapons should be allowed on Norwegian territory in peacetime. The Norwegian Prime Minister, Einar Gerhardsen, announced this principle as official policy of his government at the NAC summit meeting in December 1957. Even peacetime preparations for the use of Norwegian F-104 Starfighter aircraft in wartime in a nuclear role were ruled out in 1963.[15] The Americans (and Norway's other allies) were forced to acquiesce in this Norwegian posture, even though the defense of Scandinavian territory with tactical nuclear weapons made much more sense in view of the low density of population of parts of this region than, for example, for the densely populated Central Front. (This practical fact was recognized by the Swedes who until the early 1960s pursued a nuclear option of their own for this very reason.)[16]

Government and public attitudes were similar in Denmark, which, in the words of Nikolaj Petersen, "joined the pact somewhat halfheartedly."[17] In 1953, the Danes elected a new Social Democratic Government, which, following the Norwegian example, decided not to allow the peacetime stationing of foreign forces on its soil.[18] In December 1957, Copenhagen at the same time as Oslo proclaimed that Denmark would not allow nuclear weapons on their soil in peacetime. In 1964, the Norwegian Prime Minister Gerhardsen once again repeated its 1949 base declaration: "We do not want foreign forces and... atomic weapons on our soil so long as we are not attacked or threatened by attack." Nor do Iceland or Portugal host nuclear weapons, Iceland having demanded the withdrawal of all US military personnel from its soil in 1956, but having relinquished this demand shortly thereafter.[19] France forced a withdrawal of all foreign forces (i.e. mainly Americans) from its territory in 1966, with effect from January 1, 1967, all objections proving vain. Spain, which of course joined NATO only in 1982, does not allow nuclear weapons on its territory, although the United States have used its ports with nuclear-armed vessels since before this date on the basis of special bilateral arrangements.[20]

Whereas these countries refused to let American nuclear weapons into their borders, and whereas NATO countries are not obliged to grant American air forces overflight rights, these constraints are largely offset by the early decisions of Britain and Canada (during the Second World War), the FRG, the Netherlands, Belgium, Italy, Greece, and Turkey (Greece revoking this permission in the 1970s) to allow US forces and nuclear weapons on their territory. On balance, however, it is clear that as members of NATO state governments do not forego the option of modifying their defense relationship with the United States, and even when the threat of WTO invasion was looming large the United States could not use force to change its Allies' respective stances. Although it did have available diplomatic and economic tools, including in particular the leverage of arms supplies, transfer of technology, and the withholding or sharing of intelligence, it did not manage to impose a change of policy on Norway, Denmark, or Greece.

Those NATO member states that agreed to host US nuclear weapons, or on whose territory US nuclear weapons might have been used, exercised a growing influence in the Alliance. They repeatedly managed to persuade the United States to revise its operational doctrines and nuclear deployment plans. Most notably, the Germans gradually persuaded the Americans and the British to move their imaginary line of defense ever further east in Central Europe, from early plans for a defense of the Rhine (which would have left parts of the Netherlands and almost all of the FRG undefended) to a defense in the depth of the territory of the FRG under the motto of "forward defense" and then "defense at the front" (*vorne*).[21] The Germans also persuaded the British and other allies to accept the idea of early nuclear use by NATO, including even initial use, being targeted deep into WTO territory, possibly even into Soviet territory. The FRG's nuclear allies initially much preferred planning for nuclear use on FRG territory. French short-range nuclear forces notoriously could only reach West German (or Belgian) territory, if fired from French soil. This repeatedly led to strong German government protest and to a keen interest in changing French planning. But it was only with the end of the Cold War that German protests resulted in French relinquishment of these short-range weapons.

The US veto over the use of weapons earmarked for allied use in wartime

The US veto over the use of those of its weapons that were made available to the Alliance from the mid-1950s had in principle existed from the beginning. It is now generally accepted that during the second Eisenhower administration, the American control or oversight of its Europe-based nuclear weapons earmarked for allied use in wartime was fairly flimsy. In November 1957, the French government was aware that US custody of such weapons was intentionally nominal, designed to satisfy the requirements of US legislation, but also to give the Allies the assurance that they could lay their hands on these weapons *and use them* in times of crisis and war.[22] It is not clear, however, that the Allied governments were always aware of the implications of this.

In 1965 NATO adopted an arrangement whereby American-owned nuclear weapons in nine NATO countries were placed on Quick Reaction Alert (QRA), meaning that they would be ready for launching at 10–15 minutes' notice. The countries concerned were Canada, the United Kingdom, Belgium, the Netherlands, France, the FRG, Italy, Greece, and Turkey, with Canada and France withdrawing from the arrangement again. As some of these QRA weapons were air-launched, only some armed US guards would stand between non-American Allied airmen and their ability to fire or drop these American nuclear weapons from non-American Allied aircraft.[23] This does not mean, however, that they could have achieved a nuclear detonation of these weapons.

From about the same time that QRA was adopted, the release mechanisms for such US nuclear weapons made available to Allies were carefully controlled by the United States, and effectively constituted a US veto over their use. Permissive Action Links (PALs), code-based devices that allowed the United States to enable or disable nuclear weapons, were adopted under the Kennedy administration to prevent the seizure and unauthorized use by other NATO members (or anybody else) of American weapons, reflecting the concern of Kennedy's advisers about accidental or unauthorized use.[24] This was part of a new policy of extreme dislike of nuclear sharing, associated mainly with Robert McNamara and his advisers, which emphasized the need for central control so as to improve crisis stability. Ideally, McNamara wanted America's Allies to get out of the nuclear business altogether, which is why he was so displeased with the outcome of the Nassau meeting of December 1962 between Kennedy and the British Prime Minister Harold Macmillan, which ensured the survival and modernization of the British nuclear forces for another generation.

US custody of American nuclear bombs and warheads on Allied territory, prior to matching warheads with missiles or deploying missiles and bombs on Allied aircraft, was also stepped up considerably in the 1960s and 1970s. In Britain, for example, US air bases and the depots for air-launched nuclear weapons were and are very strongly guarded, eliciting angry responses (and long "sieges") not only from anti-nuclear protesters but also from ardent defenders of British sovereignty against foreign encroachments.[25] The same was true for Spain in the years immediately after Franco's death, and even in the early 1980s, Spanish anti-Americanism and anti-NATO protests focused on American air bases in Spain, the permissions for the establishment of which having been granted by Franco to Truman early in the Cold War, when both were united in their anti-communist crusading fervor.[26]

The US veto over the use of US nuclear weapons earmarked for use by the Allies in times of war was thus one of the longstanding grievances of certain European members of NATO, namely those with common frontiers with the WTO, from Turkey on the Southern flank to Norway in the North. Highlighted by the lack of US nuclear support for European policies in France's defeat in Indochina in 1954 and Britain's and France's checkmate in Suez in 1956 and by McNamara's attempt to restore the American nuclear monopoly within NATO, Europeans and Turks from time to time worried about excessive US *reluctance* to use nuclear weapons. Britons since the Second World War, but also Frenchmen, Italians and West Germans after the Suez Crisis in late 1956 were very keen on nuclear weapons independent from a US veto. London and Paris procured their own respective nuclear arsenals, whereas Italians and Germans attempted (but failed) to realize their joint project for a European nuclear force free from an American veto.[27]

Perceptions of the US President's unilateral control over American-produced nuclear weapons depended on the rhetorical posture of US governments, which fluctuated wildly throughout the Cold War period. On occasion, the extent of US control of nuclear release in NATO was welcomed in Europe. A perception that the United States would err on the side of caution comforted those who were afraid of unnecessary or premature use of nuclear weapons in a crisis or conflict. On other occasions, a perception of US nuclear trigger-willingness if not trigger-happiness was seen as enhancing deterrence. Any US administration, without the need for internal government or cabinet consultation on nuclear use due to the President's exceptional powers in such an emergency, could act much faster, unilaterally, to release and use its own nuclear weapons than NATO could collectively, or than the co-owners of any European nuclear force might have. In some Cold War contexts this could be reassuring to the Europeans and Turks, as it might mean a stronger deterrence posture. In other contexts, the perceived US nuclear trigger-happiness was seen as very dangerous in Europe, such as during the Quemoy–Matsu Crisis in 1957, when it was feared that an incident in the Far East might through an overly bellicose American reaction result in a more general nuclear conflagration that might not be contained in that part of the world.[28]

American secretiveness challenged

The imbalance between the United States and its Allies was aggravated by American secretiveness. During the first decade-and-a-half of the Cold War, US information sharing with Allies was fettered by the McMahon Act prohibiting the sharing of nuclear know-how with any other country (amended in 1958 to accommodate Britain or, more generally any Allied country that had by itself achieved an advanced stage of nuclear expertise). Consequently, Americans were very chary of telling their Allies anything about the workings of American arms, of their targeting plans, or even the location of American nuclear weapons. Famously, this humiliated and angered de Gaulle when he returned to power in 1958 and significantly contributed to his incremental policy culminating in his 1966 decision to turn all foreign (and especially US) forces out of France.[29] Less famously, this worried the Canadians even in 1950, when at the outbreak of the Korean War they had to face up to the crucial importance of Goose Bay, Labrador, to the delivery of US nuclear weapons to strategic targets in the Soviet Union, should the war escalate to involve America and the USSR directly. While they were happy for the United States to retaliate instantly to any "major outright Soviet attack against continental North America" with nuclear weapons, including the use of air bases in Canada, the Canadians strongly preferred to be given the right to veto the storage of US nuclear weapons on their territory, and to be consulted, not merely informed, about the delivery of nuclear weapons from Canadian territory in case of a less extreme conflict scenario.[30] The West Germans were by far in the worst position. While their political and military leaders became aware through joint NATO exercises that the Americans (and the British) intended to use nuclear weapons against WTO invaders on German (including West German!) soil, the extent of the destruction this would have entailed in Germany only became clear by and by. The famous *Carte Blanche* exercise of June 1955 and the *Lion Noir* exercise of 1957, both of which were reported upon in the press, included millions of putative deaths among German civilians in their scenarios, which occasioned an uproar in the FRG.[31]

At the beginning of 1962, the West Germans did not even know how many US nuclear weapons were deployed on their soil.[32] Around the time of the Cuban Missile Crisis of the end of 1962, Atomic Demolition Munitions (ADMs) were furnished to US forces in Europe, especially along the Central Front. Still the Germans were not told what the American plans were for these ground-burst nuclear weapons with their extremely high development of nuclear fall-out (and consequently, contamination of all local human and animal life as well as vegetation for years to come).

In 1964–65, West German and American military planners jointly conducted a study on how the Americans might use ADM in Germany. Much to the horror of their German colleagues, the US planners (at least for the purpose of this study) deployed ADM into a depth of up to 200 km within the FRG. They wanted to distribute ADM in all three zones, very often in built-up areas. Their intention was to detonate many of them in West German villages and even towns, to create mounds of debris, destroy harbors, railway junctions, and centers of supply and energy production. Apart from this very different choice of target, in itself completely unacceptable to the Germans, the American proposals included yields of up to 45 kilotons TNT. The consequence would thus, again, have been several millions of civilian deaths within the FRG.[33]

In 1963, the West German Ministry of Defense suggested that all NATO nuclear forces should be controlled by a "NATO Nuclear Executive Committee," attached to the NAC, of which the FRG should of course be a member – one of the many European initiatives of the early 1960s which culminated in the American concession that a NATO NPG had to be formed in 1967. Like the Canadians and the British before them, the Germans also pressed for a veto on American use of nuclear forces *from* their territory, but the West Germans were singularly desperate in their attempts to acquire a veto power against use *on* German territory, which Bonn took to include also the German Democratic Republic (GDR).[34] Understandably, the West Germans, who often had relatives in East Germany, felt uneasy when confronted with US or Allied plans for the nuclear bombing of the GDR.[35]

Between 1949 and 1967, then, America's Allies fought a hard but ultimately relatively successful campaign of persuasion to induce the Americans into sharing more information about the location of American nuclear weapons, and American plans for their use. From 1967 and the constitution of the NPG onwards, America's Allies compelled US administrations to air their principles governing nuclear use against the WTO in NATO committees and to accept Allied criticism of these plans. Indeed, they managed to prevail upon the Americans to agree to the joint formulation of such principles that were to govern nuclear use in the context of NATO. America's Allies thus managed to gain a substantial influence on the quality and the quantity of US nuclear forces in Europe and were not forced to accept the preferences of the "hegemon," in all their permutations.

Whereas WTO procurement policy was decided unilaterally in the Soviet Union, the American arsenal assigned to NATO was increasingly configured according to European as well as American wishes. Still, there are some points of comparison. Hope Harrison has shown very persuasively that from 1955 to 1961, the relative strength of the GDR's government within the WTO had commonalties with that of the FRG's in NATO. This waned for a while when the building of the Berlin Wall and the fortifications along the inner-German border in 1961 put a stop to migration from East to West Germany and thus to the argument that sacrifices had to be made by Moscow and the WTO to appease the East German population.[36] But Vojtech Mastny argues that East Germany once again wielded substantial influence under Honecker from 1971.[37]

The degree of secrecy about nuclear weapons-related issues (including strategic, operational level, and tactical planning) which the Soviet Union was able to uphold concerning vis-à-vis its allies right until the last decade of the Cold War differs greatly from that in NATO. The contrast between NATO after 1967 and the WTO could not be greater. The leadership of the GDR was merely informed when Soviet forces first deployed nuclear weapons to be fired by special forces of the East German National People's Army (*Nationale Volksarmee*, NVA). Officers of the WTO countries who were invited to study at Soviet military academies were barred from sitting in on lectures and other classes dealing with overall strategy, as opposed to operational art and tactics. In the 1980s, staff exercises involving the "played" use of nuclear weapons were conducted on two levels: on the lower level, many of the highest-ranking officers of countries allied to the USSR never knew that nuclear use was part of the upper level scenario, to the point where a NVA general of the GDR claimed at a conference in March 2003 that WTO strategy did not provide for any nuclear use.[38] In my article on WTO doctrine of 1993, I wrote that the exercise *Stabstraining-89* did not contain a nuclear element, which all the documents on it then available at the interim archive in Potsdam seemed to suggest.[39] Shortly thereafter, however, I found a set of documents in Russian relating to the same exercise, obviously furnished to "players" on a higher level, which contained information on the "played" nuclear bombing of 76 targets in northern Germany with nuclear weapons of 10–500 kiloton yields.[40] A further example of WTO secretiveness is that the member states compiled annual diaries of their militaries' activities, which were treated as top secret – to the extent that one of several Vice-Ministers of Defense of the GDR, General Joachim Goldbach, and several of his lower-ranking fellow generals, asked about these documents (which intriguingly carried the title "War Diary" in 1979 and 1983) in an oral history session conducted by myself in 1995, did not even know that they existed.[41]

Expertise

Another structural inequality in the negotiation process leading to the adoption of common strategies, policies, and other decisions arises from the varying degrees of expertise in the respective member states' governments. The United States largely took the lead on many technical issues, providing its allies with information that the US could select with a view to supporting its own policies. As Scilla McLean noted toward the end of the Cold War, "Many European ministers lack interest, expertise, skilled back-up or the intellectual resources required to challenge American input into N[uclear] P[lanning] G[roup] deliberations."[42] Throughout the Cold War, Britain as a nuclear power did have engineers and other scientists who were experts on most of the technical matters that needed to be resolved in the context of formulating and revising NATO's nuclear posture. West Germany, with a range of generously funded think tanks, just about kept abreast with the major issues. (This did not mean, however, that the intimate acquaintance with American strategic and technical jargon helped German defense experts explain the rationale behind weapons and doctrine to their own politicians, let alone their own public. The more German defense specialists delighted in their mastery of American and NATO acronyms and jargon, the less they could make themselves understood in non-expert circles or persuade the anti-nuclear campaigners of the rationality of their stance.) The other countries represented in the NPG had a more difficult stance with regard to both expertise and input into doctrinal discussions.

A late example of the American monopoly in expertise, but also of information sharing, is the working of the High Level Group in NATO, 1977–79. At the NATO summit in May 1977 in London, President Carter initiated a Long Term Defense Program. Ten different working groups were assigned to drafting it, one of which being charged with looking at nuclear issues, and this Task Force 10, due to the high ranks of the government representatives charged with this study, became known as High Level Group (HLG). The main body of information on the options available by way of American nuclear technology was provided to the HLG by a US administration inter-departmental group, referred to as PRM-38, created under the US President's mandate in June 1978, which presented its set of "military options" papers to the HLG in October 1978.[43] The land-based option was agreed upon by the HLG and subsequently by the NPG because, thus the argument ran, "land based systems could be targeted with greater accuracy than sea-based systems, and hence could be configured to carry warheads with a lower yield, and by being based on countries' soil" symbolized their direct involvement in NATO's deterrence posture.[44] In September 1979, the HLG reported to the NPG, based on 2 of the 4 options that PRM-38 had outlined, both involving the deployment of *Tomahawk* cruise missiles and *Pershing II* ballistic missiles as

"Theatre Nuclear Forces" (TNF, in American parlance) in Europe.[45] Interestingly, from the point of view of democratic Alliance decision-making, as we shall see, the HLG's report did not recommend the option most favored by the Americans at the outset of these negotiations. Such an outcome would have been inconceivable in the WTO.

NATO's command structure

Another long-term structural factor with which the Europeans had to contend was that the Supreme Allied Commander of the European theater of NATO, SACEUR, and also of course the Supreme Allied Commander of the Atlantic theater, SACLANT, were always Americans. Both were "dual-hatted," that is, simultaneously held the posts of American commanders-in-chief of these two theaters, respectively CINCEUR and CINCLANT. *De facto*, successive SACEURs tended to become sympathetic very soon to European concerns within the Alliance. SACEUR's headquarters, SHAPE, was originally installed in Fontainebleau near Paris, and after de Gaulle "expelled" NATO forces from France in 1967, they were moved to Mons in Belgium. A former chief of the West German armed forces commented: "SACEURs come as Americans but become Europeans; they look at European maps, work with European soldiers, meet European policy-makers and thus understand and often embrace European causes."[46] This was especially true for General Lauris Norstad (SACEUR 1956–63), who, appointed by US President Eisenhower, clashed fundamentally with President Kennedy and his advisers, and for General Bernard Rogers (SACEUR 1979–87).

Below the level of SACEUR, however, top command posts are shared throughout the Alliance with a view to the military and geographic weight of member states. The actual structure has changed a few times, but important command posts are held by British, (West) German, Italian and, until 1967, French officers.

Admittedly, all nuclear weapons in NATO were always under a chain of command of officers from the state that had supplied them (United States and United Kingdom respectively), with additional input made possible for some weapons from the governments of the countries in which they were deployed through the "dual key" structure (i.e. both owner and host could veto their use). But with an overwhelming preponderance of nuclear weapons being owned by the United States, the strange situation arose in the late 1950s, with the deployment of battlefield nuclear weapons (very short range missiles and ADM) that it might very well not be possible for commanders to consult SACEUR or even Washington about permission to use them, let alone for consultation to pass through NATO committees. Therefore, when Eisenhower was in his second term, and Norstad was SACEUR, the US had a policy of pre-delegating the authority to use battlefield nuclear weapons to local commanders, especially on the Central Front. Much secrecy has shrouded this matter, but the historians Marc Trachtenberg and Klaus Maier with their relentless archival spadework have unearthed conclusive documents that pre-delegation was indeed standard US policy until the advent of the Kennedy administration in 1961.[47]

The period from the second Berlin Crisis and the Cuban Missile Crisis, 1957–62 is that for which pre-delegation of the authority to order the use of certain nuclear weapons existed, at least among American commanders, within NATO.[48] Many tactical nuclear weapons deployed with NATO forces during this period, including ADM, were "forward-based," that is deployed near NATO borders with the WTO's member states, and were likely to be overrun quickly if they were not used early on in a confrontation, leading to a "use them or lose them" logic.

Oddly enough, in the particular circumstances of the time, this worked both in favor of Americans and Europeans. Since 1949, the threat scenario on which NATO strategy was based was one in which the WTO would attack NATO massively, at least on the Central Front (Germany) or even on all fronts (also Norway, Denmark, Greece, Turkey, and Italy through Yugoslavia). Western planners expected that the WTO would attack with all the forces at its disposition, probably including nuclear weapons. In such circumstances, it made sense for the United States (and through it, NATO) to have a massive response, both tactically on the battlefield and strategically, including a massive nuclear response posture. Should Moscow be planning for such an all-out war, it would be best to let Moscow know that the most destructive response possible would await them.

But besides an all-out attack scenario, the events of 1956 had forced Western government defense planners to take on board further planning scenarios, which generically fell under the category of a more limited conflict along a NATO border with the WTO. The strategy adopted by NATO in 1957, MC 14/2 or "Differentiated Responses,"[49] also included a local defense scenario, without nuclear weapons, provided Soviet forces were not directly involved in the border clash.

Gradually, between 1952 and 1961, Western government defense planners very slowly came to believe that no rational leadership in Moscow could willingly plan for an all-out war, if they knew what NATO's reaction would be. The question this raised was, how could a war break out? The defense planners and their intelligence and diplomatic advisers gradually agreed that this could only be by accident or miscalculation. By miscalculation, if Moscow thought that either, its war aim was so limited that the West would not risk all-out war to reverse a minor *fait accompli*, or by accident, in which case the West should try to contain the damage by negotiating for a quick armistice with Moscow, presumed, in case of an accident, also to be adverse to further war. In other words, NATO had to be prepared not only for the all-out scenario, which was seen as decreasing in likelihood, but also for smaller clashes, for which it had to come up with proportionately smaller, and above all not self-deterring, solutions. If a more limited scenario seemed more likely, it made less sense to enable local commanders to use nuclear weapons, thereby escalating the conflict, when a quick armistice might be a real alternative. Both European and American governments were thus keen, from about 1961 onwards, to avoid unnecessarily escalatory nuclear use. But among the defense planners of the FRG, there was also the fear that reluctance to use nuclear weapons would result in a destructive conventional war on Germany soil, rather than in a restoration of deterrence through early battlefield nuclear use.[50] In 1963, in the face of Washington's centralizing measures and keenness to raise the nuclear threshold, the West German Ministry of Defense proposed that certain scenarios should be defined in which a NATO Committee or even SACEUR could unilaterally decide on nuclear release and use.[51] This was eventually translated into NATO operational arrangements: henceforth any NATO member or any major NATO commander (SACEUR, SACLANT, CINCHAN – that is Commander-in-Chief Channel, until the abolition of this command in the late 1990s, always a Briton) could request permission to use nuclear weapons. Once this permission was granted by NATO (the North Atlantic Council or under it the Defense Planning Committee (DPC)) or unilaterally by the United States or the United Kingdom, it was up to the military commander to decide on the timing and the targets, unless he were given further instruction by the political authority that had approved the release.

To parallel US pre-delegation of the authority to use nuclear weapons, historians have unearthed evidence that in the context of the Cuban Missile Crisis, the Soviet government delegated a similar authority to commanders of the Group of Soviet Forces in Cuba:

> In a situation of an enemy landing on the island of Cuba and of the concentration of enemy ships with amphibious forces off the coast of Cuba in its territorial waters, when the destruction of the enemy is delaying [further actions] and there is no possibility of receiving instructions from the USSR Ministry of Defense, you are permitted to make your own decision and to use the nuclear means of the "Luna," IL-28 or FKR-1 as instruments of local warfare for the destruction of the enemy on land and along the coast in order to achieve the complete destruction of the invaders on the Cuban territory and to defend the Republic of Cuba.[52]

Here it was clearly technology that dictated a policy on both sides of the Cold War divide and not culture: equally, both the United States and the USSR later pulled back from this risk-prone policy. On the NATO side, it was ensured that all nuclear use that could be requested by the major military commanders of NATO still had to be approved by the North Atlantic Council and the government of the owner state of the weapons concerned, (or at any rate the latter). On the side of the USSR, all nuclear release was to be authorized only by the top Soviet leadership.

Structures and culture of negotiations

NATO's decision-making processes, based on inter-governmental negotiations conducted on behalf of governments in the Headquarters of NATO in Paris until 1966, and since 1967 at Evère in Brussels, are also influenced by some constants. One is the enduring politico-military preponderance of the United States, which simply gives its representatives' voices more weight than to those of its Allies. This weight is aggravated strongly, however, by a factor which is not at first self-evident. And this is the acrimonious decision-making process in Washington, carried out through a very public debate and the taking of sides by major players on some important subjects, among which military ones are particularly prominent. As a result, policies agreed upon within US administrations, or even between the respective administration and Congress, tend to be finely honed compromises, to which American presidents are then publicly committed. This gives US government representatives in NATO a much smaller room for maneuver and scope for negotiations than just about all their colleagues. It makes US representatives come across as intransigent negotiators, even as errand-boys, who have no power to make concessions and who slavishly follow instructions from Washington line-by-line to insist on specific wordings of NATO agreements and policy statements.

The largely "closed," that is, very secretive and non-public, decision-making process in Britain is the extreme opposite.[53] This usually allows British representatives to put forward many alternative solutions that aim to find compromises between the rigid American instructions and the sometimes also restricted policy options of some of the European Allies, notably those with coalition governments or great public sensitivity to nuclear or other defense issues. As a result, NATO decisions, doctrines, and policies tend to be (often British-brokered) compromises between diverging aims and concerns on the respective sides of the Atlantic, negotiated in committee sessions most similar in style and tone to the committee system by which Britain is governed. This gives NATO doctrines, policies, and public statements a distinctively British flavor, over and beyond the obvious factor that they are written in the Queen's English, with a disproportionately high number of Britons working in NATO's International Staff at the Headquarters of NATO. NATO doctrines, strategies, and policies are also permeated by the deliberate ambiguity (deliberate, at the time of reaching the agreement on the language) that is typical for political compromises, and that is often well-nigh impossible for officials and military alike to implement. As the historian and specialist on national cultures, George Schöpflin, has commented so aptly about this central feature of British political culture, the pragmatic compromise, it is reached with that central feature of British thinking, common sense. Common sense persuades British politicians and officials to "concentrate on what is immediately in front of us" to reach a pragmatic agreement. Pragmatism is built on agreement to disagree but to concentrate on what can be agreed upon. A pragmatic agreement is therefore usually a compromise in which fundamental disagreements, which of course remain just below the surface, are papered over by the deliberate ambiguity of compromise language. The problem with this is that the resulting policies, strategies, and doctrines are nothing if not ambiguous, which only rarely can be turned into a strength.[54] As Ivo Daalder, the leading academic expert on the nature and practice of NATO Strategy document MC 14/3 (which I call "Flexible Escalation," as it was referred to as "Flexible Response" like its predecessor MC 14/2), has concluded, ambiguity is its essence.[55] Marco Carnovale has rightly concluded in his study on the control of

NATO nuclear forces:

> To keep the requirements ambiguous may help to conceal interallied divergences in peacetime, but it could hardly smooth collective decision-making and contribute to the common security against an enemy in an emergency. That this has long been accepted practice does not justify its perpetuation.[56]

There is another element in the patterns of NATO negotiations, which can be seen as either justifiable in terms of democratic–demographic representation or as undemocratic in terms of the representation of states members. This is NATO's "Quad" – the informal meeting of the United States, British, French, and (formerly West) German ambassadors to agree on key issues in advance of putting them before the NAC as a whole. In January 1979, the Quad even had a summit meeting in Guadeloupe on the question of the deployment of the Euromissiles, and French President Valery Giscard d'Estaing as host, US President Jimmy Carter, British Prime Minister James Callaghan, and FRG Chancellor Helmut Schmidt agreed on this matter, followed only in November 1979 by a consensus decision in the NPG.

All this contrasts very much with the inner workings of the WTO. Initially, the WTO took the form of bilateral relationships between Moscow and the other member states. As Vojtech Mastny has shown, it was only in the 1960s that the WTO adopted something of a *collective* defense alliance character, and little by little, over the following two decades, the periodic meetings of defense ministers, foreign ministers, chiefs-of-staff, and heads of state and government turned from very formal meetings in which each representative read out a prepared paper into meetings allowing for questions and answers.

Only the respective roles assumed by France and Rumania in NATO and the WTO are very comparable. The protocols of the meetings of heads of government and state, of defense chiefs, defense ministers, and foreign ministers, of the WTO, show many instances of Rumanian opposition to Soviet policies, which seem to have been met with stony silence most of the time. Nevertheless, Ceauşescu managed to claim for his country a large set of privileges, a policy that was easier to follow in the absence of Soviet forces on Rumanian soil. Cooperation with the rest of the WTO in joint exercises, joint planning, joint air defenses were thus invariably a matter for unilateral, and fairly free decision-making for Bucharest, much as it was for France in NATO.

Peacetime consultation on strategy

Notwithstanding the overpowering military weight of the United States among Alliance members and its intransigent negotiation style within NATO, there are many instances in which members other than the United States have had a decisive influence on decisions and doctrines adopted. The most prominent members in this respect, not surprisingly, are the United Kingdom and the FRG. Britain successfully initiated strategy reviews in 1952–53 and 1956, even though the product of the 1956–57 review, MC14/2 (which I call "Differentiated Responses" as confusingly, it was also known at the time as "Flexible Response," like its successor MC 14/3 – see earlier), was not to Britain's liking. British government strategists' views prevailed in the negotiations leading to the November 1979 Euro-missile deployment decision: here it was the British, led by HLG member Michael Quinlan, who insisted on a land-based option, while US Defense Secretary Harold Brown and Federal Chancellor Helmut Schmidt would have preferred sea-based options.[57]

As far as West Germany is concerned, in the words of historian Saki Dockrill, "Even between 1949 and 1955, when West Germany was not yet a member of NATO, the Bonn Republic was already in a position to influence NATO's rearmament policy with its potential military and industrial power." Once a member, the FRG, because of its key strategic position and its manpower contribution, began to play a role of considerable importance within the Alliance.[58] The tensions between US unilateralism and Alliance dynamics were highlighted immediately. When the FRG first joined NATO in 1955, its government was seriously wrong-footed. Its government had been encouraged to join NATO and had since 1952 been encouraged to build up a large army on the assumption that this tallied with NATO's strategic posture (which had been the case in 1952). West German Chancellor Konrad Adenauer and his government had not been kept abreast of more recent developments in strategic thinking within the Alliance (essentially, the rationale of MC-48, "Massive Retaliation") and with thinking within the US administration. Both of these had since 1953 been moving towards a reduction of US manpower and an increasing reliance on battlefield nuclear weapons to offset the recently founded WTO's unabated strengths in conventional (including human) forces. US intentions to reduce personnel in Europe, a plan championed above all by US Admiral Arthur Radford, were leaked to the press in July 1956 (a typical feature of democracy), and triggered a furore in the West German public debate about the armament of the FRG. What point was it to rearm Germans, if the Americans were reducing their forces? Did this mean that the German soldiers would be used as canon-fodder in the nuclear battles between the United States and the Soviet Union? The Adenauer government slowed down the build-up of the Bundeswehr, and subsequent Bonn governments proved determined not to be caught out again, and to have their say in NATO strategy. From this point onwards, the weight gained by the FRG, as the most exposed state on the Alliance's Central Front, never ceased to be felt.

Joint pressure from Bonn, London, Rome, and other Alliance capitals forced the Americans to agree to the establishment of a committee within NATO in which the United States would explain their nuclear targeting and use rationale and open themselves wide to Allied criticism. Indeed, the US agreed to binding joint guidelines on nuclear use. In 1969, after years of debate, NATO Allies minus France agreed with the PPGs that initial nuclear use should have a political signaling function, and should not be designed to assure a battlefield victory for NATO.[59]

This was a victory for European preferences, and was reiterated in the GPGs of 1986. In the interim period, successive US administrations repeatedly tried but were not able to get their war-fighting strategy preferences accepted by NATO against European opposition. The European members consistently insisted that initial and follow-on nuclear use by NATO must be primarily a political signal, and that no effort should be made to defeat WTO forces in nuclear war, as the collateral damages to Europe resulting from this were deemed unacceptable. In 1973 the NATO NPG agreed that:

> follow-on use of TNF [theatre nuclear forces] by NATO in the form of selective strikes against Warsaw Pact forces could result in a short-term military advantage in the area concerned, and quite possibly a pause in the conflict; but if the Warsaw Pact responded with a nuclear attack on a similar (or greater) scale, neither side would gain a significant advantage as a direct consequence of using nuclear weapons (save in some special circumstances such as using them to halt an amphibious landing).[60]

By about 1973, due above all to German pleading, it would seem, NATO relinquished the option of carrying out ground bursts on NATO territory, which among other things meant the elimination of ADM, which happened in the early 1980s. The maximum yield of weapons that might be used *above* NATO territory was limited to 10 kilotons.[61]

The Allies had no problems agreeing in their Nuclear Operations Plan that all NATO nuclear targets should be military, "and that their selection" should be "based on the twin criteria of achieving essential military objectives while minimizing civilian casualties and collateral damage," in the words of SACEUR General Andrew Goodpaster in 1974.[62] The objective of minimizing civilian casualties was clearly a bow in the direction of the anti-nuclear movements in Europe, who since the mid-1950s had not merely drawn their strength from fear of nuclear war, but also from retrospective revulsion against the two only nuclear bombings in history, against the hapless populations of Hiroshima and Nagasaki. The Europeans at the same time clung to the commitment made by the NATO members in the PPGs to regard initial and even follow-on nuclear use by NATO as serving political signaling aims, not aiming at military victory.

The GPGs thus reflected West German preferences over America's preference for conventional war or war-fighting tactical nuclear use with its twin political deterrent and military operational aim of forestalling enemy advances on the battlefield. SACEUR General Galvin commented retrospectively:

> What those guidelines also show is a history in which there is a movement away from thinking of nuclear weapons as something that would be used in war fighting and more toward nuclear weapons as a political statement, which would provide for deterrence ... And with the longer range weapons you can send a political message to the people who sent those forces in the first place.[63]

Historian Thomas Halverson concluded, "GPG guidance included parameters for SACEUR to take into account when planning his nuclear strikes. These clearly derived from Bonn's political considerations, like collateral damage and civilian casualty constraints."[64]

A similar degree of influence by one of the Soviet Union's allies on WTO procedures can perhaps only be found in the Czechoslovak request of 1983, which resulted in the WTO's first training for actual defense (before starting the counteroffensive) in the exercise SHIELD 84![65]

Crisis and wartime consultation

According to Marco Carnovale, "the first formal arrangements for nuclear consultation" not only between the United States, Britain, and Canada but also with other NATO members were approved by the North Atlantic Council on March 2, 1955.[66] This was far from satisfactory for America's Allies. The "three wise men" (the Canadian Lester Pearson, the Italian Gaetano Martino, and the Norwegian Halvard Lange) who were asked to comment on the persistent problems in the following year could thus report that:

> Consultation within an Alliance means much more than exchange of information, though that is necessary. It means more than letting the NATO Council know about national decisions that have already been taken, or trying to enlist support for those decisions. It means the discussion of problems collectively, in the early stages of policy formation, and before national positions become fixed. At best, this will result in collective decisions on matters of common interest affecting the Alliance. At the least, it will ensure that no action is taken by one member without a knowledge of the views of the others.[67]

At the Athens NAC meeting in May 1962, the famous Athens Guidelines were laid down, which have been summed up as a commitment to mutual consultation on nuclear use, "time and circumstances permitting." In case of a Soviet nuclear attack against the NATO area, it was agreed in the PPGs that little time would probably be left for consultations. In case of a full-scale Soviet conventional attack, it was hoped that time would be left for consultation before NATO would resort to a nuclear response. If the Soviet attack was neither nuclear nor drew on overwhelming conventional forces, NATO members committed themselves to consulting in the NAC before resorting to the use of nuclear weapons.[68]

In the PPGs it was agreed that if NATO were attacked, short of the attack being an all-out nuclear one, negotiations about the release and use of nuclear forces would take place both in the North Atlantic Council (delegated to its DPC) and bilaterally between the US government and the government from whose or on whose territory nuclear weapons would be used.[69] This and all subsequent set of guidelines on the use of nuclear weapons by NATO acknowledged, however, that ultimately, the decision on the use of nuclear weapons lies with its owners, even though the United States and the United Kingdom would try hard, as far as time and circumstances permitted, to take their Allies' views and concerns into consideration, particularly where their territory and/or forces might be affected.

Government policy and public opinion

NATO and its member states' governments fell well short of wider definitions of democracy, such as the publication of sufficient information to allow an educated public debate on major decisions, not to mention the encouragement of public debates. Even in the mid-1950s, NATO was not yet a decade old, sections of the public concerned about government policies particularly in the nuclear domain began to demand more information and formed vocal anti-nuclear campaigns, especially in Britain, West Germany, the Netherlands, Norway, and Denmark. The anti-nuclear movements were less active during the period of détente in the 1960s and 1970s, but at the end of the 1970s, with the neutron bomb issue and the NATO decision to procure *Tomahawk* cruise and *Pershing II* missiles, they became very strong again, forcing very public debates on these issues, which led to the fall of at least one government (that of Helmut Schmidt in the FRG). Although the nuclear protesters were regarded with deep suspicion by NATO member states' governments, and although internal security and intelligence services took an interest in them which at least in their view was quite undemocratic, this led to no imprisonment or serious persecution. I would argue that the democratic nature of the NATO member states was confirmed and enhanced by the power and influence of these protest movements, and by their insistence on public debates and on the disclosure of more information to the public at large than NATO governments would normally have liked to provide. There is a significant difference here between NATO and the WTO states where peace protesters were often jailed and their families were often harassed in ways which included barring their children from university education and barring them and their relatives from a host of jobs.

Defense analyst Scilla McLean argued that it was an error of political judgment on the part of NATO "to assume that governmental consultation on nuclear planning is the same as public consent for nuclear plans." The failure of the governments to communicate persuasively the reasons for NATO policies supported by them to their own publics underlines this criticism. McLean went on to postulate that "what is required to gain public support for NATO decisions are visible, democratic and authentic forms of reassurance of peaceful intent." Instead, democratic processes were clearly felt to be wanting in the late 1970s and early 1980s. As an article in the *Guardian* noted, right in the middle of the Euro-missile Crisis (October 14, 1983): the revival "of the peace movement since 1979 has gone a long way to undermining the decision-making process in the Alliance, which for all the mention of participational democracy in the Atlantic Charter has always been the responsibility of a very narrow élite."[70]

Increasingly over the years, public opinion in NATO countries was thus at once a constraint on the policy-making of individual governments within NATO, as it was on the Alliance as a whole. As far as I am aware, no similar pattern of public influence through an open discourse in the press and demonstrations can be detected in the WTO's countries.

Conclusions

The preceding considerations seem to indicate that NATO as an Alliance of democracies in its attitude towards nuclear deterrence only in part reflects the distribution of nuclear resources and military might within it. In the early days and indeed in the first decade of NATO's existence, the United States showed many traits of hegemonic rule that conform with Realist theory. But even then, and increasingly in the following decades, NATO's Allies began to voice their own concerns, and Washington had to listen. Just as NATO's defense plans in the 1980s centered on the hope that WTO solidarity would prove fragile and that individual WTO members would declare their neutrality in the case of war,[71] most NATO members understood the importance of solidarity among their own ranks. And solidarity would be severely undermined if the United States imposed its arsenals, strategies, and unilateral decisions upon reluctant Allies. Resulting strategies may have been marred by ambiguity but the Alliance kept together – voluntarily. It continues to exist today, even though the WTO's members agreed to dissolve that organization in 1991. The main reason, I maintain, is that NATO is not a means of American hegemonic control but a forum for transatlantic debate. The nature of this debate carries aspects of democracy, most notably the right for every member to voice its opinion (even though etiquette demands that the Luxembourgeois and the Icelandic representatives keep their interventions short and rare) and the need for consensus for any joint position adopted. American unilateralism under the George W. Bush administration has crucially not been able to instrumentalize NATO as force multiplier for its hegemonic ambitions. The reason for this lies in the nature of the Alliance.

Notes

1 For the details of this, see Beatrice Heuser, "Yugoslavia in Western Defence Strategy, 1948–1955," in *Yugoslavia's Security Dilemmas*, eds, Marko Milivojevic, John B. Allcock, and Pierre Maurer (Oxford: Berg, 1988), pp. 126–63.
2 Heuser, "Yugoslavia in Western Defence Strategy, 1948–1955"; and Beatrice Heuser, *NATO, Britain, France and the FRG: Nuclear Strategies and Forces for Europe, 1949–2000* (Basingstoke: Macmillan, 1997), chapter 2.
3 Quoted in Milton Leitenberg, "Background Information on Tactical Nuclear Weapons," in *Tactical Nuclear Weapons: European Perspectives*, ed., Swedish International Peace Research Institute (SIPRI) (London: Taylor & Francis, 1978), pp. 88f., see also Marco Carnovale, *The Control of NATO Nuclear Forces in Europe* (Boulder, CO: Westview Press, 1993), p. 56.
4 On the joint targeting plans, see John Baylis, *Ambiguity and Deterrence: British Nuclear Strategy 1945–1964* (Oxford: Clarendon Press, 1995); Ian Clark, *Nuclear Diplomacy and the Special Relationship: Britain's Deterrent and America, 1957–1962* (Oxford: Clarendon Press, 1994).
5 Quoted in Carnovale, *The Control*, p. 52.
6 Department of Defense, *Report to Congress*, FY 1978, p. 82, quoted in Ivo Daalder, *The Nature and Practice of Flexible Response: NATO Strategy and Theater Nuclear Forces since 1967* (New York: Columbia University Press, 1991), p. 135.

7 Philip Bobbit, Lawrence Freedman, and Gregory Treverton, *US Nuclear Strategy: A Reader* (London: Macmillan, 1989), pp. 338–426, especially Philip Bobbit's introduction pp. 338–46.
8 Carnovale, *The Control*, pp. 63f.
9 "General Rogers: Time to Say 'Time Out'," *Army* (September 1987), quoted in Thomas Halverson, *The Last Great Nuclear Debate: NATO and Short-Range Nuclear Weapons in the 1980s* (Basingstoke: Macmillan, 1995), p. 92.
10 Halverson, *The Last Great Nuclear Debate*, p. 93.
11 Carnovale, *The Control*, p. 40.
12 Rolf Tamnes, "Defence of the Northern Flank, 1949–1956," in *Das Nordatlantische Bündnis 1949–1956*, eds, Klaus A. Maier and Norbert Wiggershaus (Munich: Oldenbourg, 1993), p. 191; Kjetil Skogrand and Rolf Tamnes, *Fryktens likevekt: Atombomben, Norge og verden 1945–1970* (Oslo: Tiden, 1997).
13 Carnovale, *The Control*, p. 77.
14 Tamnes, "Defence of the Northern Flank," pp. 191f.
15 Kjetil Skogrand, "Norwegian Nuclear Policy, 1945–1970," in *The Cold War, Military Power and the Civilian Society*, ed. Karl Kleve, *Norwegian Aviation Museum Series* No. 5 (Norwegian Aviation Museum: Bodø, 2003), pp. 100–20.
16 Wilhelm Agrell, *Alliansfrihet och atombomber – kontinuitet och förändring i den svenska försvarsdoktrinen 1945–1982* (Stockholm: Liber, 1985); Tor Larsson, "Swedish Nuclear and Non-Nuclear Postures," in *Dividing the Atom: Essays on the History of Nuclear Sharing and Nuclear Proliferation*, eds, Cyril Buffet and Leopoldo Nuti, special Issue of *Storia delle relazioni internazionali*, year XIII, No. 1 (1988), pp. 101–20.
17 Nikolaj Petersen, "The Dilemmas of Alliance: Denmark's Fifty Years with NATO," in *A History of NATO – the First Fifty Years*, vol. 3, ed. Gustav Schmidt (Basingstoke: Palgrave, 2001), p. 277.
18 Tamnes, "Defence of the Northern Flank," p. 193.
19 Winfried Heinemann, "Politische Zusammenarbeit im Bündnis," in *Von Truman bis Harmel*, ed. Hans-Joachim Harder (Munich: Oldenbourg, 2000), pp. 174–7; Winfried Heinemann, "1956 als das Krisenjahr der NATO," in *Das Internationale Krisenjahr 1956*, eds, Winfried Heinemann and Norbert Wiggershaus (Munich: Oldenbourg, 1999), pp. 617–21, 625–8; Winfried Heinemann, *Vom Zusammenwachsen des Bündnisses* (Munich: Oldenbourg, 1998).
20 Carnovale, *The Control*, p. 77.
21 Bruno Thoss, "Forward Defence," in *GIs in Germany*, ed. Detlev Junker (Washington, DC: The German Historical Institute, forthcoming).
22 Marc Trachtenberg, *A Constructed Peace* (Princeton, NJ: Princeton University Press, 1999), pp. 194–200.
23 Carnovale, *The Control*, pp. 38, 78.
24 Ibid., p. 68.
25 Philip Sabin, *The Third World War Scare in Britain* (Basingstoke: Macmillan, 1986); Simon Duke, *US Defence Bases in the United Kingdom* (Basingstoke: Macmillan, 1987).
26 Jill Edwards, "Spain, *Drumbeat* and NATO: Incorporating Franco's Spain in Western Defence," in *Securing Peace in Europe, 1945–62: Thoughts for the Post-Cold War Era* eds, Beatrice Heuser and Robert O'Neill (London: Macmillan, 1992), pp. 159–72.
27 Cyril Buffet and Leopoldo Nuti, eds, *Dividing the Atom: Proliferation and Nuclear Politics, 1957–1969*, special Issue of *Storia delle Relazioni Internazionali* (Florence, 1998).
28 For example, see David N. Schwartz, *NATO's Nuclear Dilemmas* (Washington, DC: The Brookings Institution, 1983); for all these views being reflected within one country's political debate see Catherine M. Kelleher, *Germany and the Politics of Nuclear Weapons* (New York: Columbia University Press, 1975).
29 Jean Lacouture, *De Gaulle*, vol. 3, *Le Souverain, 1959–1970* (Paris: Seuil, 1986), p. 466.

30 For details, see Beatrice Heuser, "What Price Solidarity? Nuclear Interdependence in NATO," in *The United States and the European Alliance since 1945*, eds, Kathleen Burk and Melvyn Stokes (Oxford: Berg, 1999), pp. 155–61.
31 Hans Henrich, "Sozialer Faktor Atombombe," *Frankfurter Rundschau* (April 24, 1957); "Frankfurt gegen Atomwaffenversuche," *Stuttgarter Zeitung* (April 27, 1957).
32 "Sprechzettel für den Besuch des Herrn Ministers bei General Norstad" (March 5, 1962), NHP collection Bonn Document 88, p. 5.
33 For details of this study, see Beatrice Heuser, *Nuclear Strategies and Forces for Europe, 1949–2000*, chapter 5.
34 Ibid.
35 Johannes Steinhoff and Reiner Pommerin, *Strategiewechsel: Bundesrepublik und Nuklearstrategie in der Ära Adenauer-Kennedy* (Baden-Baden: Nomos, 1992), pp. 38–42.
36 Hope Harrison, "Ein Superalliierter und eine Supermacht? Sowjetisch-ostdeutsche Beziehungen, 1953 bis 1961," in *Militär, Staat und Gesellschaft in der DDR*, eds, Hans Ehlert and Matthias Rogg (Berlin: Ch. Links Verlag, 2004), pp. 83–96.
37 Vojtech Mastny, *Learning from the Enemy: NATO as a Model for the Warsaw Pact* (Zurich: Forschungsstelle für Sicherheitspolitik und Konfliktanalyse der ETH, 2001).
38 Conference on the NVA in the WTO, organized by the Bundeswehr's Military History Research Institute (MGFA) in Potsdam, March 2003.
39 Beatrice Heuser, "Warsaw Pact Military Doctrines in the 70s and 80s: Findings in the East German Archives," *Comparative Strategy*, Vol. 12, No. 4 (October–December 1993), pp. 437–57.
40 "Operativnaia Direktiva" in Russian, accompanying "Stabstraining-89," Bundesarchiv Militärarchiv Freiburg/Breisgau, DVH 27/50214, p. 61.
41 Oral History Session, organized with the help of Colonel Prayon, Commandant of the Academy for Information and Communication of the Bundeswehr, Strausberg, April 20, 1995, minutes taken by Michael Ploetz.
42 Scilla McLean, ed., *How Nuclear Weapons Decisions are Made* (Basingstoke: Macmillan, 1986), p. 230.
43 McLean, *How Nuclear Weapons Decisions are Made*, p. 226.
44 Daalder, *The Nature and Practice of Flexible Response*, p. 191.
45 For the details, see Daalder, *The Nature and Practice of Flexible Response*, p. 191.
46 Quoted in Carnovale, *The Control*, pp. 45f.
47 Marc Trachtenberg, *A Constructed Peace: The Making of the European Settlement, 1945–1963* (Princeton, NJ: Princeton University Press, 1999), pp. 146–200; Klaus Maier, "Die politische Kontrolle über die amerikanischen Atomwaffen als Bündnisproblem der NATO unter der Doktrin der massiven Vergeltung," in *Von Truman bis Harmel*, ed. Hans-Joachim Harder (Munich: Oldenbourg, 2000), pp. 39–54.
48 Conclusive documents on this matter can be found on the website of the National Security Archive: http://www.gwu.edu/~nsarchiv/news/predelegation/pd01_01.htm, accessed 26 November 2003.
49 At the time referred to as Flexible Response, which is confusing for us retrospectively as two other strategies would be given that name in the next ten years – see Heuser, *Nuclear Strategies and Forces for Europe, 1949–2000*, chapter 2.
50 Bruno Thoss, *NATO Strategie und Nationale Verteidigungsplanung in den Aufbaujahren der Bundeswehr, 1956–1961*, Part 1 (Munich: Oldenbourg for the MGFA, 2005).
51 "Vorschlag für Einleitungsvortrag Minister" (for von Hassel talks in Pentagon, February 1963), NHP Bonn Document 128, pp. 36f.
52 Memorandum from Malinovskii and Zakharov to Pliev, 8 September 1962, http://www.gwu.edu/~nsarchiv/nsa/cuba_mis_cri/620908%20Memorandum%20from%20Malynovsky.pdf accessed on 26 November 2003.
53 Zara Steiner, "Decision-making in American and British Foreign Policy: An Open and a Shut Case," *Review of International Studies*, Vol. 13 (1987), pp. 1–18.

54 Baylis, *Ambiguity and Deterrence*; Carnovale, *The Control*, p. 56. See also my criticism of the deliberate ambiguity in a central NATO tenet, "Die No-first-use Debatte," *Soldat und Technik* (February 1999).
55 Daalder, *The Nature and Practice of Flexible Response*, p. 70.
56 Carnovale, *The Control*, p. 61.
57 Daalder, *The Nature and Practice of Flexible Response*, p. 190; Sir Michael Quinlan, "The UK/FRG Defence Relationships, 1968–1981," in *Britain and Germany*, ed. Manfred Görtemaker (Houdsmills: Palgrave, forthcoming).
58 Saki Dockrill, "No Troops Please, We Are American," in *Von Truman bis Harmel*, ed. Hans-Joachim Harder (Munich: Oldenbourg, 2000), p. 135.
59 For the development of NATO threat scenarios and strategy, see Heuser, *Nuclear Strategies and Forces for Europe, 1949–2000*, chapters 1 and 2.
60 Michael Legge, "Theater Nuclear Weapons and the NATO Strategy of Flexible Response," *RAND Paper* R-2964-FF (1983), p. 26.
61 Daalder, *The Nature and Practice of Flexible Response*, p. 98.
62 Quoted in Daalder, *The Nature and Practice of Flexible Response*, p. 96.
63 Quoted in Thomas Halverson, *The Last Great Nuclear Debate: NATO and Short-Range Nuclear Weapons in the 1980s* (Basingstoke: Macmillan, 1995), p. 72.
64 Ibid.
65 Bundesarchiv-Militärarchiv, formerly Strausberg, AZN32908, Protocol of the 29th Meeting of the Military Council of the WTO, Prague, April 24–27, 1984, p. 196.
66 Carnovale, *The Control*, p. 58.
67 "Report of the Committee of Three on Non-Military Co-operation in NATO" of 1956, *The North Atlantic Treaty Organisation: Facts and Figures* (Brussels: NATO Information Services, 1989), p. 389.
68 Carnovale, *The Control*, pp. 59f.
69 Ibid.
70 Quoted in Scilla McLean, *How Nuclear Weapons Decisions are Made*, p. 229.
71 General Sir John Hackett, Air Chief Marshal Sir John Barraclough, Sir Bernard Burrows, Brigadier Kenneth Hunt, Vice-Admiral Sir Jan McGeoch, and Major-General John Strawson, *The Third World War* (London: Sphere Books, 1978) and following editions of 1983 and 1985.

9 Securing small-state interests
Norway in NATO

Kjell Inge Bjerga and Kjetil Skogrand

Introduction

This essay is about NATO planning processes, decision-making, and command structures from a small-state perspective with an emphasis on Norway. First, we will present a basic outline of NATO's planning structures and the procedures of the allied force goal process. Thereafter, the principal channels of influence for a small state like Norway will be discussed. These two parts form the basis for five case studies which all illustrate the challenges in striking a balance between national control and allied integration for a small state. We will examine the establishment of an integrated command structure, national access to allied nuclear strike plans, the question of a Norwegian nuclear veto, control over Norwegian aircraft, and command arrangements during exercises.

The policies of the Norwegian government in principal NATO questions have already been a topic of extensive research.[1] Thus, it is well established in the research literature that Norway, despite being loyal to the main lines of development in the Alliance, adopted a somewhat oppositional attitude in various questions concerning issues such as arms control and membership extensions.[2] The Norwegian views were sometimes a source of irritation and impatience among other allies, but only seldom did the relationship between Norway and other member countries become seriously strained. This was because the Norwegian views were normally not voiced publicly but instead presented in a careful manner in internal meetings. Moreover, Norway would usually fall into line after voicing initial dissent. The most important exception to this rule was the question of Spanish membership in NATO, which was effectively blocked by Norway until the death of Francisco Franco in 1975.[3]

This chapter will, however, not focus on NATO-wide issues that were on the agenda of summit meetings among ministers and heads of state. Our case studies concern the relationship between national authorities and allied structures in the practical implementation of principal decisions, particularly command arrangements. Such questions sometimes demanded the active involvement of cabinet ministers, at least in a small country like Norway. However, military staffs and bureaucracies primarily handled these issues, and such questions are interesting to historians because they illustrate the practical day-to-day functioning of the Alliance.

NATO's planning structures – a brief outline

On top of the NATO planning hierarchy were the strategic concepts and the documents giving a principal outline of how to implement the concepts. These documents were normally first adopted by the Military Committee and then officially approved by all member governments at summit meetings. The strategy documents formed the principal starting point for both force goals and operational planning.

In the early years of the Alliance such strategic documents were developed *ad hoc*. There was no clear hierarchy of documents, and some of the documents were partly overlapping. The first strategic concept was adopted as DC 6/1 in December 1949 only to be followed by a number of documents in the years to come.[4] From the late 1950s onward the hierarchy of strategic documents became clearer. NATO settled on a structure with two principal strategy documents: the MC 14-series constituted the overall strategic concept, whereas the MC 48-series discussed the measures to implement the concept. MC 14/2 and MC 48/2 were approved in 1957. They both constituted a refined version of the doctrine of massive retaliation, which had been introduced four years earlier. In 1967, after heavy discussion, both documents were revised and flexible response was officially introduced as the strategy of the Alliance. In practice, however, flexible response had already characterized allied operational planning since the early 1960s. The new documents, MC 14/3 and MC 48/3, remained the principal NATO strategy for the rest of the Cold War all the way to 1991 and the introduction of a post–Cold War strategy.[5]

On the next level of NATO's planning hierarchy were the plans of the principal NATO commanders, the Supreme Allied Commander Europe (SACEUR) and Supreme Allied Commander Atlantic (SACLANT). These documents were known as Emergency Defense Plans and were revised annually. An important annex of the Emergency Defense Plan was the Atomic Strike Plan (ASP), later known as Nuclear Strike Plan (NSP) and General Strike Plan (GSP). This annex described operational concepts for nuclear operations, assigned forces, and targets earmarked for destruction in the event of war.[6]

The level underneath SACEUR's plans was the defense plans for NATO's regional commands. The Northern European Command, under the Commander in Chief Allied Forces Northern Europe (CINCNORTH), was responsible for Norway, Denmark, and the northern part of the Federal Republic of Germany (FRG). CINCNORTH's regional Emergency Defense Plans included regional ASPs.[7]

Bureaucratization of NATO planning processes

In addition to the defense plans, NATO established common *force goals*. As with the development of doctrines, this process was gradual and spasmodic at first. After the outbreak of the Korean War, the level of international tension seemed to call for a massive growth of military spending, at a time when the European member states had hardly recovered from the last world war. At a summit in

Lisbon in 1952, NATO decided on highly ambitious force goals for the following years. It turned out that it was politically impossible to appropriate the necessary resources for these ambitious force goals. The Alliance therefore searched for new and more cost-effective ways of matching the clear conventional lead of the Soviet bloc. The answer was found in nuclear weapons that would give "more bang for the buck." In 1958, the defense ministers of the Alliance adopted force goals for the period 1958–63 based on introduction of nuclear weapons in the armed forces of the European member states, in a document known as MC 70.[8]

In the mid-1960s the Western Alliance created a more regular force goal process. It was acknowledged that the Cold War confrontation was a lasting phenomenon, and NATO had to plan for the long haul. Moreover, the *ad hoc* practices of NATO's early years were no longer suited to meet the requirements of a gradually more complex and bureaucratic alliance.

The development of allied planning procedures in the 1960s was a part of an international quest for more effective and rational methods of analysis and planning within the military system. The aim was to adopt a putatively "more scientific" approach to warfare and planning, which in practical terms meant applying quantitative methods. Defense planning became dominated by the so-called bellometricians, and the planning process in the Unites States and Western Europe became almost exclusively focused on counting, weighting, and calculating. The US Secretary of Defense, Robert McNamara, was a driving force behind the new approach largely based on methods developed by the RAND Corporation in California. Some have spoken of a revolution in the military planning system.[9]

One of the most important goals for McNamara and his followers was to strengthen political and economic control over the armed forces and increase efficiency. However, the actual result was often an extensive bureaucratization of the planning process. NATO's planning efforts followed the general trend in this respect.

In 1966 NATO launched its first five-year plan, covering the years 1966–71. During the work on this first five-year plan, the Alliance concluded that a continuous *force planning process* was needed. Thus the Alliance started developing bureaucratic procedures for continuous force planning. The procedures were ready in 1971.[10]

NATO's force planning process was in fact two parallel processes: the *force goal process* and the *annual defense review*. The most important element in the force planning process and the annual examination of the five-year plan was determining the *force goals*. The force goals were ambitious targets that the allied countries could aim at in their own national defense planning. The force goals were also an important tool in the effort to harmonize the force structures of the Alliance so that the capabilities of the individual member countries formed a balanced totality.

The new force goal process was conducted within the framework of the integrated allied chain of command, which we return to later. The lower levels in the allied command chain, that is the operational headquarters at the Principal Subordinated Command (PSC) level, presented the initial proposals. The headquarters reported how large forces and what kind of equipment they needed to fulfill their tasks. The proposals from the lower levels were processed through the allied chain of command until they reached the highest level, the military strategic level with the two major NATO commanders, SACEUR and SACLANT. On this level the different reports were coordinated and made into overall *force proposals* for the Alliance.[11]

The annual defense review process became even more bureaucratized than the force goal process. In the annual defense review each country formulated its national defense plans, taking into account the NATO force goals. The national plans were forwarded to the Alliance where they were subject to scrutiny. The Military Committee contributed to the examination with evaluations of the country proposals from a military point of view. On the basis of this, the Defense Review Committee reported to the Defense Planning Committee on how far the countries had been able to meet the force goals. This process resulted in a recommended five-year force plan, which was submitted to the ministers. The approved force plan was then supposed to form the basis of the force planning of each member state throughout the five-year period.

Channels of influence

Norway could influence decision-making in NATO through a number of channels on different levels. On the top level were the summits and the ministerial meetings. When the Military Committee met in Chiefs of Staff Session, the Norwegian Chief of the Defense Staff represented Norway (from 1963 known simply as the Chief of Defense). The member states also had permanent diplomatic representation in the civilian and military bodies of the Alliance. Norway had a NATO ambassador who was the national representative in the Permanent Council, and the head of the Military Mission represented Norway in the regular proceedings of the Military Committee.

In addition, Norway had a permanent military representative to Supreme Headquarters Allied Powers Europe (SHAPE). On various levels a number of Norwegians held positions in the NATO bureaucracy and in the joint combined command structure. Even if these were not formally Norwegian representatives, they could promote Norwegian views and interests in an indirect way. There are indications, however, that Norway exploited this potential in a less systematic way than other member states.[12]

Another important channel of influence was through formal NATO consultations on planning issues with Norwegian military authorities, in particular the Norwegian Joint Chiefs Committee. For example, the Norwegian Joint Chiefs in their comments to NATO's Emergency Defense Plan Northern Europe several times stressed the need to assign larger allied forces to Norway than in the original drafts.[13]

Norway also nurtured bilateral contacts within the Alliance, in particular with the United States and the United Kingdom. The special relationship between the United States and Norway has been labeled an "alliance within the Alliance."

These contacts reflected the fact that the United States, together with Britain, was perceived as the principal guarantor of Norwegian independence. In addition, Norway also kept close ties to other "like-minded" NATO members, for example, Canada, the Netherlands, and Denmark. The importance of such bilateral ties was reinforced by the bilateral aid received from the United States, notably the Military Development Assistance Program as well as generous grants to the Norwegian Military Intelligence Service. The United States was also the chief contributor to the NATO Infrastructure Program from which Norway was a great recipient. In many cases, the distinction between formal NATO processes and bilateral cooperation thus became somewhat blurred.

What kind of influence could Norwegian authorities have in NATO's decision-making process? When overarching NATO plans and guidance documents were formulated, it seems that the processes were often top-down and dominated by the great powers, notably the United States. The general content and structure of such documents had in many cases already been decided by the time when a draft was presented to the small member states. Admittedly, the small allies frequently suggested minor adjustments to the text. But only very seldom were there any discussions about the basic principles or content of the drafts that were presented. The real power was hence concentrated on those responsible for drafting the documents.

The lack of discussion about the main content of such documents may have reflected broad agreement or perhaps a feeling of resignation. For a small state, the most rational strategy was to focus on details and push for a slightly different phrasing. In the case of a small country like Norway, such a myopic attitude to planning or policy documents may also have reflected the fact that national authorities primarily focused on issues that had a direct impact on the defense of their own country or flank. The great powers had wider strategic interests and bureaucracies large enough to take on larger issues of strategic importance.

As opposed to the decision-making processes in principal questions of doctrine and structure, the force goal process was a bottom-up procedure. This allowed for substantial influence even from military staffs on a sub-national level. In Norway, the operational headquarters of North and South Norway developed the initial contributions to the force goal process. These were national headquarters in peacetime but would become parts of the allied chain of command in wartime. The regional Norwegian commanders were thus double-hatted; that is, they both had a position in the national and the allied chain of command. In the latter capacity the commanders were entitled to submit their force proposals through the allied chain of command.

In the first years of the force goal process, the regional Norwegian commanders conscientiously reported their force requirements directly to CINCNORTH, without consulting their superiors on a national level.[14] Norwegian political and military authorities could thus be confronted by Norwegian force goals in the NATO system that they had never seen before and which did not correspond with overall national defense plans.[15] Even worse, the Norwegian government could be met by allied criticism for failing to fulfill these goals. The Norwegian Ministry of

Defense therefore instituted a practice where the regional commander's proposals to the force goal process had to be coordinated with central authorities *before* they were forwarded to the Alliance.

Investigating different aspects of the planning process gives us an idea of some practical implications of allied structures and working methods. We now briefly present some case studies that can shed light on the role of a small state like Norway in the complex web of allied cooperation. In the following we focus on several issues characterized by tensions between various considerations and needs in Norway on the one side and within the Alliance on the other.

Integrated command structure – commanders in Norway

The process of establishing a Norwegian–allied integrated command structure started in 1951 and was completed in 1958. The outbreak of the Korean War in the summer of 1950 had reinforced the Western perception of an aggressive communist bloc which constituted an acute military threat. The Alliance lacked both manpower and equipment to stand up against the perceived threat and there were no command and control systems to coordinate and conduct even the modest forces in place. This recognition led to the transformation of the original North Atlantic Treaty from a loose political framework to a tightly knit organizational structure.

US Secretary of State Dean Acheson pushed for closer military integration of the Alliance, and he made it clear that one of the most important efforts was establishing an integrated command structure serving the military forces.[16] In December 1950, General Dwight D. Eisenhower was appointed as the first SACEUR. On the level below SACEUR, the Alliance's command structure was divided into three major regions: The Central Region covered the heart of the Continent; the Southern Region consisted of Italy and the Mediterranean, and was expanded by Greece and Turkey in 1952; and the Northern Region covered Scandinavia and northern Germany.[17] In the southern and northern regions Eisenhower appointed joint commanders-in-chief (CINCSOUTH and CINCNORTH). In 1951, CINCNORTH and his staff in the north set up a headquarters at Holmenkollen in Oslo, and three years later they moved into a new atomic-proof headquarters situated in the Kolsås Mountain just outside the Norwegian capital.

Norwegian authorities saw it as very desirable, both in political and military terms, to have a major NATO headquarters located in Norway.[18] In the view of Norway's Minister of Defense, Jens Christian Hauge, a NATO headquarters on Norwegian soil would be a visible proof of the American and British interest in supporting Norway and an acknowledgment of her geostrategically important position between east and west.[19] At the same time, Norway would demonstrate her political will to fulfill the obligations in the North Atlantic Treaty through welcoming such a headquarters.

From a Norwegian point of view it was also important to have high-ranking allied officers in Norway on a permanent basis so that they could get to know

Norway and become familiar with the serious security challenges in the north. In addition, it was believed that the high-ranking allied officers that served in Norway during peacetime would do their best to secure allied support for the country in wartime. In the Norwegian view, the allied headquarters would serve as a "hook in the nose" that would pull in allied reinforcements.[20]

The establishment of a regional NATO command in Oslo made it necessary to strike a balance between national control and the effectiveness of allied cooperation. In the years 1951–53 this question was the subject of debate among leading civilian and military officials. This resulted in the creation of a very complex Norwegian–Allied command structure, completed in 1958. The complexity of the command structure was a direct result of tensions between national considerations and allied objectives. Some Norwegian political and military circles harbored substantial skepticism toward the Northern European Command in Oslo and Norway's participation in NATO's integrated command structure. In the view of some national conservative politicians, like Carl Joachim Hambro, president of the Norwegian Odelsting 1945–57, Norway's comprehensive participation in the Alliance could imperil the constitutional principle of national sovereignty in military matters.[21] Left-wing factions within the ruling and basically pro-NATO Labor Party were also critical of the Norwegian participation in the allied command structure, partly for the same constitutional reasons as the national conservatives, and partly rooted in a general skepticism toward NATO and the United States.

In addition, some conservative Norwegian officers, mostly in the army and navy, rejected what they believed to be too close an integration into the Alliance. These officers were particularly skeptical toward the allied priority of offensive air power in the wake of the introduction of the strategy of massive retaliation from 1952–53 onward. Major General Odd Lindbäck-Larsen, Commander Armed Forces North Norway (1952–58), stated that it seemed as if great power interests and modern air strategies were more important than the basic need of defending Norwegian territory against the Russians.[22] However, the resistance against integration stemmed mainly from an older generation of Army officers who retired in the late 1950s and early 1960s.

In peacetime the allied command structure developed plans and conducted exercises. With a few exceptions, Norwegian units remained under national command in peacetime. In wartime the integrated command structure was meant to assume command over Norwegian forces, following a formal transfer of power from the Norwegian government. This meant that wartime command structures would be different from peacetime structures. At one level, however, allied and national command structures would have to be combined. Some Norwegian officers would have to take up command posts in the allied command structure under CINCNORTH and lead Norwegian forces in accordance with allied directives. The question was which of the Norwegian officers would be assigned such a task. This problem was solved differently in North and South Norway.

In South Norway the three single service chiefs (i.e. army, navy, and air force) originally had operational command over the forces of their services, that is land, sea, and air. The service chiefs were placed directly under the Minister of

Defense. A Joint Chiefs of Staff system provided contact and coordination between the three service chiefs. When Norway entered NATO's integrated command structure, this system was reformed. The most important change was that the three service chiefs lost operational command over their forces in wartime. Instead their deputies were designated as operational commanders in the new integrated allied chain of command. In peacetime, the service chiefs still had operational command over their forces. However, if the Norwegian government decided to transfer operational authority over Norwegian forces to NATO in wartime, the deputy service chiefs would step forward and become *operational commanders*, placed under the regional NATO commander, CINCNORTH, whereas the service chiefs themselves would function as *military advisers* to the Norwegian government. The architect behind this solution was Admiral Sir Patrick Brind, who held the position as CINCNORTH from 1951 to 1953. Brind's main objective was to avoid a combination of the functions as *national adviser* and *allied commander* in one hand.[23]

No wonder, this arrangement caused no enthusiasm among the Norwegian service chiefs. They claimed that it would seriously weaken their positions if operational wartime command were given to their peacetime deputies.[24] The anger over the new allied command arrangement was particularly strong in the navy, partly based on the view that NATO had failed to acknowledge the importance of sea power in general, and the importance of the Royal Norwegian Navy in particular. In July 1951 Vice Admiral Edvard Christian Danielsen, chief of the navy, and Commodore Gunnar Hovdenak, chief of the Naval Staff, both filed their resignations as a protest against the low priority assigned to Norwegian naval capacities both among national and allied authorities. In March 1952 the new naval chief, Vice Admiral Skule Storheill, objected to transfer command of naval forces to the Northern European Command because this would mean that a foreign officer became the principal commander of Norwegian maritime forces.[25] However, higher authorities, the Defense Staff and the Ministry of Defense, overruled Storheill's decision, and he fell into line without further objections.

The Norwegian–allied command system created in North Norway was quite different from the command system in the south. Because of the significant geographical distance between South and North Norway and the rugged Norwegian terrain, it was not improbable that the lines of communications between the two geographical regions would be cut in case of a major war. The distance and the topography would also make coordination between CINCNORTH's subordinated headquarters in the south and fighting forces in the north extremely difficult. These considerations led to the incorporation of no less than *four* northern national commands into NATO's chain of command in 1958. The commanders and their headquarters remained national in peace and would assume allied status only in wartime. The Commander Armed Forces North Norway would enter the allied chain of command under the title of Commander Allied Task Force Northern Norway, and would serve the regional joint commander on the operational level, placed directly under CINCNORTH. In addition there would be two allied single service commanders: Commander Allied Tactical Air Force North

Norway and Commander Allied Naval Forces North Norway. In peacetime, these two officers were national regional commanders for the air force and the navy.[26]

Despite several difficulties in the creation of a Norwegian–allied command structure in the 1950s, the structure apparently functioned well during the Cold War and no serious disagreements between national and allied authorities appeared. However, the command structure was very complex and it is an open question whether it would have worked in wartime or not. Furthermore, one may wonder whether allied reinforcements would have relied on the intricate Norwegian–allied structure in a real war, or if they would have brought their own command components. Several high ranking Norwegian officers, among them Major General Odd Lindbäck-Larsen and Vice Admiral Skule Storheill who both held the position as Commander Armed Forces North Norway in different periods, feared that the Norwegians would not manage the leadership of allied reinforcements in a major war.[27]

Nuclear planning

Norwegian military authorities insisted on the right to be consulted about all kinds of allied planning pertaining to Norwegian territory. In 1955, the Norwegian Joint Chiefs Committee demanded access to CINCNORTH's ASP and the right to approve the plan before it was passed on to SACEUR. It seems that the Northern European Command accepted this and, throughout the latter part of the 1950s, the Norwegian Joint Chiefs did obtain a copy of the revised nuclear plans and suggested some alterations. However, when the Joint Chiefs received the revised edition of the regional defense plan in 1960, the ASP had been left out. The reason was said to be security concerns.

The Norwegian Joint Chiefs Committee reacted strongly to this decision. The Committee emphasized that the ASP "touches on important and central national interests both of a political and a military nature." The fact that the Joint Chiefs had not been given the ASP did not mean that *all* Norwegian officers were kept ignorant, however. Those Norwegians who held positions in the allied command structure had received the plan in that capacity. The Joint Chiefs could thus contact these colleagues and receive information about the content. They were, however, blocked from the possibility of presenting comments or suggest alterations. From available sources it is difficult to tell whether CINCNORTH accepted the demand from the Norwegian Joint Chiefs and gave them access to the next revised edition of the plan, but the question seems not to have been raised later.[28]

A nuclear veto?

Norwegian authorities insisted as a general principle that any decision to use nuclear weapons should be a political one. If NATO decided to cross the nuclear threshold, this should preferably be discussed in the NATO Council. If such a procedure proved impossible, Norway still held that political authorities should make the decision. However, in the Norwegian view the power to use the most powerful weapon in the allied arsenal should not be granted to any government on the European Continent. The Norwegian view was that the final decision should always rest with the American president. Norway was dead against any delegation of nuclear release authority to allied military authorities.[29]

Even more important to Norwegian authorities was the right to approve of allied nuclear bombing on Norwegian territory in the event of war. This demand surfaced for the first time in 1953, when the Norwegian Ministry of Defense insisted that all types, that is, not only nuclear, of allied bombing in occupied parts of Norway should be subject to prior approval by Norwegian authorities. Later, the emphasis was placed on nuclear bombing.[30]

When it came to the regional NATO commander, CINCNORTH, Norwegian authorities succeeded in establishing procedures that would give the Norwegian government the right to veto any nuclear attacks in Norway. Such an arrangement was explicitly referred to in a document from 1958, and it seems that the arrangement was already well established at that time. The use of nuclear weapons in Norway would normally involve the regional NATO commander; so Norwegian authorities had thus secured a national veto in almost all conceivable scenarios where allied nuclear attacks in Norway would be considered.[31]

Norwegian authorities were still not satisfied, however. They wanted the Norwegian nuclear veto to be explicitly acknowledged in SACEUR's Emergency Defense Plan. The Norwegian Joint Chiefs Committee repeated this demand throughout the latter half of the 1950s but with no success. At the time, the planning processes of the Military Committee was led by an executive agency, the NATO Standing Group, consisting of the United States, France, and Britain. In 1957, the Standing Group suggested a passage in SACEUR's defense plan that envisaged that nuclear weapons should be used "in coordination with other commands." It was not at all clear if this meant that national political authorities would be consulted or if SACEUR would only seek military information prior to such a decision.[32]

Two years later, Norwegian authorities once again complained that SACEUR's Emergency Defense Plan failed to acknowledge a Norwegian right to be consulted in nuclear matters. This time the Standing Group discussed the Norwegian complaint, and Norwegian authorities received an answer in March 1960. The Standing Group had consulted with SACEUR, who advised that the most practicable channel of communication between the Norwegian government and SACEUR would go through CINCNORTH. If the use of nuclear weapons on Norwegian territory were contemplated, SACEUR would communicate directly with CINCNORTH who would then talk to Norwegian authorities. In other words, the Norwegians were advised to do what they had already done, that is, establish a consultative arrangement with the regional allied commander.

In the reply to Norway, the Standing Group also underlined that any NATO commander who authorized nuclear strikes on allied soil would seek prior approval from national authorities. However, the obligation to consult affected governments was moderated by phrases like "to the maximum practicable extent" and "as fully as practical." In other words, there were no guarantees.[33]

A promise that Norwegian authorities would be consulted if possible was of course very different from a formal right to veto nuclear attacks. However, available sources indicate that Norwegian authorities failed to obtain any further guarantees at this point. The year after, in 1961, the Germans were under the impression that the Norwegians had indeed succeeded in securing an exclusive nuclear veto right from SACEUR, but this cannot be confirmed on the basis of available sources. A common allied solution to these problems did not occur until 1968, when it was decided that the Alliance would consult the country where the warheads were stationed, the country from which an attack would be launched, and the country where the targets were located.

In the meantime, Norwegian authorities had to rely on contacts with CINCNORTH's headquarters when it came to national influence over possible allied nuclear bombing of enemy targets on Norwegian territory. One possible way would be to act through the Norwegian officers who held positions in the integrated allied command structure. The most effective way to exercise influence, however, would be through direct and formal contact between the government and CINCNORTH. In 1953, it was decided that a representative of the Norwegian government should be present in the regional allied headquarters in wartime in case communication lines were broken. A member of the government could also be sent to the headquarters of the Commander Armed Forces North Norway.[34] Later on, in the 1960s, this was turned into a permanent arrangement with a representative from the Norwegian government stationed in North Norway.

Control over Norwegian aircraft

An illustrating example of the tensions between national control and the integrated command structure is the use of Norwegian fighter aircraft, especially in northern Norway. From the latter half of the 1950s and throughout the 1960s, Norwegian fighter squadrons were assigned tasks in support of the allied nuclear offensive that would take place in the event of war. Norwegian forces did not have nuclear capacity themselves but they were going to aid nuclear attacks by performing conventional tasks. Thus, Norwegian fighter–bombers would attack enemy air control systems with conventional weapons, whereas Norwegian reconnaissance fighters would gather intelligence before and after allied nuclear strikes. The targets were in northwest Russia, Finland, the Soviet Baltic republics, Poland, and the German Democratic Republic (GDR). The codename of these operations was *Snowcat*, which stood for Support of Nuclear Operations with Conventional Attacks.[35]

If war broke out it was expected that the Norwegian government would authorize the transfer of Norwegian operative forces to allied command. Units of the Norwegian Air Force would then be placed under the Commander of the Air Forces of the Northern European Command (COMAIRNORTH) who was an American general. In allied defense plans, Snowcat operations had priority over defending Norwegian territory against invading forces. In the event of a Soviet attack on Norway, it was therefore conceivable that COMAIRNORTH would not employ the aircraft in the defense of Norway but rather hold them back pending the possible execution of the nuclear plans. This was a source of concern in parts of the Norwegian military leadership.[36]

A further source of concern was that the Snowcat operations were extremely risky for the forces involved. CINCNORTH in the period 1958–61, General Sir Horatius Murray, once admitted to the Norwegian Minister of Defense Nils Handal that the attacks would be a kind of suicide missions.[37] In other words, there was a chance that the Norwegian squadrons would be wiped out in operations over Eastern Europe and the Soviet Union in the opening phase of a war and never contribute to homeland defense. These concerns were aggravated by the limited prospects of receiving fast allied reinforcements that could compensate for the losses.

The situation seemed particularly difficult in northern Norway. After command had been transferred to the Alliance, the Commander Armed Forces North Norway would have to ask permission from the Regional Allied Air Force Commander in order to use the earmarked Norwegian squadrons for invasion defense. In 1959, the Commander Armed Forces North Norway asked that the command arrangements be altered so that he could obtain the right to use the available aircraft against an invasion force without prior consent from an allied superior. While expressing understanding for the concerns of the Commander Armed Forces North Norway, CINCNORTH declined the request. The Norwegian Joint Chiefs Committee also sympathized with the Commander Armed Forces North Norway, but after long deliberations they ended up supporting CINCNORTH. The defense of Norway had to be viewed in a wider perspective, as part of a regional allied effort. Seen from such an angle, the successful execution of a coordinated nuclear offensive was a more important concern than the defense of Norwegian territory in order to achieve a decisive victory in Europe.[38]

The Norwegian decision was still marked by considerable ambivalence. Norwegian army generals doubted that the offensive value of the Norwegian aircraft was so great that they could not be relieved of their missions in support of the nuclear attacks. The army held on to a traditional defensive strategy in the far north and would have preferred that the Norwegian Air Force contribute to holding the prepared defensive line in the Troms area, rather than perform offensive operations abroad. The holders of the position as Commander Armed Forces North Norway also kept being skeptical to a command structure that denied them the right to deploy all available aircraft in defense of the region against an attack. The debate thus continued further into the 1960s.

The question became more complicated as the doctrine of massive retaliation came under mounting criticism within NATO. Already from the mid-1950s there was a growing concern about the possibilities of *limited war on the flanks*, for instance an isolated attack on northern Norway. In such a scenario, the swift, single, crushing nuclear blow envisaged in massive retaliation seemed less appropriate and less credible, at least as an initial reaction. From the early 1960s more flexible defense strategies began to mark allied defense plans, even if the formal change of the NATO doctrine to flexible response did not take place until 1967.

As the prospect of an initial massive nuclear offensive subsided, there was reason to reassess the use of the Norwegian fighter squadrons. If North Norway became the victim of a limited Soviet attack that was not part of a general war, it would make even less sense to hold back squadrons pending a nuclear offensive that would perhaps never take place.

CINCNORTH's war plans gradually adapted to new scenarios. In 1965 it was underlined in the plan that allied commanders should not keep back the main part of their forces in the case of a limited attack, but units earmarked for contributing to the NSP were still an exception. At this point of time, however, it was generally expected that the allied commanders would indeed deploy all available Norwegian aircraft in defense against a limited Soviet attack on northern Norway, including those that were earmarked for offensive operations. This expectation was later confirmed in allied exercises. The Snowcat plans were finally shelved in the mid-1970s.[39]

Increasing exercise activity

Some challenges that surfaced in connection with the allied exercise activity in Norway supply further examples of tension between the Alliance and Norwegian authorities.

Upon signing the North Atlantic Treaty in 1949, Norway had stated: "We are not going to open up bases for foreign armed forces on Norwegian territory unless we are attacked or subjected to threat of attack."[40] Allied participation in exercises was accepted, however, and due to the lack of permanently stationed allied troops, Norwegian authorities even encouraged such exercises. NATO exercises in Norway served as a symbolic expression of the allied commitment to the northern flank. Such exercises would also make it possible for allied reinforcements to get acquainted with the particular challenges posed by operating under sub-arctic and alpine conditions.

The object of the allied exercises was to prepare Norwegian and allied forces for Article V operations, which meant large-scale operations where a united Alliance was fighting a common enemy with all means. For example, an Article V scenario formed the basis for exercise "Main Brace" in 1952 as well as in "Arrowhead Express" 36 years later, that is, in 1988. However, during the decades the all-out war scenario changed characteristics, reflecting the shift from massive retaliation to flexible response. Before 1960 the dominating scenario in all of the major allied exercises was all-out war from day one. From 1962 onwards most of the scenarios were based on a limited conflict, which gradually escalated into all-out war.

From 1952 onwards most of the major exercises in Norway included an allied element. However, this element was limited in the 1950s and the early 1960s, and only rarely included substantial ground forces. From the mid-1960s onwards, however, allied activity increased. Among the most important participants were the United States, Canada, Great Britain, the Netherlands, and Italy, but there were also several other allied countries sending their troops to the north.

The increased allied activity of the 1960s reflected the shift in NATO strategy from massive retaliation to flexible response, which brought flexible and deployable forces into focus. Hence NATO created the Allied Command Europe Mobile Force (AMF, also known as the "Fire Brigade"). The AMF was multinational, lightly armed, and based on air transportation. It was composed of a land force of the size of a brigade, AMF (L), and an air force, AMF (A), which consisted of three fighter squadrons.[41] The actual fighting capacity of these forces was clearly limited, but the Fire Brigade would serve as a useful deterrent against minor Soviet incursions on the flanks.[42]

In the 1970s NATO introduced the Rapid Reinforcement Concept. In addition to token forces like the AMF, the Alliance, notably the United States, now assigned substantial conventional military forces to reinforce the defense of Europe, including the northern flank. Thus the volume of the allied exercises increased. At the same time the exercises became more frequent and regular. In terms of volume, the exercises in Norway reached a peak in 1984 with the combined AMF/Rapid Reinforcement exercise "Avalanche Express/Teamwork," which had more than 24,000 participants from several allied countries.[43]

Norwegian–allied exercises can be split into two categories. The first was staff exercises or "paper exercises" – that is, simulations without actual troops in action. Back in the 1960s the exercise series *Keep Keen* was essential, but this series was gradually replaced by the *Fallex* exercises, the *Three Sword* exercises and the *Wintex-Cimex* exercises. These exercises were an opportunity for the staffs and the military leadership to handle different scenarios without involving real military forces. The purpose was to test central decision-makers and the command and communications facilities under heavy pressure. From a Norwegian point of view, staff exercises were a way to develop joint operational expertise at a national level. Such an expertise was considered crucial in order to exercise strict Norwegian control over allied forces operating in Norway. Norwegian authorities in general also saw it as very important to develop close relations with allied commanders and officers assigned to Norway in wartime.[44]

During the many staff exercises, Norwegian–allied tensions only rarely surfaced. Such tensions were first and foremost pronounced during planning and execution of field exercises. The main exercise series affecting the Norwegian–allied relations was the *Express* exercises. NATO's European headquarters and the regional Northern European Command at Kolsås arranged these exercises. The first Express exercise, "Northern Express," was held in the autumn of 1964, 3 years after the creation of the "Fire Brigade." In this exercise the AMF force cooperated closely with the Norwegian Brigade North Norway (Brig N) and personnel from the South Varanger Garrison in Kirkenes. From the 1970s onwards NATO's Rapid Reinforcement Concept lead to the organization of reinforcement forces that were much more voluminous and heavier equipped than the Fire Brigade. Hence reinforcement forces composed of units from the US Marine Corps (USMC), and the Royal Marines joined the Express exercises together with the AMF.

The increased exercise activity in Norway, primarily North Norway, from the 1960s onwards raised three questions, which all illustrated the tensions in the intersection between national considerations on the one hand and allied integration on the other. First, Norwegian authorities were anxious to avoid allied activity in the north in general, and particularly in the county of Finnmark, the easternmost county bordering on the Soviet Union. It was feared that allied presence in this region could provoke the Soviets and increase tension.[45] Thus, Norwegian authorities put restrictions on allied activity in Finnmark. As an alternative, allied forces were invited to exercise extensively in Troms and Nordland, two of the three northernmost counties.

Second, limited Norwegian staff capacity proved to be a major challenge. In the late 1970s, Lieutenant General Tønne Huitfeldt, Commander Armed Forces North Norway, noted a "very strong interest" among the Allies to send units on arctic and alpine warfare training in Norway, including forces that were not earmarked for Norway in wartime.[46] This interest resulted in an extensive and continuous allied activity in northern Norway that naturally affected Norway's national military functions in the region. The limited Norwegian staff capacity was tied up in allied activity and national mobilization exercises could not be conducted to the extent desirable. Still national defense authorities chose to maintain a comprehensive NATO activity in Norway. In their view this was an important contribution to Norwegian security, perhaps more important than refresher exercises for Norwegian reservists.[47]

Third, Norwegian defense authorities were faced with serious challenges, as the USMC in the 1970s became an important element in the defense planning on the northern flank and began exercising on a regular basis in Norway. Two problems deserve attention in this context.

The first problem was the size of the area where the commander of an amphibious operation, according to USMC doctrine, needed full command authority on land, at sea, and in the air. In the American view, such authority was necessary to achieve sufficient force protection during the short but vulnerable amphibious landing phase. In the narrow and confined area of North Norway, so called *Amphibious Objective Area*, a standard USMC would cover major parts of the Commander Armed Forces North Norway's area of responsibility and extend far into neighboring Sweden. No wonder, the American practice was politically indigestible for the host nation. However, on the Norwegian side there was a strong political wish to engage the Marines in the defense of Norway, and it became necessary to strike a balance. Hence the problem was not voiced publicly but discussed quietly on a practical level and solved on *ad hoc* basis. The Amphibious Objective Area was decreased in size and adjusted to the local topography from exercise to exercise but in fact the problem was never solved on a permanent basis and it is not possible to say how this challenge would have been met in a real war.[48]

The second problem also arose on the practical level. The USMC exercising in Norway consisted of a land and an air element: it was a so-called Marine Air Ground Task Force (MAGTF). According to USMC doctrine, the priority mission of the MAGTF air element was tactical air support to the MAGTF land element. The land element was lightly equipped, lacked sufficient artillery, and was hence dependent on close air support. The Commander Armed Forces North Norway, on the other hand, wanted maximum flexibility in the employment of all forces allocated to him. He thus wanted to integrate the MAGTF air element with the other air forces under his control. In the same way he also wanted to integrate the land element of the MAGFT with other land forces under his control. To the Americans this was unacceptable. First, they refused to deviate from doctrine and split the MAGTF. Second, they pointed out that splitting the MAGTF went beyond Commander Armed Forces North Norway's formal command authority, which was restricted to so-called *operational control*. However, the Norwegians and Americans reached a compromise to the effect that the USMC was willing to make "excess sorties," that is, fighter aircraft not currently employed in support of the MAGTF, available to the Norwegian commander.[49]

The official position of the Norwegian government was that allied forces operating in Norway should always fall into line with Norwegian views and considerations. However, the efforts to find practical solutions regarding the USMC were consistently held at an operational military level and rarely reached the government. Even at the operational level, however, it proved very difficult to find permanent solutions acceptable to both parties. Thus, the command and control problems had to be dealt with bilaterally from exercise to exercise.

Perhaps this *ad hoc* way of dealing with the command issue was a revealing illustration of what might have occurred if allied reinforcements had arrived in a real crisis. This brings us back to the question of whether the intricate command arrangements would have been reliable in wartime and whether the major allies would have conducted operations in Norway in their own way.

Concluding remarks

This chapter has discussed NATO planning, decision-making, and command structures in a small power perspective. We have examined five particular questions where Norwegian and allied interests had to be reconciled: the establishment of an integrated command structure, access to NSPs, the question of a Norwegian nuclear veto, control over Norwegian aircraft, and command arrangements during exercises. The tug of war that characterized these issues could be viewed in the light of some general traits of Norwegian security policies in the latter half of the twentieth century.

First, within the NATO Alliance Norway pursued policies of both *integration* and *screening*, that is, trying to bolster the allied security guarantee through intimate cooperation, while on the other hand limiting the extent of allied infringement.[50] The Norwegians had no possibility of defending themselves on their own against a Soviet attack and sorely needed allied reinforcements. It was particularly important to commit the Western great powers to the defense of Norway. The appointments of a British flag officer as commander in chief of the regional command and an American general as head of the air forces thus were very satisfying to the Norwegians. On the other hand, the fear of being abandoned was tempered by the fear of being dominated. Therefore, Norway insisted on regulations that limited allied influence.

Second, Norwegian policies towards the Soviet Union were also marked by a balancing trick. Being a member of NATO, accepting a regional allied headquarters on Norwegian soil, and conducting allied exercises were all part of a *deterrence strategy*. However, these policies were balanced by *reassuring measures* in relation to the Soviet neighbor, such as banning permanently stationed foreign troops and nuclear weapons in peacetime and restricting allied exercises in the border region. The actual outcome may have been a curious mix of contradictory efforts, but it could be argued that Norwegian policies were successful in keeping the High North as an area of relatively low tension during the Cold War.[51]

We shall now sum up some of our findings. We started by presenting NATO's planning structures and the formal and informal channels of influence for small states. We then went on to show how NATO force planning for many years was conducted in a spasmodic *ad hoc* fashion until it became gradually more formalized and marked by a growing bureaucratization from the mid-1960s.

On a practical level Norway's attitude to the development of NATO's force structure was positive but guarded. It seems as if Norway was more comfortable with the bureaucratic decision-making system that had developed within the Alliance by the mid-1960s than with the previous spasmodic practice. The *ad hoc* approach could of course from time to time open windows of opportunity for the small state. However, the lack of predictability implied a fundamental uncertainty that was not in the interest of a small state that would have to adopt to whatever the great power allies decided. The systematic force goal process was safe and predictable. Moreover, the bureaucratization also meant more reliable and more permanent channels of influence.

From the Norwegian point of view, the question of national control was a vital issue. As a small state on a strategic flank, Norway had interests that did not necessarily coincide with the Alliance as a whole. Thus it was important to establish arrangements that could prevent allied actions that would make sense in a NATO-wide strategic perspective but nevertheless would constitute a national catastrophe for Norway. For example, it was perfectly conceivable that an allied commander would call a swift retreat from parts of the country or order a nuclear attack on a Norwegian city that had been seized by the enemy. Whereas such actions might be accepted by Norwegian authorities under certain circumstances, they reserved the right to be consulted, and, in case of nuclear attacks, the right to veto. One way of securing national control was by allied command arrangements that put a Norwegian in charge. The official policy was that allied reinforcements should always be placed under a Norwegian commander in the NATO chain of command. There was also a Norwegian requirement that allied reinforcements to Norway had to transfer authority to the Alliance before they were authorized to commence operations in Norway. In practice, the issue was more complicated and had to be solved on an *ad hoc* basis.

The outcome of the questions examined in this chapter could be interpreted in different ways. The Norwegian service chiefs did not appreciate loosing operational command over their forces in wartime, but apart from them, there was widespread satisfaction among the Norwegians with the allied command structure as it was developed in 1951–58. However, the allied command structure in Norway became so complex that it remained an open question whether it would actually have worked in an actual war. Fortunately, it was never put to the test.

The Norwegians did obtain an arrangement that would presumably give them decisive influence if the regional NATO commander should contemplate an actual nuclear strike against a target in Norway. But once again, the realism of the arrangement in a war can be questioned. Moreover, until the NATO-wide decision in 1968, no parallel arrangement was in place when it came to the principal commander in Europe, SACEUR. Thus the arrangement fell short of an actual, watertight right to a veto.

On the Norwegian side the question of control over Norwegian aircraft seemed different according to the position of the viewer. In the Royal Norwegian Air Force, the general attitude was to view the defense of Norway as indivisible from the general defense of Europe. During the years of massive retaliation, the corollary was that Norwegian fighter–bombers and reconnaissance aircraft were best exploited by using them as part of the large nuclear offensive that would hopefully cripple both the ability and the will to fight on the side of the Warsaw Pact. In order to coordinate such an attack, the command had to be centralized. The Norwegian Army was more concerned with the direct defense of Norwegian territory, and the Commander Armed Forces North Norway wanted to control air-craft in his own area of responsibility. Perhaps this demand reflected rational mil-itary judgments. However, it could also be interpreted as an illustration of the archetypical tendency of protecting one's own power, a tendency that has been so succinctly illuminated by Graham Allison: where you sit is where you stand.[52]

The debates about Snowcat illustrate the potential conflicts between small state national interests and the Alliance. Leaving the defense of the country to allied commanders could be a double-edged sword. On the one hand, the regional American allied air force commander seated in Norway had the power to call for allied reinforcements and actually succeed in obtaining them, even in the heat of battle. On the other hand, he might direct Norwegian squadrons to offensive oper-ations outside of Norway even if Norwegian territory was under attack. Norway had much to gain by joining the integrated command structure. But it also meant that Norwegian authorities lost much of their freedom of maneuver in a crisis.

Another illustration of challenges for a small state like Norway is the many problems posed by allied exercise activity. However, even rather fundamental problems like the disagreements with the Americans over command arrange-ments were solved on a practical, military level and did not become major obstacles for the Norwegian–allied cooperation.

Finally, we hope that this chapter demonstrates the potential in studying Alliance cooperation on the level *below* presidents, cabinet ministers, and secretary-generals. We have still only started to comprehend and analyze how the integrated multilateral machinery of NATO actually functioned. At the day-to-day level the tensions and predicaments of the common security structures appear even clearer. Heated discussions and tugs-of-war were commonplace. Still, the amazing thing was the ability of the system to produce acceptable compromises and design practical solutions. Despite diverging interests, the NATO structure managed to find common ground. If the Alliance is searching for a lesson of history in the present situation, it might be here.

Notes

1 Jakob Sverdrup, *Inn i storpolitikken 1940–1949* [Into Great Power Politics 1940–1949] (Oslo: Universitetsforlaget, 1996); Knut Einar Eriksen and Helge Ø. Pharo, *Kald krig og internasjonalisering 1949–1965* [Cold War and Internationalization 1949–1965] (Oslo: Universitetsforlaget, 1997); Rolf Tamnes, *Oljealder* [Age of Oil] (Oslo: Universitetsforlaget, 1997); Kjetil Skogrand and Rolf Tamnes, *Fryktens likevekt. Atombomben, Norge og verden 1945–1970* [Equilibrium of Fear. The Atomic Bomb, Norway and the World 1945–1970] (Oslo: Tiden, 2001); Olav Riste, *Norway's Foreign Relations – A History* (Oslo: Universitetsforlaget, 2001); Kjetil Skogrand, "Norwegian Nuclear Policy 1945–1970," in *The Cold War, Military Power and the Civilian Society*, ed. Karl L. Kleve, Norwegian Aviation Museum series, no. 5, 2003, pp. 101–23; Kjell Inge Bjerga, "Political Signals and Operational Necessity in the Arctic. The Commander Armed Forces North Norway in a Regional, National and International Perspective during the Cold War," in *The Cold War, Military Power and the Civilian Society*, ed. Karl L. Kleve, Norwegian Aviation Museum series, no. 5, 2003, pp. 11–23.
2 Eriksen and Pharo, *Kald krig og internasjonalisering 1949–1965* [Cold War and Internationalization 1949–1965], pp. 31–54, 193–258.
3 Ibid., pp. 47–9, 256–8; Hilde Haraldstad, "Norsk nei til Franco i NATO" [Norwegian No to Franco in NATO] in *Forsvarsstudier*, no. 4 (1995), pp. 5–64.
4 Gregory W. Pedlow, "The Evolution of NATO Strategy 1949–1969," in *NATO Strategy Documents 1949–1969*, ed. Gregory W. Pedlow (Brussels: NATO, 1997), pp. 11–25.
5 Ibid.
6 Skogrand and Tamnes, *Fryktens likevekt* [Equilibrium of Fear], pp. 184–7.
7 Ibid., pp. 206–7.
8 The North Atlantic Treaty Organisation 1949–1989. Facts and figures (Brussels: NATO, 1989); Tamnes, *Oljealder* [Age of Oil], pp. 40–1, 67; Skogrand and Tamnes, *Fryktens likevekt* [Equilibrium of Fear], pp. 38–9.
9 Olav Njølstad and Olav Wicken, *Kunnskap som våpen. Forsvarets forskningsinstitutt 1946–1975* [Knowledge as a Weapon. The Norwegian Defense Research Establishment 1946–1975] (Oslo: Tano, 1997), p. 311.
10 The North Atlantic Treaty Organisation 1949–1989. Facts and figures, pp. 219–26.
11 Ibid., p. 221.
12 Rolf Tamnes, Jacob Børresen, and Gullow Gjeseth, *Norsk forsvarshistorie*, bind 5, *Allianseforsvar i endring, 1970–2000* [A History of Norwegian Defense, Volume 5, Alliance Defense under Change, 1970–2000] (Bergen: Eide, 2004).
13 Norwegian Joint Chiefs Committee minute, February 26, 1953, Semi-Current Secret Records 1953, Defense Staff Norway.
14 Commander Armed Forces North Norway's annual reports 1970–75, Semi-Current Secret Record, Regional Headquarters North Norway.
15 Rolf Tamnes, Jacob Børresen, and Gullow Gjeseth, *Allianseforsvar i endring, 1970–2000* [Alliance Defence under Change, 1970–2000].
16 Rolf Tamnes, *The United States and the Cold War in the High North* (Oslo: ad Notam, 1991), p. 112.
17 Ibid., p. 7.
18 Memorandum on Defense Program 1951–1954: Main Issues, Semi-Current Secret Records, Norwegian Ministry of Defense.

19 Jens Christian Hauge, "Present at the Creation," in *Kommandospørsmålet på Nordflanken. Utviklingen i to formative perioder* [The Command Issue on the Northern Flank. The Development in Two Formative Periods] ed. Rolf Tamnes, *IFS Info*, no. 4 (2001).
20 Morten Aasland, " 'A hook in the nose of the US Air Force'. Norge og opprettelsen av NATOs Nordkommando 1950–51," *PRIO Report*, no. 8 (1984).
21 Eriksen and Pharo, *Kald krig og internasjonalisering 1949–1965* [Cold War and Internationalization 1949–1965], p. 25.
22 Memorandum from Major General Odd Lindbäck-Larsen, Semi-Current Secret Records 1954, Regional Headquarters North Norway.
23 Speech delivered from the Chief of the Defense Staff to the Norwegian Defense Council, June 19, 1952. Attached to the speech, Admiral Brind's proposal dated December 3, 1952, Semi-Current Top Secret Records 1952, Defense Staff Norway.
24 Norwegian Joint Chiefs Committee, minute June 13, 1952, Semi-Current Secret Records 1952, Defense Staff Norway.
25 Torkel Lindeland, "Forsvarets øverste ledelse 1945–1961" [Central Organization of Defense 1945–1961], in *Forsvarsstudier*, no. 2 (1999), pp. 57–8.
26 Kjell Inge Bjerga, "Sikkerhetspolitikk, militærstrategi og kommandoordning" [Security Policy, Military Strategy, and Command Structure], in *Kommandospørsmålet på Nordflanken. Utviklingen i to formative perioder* [The Command Issue on the Northern Flank. The Development in Two Formative Periods], ed. Rolf Tamnes, *IFS Info*, no. 4 (2001).
27 Note from Major General Odd Lindbäck-Larsen, October 10, 1955, Semi-Current Secret Records 1955, Defense Command North Norway; letter from Vice Admiral Skule Storheill, February 16, 1966, Semi-Current Secret Records 1966, Defense Staff Norway.
28 Defense Staff to Minister of Defense, August 27, 1955; Norwegian Joint Chiefs Committee, document no. 16, 1958 and document no. 10, 1960; Norwegian Joint Chiefs Committee, minutes, January 23, 1959, August 19, 22, and 23, 1960, and September 23, 1960, Semi-Current Secret records, Defense Staff Norway; Skogrand and Tamnes, *Fryktens likevekt* [Equilibrium of Fear], pp. 195–6. Regrettably, no oral sources can enlighten the outcome.
29 Skogrand and Tamnes, *Fryktens likevekt* [Equilibrium of Fear], pp. 112–3.
30 Norwegian Joint Chiefs Committee, minute, August 14, 1953, Semi-Current Secret Records, Defense Staff Norway; Skogrand and Tamnes, *Fryktens likevekt* [Equilibrium of Fear], pp. 207–9.
31 SH-3494/58–001, July 4, 1958, Semi-Current Top Secret Records, Defense Staff Norway.
32 Defense Staff to Minister of Defense, August 27, 1955; Major General Harald Løken to head of the Norwegian Military Representative Washington, September 30, 1959 with attached memorandum, September 29, 1959, Semi-Current Records, Defense Staff, NATO Archive, copy books, Defense Staff Norway; Norwegian Joint Chiefs Committee, minutes September 10, 1956 and August, 19, 22, and 23, 1960, Semi-Current Secret Records, Defense Staff Norway.
33 Skogrand and Tamnes, *Fryktens likevekt* [Equilibrium of Fear], p. 208.
34 Cabinet Security Committee, October 5, 1962; Major General Harald Løken to head of the Norwegian Military Representative Washington, September 30, 1959 with attached memorandum, September 29, 1959, Semi-Current Secret Records, Defense Staff, NATO Archive, copy books, Defense Staff Norway.
35 Skogrand and Tamnes, *Fryktens likevekt* [Equilibrium of Fear], pp. 197–206.
36 Norwegian Joint Chiefs Committee, minute February 2, 1960, Norwegian Joint Chiefs Committee document no. 10, 1960, Semi-Current Secret Records, Defense Staff Norway.
37 General Sir Horatius Murray to Minister of Defense, Nils Handal, January 15, 1959, UD 33.2/64, AFNE, Norwegian Ministry of Foreign Affairs Archive.

38 Memorandum from Chief of Operations to Chief of Defense Staff, August 31, 1959, Semi-Current Records, Defense Staff, NATO Archive, Defense Staff Norway; SH-4363/59-315, Major General Harald Løken to Chief of Air Force, September 22, 1959; SH-447/60-315, Attachment to letter from the Air Force Command, January 25, 1960, Defense Staff, Top Secret NATO Archive; Norwegian Joint Chiefs Committee, minutes September 11, 1959, August 9, 10, and 11, 1960, October 28, 1960, Semi-Current Secret Records, Defense Staff Norway.

39 SH-2669/65-315, Vice Admiral Storheill to several addressees, April 30, 1965, AFNE, Frisby to several addressees, April 2, 1965, Semi-Current Records, Defense Staff, Top Secret NATO Archive, Defense Staff Norway; Interview with Lieutenant General Nils W. Arveschoug, May 1999.

40 Jens Christian Hauge, "Present at the Creation," in *Kommandospørsmålet på Nordflanken. Utviklingen i to formative perioder* [The Command Issue on the Northern Flank. The Development in Two Formative Periods], ed. Rolf Tamnes *IFS Info*, no. 4 (2001), s. 7.

41 In 1967 NATO also created a multinational naval "Fire Brigade" called Standing Naval Force Atlantic, best known under the acronym Stanavforlant.

42 Rolf Tamnes, "The Strategic Importance of the High North during the Cold War," in *A History of NATO: The First Fifty Years*, vol. 3, ed. Gustav Schmidt (Basingstoke: Palgrave, 2001), p. 267.

43 Kjell Inge Bjerga, *Enhet som våpen. Øverstkommanderende i Nord-Norge 1948–2002* [Unity as a Weapon. The Commander Armed Forces North Norway 1948–2002] (Bergen: Eide, 2002), p. 169.

44 Commander Armed Forces North Norway annual reports 1975–80, Semi-Current Secret Records 1980, Regional Headquarters North Norway.

45 Norway's military self-imposed restrictions fell into seven categories. First, permanently stationed foreign troops were banned on Norwegian soil in peacetime. Second, there were restrictions on nuclear and chemical activity, of which the ban on storing nuclear warheads on Norwegian soil in peacetime was the most prominent. Third, the Norwegians demanded that all intelligence and surveillance activity in the North should be under firm national control. Fourth, there were restrictions on German participation in the defense of the Northern flank. Fifth, based on the Svalbard Treaty of 1920, military activity on the Spitzbergen archipelago, both allied and national, was almost totally banned. Sixth, from 1976 Norway stated that naval vessels were not allowed to call at Norwegian ports if they were carrying nuclear weapons. Since allied vessels would neither confirm nor deny that they carried such weapons, Norwegian authorities in practice just had to assume that this restriction was observed. Seventh, there were restrictions on allied activities in northern Norway. Ground troops were banned from exercising in Finnmark. Allied aircraft or vessels were not allowed to exercise east of the 24th parallel. The latter restrictions were still practised with some flexibility. The self-imposed restrictions had three main motives: first, a general desire to keep the High North as an area of low tension; second to placate the Soviet Union, and third to avoid domestic protests. See Anders Jølstad, "Det tyske problem: norsk sikkerhetspolitisk samarbeid med Vest-Tyskland fra 1955 til 1965" [The German Problem: Norwegian–German Security Policy Cooperation 1955–1965], in *Forsvarsstudier*, no. 5 (1995); Knut Egeland Moen, "Selvpålagte restriksjoner i nord 1945–1965" [Self-Imposed Restrictions in the North 1945–1965], in *Forsvarsstudier*, no. 5 (1998).

46 Commander Armed Forces North Norway's annual report 1980, Semi-Current Secret Records 1980, Regional Headquarters North Norway.

47 Bjerga, *Enhet som våpen. Øverstkommanderende i Nord-Norge 1948–2002* [Unity as a weapon. The Commander Armed Forces North Norway 1948–2002], pp. 173–4.

48 Ibid.

49 Thanks to commodore Jacob Børresen, former Deputy Chief of Staff Operations, Defence Command North Norway (1990–93), who has been most helpful to us on this very complex military issue.

50 Rolf Tamnes, "Integration and screening: The Two Face of Norwegian Alliance Policy 1945–1986," in *Defence Studies VI* (Oslo: Norwegian Institute for Defense Studies, 1987), pp. 59–100.
51 Johan Jørgen Holst, "Norsk sikkerhetspolitikk i strategisk perspektiv" [Norwegian Security Policy in Strategic Perspective], in *Internasjonal Politikk*, no. 5 (1966).
52 Graham T. Allison, "Conceptual Models and the Cuban Missile Crisis," in *The American Political Science Review*, vol. LXIII, no. 3, September 1969, pp. 689–718. Also published as a book: Graham T. Allison, *Essence of Decision: Explaining the Cuban Missile Crisis* (New York: Harper Collins Publishers, 1992).

10 How strong was the "weakest link"?

Danish security policy reconsidered

Jonathan Søborg Agger and
Trine Engholm Michelsen

Introduction

In the spring of 1945, Soviet troops controlled more than a thousand miles of the Baltic coast and held the Danish island Bornholm in the western Baltic. After 5 years of German occupation, Denmark became a frontline state between East and West. By signing the North Atlantic Treaty in April 1949, Denmark abandoned more than a 100 years of non-alignment. The question remains, however, to what extent elements of acquiescence and non-provocation survived in Danish policy. Would fear of political and military retaliation from the East make Danish policy a low-key affair? Would Danish decision-makers succumb to Soviet pressure and abstain from military integration with NATO? To what extent did Danish decision-makers restrict or postpone military integration because of domestic concerns, political or ideological disagreement with official NATO policy, or the avoidance of unnecessary conflicts?

These issues have been the subject of much animated political and scholarly discussion. Greater access to the archives of Danish ministries is now providing a unique insight into the internal deliberations of the Danish authorities and decision-makers. Knowledge of these deliberations regarding how to deal with the continuous political pressure from the Kremlin sheds new light on how Soviet policy affected Denmark's security policy and on the extent of Danish political vulnerability to the Soviet Union.

This chapter begins by discussing the impact on Denmark of Soviet attempts to obtain Danish neutrality or at least Denmark's partial detachment from the Western Alliance. The focus is on the government's adjustments in its relationship with NATO, as well as in Danish public life, in coping with overt and covert Soviet campaigns. The chapter then examines Danish deliberations on how to deal with expected or specific reactions from the Kremlin with regard to Danish defense measures and NATO military initiatives in the Danish and Baltic regions. The focus is particularly on the extent to which Denmark's restraint and hesitations arose from considerations concerning potential Soviet reactions. Finally, brief reflections are presented on the extent to which Danish restraint actually limited the country's military readiness, damaged its political relationship with its Alliance partners, and weakened the Western Alliance.

Danish scholars have not achieved consensus on the topic of the Soviet impact on Danish Alliance policy. A striking example of the broad spectrum of interpretations is the difference between the views of Bo Lidegaard and Bent Jensen. While, generally speaking, the former considers Denmark to have been a completely loyal member of the Alliance, whose minor reservations were generally accepted by the United States, the latter sees Denmark as a more ambivalent member of NATO with low defense capabilities because of Soviet intimidation. Poul Villaume also considers the Danish policy toward the Alliance to have been one of reserve, though he does see the Danish position as having been stimulated by a desire to maintain the Nordic region as one of relatively low tension. He also stresses the significance of lacking Danish trust in the outlook of American foreign policy.[1]

Soviet goals, strategy, and campaigns in Denmark

The Soviet Union considered Scandinavia to be of essential strategic interest. The region constituted a buffer zone for the Soviet homeland from the north and northwest, while the Danish straits were essential for free access to the Baltic Sea and the Atlantic Ocean.[2] Denmark's participation in any kind of Western coalition or Alliance weakened Soviet security, since it prevented control of the area during a future crisis or war.[3] Since 1948, when Scandinavia's integration into Western military Alliances was placed on the agenda of Nordic governments, Soviet aims were clear: first, to prevent Danish membership and, after 1949, to bring about a Danish withdrawal from the Alliance. The second was to weaken Danish and Western military capacity in the Baltic region. Moscow did not consider the first aim realistic and therefore only seriously worked on the second.[4]

Soviet attempts to influence Danish decision-makers consisted in formal and informal approaches to governments, relevant ministries and ministers, politicians and civil servants.[5] Diplomatic pressure on the Danish government to withdraw from the Alliance was limited. The Soviet Union addressed a protest note directly to the Danish government in April 1949, days before the latter was due to sign up to the NATO Alliance in Washington. In the following years, Soviet official protests concerning Denmark's steps towards further military integration became more frequent. These protests took a number of forms and were aimed to isolate Denmark within NATO. The goals were both military and political, consisting partly in preventing Denmark from benefiting from Western security guarantees, and partly in attempting to drive a wedge between the United States and a European member of the Alliance. After Denmark joined the Alliance, the Soviet embassy in Copenhagen suggested in its reports to Moscow that the Soviet Union demand new rules for foreign fleets in the Baltic Sea. Thereafter, Moscow developed the thesis of the Baltic as a *mare clausum*, suggesting that only the fleets of the littoral states – that is, Denmark but not the other NATO allies – should be allowed into the Baltic Sea.[6] Moscow published a number of articles on the subject but never went as far as to demand new international rules officially.

In the late 1950s, Denmark became subject to diplomatic pressure over its NATO commitment. Danish governments received a number of proposals in which Denmark was to be included in peace zones that the Soviet Union alternately termed "neutralized" and "nuclear-free." The first formal proposals appeared in Premier Nikolai A. Bulganin's letters of December 12, 1957, and January 8, 1958. East German officials also proposed a Nordic Nuclear Weapon Free Zone to Danish parliamentarians during visits of their delegation to the German Democratic Republic (GDR). From 1959, Moscow became even more explicit in its approaches to the Danish government in speeches and in press campaigns proposing that the whole of Scandinavia be transformed into a neutral zone.

Soviet attempts to influence Danish policy through public campaigns were more frequent and more comprehensive than attempts to influence Danish governments directly at the diplomatic level. One aim of the strategy was to influence as many Danes as possible – parliamentarians, journalists, civil servants, trade unionists, intellectuals, etc. – to support Soviet policy and ideology. A shift in public mood in Denmark in favor of the Eastern bloc could, Moscow hoped, put pressure on the country's NATO membership, as well as on Denmark's political and economic ties with the Western Alliance.

Moscow considered active measures in Denmark worthwhile, since the Danes, with their tradition of neutrality, were expected to be susceptible to influence when it came to security issues.[7] Soviet-inspired public campaigns were aimed at influencing a number of groups in Western societies, stimulating public skepticism regarding NATO and creating discontent with the Western democratic system. In 1949, communists in Western Europe stirred up a massive "peace campaign" masterminded by the Cominform, the Soviet-dominated body for the management of European communist parties. International front organizations acted as the main channels of propaganda. During the war in Korea, the propaganda disseminated by these organizations sought to intimidate Denmark and the other European NATO allies by raising fears of Soviet reactions to American imperialism and aggression.

In addition, Moscow took a number of specific steps to encourage neutralist sentiments in Scandinavia, including bilateral agreements, invitations of official delegations to Warsaw Pact countries, and exchanges of military visits.[8]

In the late 1950s, following West Germany's accession to NATO, the task of organizing public campaigns calling for the "Baltic as an inner sea of peace" was delegated to the GDR and Poland. The tone of these campaigns shifted from denunciations of NATO to an emphasis on common interests and "coexistence" among "Baltic neighbors." The main tool, apart from Polish and East German public statements, was popular propaganda, conducted principally by the GDR and aimed at all the Scandinavian countries as well as the Federal Republic of Germany (FRG).[9]

Danish reactions to Soviet campaigns

In the 1950s, all Danish governments were careful not to weaken their relationship with NATO. They characterized Danish territory as difficult to defend because of its exposed geography and poor natural resources. Danish officials felt that the country was dependent on Western deterrence and thus on NATO membership. In 1954, the Foreign Ministry perceived NATO's greatest value for Denmark in its preventive effect: Danish main interests were guaranteed by official US statements of readiness to retaliate any aggression against the free world.[10] According to the Foreign Ministry, Denmark could not be 100 percent sure of American help when it came to crisis or war. It was stated, however, that

> it is probably the interest of the Soviet Union that people in Western Europe only see two alternatives: a light and smiling co-existence or an absolute darkness of atomic war and not the semidarkness in which smaller aggressions could take place without any warning. For the time being, such acts of semidarkness are blocked by the NATO alarm system.[11]

Danish attitude towards the Soviet Union took the form of a reassurance policy. Danish decision-makers chose not to be sensitive to any Soviet proposals of semi-neutrality. Proposals for "nuclear-free" or "peace" zones were either ignored or explicitly rejected. Although they felt uncomfortable, Danish officials remained unimpressed by the formal approaches, letters, and notes flowing from Moscow, as well as by informal diplomatic approaches. At the same time, they reacted politely and reassuringly. The aim of successive Danish governments seemed to be to prevent conflict and maintain a good bilateral relationship with the Soviet Union. After 1957, however – a year which heralded Khrushchev's more offensive diplomacy and insistence that Scandinavia become a nuclear-free zone – Danish governments expressed themselves more unsympathetically. They stressed that peace was the responsibility of the Great Powers and – referring to Soviet proposals for nuclear-free zones in Scandinavia and an inner sea of peace in the Baltic – pointed out that Russia was the only power that had nuclear weapons stored in this area. Semi-neutral zones in Scandinavia therefore demanded prior Soviet disarmament.[12]

By contrast, Danish officials felt much more vulnerable to the effect on Danish public opinion of Soviet-inspired "peace propaganda." The authorities worried about a possible political convergence of radical pacifist and communist attitudes among Danes. In this respect, Danish governments did not fear "communist attitudes" as such. According to the Foreign Ministry's analysis, Danes were not attracted to communist ideology, since political and material conditions in Denmark limited its influence.[13]

Early in the Cold War, Danish governments adopted measures to prevent the communist movement from spreading. Governments, both Social Democratic and Liberal, chose socialist-leaning economic policies, which were aimed to appeal to potential communist supporters. Furthermore, Danish governments co-operated with the Marshall Plan in campaigns presenting an attractive image of the "American Way of Life."[14]

The worries concerned therefore not so much the subversive activities of the Danish Communist Party (DKP), which the government believed had been countered by laws on fifth columnists in the early 1950s. Police and defense intelligence services carried out strict surveillance of communist-inspired front organizations throughout the decade. It was Soviet psychological warfare that worried governments, as a Danish civil servant in NATO expressed the matter: "While there is no threat of influence from the DKP, Denmark's relationship with the Soviet Union is something quite distinct and concerns the military imperialism of this mighty power."[15]

There was a certain anti-militarist and defense-hostile sentiment among the general public and in parliament, in particular in the Social Liberal Party. Whereas the Social Democrats despite many anti-militarist voters in the party had joined the right wing in favor of Danish membership of the Alliance, the Social Liberals had voted against. The fact that the latter party's decision to maintain an anti-militarist profile dated back to before the Second World War and was not the result of Soviet influence allowed it to develop a distinctive image and to have a decisive influence on the debate. In parliament, the Social Liberals, as well as some Liberals and Social Democrats, recalled the reasons for Denmark's tradition of neutrality, which had been brought to an end in 1949.

Competition between the Social Democrats and the Social Liberals for the votes of those who were skeptical regarding defense issues intensified in 1953, when the Social Liberals came out in favor of some Soviet proposals, in particular the nuclear-free zone. However, despite its opposition to NATO membership in 1949, the party rarely explicitly voiced support for Moscow's alternative security proposals but rather favored UN-inspired solutions. During the party's participation in the government from 1957 to 1961, it silently assented to NATO and also voted for the defense act in 1960.

Public opinion polls indicated some public skepticism towards an active Danish NATO policy. Those favoring NATO membership amounted to only around 50 percent throughout the period. A little more than 25 percent were against NATO membership, and the rest was undecided. However, governments regarded this skepticism as being almost purely homegrown and not Soviet-inspired, just like the profile of the Social Liberal Party. After 1956, and during the early détente period, although those rejecting membership amounted to less than one-fifth, it was the "don't knows" rather than those in favor who increased in number. It is therefore unclear how strongly Danes were opposed to Denmark's policy in NATO. The low level of "pros" might reflect the low public interest in foreign policy. Opinion polls also show that defense skepticism resulted from budgetary concerns. In postwar Denmark, there was a consensus from right to left that a high priority should be given to social policy. This sometimes led to debates on the impact of defense expenditure.[16]

In order to prevent withdrawal from NATO membership becoming a political issue, the authorities developed methods to prevent Danish criticism of it from growing. To manage the anti-militarist mood, governments frequently stressed that Denmark perceived NATO as a strictly defensive Alliance. They also underlined that having a low-profile member such as Denmark in NATO contributed to a general relaxation of tensions. Within NATO, Danish governments were also careful to propose that Soviet initiatives be responded to politely.[17] Such reassuring signals became even more explicit during the late 1960s, when public skepticism regarding NATO was increasing.[18]

Another way of reassuring the Danish population that Denmark was a moderate NATO member working in favor of détente was to link Danish security policy to NATO members with whom Denmark traditionally had close ties. The aim was to stress that Denmark was not totally dependent on American political and strategic thinking, which, in the eyes of some pacifists, was aggressive towards the East. Some research on Danish management of Soviet pressure during the early Cold War indicates the existence of a "strategic alliance" between Danish Social Democrats in government and the United States. The thesis is that the US relied on the strong anti-communism of Danish Social Democrats to contain Soviet influence in the area. In return, the US tolerated Denmark's low military and ideological commitment to NATO. This thesis has some relevance for the first few years of the Cold War, when communism as such was still playing a part in Danish policy. A policy oriented toward a Nordic and to some extent to a British context, at least in the official presentation of Danish policy, seems to cover the whole period being scrutinized here.[19]

Besides, in order to defuse pro-neutrality and isolationist propaganda, it was standard policy to allow front organizations to carry on their peace activities freely. All governments felt obliged to adopt a liberal policy of public expression, not daring to inhibit such activities for fear of being accused of anti-democratic measures.[20] The covert part of this diffusion strategy included secret material prepared by the government and planted in Danish newspapers, as well as support for so-called private pro-Atlantic propaganda initiatives. These discrete counter-propaganda measures often consisted in nothing more than systematically ignoring the peace propaganda, because, in the Danish political environment, arguing in favor of a pro-Atlantic posture was regarded as counter-productive.[21]

Moscow failed in its attempt to effect changes in Denmark's overall security policy. But its campaigns to minimize the impact of Western military measures in the Danish and Baltic regions did apparently enjoy some degree of success. In so far as this happened, the degree to which the Eastern bloc's political pressure influenced Danish actions in ways that furthered the Soviet agenda must be examined.

In order to evaluate the significance of the pressure from the East, a number of cases where Moscow brought extensive pressure to bear on the Danish government will be discussed. The four cases are:

1 the stationing of foreign aircraft on Danish soil (1952–53)
2 NATO military activity and the island of Bornholm (1952–53)
3 the storage of nuclear warheads on Danish soil (1957–60)
4 Danish–West German military cooperation and integration (mid-1950s to 1961).

In order to estimate the extent and significance of the Soviet impact, all major Danish concerns influencing the decision-making process must be taken into account and their individual impact on the chosen Danish policy compared and discussed. Needless to say, making such an estimate is difficult, since any decision-making process is often a conglomeration of numerous, partly interacting elements. Nevertheless, the extensive source material now available, especially from the archives of the Danish Foreign Ministry, demonstrates to some extent the relative importance of the different considerations in the decision-making process.

Foreign aircraft on Danish soil

In early 1952, NATO's military authorities and the United States discreetly proposed to the Danish authorities the stationing of US Air Force units on Danish territory in peacetime.[22] In late January 1953, these negotiations more or less collapsed and were never seriously resumed. After an impasse lasting approximately 6 months, the matter was brought to a close with an announcement that the suggestion was being declined "under the present circumstances."

In 1952 and 1953, the Kremlin sent a number of strong-worded notes to the Danish government, warning it not to accept the US proposal. Bent Jensen argues that it was these Soviet protests that led to the Danish refusal and that Moscow thereby succeeded in obstructing the establishment of military bases for foreign troops.[23] However, in fact, the Danish government showed considerable resolve in facing the Soviet intimidation, and considerations other than Soviet pressure influenced the Danish government's rejection of the stationing of US aircraft on its soil.

Although the Danish government received the proposal to station allied aircraft positively, it was considered vital to keep the matter secret for as long as possible. In February 1952, Danish Foreign Minister Ole Bjørn Kraft stated that it would be "unfortunate" if an agreement were reached a year before the airfields had been built and the aircraft were available.[24] The Soviet Union should be kept unaware of the agreement until all the necessary preparations had been made. According to the Foreign Ministry, the only certainty about the potential risk of war was that this risk would increase in the period between the Soviet Union learning of a Danish acceptance and the actual deployment.[25] In March 1952, the Danish Defense Minister stated that the risk of antagonizing the Soviets was an important issue for Denmark. The logical development, he argued, would be to take the necessary steps when the military forces and external assistance were both ready, since this would lessen the risk.[26] But there were other reasons than Soviet reactions for postponing an agreement. Danish public opinion had to become accustomed gradually to the thought of foreign troops being stationed on Danish soil. The general public was expected to have reservations about the prospect of having US soldiers stationed in Denmark. Therefore, as the Foreign Ministry noted in May 1952, several key ministers attempted to prepare the public for this in their speeches on the subject. However, apparently these preparatory measures had to be discreet and somewhat non-factual in order to avoid any premature public debate on the peacetime stationing of US forces.[27]

In mid-1952, public debate on the stationing of US forces began to take shape. In October 1952, the Soviet Union addressed a strongly worded protest note to the Danish government, warning it not to accept the stationing of US aircraft. Despite the fact that the Danish authorities seemed inclined to dismiss the Soviet warning, the Kremlin did influence the Danish public debate in late 1952 by raising public awareness further and by contributing to public debate on the matter. Also, rather than interpreting the Soviet memorandum as an omen of an impending attack on them, the authorities saw it as an attempt to influence the forthcoming debate in parliament by creating domestic political difficulties for the Liberal–Conservative government.[28] Communists and Social Liberals vocally opposed any suggestion of stationing foreign military units in Denmark. By the fall, factions within the Social Democratic Party also seemed inclined to agree with the skeptical parties. Nevertheless, the Soviet impact on actual decision-making was more obscure. Thus, Social Democratic Chairman Hans Hedtoft told the American ambassador that the Soviet October memorandum had actually strengthened his position *vis-à-vis* his opponents within the party. According to Hedtoft, neither he nor any of the party chairmen would give in to Soviet pressure.[29] Also, according to Kraft, the case was further supported by the expectation that the Kremlin would otherwise get the impression that it was possible to intimidate Denmark. Also, a Danish backing out would have negative repercussions for Denmark's relations with its NATO allies.[30] Despite the generally non-provocative sentiment inherent in Denmark's security policy and defense posture, Danish decision-makers were ready to accept the American proposal in the fall of 1952.

In early 1953, the Kremlin sent yet another note of protest to the Danish government. However, it was not this that caused the breakdown of negotiations. In late 1952, the positive Danish attitude towards the stationing of US aircraft had begun to change when the United States refused to guarantee that the units would be deployed for Denmark's defense. Instead, SHAPE could use them anywhere in the European theater without Danish consent.[31] For the Social Democratic Party, it was a sine qua non that Denmark should have the right to veto any engagement of US Air Force units stationed in Denmark in conflicts outside Danish territory. In the early fall of 1952, the Social Democrats had already been somewhat less eager than the government to accept the agreement.[32] Given the political disadvantages in peacetime and the increased risk of Soviet bombing in time of war, the security advantage was now considered too modest to be worthwhile. Considering the weakened prospect of strengthening the allied defense in Schleswig-Holstein by West-German accession to the European Defence Community (EDC), the overall military advantage was dubious, the Social Democrats argued.[33] In all likelihood, discomfort with the foreign policy outlook announced by the Eisenhower government, not least its "rollback strategy," served as an impetus for the Social Democratic demand.[34] The government acknowledged that the Social Democratic argument was true in so far as the stationing of US air force units would not now lead to a substantial improvement of Danish security.[35] Rather, Denmark would be more exposed in respect of the peacetime stationing of aircraft, which actually might be removed in time of war.

Furthermore, in February 1953, the Secretary-General of the Foreign Ministry, Nils Svenningsen, stated that the Soviet approach of late January should not influence the government's attitude, not least since, according to the Foreign Ministry, the Soviet aide mémoire did not contain any alarming diplomatic expressions.[36] Denmark was ready to risk antagonizing the Soviets as long as the stationing proposal meant an overall improvement in Danish security.

Now, however, the picture had altered slightly. Also, since the Liberal-Conservative government was dependent on Social Democratic parliamentary support for any stationing agreement to go ahead, the negotiations were put on hold, despite the fact that the government was still inclined to accept a stationing agreement on US terms.

Domestic considerations reached further than the government's dependence on the Social Democratic Party. The Social Democratic dismissal of the American stationing proposal was stimulated by domestic political concerns. With the national election approaching in mid-1953, Social Democratic leaders considered it essential to strengthen their image on security issues, especially since they needed the parliamentary backing of the pacifist Social Liberals to get back into government.[37]

Finally, the change in the international climate in the wake of Stalin's death made a stationing seem less necessary and potentially politically counter-productive, since the Danish population would have difficulties in accepting the overall necessity of such a military measure.[38]

Bornholm: the chink in the armor?

In the Soviet note of January 1953, the Kremlin had accused Denmark of breaking a promise from 1946 that Bornholm would be kept under Danish administration. In fact, Nils Svenningsen argued that Moscow's goal was to prevent foreign troops from being stationed on Bornholm, rather than the stationing of foreign aircraft in Denmark proper, that is, in Jutland. Ministry officials argued that the Soviet Union had shown a special interest in areas within the Western zone that could be used for forward bases. And Bornholm was just such an area. Despite the fact that the Danish authorities did not consider the 1946 statement on Bornholm's status to be binding regarding the presence of foreign troops there, the protest from Moscow led to serious thinking about how to escape from the predicament without making "dangerous concessions to the Russians."[39] Although Pentagon planning included the use of Bornholm for military installations,[40] no Danish–American negotiations were pursued regarding a US presence on Bornholm, and the Danish authorities did not expect future stationing of US forces there. Therefore, a statement on non-acceptance of foreign troops on Bornholm would not actually mean any real concession to the Soviets, Svenningsen argued.[41] Eventually, the Danish government decided not to give a formal answer to the Soviet note. Instead, during a visit to Bornholm the Danish Foreign Minister made a public statement, meant to reassure both the Danish public and the Soviets, in which he emphasized that the government was paying attention to the special situation of Bornholm. However, he did not make any explicit promises regarding future stationing of foreign troops on the island.[42]

There was some disagreement in the Foreign Ministry regarding Bornholm's strategic importance to the Soviet Union and the likelihood of an isolated Soviet attack on the island. Even though it was argued that Bornholm had greater significance in terms of political leverage than as a strategic asset, it was acknowledged that the possibility of an attack could not be ruled out.[43] Although the Danish authorities assumed that the Foreign Minister's statement regarding the stationing of foreign forces on Bornholm would reassure the Russians and might help to ease bilateral tensions, they did not consider the statement likely to cause the Kremlin to abandon the issue of Bornholm as such. According to Nils Svenningsen, Moscow was not concerned with NATO deterrence on such minor issues as the status of Bornholm. The Russians knew that, among the European NATO countries, there were strong forces ready to go to great lengths to placate Moscow in order to avoid a confrontation.[44] In other words, the West was not ready to go to war for the sake of Bornholm. Svenningsen's fear was increased by the belief among Danish decision-makers that, in case of war, there was little hope of an allied defense of Denmark. The Danes knew that, until the late 1950s, Jutland would be exposed to an eastern attack, as NATO military authorities did not anticipate holding Western Europe east of the Rhine-Ijssel line.[45] Nevertheless, the main reason for Denmark's membership of NATO was that core Danish decision-makers generally believed in the effectiveness of deterrence. As a strategic concept, deterrence was considered the only way to ensure that the Russians would think twice before contemplating aggression.[46] Still, the dawn of the nuclear age gave rise to doubts. If deterrence failed, would the nuclear defense work? According to one senior civil servant, it was likely that, "hypnotized by the threat of nuclear bombs...the population of a great power [would] be less prepared than ever to 'die for Danzig'."[47]

In general, the Danish worries were most pronounced with respect to Bornholm. The British acknowledged that the Danes were particularly anxious about the island. But, as a British foreign office memorandum from mid-1953 noted, "despite a certain tendency to timidity...the Danes had remained firm when confronted with the recent Russian notes [concerning the stationing of US aircraft]."[48]

The Soviet reference to the 1946 Danish statement on Bornholm was not without precedence. In the fall of 1952, NATO's *Main Brace* exercises had demonstrated similar Danish vulnerability concerning Bornholm. Consideration for Soviet concerns eventually led to some changes in the allied plans regarding the geographical scope of both sea and air operations. The negotiations over *Main Brace* highlighted Anglo-American disagreements over how far NATO should go to placate the Soviets. While the British found the exercise "dangerously provocative" and suggested complete abandonment of the portion that was scheduled to take place in the eastern Baltic, the US administration stood firm: it was important not to give in to Soviet pressure, especially since it would create a precedent. Nevertheless, the Americans stressed that everything possible should be done to avoid anything that might appear provocative to the Soviets.[49]

The Danish authorities understood and appreciated the American concern. This was due not least to the risk of creating a precedent with respect to the forthcoming negotiations on the stationing of US Air Force units in the country.[50] But the Danes also shared the British concern and even calculated the risk of a Soviet occupation of Bornholm once the exercises had been concluded. It is worth remembering that this was at the time of the Korean War, which cast long shadows of fear. Following *Main Brace*, the geographical limitations imposed by Denmark on allied military exercises on and to the east of Bornholm were adopted as permanent peacetime constraints.[51]

It is difficult to gauge the politico-military implications of the Danish restrictions relating to Bornholm. The consequences and the level of Denmark's need to placate Moscow may be somewhat overestimated, since the restrictions did not apply to Danish vessels but only to those of the allies. The Danish navy maintained a rather high profile around the island and made expeditions deep into the Baltic Sea and the Gulf of Bothnia. Moreover, the Danish Ministry of Defense and Danish military authorities emphasized the military importance of NATO allies being familiar with the waters around Bornholm. Nevertheless, the Danish Foreign Ministry stood by the conviction that such activities were not of sufficient strategic importance to counter-balance the politico-military consequences of challenging the Soviet Union over Bornholm. Therefore, it was deemed prudent to avoid incidents that could develop in a dangerous direction. Activity on Bornholm in particular was expected to cause new Soviet reactions.[52]

Danish decision-makers proved to be quite vulnerable to Kremlin pressure concerning Bornholm and the eastern Baltic. The military consequences of this vulnerability were apparently rather modest. The political consequences to Denmark's reputation within NATO also seemed to be minor, due mostly to Britain's clear expressions of understanding about the complexity of the Bornholm issue. Probably the most significant consequence of the restrictions was that it encouraged the Kremlin, as had also been the case with the stationing of foreign aircraft. The unavoidable Soviet impression must have been that the Danes were susceptible to pressure. Furthermore, strategic considerations aside, NATO emphasized that the restrictions would imply a tacit acceptance by the West that these waters were exclusively reserved for Soviet activity.

The level of Danish concern, which prompted the decision to restrict allied activity on and around Bornholm, apparently did not change significantly after Stalin's death although, as Vojtech Mastny has emphasized, the Soviets did not by this time have much appetite for risky adventures in Western Europe.[53]

Nuclear policy

In mid-1956, NATO decided to equip the shield forces with nuclear weapons. A few months later, NATO military authorities suggested the nuclear armament of Danish military forces to key Danish decision-makers. Secret discussions with the US and NATO military authorities on the delivery of "atomic artillery" went on for nearly half a year before the question became public.

The final US proposal was for the deployment of rockets (HONEST JOHN) and guided missiles (NIKE) with nuclear capabilities. Transcripts of internal Danish deliberations show a surprisingly modest concern for the Soviet Union. The US authorities estimated that "Denmark will ultimately accept NIKE. However, it does not appear that Denmark will make a final decision until the political situation is cleared or until the total cost to Denmark has been determined."[54] The political situation concerned the forthcoming national elections in May 1957. The Danish authorities focused on the potential impact on public opinion.[55] Not the least of the problems was the prospects of having US troops guard the nuclear missiles, as this would clash with the basic principles of Danish stationing policy. According to a Gallup Poll, 44 percent of the Danish population was against the permanent stationing of troops from another NATO country on Danish soil. Furthermore, given especially the Social Liberal Party's animosity toward the military, nuclear armament was not expected to be popular. This might pose a problem for the Social Democratic government, which relied on Social Liberal backing. With regard to the economic perspectives, the US delegation assured the Danes that acceptance would not result in extra expenditure for Denmark.

It must be stressed that the US offer covered only the delivery units (rockets and guided missiles), not the actual nuclear warheads, as this was ruled out by US law on nuclear energy at the time. Although the weapons systems could in principle be used for conventional purposes, their tactical range was highly problematic. For instance, due to its low accuracy HONEST JOHN demanded a very wide range of impact. The Danish authorities were clearly aware of the serious problems involved in using such weapons without nuclear warheads. Nonetheless, they showed considerable interest in the dual-purpose facility. In all likelihood, this prospect mainly served as leverage for domestic acceptance of the missiles.

In March 1957, the Danish government accepted in principle the delivery of the missiles (NIKE). After the matter became public later that month, the government received a rather aggressive letter from Soviet Minister Bulganin, who warned Denmark strongly against allowing the presence of US troops equipped with nuclear weapons on her soil. The Danish decision-makers did take the letter quite seriously, but despite some anxiety in the Foreign Policy Committee with regard to sentences about Denmark exposing herself to an unavoidable nuclear strike, the Danish government dismissed the Soviet approach quite sharply. The Danish resolve may have been increased by the fact that the Kremlin had sent similar warnings to several other NATO countries. In conversations with the US Embassy, Prime Minister H.C. Hansen described Bulganin's letter as stupid and senseless, and stressed the Soviet desire to restore relations to their pre-Hungary status. Although Hansen's interpretation must be seen partly as an attempt to reassure the Americans that Denmark was not susceptible to Soviet pressure, similar interpretations flourished in internal Danish discussions of the Soviet approach. Also, the Danish press almost unanimously reacted to the Kremlin's warning in a chilly fashion and emphasized that the Soviet approach should not influence Danish policy.

Although the precise impact of the Soviet approach is unclear, it may have had a greater impact on decision-making than a cursory look at Danish thinking on the issue would reveal. Along with rumors in the press that Denmark might have accepted nuclear-capable guided missiles, Bulganin's letter from late March prompted the Danish Communist Party to bring up the nuclear issue in the election campaigns, leading to a sharp clash between the Social Democrats and the Communists. Thus, the way in which Hansen handled the Soviet approach limited his choices and to some extent locked him into a particular political course. Given the domestic political equation at that time, allowing nuclear warheads to be stored in Denmark was considered politically harmful. The Social Democrats were caught in a tactical electoral ploy where the Social Liberal Party's anti-militarist feelings were allowed to influence the Social Democratic position. During the following general election campaign, Hansen stated that, in his personal opinion, Denmark would have rejected any offer of nuclear warheads for the guided missiles. The newly formed coalition government, which included the Social Democratic and Social Liberal parties, issued a statement that nuclear weapons would not be permitted "under present circumstances."[56]

In December 1957, the Danish government decided to maintain the existing policy and made an official statement in NATO on the rejection. That same month, the Danish government received yet another threatening letter from Bulganin, which has been seen as providing the impetus for the Danish government to maintain the existing policy of non-acceptance.[57] However, the letter actually arrived a few days after the policy had been agreed. In addition, it is highly likely that the Kremlin knew about the Danish decision before Bulganin's letter was sent. In all likelihood, the Soviet goal was to give the impression that Moscow was able to affect Danish policy-making.[58] However, this is not to say that Danish decision-makers did not consider the consequences for the Danish–Soviet relationship when formulating their nuclear policy: in fact, they did. As regards the possibility of intermediate range ballistic missiles being based in Denmark, the government felt that this would be unacceptably provocative, although, during the very same discussions, the avoidance of provocation was never mentioned in debating the potential stockpiling of tactical nuclear warheads for the Danish armed forces. However, in all likelihood the Danish decision-makers did to some degree consider this perspective when deciding to maintain the policy.[59]

In the late 1950s, the Danish authorities seriously considered changing Danish nuclear policy in peacetime and storing nuclear warheads on Danish soil. The Danish government kept this option open by maintaining maximum flexibility in phrasing its nuclear policy. According to high-ranking officials in spring 1958, a future change of policy was inevitable. In late 1958, the necessity for flexibility was demonstrated when the American government began to bring pressure to bear on the Danes to agree to nuclear stockpiling. Therefore, the foreign minister and the defense minister deemed it prudent to express a positive attitude towards nuclear armament. At the same time, Denmark ensured that it took all the steps necessary to facilitate the introduction of nuclear weapons if circumstances should change. One of these steps was the preparation of storage facilities for nuclear warheads. According to negotiations between NATO military authorities and the Danish Ministry of Defense, it was agreed that Denmark was not committing itself to future nuclear stockpiling simply by establishing NATO financed storage facilities. Furthermore, until there was a change in nuclear policy, the stores could be used for conventional stockpiling. For domestic political reasons, Foreign Ministry officials were doubtful about proceeding with the actual establishment. With regard to foreign political concerns, there would hardly be any reservations. This despite the fact, that criticism could be expected from the Soviet Union. Thus, the expected Soviet criticism of nuclear storage facilities did not carry sufficient weight to raise Danish reservations over the agreement itself. The Foreign Ministry reckoned that, despite its explicit reservations concerning future nuclear deployment, Denmark would in fact accept a future change in its policy of refusing to accept nuclear warheads. Therefore, the Foreign Ministry expected the agreement over storage facilities to reduce the Danish government's political maneuverability with respect to NATO and the Soviet Union.[60]

In late 1959, the Social Democratic-led Danish government finally decided to abandon the stockpiling of nuclear warheads in peacetime. Although future nuclear armament was still a remote possibility due to the flexible wording mentioning the "present circumstances," the prospect of peacetime storage was in fact buried. A few weeks earlier, Hansen met the Soviet ambassador, who advised the Danes strongly against any change in their nuclear policy. The renewed Soviet warnings of Soviet countermeasures may have prompted the Prime Minister's decision to maintain the Danish veto on stationing nuclear weapons on Danish soil. However, Hansen's personal memorandum of the meeting indicates his impatient, almost ironic tone in addressing the Soviet ambassador.[61] Furthermore, although Danish–Soviet relations had been stable since early 1958, Soviet displeasure at the thought of potential nuclear stockpiling in Denmark can hardly have surprised the Danish authorities.

Apparently, the main reason for the Social Democratic decision to maintain the Danish veto was that negotiations over the National Defense Act showed it was prudent to do so. Despite constant political pressure, nuclear armament proved not to be a sine qua non for the Liberal–Conservative opposition. And, in late August 1959, the Social Liberal Party decided not to support any change in nuclear policy. As the US Embassy noted, the Social Liberals' negative stand would make acceptance more difficult in the near future. Furthermore, since late spring 1959, the American authorities had reduced their political pressure on the Danish government. The American reasoning was that the discussions over the Danish National Defense Act regarding nuclear stockpiling should continue without any US interference, since the change in the Danish attitude should take place without any prodding from outside, which might have the effect of scaring the Danes off.[62] This had been one of the lessons the US drew from the earlier discussions on the stationing of foreign aircraft on Danish soil. Finally, as late as June 1959, Hansen stressed that nuclear armament should be considered if the international situation should deteriorate. In September 1959, the international climate emerging from the meeting at Camp David between Eisenhower and Khrushchev could hardly be seen as a deterioration of international relations.

In the spring of 1960, Denmark and Norway were to present the reasoning for their nuclear policies within NATO. In a memorandum in late March issued during the ministerial preparations for this, Foreign Minister Jens Otto Krag stressed that taking Soviet reactions into account was the most important argument against nuclear armament.[63] In Danish research, this remark has been used to argue that the continuous Soviet pressure was the single most important reason for Denmark's rejection of the US offer to store nuclear warheads on Danish soil.[64] However, there is a significant difference between the motives for creating a policy and the motives for maintaining it. Undoubtedly it became increasingly difficult for the Danish government to abandon its veto on nuclear warheads. Not least from a Soviet point of view, changes in the policy would have been considered most provocative – probably considerably more provocative than an original acceptance.

These considerations aside, the actual meaning of the foreign minister's comment is in itself somewhat blurred and open to discussion. The impetus for Krag's remark was a Norwegian draft emphasizing the potential Soviet responses to Finland and Sweden as a leading motive of Norwegian nuclear policy. In Krag's opinion, Denmark could not use such arguments. With regard to potential Soviet responses, Soviet reactions directed toward Denmark carried more weight and had to be the most important argument against nuclear armament.[65] Possibly, the phrase "argument" should not be understood as the reasoning behind the policy, but as the argument to adduce when explaining the policy to Denmark's NATO partners. Counter to this interpretation is the fact that a few days later Krag rejected a similar argument drafted by Foreign Ministry officials, arguing that such statements should only be made in case of strong pressure from the NATO partners. This argument may be seen as weakening the thesis that Krag's comment on Soviet reactions towards Denmark is really referring to arguments within NATO. However, Krag actually rejected several other arguments, which he himself had outlined in the memorandum, for example, considerations for détente between East and West, which was otherwise mentioned as an argument. In all likelihood, Krag eventually came to the conclusion that the Danish presentation should be as brief as possible.

Krag's comment from March 1960 can hardly be considered definite proof of the reasoning behind the Danish nuclear policy. Nevertheless, the considerations in connection with the adherence to this policy demonstrate that there was a desire not to provoke the Soviets. Moreover, the government most likely considered the non-provocative aspect an advantage of the policy. But apparently, avoiding provocation was not the key issue in the Danish rejection of nuclear stockpiling for the dual-purpose missiles: the government's nuclear policy was at least as dependent on domestic considerations.

Danish–West German military cooperation

After the accession of West Germany to NATO in 1955, Danish military co-operation with West Germany began to take shape. From the outset, the negotiations attracted Moscow's close attention. Nevertheless, Denmark's unequivocal stand was that, although there were good arguments for displaying some reservations regarding Danish–German military cooperation, concern for the Soviet Union should hardly obstruct necessary military cooperation between the two NATO partners in a decisive manner.[66] Furthermore, the Danish authorities acknowledged that neither the United States nor Britain would welcome a reluctant attitude toward Germany on the part of Denmark.[67]

In the early 1960s, when Denmark was about to accept the establishment of NATO's Unified Command for the Baltic Approaches (COMBALTAP), the Kremlin reinforced its campaign to prevent, or at least slow down, Danish–German military cooperation. When it was on the brink of accepting the establishment in late 1961, the Danish government received a strongly worded Soviet warning. Foreign Minister Krag reckoned that the Soviet approach was aimed at scaring Denmark so much that Denmark would pull out of the Unified Command and thus also out of NATO.[68] Nevertheless, Krag observed in his diary that

> Soviet pressure must not stand in the way of an unavoidable process. . . . There can be no doubt that we must stand firm. Compliance will only lead to new demands until we end up in neutrality and stand defenseless . . . but, of course, the whole situation causes severe worry.[69]

Apparently, the most worrying aspect was the explicit Soviet references to Bornholm. A few years earlier, the Foreign Ministry had supposed the goal of Soviet policy to be the establishment of "crisis areas" around the world. Should a critical situation arise from a Soviet perspective, Moscow could shift attention to a different area of the world. Thus, Denmark should constantly be prepared for Bornholm becoming the object of Eastern attention if international events should take an unfortunate turn.[70]

In late 1961, the still vivid recollections of the Berlin Crisis and the Finnish Note Crisis shed a somewhat sinister light on the Soviet Union's aggressive approach. Nevertheless, the Foreign Ministry stood firm and stated that concern for Bornholm could not stand in the way of Danish accession to the Unified Command. And, despite its considerable nervousness, the government held to its course through a combination of defensive preparations and non-provocative measures. The Danish armed forces were to be held ready at Karup and on Bornholm, but they should not take any action. During a meeting with NATO's military authorities, Danish Chief of Defense Admiral Qvistgaard emphasized that he did not want any allied naval activity near Bornholm, although he would appreciate swift NATO reinforcement in the case of a Soviet attack. Denmark's NATO partners offered reassurances, explaining that such an attack was unlikely, but promising allied intervention in the case of Soviet aggression.[71]

Nevertheless, on several occasions the Danish government attempted to reassure the Soviets by making cosmetic changes when establishing COMBALTAP. First, American officers were excluded from the Command. Their presence was considered an unnecessary provocation, in the light of Soviet fears that the

United States and West Germany were trying to assume a dominant influence in West European politico-military affairs. Second, the Danish authorities carefully considered the name for the Danish–West German command, rejecting the term "Baltic Command" since it was thought that this might upset the Russians. Instead, COMBALTAP became commonly known by the innocuous title of "Unified Command" ("Enhedskommandoen").[72]

In addition to these cosmetic changes, a few actual constraints were placed on military activities to avoid any unnecessary provocation. This was not least since the Foreign Ministry expected foreign political concerns to increase along with the increase in German participation in the exercises.[73] Therefore, in the late 1950s, the Danish authorities imposed a number of restrictions on West German participation in military exercises. These restrictions were in addition to the 1953 guidelines for naval exercises around Bornholm. Furthermore, immediately after Moscow sent a strongly worded protest against the establishment of COMBALTAP in late 1961, the Danish government issued a statement making it clear that the establishment would not mean any changes in the current situation, where only Danish troops, under Danish command, were stationed on Bornholm. In other words, the COMBALTAP would not result in West German presence on the island. This prompt Danish reaction was due to Soviet references to the Danish statement from 1946 on establishing a purely national administration of the island without the support of foreign troops.[74] However, this reassurance was not expected to restrain the Soviet Union from launching an attack against Bornholm. This was still perceived to be a potential outcome of the tense situation in late 1961.

The Soviet attempts to obstruct the establishment of COMBALTAP occasionally proved counter-productive, not least because of the often clumsy and harsh approach used. Thus, the final Soviet memorandum led to a sudden strengthening of Social Democratic efforts to force the Social Liberals to accept the Command, even though its initial effect was to increase the Foreign Ministry's concerns about the disadvantages of the impending decision.[75] For years, the Social Democratic Party, whose policy was especially based on concern for public reaction, took shelter behind the Social Liberal Party's objection to the establishment of COMBALTAP. Ironically, Soviet pressure was used as leverage in its final acceptance. Other factors influencing acceptance included the decline in public animosity toward Germans, which had recently heightened public awareness of the need for protection. Furthermore, the Berlin Crisis led to stronger allied pressure on the Danes to accept the establishment of the COMBALTAP.[76] This development ran counter to Soviet expectations, even though the Soviet ambassador had warned that it was inevitable. The Kremlin had assumed that the Social Liberal ministers would bring their influence to bear and persuade the government to resist West German pressure.[77]

Although the Soviet assessment of the Social Liberal influence proved wrong in late 1961, domestic concerns did play a predominant role in the extent of Danish–West German military cooperation. Copenhagen repeatedly responded to allied demands with hesitation and stalling tactics. In 1956, during a discussion about German officers being stationed on Danish soil, Vice Foreign Minister

Ernst Christiansen stated that concern for Danish emotions arising from the memory of the German occupation of the Second World War dictated that the government stall as long as possible.[78] In fact, this reasoning formed the backbone of the Danish reaction to the development of military integration with West Germany. In some cases, taking public opinion into account completely overshadowed the concern for the Soviet Union's interests. In the case of the establishment of West German storage facilities on Danish soil, Moscow's loud displeasure never became an argument for a re-evaluation of the Danish position. This is especially interesting considering that, in a similar situation, Norwegian officials discussed whether regular NATO storage facilities would be more acceptable to Moscow than West German stores on Norwegian soil.[79]

The Danish position, on the other hand, was mostly the result of the expected public disapproval of a conspicuous German presence.[80] This was why the Danish authorities initially conducted their negotiations with West Germany with a maximum of discretion. Also, when the matter was later leaked to the press, consideration for public opinion was the main argument for shelving the discussions for half a year. And finally, when the Danish government avoided making a bilateral agreement with West Germany by agreeing instead to establish NATO storage facilities for West German forces, once again concern for Danish domestic reaction was the key factor. However, economic considerations also played some part in the Danish policy of making West German military stores on Danish soil a NATO matter, since this would enable joint NATO financing of the stores and thus reduce Danish expenditure.[81]

Besides the public's – and to some extent their own – lingering animosity towards Germany, Danish policy-makers' decisions regarding military cooperation with the forces of their former occupier were influenced by considerations of the relative strength of the various parties in parliament. First, anti-NATO elements, especially the Communist Party, would no doubt exploit the unpopularity of military cooperation involving West German troops for political gain.[82] Second, it was necessary to make concessions to the Social Liberal Party on several occasions, for example, in the elections of 1957 and 1961, when the Social Democratic-led government explicitly mentioned the forthcoming elections in its refusal to make any decisions regarding the development of military cooperation with West Germany.

Conclusion

The impact on Danish policy of Soviet campaigns for neutrality and "peace zones" was low in the period being treated here. As perceived by the Danish government, the impact was indirect, running the major risk of encouraging the internal political debate on Denmark's commitment to NATO and, ultimately, membership in it. This does not imply that the Danish government paid any serious attention to Soviet security proposals. Instead, the nation's governments were careful to stress in public and toward the Soviet Union that Denmark conducted a moderate NATO policy. They also chose to tolerate public manifestations of skepticism about NATO.

Throughout the early Cold War Denmark's policy toward NATO seemed to have been characterized by attempts to reject or postpone certain aspects of military integration. To the extent that this was true, it was not particularly due to the considerable Soviet political pressure on Denmark. Even though Danish decision-makers constantly kept Moxcow's attitude in mind and considered consequences for the bilateral Danish–Soviet relationship, this never led to refraining from military measures that were considered *necessary* for national security. Instead, the Danish authorities showed considerable endurance in the face of Soviet attempts to influence the country's security policy.

Regarding the security policy cases discussed in this chapter, it is true that it was only with respect to Danish–West German military co-operation that the Danish authorities carried out the associated military measures in a generally unrestrained manner. Nevertheless, the rejection of Soviet influence did not only apply to COMBALTAP: to a large extent, it also covered the decision to reject the stationing of foreign aircraft and the storing of nuclear warheads on Danish soil. Probably the most significant reason for abstaining from full-scale acceptance of these military measures was the calculation that acceptance would not result in any decisive improvement of security. Moreover, public opinion and the composition of parliament often gave rise to reluctance and reservations when developing security policy. In all likelihood, the Danish government would have accepted nuclear warheads and the stationing of US Air Force Units if it had expected these measures to make the difference between victory and defeat. This was not the case. Instead, the government prepared for the future removal of these policy restrictions by taking all the steps necessary to change course. One of the arguments for adopting such a flexible posture was the expected positive reaction within the Alliance. Such considerations also appeared in Danish reflections on the issue of co-operation with West Germany.

It must be stressed that the Danish government attempted to mollify the Russians on several occasions with declarations aimed at defusing the tensions arising from Danish security measures. The prospect of upsetting the Soviets often appeared in the government's deliberations and was considered an item in the overall balance of advantage and disadvantage. Although the Danish authorities strove to follow the principle of studied indifference to Soviet declarations of interests and Soviet pressure regarding important military matters, they understood that consideration must be given to how, and to what extent, the Kremlin would react. Nevertheless, their basic assumption was that the Soviet Union's potential reactions could be taken into account in formulating Danish positions as long as reassuring the Kremlin did not put any necessary strategic measures at risk.

What, then, led to Denmark's occasionally self-imposed restrictions and reluctance to accept certain NATO policies? Besides doubts as to whether the measures would in fact increase national security, domestic politics seem to have been a consistent factor. Two aspects in particular alternated in dominating the political considerations behind Danish security policy. One was public opinion, especially the voting public; the other was the specific composition of parliament.

However, any evaluation of the Soviet impact on Danish security policy must also take into account the fact that the Kremlin deliberately tried to mobilize Danish voters. Soviet strategy consisted partly in swaying government attitudes by influencing public opinion and opposition politicians. The goal was to create public pressure on the government to reject allied plans for military measures in the Danish or Baltic regions. The significance of such domestic factors should be thoroughly considered before judging the Soviet campaigns a failure. The Soviet Union invested heavily in peace campaigns and succeeded in provoking internal controversy when it chose to capitalize on issues that were already part of public debate in Denmark. However, it is almost impossible to estimate the effect of these Soviet campaigns because of the existing public animosity to a strong defense policy. Furthermore, the aggressive Soviet diplomacy was often so brutal and clumsy that it proved counter-productive. Nevertheless, to some extent Moscow succeeded in setting the agenda for Danish political debates on security issues, although in the final analysis the firm general Danish commitment to NATO integration would seem to indicate that Soviet campaigns did not have decisive influence on Danish governmental policy.

At one point, Danish resolve was somewhat weakened by Soviet political pressure. Almost every time the Kremlin raised the question of Bornholm, the Foreign Ministry reacted promptly, usually by attempting to reassure the Soviets by imposing restrictions, especially on allied activity in the area. The Danish authorities disagreed among themselves about how to stand firm in these situations, mainly because Bornholm was considered strategically more vulnerable than the rest of Denmark. Nevertheless, without ignoring Denmark's undeniable anxiety about Bornholm, it is worth asking whether the *apparent* willingness of Danish decision-makers to capitulate to Soviet pressure was at least partially caused by an awareness of other factors.

The apparent Danish concessions mainly concerned issues that were not on the Danish agenda, such as the permanent stationing of foreign troops on Bornholm or the presence of West German troops on the island. Although the restrictions did impose unwanted limits on political maneuverability, concessions to the Kremlin could be perceived as rather cheap, since they required no practical change in the modus operandi for allied activity on Bornholm. Second, Bornholm served a useful purpose in raising allied awareness of the significance of the threat against Denmark. The Danes often stressed Bornholm's strategic value and vulnerability, and a policy of accommodating the Soviets could be justified because of the interest in emphasizing further the need for an allied defense of Danish soil.

We have seen that although the Danish government displayed considerable resolve in the face of Soviet pressure, it nevertheless pursued a policy line that was close to the Kremlin's demands. These apparent Danish concessions led to a strengthening of the Kremlin's conviction that Copenhagen was susceptible to influence. Apparently, the Kremlin believed that Denmark's attitude stemmed from concerns about its relationship with the Soviet Union.[83] Furthermore, Danish rejections were exploited in international and domestic propaganda targeted at NATO, thus creating internal discomfort and resentment towards the

US-led NATO policy. This was probably the most significant political consequence of Denmark's self-imposed restrictions.

From NATO's perspective, Denmark's political signals carried more weight than the relatively minor military and strategic disadvantages of its policy. Denmark's constraints caused no serious conflicts within NATO, not least because their removal in times of crisis or war was taken for granted and prepared for. Danish airfields and storage facilities were ready for the deployment of US aircraft and nuclear warheads. Nuclear-armed NATO forces, particularly from West Germany, were expected to defend Denmark. NATO's military authorities did stress that Danish restraint might weaken the politico-military position of the West in the Baltic area. Nonetheless, the Western defense capability in the Baltic area did not suffer any substantive harm as a result. Besides, trying to reassure the Soviets in the Nordic area was no Danish specialty. The Americans and British did the same.

* * *

In terms of the adaptation theory, Denmark's security policy toward both the friend and the enemy was that of balance, not of acquiescence.[84] In relation to the Alliance, the self-imposed Danish restraints were minor adjustments in the bastion strategy of all-out commitment to NATO integration. The other side of the coin – the balancing policy toward the Soviet Union – was in effect a deterrence strategy sprinkled with a few minor concessions to reassure the opponent. The membership in NATO gave Danish decision-makers enough guts to neutralize any decisive Soviet influence.

Notes

1 Bent Jensen, *Bjørnen og haren. Sovjetunionen og Danmark 1945–1965* [The bear and the hare: The Soviet Union and Denmark 1945–1965] (Odense: Odense Universitetsforlag, 1999); Bo Lidegaard, *I Kongens Navn. Henrik Kauffmann i dansk diplomati 1919–1958* [On His Majesty's Behalf: Henrik Kauffmann in Danish Diplomacy 1919–1958] (København: Samleren 1996); Bo Lidegaard, *Jens Otto Krag 1914–1961* (København: Nordisk Forlag, 2001), Poul Villaume, *Allieret med forbehold. Danmark, NATO og den kolde krig. En studie i dansk sikkerhedspolitik* [Allied with Reservations. Denmark, NATO and the Cold War: A Study in Danish Security Policy 1949–1961] (Copenhagen: Eirene, 1995).
2 Georges-Henri Soutou, *La guerre de Cinquante Ans: Les relations Est-Ouest 1943–1990* (Paris: Fayard, 2001), pp. 132–3.
3 Report from the Soviet embassy in Copenhagen, dated March 1950, *Rossiiskii Gosudarstvennyi Arkhiv Sotsialno-Politicheskoi Istorii* [hereafter RGASPI], fond [f.] 17, opis [o.] 137, delo [d.] 129, listy [ll.] 31–88.
4 The Soviet policy as summarized in a conversation between the Danish communist Ib Nørlund and the Soviet diplomat A.S. Kaplin, the document dated September 12, 1956, *Rossiiskii Gosudarstvennyi Arkhiv Noveishei Istorii* [hereafter RGANI], f. 05, o. 28, d. 435, ll. 233–9.
5 Outline of diplomatic strategy during the 1950s. Report from the Soviet embassy in Copenhagen, dated April 19, 1963, *Arkhiv Vneshnei Politiki Rossiiskoi Federatsii* [hereafter AVPRF], f. 085, o. 48, papka [p.] 173, d. 8, ll. 1–9.

6 Report from the Soviet embassy in Denmark, dated March 1950, RGASPI, f. 17, o. 137, d. 129, Chapter VII.
7 Report from the Scandinavian Section in the Soviet Foreign Ministry (MID) to the embassy in Copenhagen, dated August 10, 1953, AVPRF, f. 085, o. 37, p. 147, d. 11, ll. 7–29; M.G. Gribanov's memorandum, MID, 1956, AVPRF, f. 085, o. 40, p. 158, d. 10, ll. 19–21. At the time of writing, Gribanov was Head of the MID's Scandinavian Department, and was later the same year appointed ambassador to Norway.
8 Reports from the Danish Foreign Ministry, dated June 12, 1957 and October 16, 1957, *Archives of the Danish Foreign Ministry* [hereafter UM],105.T.1.f/1; Intelligence Report dated November 19, 1957, box 24, lot file 86 D 232, RG 59, National Archives [hereafter NA].
9 Thomas Wegener-Friis, *Den ny nabo. DDR's forhold til Danmark 1949–1960* [The New Neighbor: GDR's Relations with Denmark 1949–1960] (Copenhagen: SFAH, 2001), pp. 97–9.
10 "New-look," memorandum dated March 26, 1954, UM 105.I.1.a/1. On this point, see also Jonathan Søborg Agger and Lasse Wolsgaard, "Pro Memoria: Atombomben er vor ven. Den danske regerings stillingtagen til og reaktioner på atomvåbnenes integration i NATOs forsvarsstrategi 1949–1956" [Pro Memoria: The Atomic Bomb Is Our Friend. The Danish government's Position and Reactions regarding Atomic Weapon Integration in NATO's Defense Strategy 1949–1956] (*Danish*) *Historisk Tidsskrift*, vol. 101 (2001), no. 2: 404.
11 Memorandum by Hessellund-Jensen, dated August 26, 1955, UM 105.I.40.b.
12 An example is a letter of February 8, 1958 from Prime Minister H.C. Hansen to Bulganin, in Udenrigsministeriet [Danish Foreign Ministry], *Dansk sikkerhedspolitik 1948–1966* [Danish Security Policy 1948–1966], vol. II (Copenhagen: Danish Foreign Ministry, 1968), vol. 2, annex 164, p. 383.
13 Discussions on counter measures, 1952–53, UM 105.M.2.g.
14 Vibeke Sørensen, *Denmark's Social Democratic Government and the Marshall Plan* (Copenhagen: Museum Tusculanum, 2001) pp. 26–7; and Marianne Rostgaard, "Kampen om sjælene. Dansk Marshallplan publicity 1948–1950" [The Battle for Minds: Danish Marshall Plan Publicity 1948–1950], *Historie*, no. 2 (Århus: Jysk Selskab for Historie, 2002).
15 The Danish representative in NATO, April 25, 1951, UM 105.K.2.a.
16 Poul Villaume, "Denmark and NATO through 50 Years", *Danish Foreign Policy Yearbook*, eds. Bertel Heurlin et al. (Copenhagen: Danish Institute for Foreign Affairs, 1999), pp. 29–61.
17 Speech by H.C. Hansen in NATO, May 5, 1958, UM 5.a.5; report from the Danish representative in NATO, January 22, 1958, UM 119.K.4.b.
18 Letter from the Danish Delegation to NATO to the Belgian Delegation, Comments on the suggested outline, July 12, 1967, The Harmel Dossier, NATO Archives.
19 Rasmus Mariager, *Trust and Warm Sympathy: Anglo-Danish Relations and the US 1945–1950–1955*, unpublished PhD dissertation, University of Copenhagen, 2003. Mariager contests the thesis of the "strategic alliance" presented in Bo Lidegaard, "Danmarks overlevelsesstrategi i den kolde krigs første år" [Denmark's Strategy of Survival in the First Years of the Cold War], *Arbejderhistorie*, 1999 (4), pp. 35–46.
20 Comments, May 27, 1952, UM 105.M.2.g; memorandum dated December 13, 1953, UM 105.T.1.f/1.
21 Memorandum dated August 1952, UM 105.M.2.g; report dated July 26, 1954, UM 5.E.95; memorandum dated July 4, 1953, UM 105.G.9. See also Villaume, *Allieret med forbehold*, chapter 9.
22 The development of this question is described in Villaume, *Allieret med forbehold*, p. 411.
23 Jensen, *Bjørnen og haren*, pp. 451–5.

24 Memorandum by Foreign Minister Ole Bjørn Kraft, dated February 21, 1952. Quoted from Danish Institute for International Studies, *Danmark under den kolde krig. Den sikkerhedspolitiske situation 1945–1991* [Denmark during the Cold War. National Security Policy and the International Environment 1945–1991] (Copenhagen: Gullander, 2005), chapter 12. Kraft made his statement to US Secretary of State Dean Acheson and Norwegian Foreign Minister Halvard Lange during a NATO Ministerial Meeting in Lisbon.

25 Memorandum dated February 8, 1952, quoted from Danish Institute for International Studies, *Danmark under den kolde krig*, chapter 12.

26 Minutes of meeting with Admiral Brind and General Taylor, March 17, 1952, quoted from Danish Institute for International Studies, *Danmark under den kolde krig*, chapter 12.

27 Memorandum dated May 28, 1952, quoted from Danish Institute for International Studies, *Danmark under den kolde krig*, chapter 12.

28 "Referat: Sovjetrussisk note til Danmark vedrørende fredstidsstationering" [Memorandum: Soviet Note to Denmark Regarding Peacetime Stationing], by H.H. Mathiesen, dated October 4, 1952, UM 105.K.7.b/3.

29 Villaume, *Allieret med forbehold*, p. 435.

30 "Samtalen i Udenrigsministeriet mandag den 8 sept. kl. 10" [Conversation in the Foreign Ministry, Monday September 8], undated Memorandum (from 1952), H.C. Hansen collection, box 21, folder 1 Arbejderbevægelsens Arkiv og Bibliotek [Archive and Library of the Danish Labor Movement – hereafter ABA].

31 "Extraktafskrift af forsvarsmøde den 6. februar 1953" [Excerpts of Defense Meeting February 6, 1953], UM 105.K.7.b/4; "Orienterende samtaler mellem danske og amerikanske repræsentanter vedrørende indholdet af en eventuel aftale om fredstidsstationering i Danmark" [Preliminary Discussions between Danish and American Representatives about Contents of a Possible Agreement on Peacetime Stationing in Denmark], memoranda dated January 23, 26, and 28, 1953, UM 105.K.7.b/4.

32 This is partly due to the uncertain Norwegian position and rumors about British support for a potential Norwegian rejection of similar proposals. The Social Democrats emphasized that Denmark could not accept the proposal without British assent. In case of a conflict of interests between the Americans and the British, Denmark could not be in a position where it was tied more strongly to the United States. A few weeks later, however, the British government assured that they would support a Danish acceptance of the proposal. "Samtalen i udenrigsministeriet mandag den 8 sept. kl. 10" [Conversation in the Foreign Ministry, Monday, September 8], undated Memorandum (from 1952), H.C. Hansen collection, box 21, folder 1, ABA.

33 For example, the foreign-policy committee, February 4, 1953.

34 For a discussion of the impact of the Eisenhower administrations "New Look" policy, see Villaume, *Allieret med forbehold*, pp. 450–60.

35 "Extraktafskrift af forsvarsmøde den 6. februar 1953" [Excerpts from Defense Meeting February 6, 1953], UM 105.K.7.b/4.

36 Udenrigsministeriet, *Dansk sikkerhedspolitik 1948–1966*, vol. 2, annex no. 125, pp. 288–90. "Den sovjetiske regerings aide mémoire af 28. januar 1953" [The Soviet government's aide mémoire dated January 28, 1953]; "Nogle bemærkninger om den russiske démarche" [Some Comments on the Russian Move], memorandum by Secretary-General Nils Svenningsen, February 3, 1953, UM 105.K.7.b/3.

37 Furthermore, the Swedish Social Democratic Party strongly advised Denmark not to accept the stationing proposal, since this would increase the risk of Soviet aggression against the neutral Nordic countries. Letter from M. Wassard to N. Svenningsen, see Danish Institute for International Studies, *Danmark under den kolde krig*, chapter 12.

38 For the significance of the change in international climate, see for example, Lidegaard, *Jens Otto Krag 1914–1961*, pp. 450–1.

39 Analysis dated February 20, 1953, quoted from Danish Institute for International Studies, *Danmark under den kolde krig*, chapter 12; memorandum by E. Schram-Nielsen, dated March 2, 1953, UM 105.K.7.b/3; comment by C.A.C. Brun, dated March 2, 1953, UM 105.K.7.b/3.

40 Villaume, *Allieret med forbehold*, p. 426.

41 "Nogle betragtninger vedrørende besvarelsen af den russiske note" [Some considerations on answering the Russian note], memorandum by Secretary-General Nils Svenningsen, dated March 12, 1953, UM 105.K.7.b/3.

42 DUPI, *Grønland under den kolde krig: Dansk og amerikansk sikkerhedspolitik 1945–68* [Greenland during the Cold War: Denmark and American Security Policy] (Copenhagen: Gyldendals Forlagsekspedition,1997) vol. 1, p. 408.

43 Memorandum by Secretary-General Svenningsen, dated July 2, 1953, UM 105.K.7.b/3.

44 "Nogle betragtninger vedrørende besvarelsen af den russiske note" [Some Considerations on Answering the Russian Note], memorandum by Secretary-General Svenningsen, dated March 12, 1953, UM 105.K.7.b/3.

45 Villaume, *Allieret med forbehold*, chapter 3; Agger and Wolsgaard, "Pro Memoria: Atombomben er vor ven", pp. 396–7.

46 Agger and Wolsgaard, "Pro Memoria: Atombomben er vor ven"; Lidegaard, *Jens Otto Krag 1914–1961*, p. 336.

47 Memorandum by Hessellund-Jensen, dated August 26, 1955, UM 105.I.40.b.

48 Meeting of HMG Ambassadors in Scandinavia, June 1953, "United Kingdom and Scandinavia," minutes dated June 18, 1953, British Foreign Office Archives (hereafter FO) 371/106109B, Public Record Office (hereafter PRO).

49 Villaume, *Allieret med forbehold*, p. 579; memorandum by Secretary-General Nils Svenningsen dated August 13, 1952, UM 105.I.5.b/1; "Øvelsen Main Brace" [Exercise Main Brace], memorandum by Secretary-General Nils Svenningsen dated August 18, 1952, UM 105.I.5.b/1.

50 Memorandum by Secretary-General Nils Svenningsen, dated August 18, 1952, UM 105.I.5.b/1.

51 Memorandum dated March 10, 1954, UM 105.I.5.a/2.

52 "NATO-øvelser i Østersøen" [NATO Exercises in the Baltic Sea], memorandum by H.H. Mathiesen dated August 14, 1953, UM 105.I.5.a/2; "Extrakt af møde i koordinationsudvalget den 21. august 1953" [Excerpts from a Meeting in Coordination Committee August 21, 1953], UM 105.I.5.a/2; "Political considerations regarding exercises," telegram from Admiral Patrick Brind to the Danish and Norwegian Chiefs of Defense, memorandum dated March 18, 1953, UM 105.I.5.a/2; "Vedrørende øvelser i Østersøen" [Regarding Exercises in the Baltic Sea], memorandum dated September 9, 1953, UM 105.G.9.

53 Personal comment to the authors by Vojtech Mastny, May 2003.

54 With respect to HONEST JOHN, the Americans reckoned that there would be "no special problems for the Danes." "Briefing Material on Denmark for General Norstad's Visit March 13–14", dispatch no. 697 from American embassy in Copenhagen to Department of State, dated March 6, 1957, 759.00/3–657 XR 740.5, NA.

55 "Forsvarsministerens møde med general Sugden den 28. December 1956 vedrørende atomartilleri til den danske hær" [Defense Minister's meeting with General Sugden, December 28, 1956, on atomic artillery for the Danish army], memorandum dated January 14, 1957, Danish Ministry of Defense Archives, 91–26/57.

56 Villaume, *Allieret med forbehold*, pp. 536–40; Jonathan Søborg Agger and Lasse Wolsgaard, "Den størst mulige fleksibilitet. Dansk atomvåbenpolitik 1956–1960" [A Maximum of Flexibility: Danish Nuclear Weapons Policy 1956–1960] (Danish) *Historisk Tidsskrift*, vol. 101 (2001), no. 1, pp. 81–4.

57 For example, Jensen, *Bjørnen og haren*, p. 514.

58 Agger and Wolsgaard, "Den størst mulige fleksibilitet. Dansk atomvåbenpolitik 1956–1960", p. 81.
59 Foreign-policy committee, December 11, 1957, appendix: "Bilag vedr. ministerrådsmødet, pkt. III" [Attachment re: Council of Ministers Meeting, pt. III].
60 "Notat til udenrigsministeren" [Memorandum for the Foreign Minister], dated January 13, 1960, UM 105.Dan.6; Memorandum dated March 3, 1958, UM 105.I.40.e; Agger and Wolsgaard, "Den størst mulige fleksibilitet. Dansk atomvåbenpolitik 1956–1960," pp. 96–7.
61 Memorandum by Prime Minister H.C. Hansen, dated September 17, 1959, UM 105.Dan.6.
62 Villaume, *Allieret med forbehold*, p. 590.
63 Memorandum by Foreign Minister Krag, dated March 30, 1960, UM 105.Dan.6.
64 Jensen, *Bjørnen og haren*, pp. 508, 548.
65 Memorandum by Foreign Minister Krag, dated March 30, 1960, UM 105.Dan.6.
66 "Nyorientering m.h.t. dansk–tysk samarbejde på forsvarets område" [New Orientation against Danish–German Cooperation in the Area of Defense], memorandum dated September 24, 1957, UM 105.K.25.
67 Agger and Wolsgaard, "Den størst mulige fleksibilitet. Dansk atomvåbenpolitik 1956–1960," pp. 94–5; "Dansk-tysk samarbejde på forsvarets område" [Danish–German Cooperation in the Area of Defense], memorandum dated February 13, 1956, UM 105.K.25.
68 Jensen, *Bjørnen og haren*, p. 586.
69 Lidegaard, *Jens Otto Krag 1914–1961*, p. 710 (entry in Krag's diary September 10, 1961, our translation).
70 "Østersøspørgsmålet m.v." [Baltic Sea etc.], analysis by the chief of the politico-juridical department E. Schram-Nielsen dated January 13, 1959, UM 105.Dan.1/2.
71 Telegram from the permanent Danish delegation to NATO (DANATO) by the Minister for Foreign Affairs, J.O. Krag, and NATO ambassador, E. Schram-Nielsen, dated December 14, 1961, UM 105.I.19b/3; telegram from London by the Secretary-General of the Danish Foreign Ministry, dated December 14, 1961, UM 105.I.19.b/3.
72 "Den officielle betegnelse for NATO-enhedskommandoen for Danmark og Østersøområdet" [The Official Term for the NATO Unified Command for Denmark and the Baltic Sea Area], memorandum dated November 29, 1961, UM 105.I.19.b/1.
73 "Forsvarsspørgsmål og Østersøen som et 'fredens hav' " [Defense Questions and the Baltic Sea as a "Sea of Peace"], memorandum dated August 24, 1959, UM 105.Dan.1/2.
74 DUPI, *Grønland under den kolde krig*, p. 417; Lidegaard, *Jens Otto Krag 1914–1961*, p. 713.
75 Statement by Torben Rønne to Danish ambassadors, October 13, 1961, UM 105.I.19.b/1.
76 Villaume, *Allieret med forbehold*, pp. 255–69.
77 Jensen, *Bjørnen og haren*, pp. 573–4.
78 Villaume, *Allieret med forbehold*, p. 238.
79 Despite the Norwegian expectations, the final outcome of creating NATO stores on Norwegian soil reserved for West German use led to Soviet expressions of strong dislike. Anders Jølstad, "Det tyske problem. Norsk sikkerhetspolitisk samarbeid med Vest-Tyskland 1955–1965" [The German Problem: Norwegian Security Policy Cooperation with West Germany 1955–1965] *Forsvarsstudier. Årbok for Forsvarshistorisk forskningssenter, Forsvarets høgskole* 5/1995 (Oslo: Tanum/Norli, 1995), p. 42.
80 Danish Institute for International Studies, *Danmark under den kolde krig*, chapter 14.
81 This was not the only time that economic considerations proved essential to the Danish position. With respect to Denmark's military integration with West German forces, the

Danish authorities acknowledged on the one hand that it was important to avoid upsetting the Germans in order to maintain beneficial trade relations. On the other hand, the Danish attitude towards military cooperation was also inspired by the need to obtain political leverage in the trade negotiations. Thus, the Danish ministers implied to their German counterparts that a solution to the growing Danish–German trade problems (which stemmed from German membership of the EEC) was imperative to a swift resolution of the delays regarding the establishing of the COMBALTAP. "Telegram af 25. januar 1961 fra udenrigsministeren til forsvarsministeren, p.t. den Kgl. ambassade i Bonn" [Telegram of January 25, 1961 from the Foreign Minister to the Defense Minister, at present at the Royal Embassy in Bonn], UM 105.I.19.b/1; "Referat af møde i forbundskanslerens hus i Bonn den 24. maj 1961" [Minutes of Meeting at the Federal Chancellor's house in Bonn May 24, 1961], UM 105.I.19.b/1.

82 "Nyorientering m.h.t. dansk–tyske samarbejde på forsvarets område" [New Orientation regarding Danish–German Cooperation in the Area of Defense], memorandum dated September 24, 1957, UM 105.K.25.

83 Dispatch from the Embassy of the Soviet Union in Copenhagen, dated April 19, 1963, AVPRF, f. 085, o. 48, d. 173, l. 8.

84 Danish Institute for International Studies, *Danmark under den kolde krig*, chapter 3.

11 "To defend or not to defend"

Drawing the line in the Netherlands

Jan Hoffenaar

In August 1952, a shock wave reverberated through the Netherlands.[1] The newspaper headlines were dominated by alarming reports that, in the event of a Soviet attack, the Netherlands would be left undefended. Many people were wondering what purpose NATO membership served, if not defense in a potential attack. Questions were asked in parliament and the Dutch government was urged to clarify the situation. The cause of the excitement was an article by Drew Middleton, the widely respected *New York Times* correspondent in Bonn. He described the growing opposition by military leaders from the Netherlands, the Federal Republic of Germany, and some other countries to the strategic views of a number of unspecified French generals who, Middleton felt, would dominate the future debate on the Allied defense strategy. The French were "interested mainly in the defense of Metropolitan France and the territories in Northern Africa." They were not interested in "holding the Low Countries and northwest Germany."[2]

The article hit at the heart of a major strategic debate in the early 1950s. At the time, the military threat posed by the Soviet Union was perceived to be very real in Western Europe, while the build-up of NATO's conventional and nuclear forces was nowhere near the stage where the West would be able to withstand a Soviet offensive. The chasm between NATO's actual and its desired and, indeed, required military capacity was formidable. True, at the beginning of 1952, the Emergency Defense Plan by the Supreme Headquarters Allied Powers Europe (SHAPE) had come into force, but the major Allied countries were nurturing their own concepts and plans regardless.

This chapter addresses the issue of how and why the Netherlands became caught in the force field of official Allied objectives and plans on the one hand, and the actual, *de facto* views and opinions that were clearly informed by national interests on the other hand. This issue may be regarded from different angles. To begin with, these build-up years were characterized by the sometimes precarious trilateral relationship between NATO, the Dutch government, and public opinion. Given that the Alliance did not have the military capability to guarantee the integrity of NATO territory – something the Dutch government knew but the Dutch people, on the whole, did not – and given the fact that the government did not want the population to be unduly alarmed, the Dutch government found itself "serving two masters," both in its policy and its statements. Second, the issue can be raised of the extent to which national interests played a role in the Allied strategic operational planning process and of what influence SHAPE exerted in this context. Third, the issue can be seen in the perspective of the ambiguous position of the Netherlands vis-à-vis NATO. While the Netherlands had a claim on NATO in that it wanted its defense and safety guaranteed, it was also accused of falling short in its own defense effort. Finally, the crucial question needs to be addressed of whether the Netherlands, in the event of a Soviet attack, would have been defended or readily given up.

Surprisingly, this equally existential and essential issue for the Netherlands has been virtually overlooked by historians. The Dutch historians Dr Jan-Willem Brouwer and Dr Ine Megens chronicled the tortuous progress of the debates held in the Council of Ministers in the period between August 1948 and March 1951 on the Dutch military contribution to NATO.[3] Dr Jan Willem Honig, moreover, shed light on the domestic decision-making regarding Dutch defense policy.[4] Both studies focus on the scope of the Dutch contribution, both in financial terms and in terms of troops and equipment. Neither of the two studies, however, pays any attention to strategic or operational aspects. The issue of the position of the Netherlands in the Allied military plans is not raised. The only exception is Dr Jan van der Harst, who touched on this subject in his, unfortunately unpublished, dissertation written in 1987.[5] At the time, he did not have access to NATO archives. Since these archives have become partly accessible in recent years, it has become possible to conduct an analysis of the strategic and operational aspects of the Dutch defense in the early 1950s.[6]

A chasm between wishes and reality

At first glance, the Dutch security situation in the second half of the 1940s looked fairly bright. The Netherlands had been closely involved in Western political and military alliances. In 1948 the Netherlands had ratified the Brussels Treaty, which was the foundation for the establishment of the Western Union. In so doing, the Netherlands bid farewell to a longstanding policy of neutrality, which had been sacrosanct for over a century. One year later, the Netherlands became one of the first original signatories to the North Atlantic Treaty. This meant that the main objective of the Dutch security policy had been achieved, namely to assure that the United States had a definite stake in the security of Western Europe. An attack on a single member state would be considered an attack on the Alliance. This instilled a sense of security.[7]

The official plans likewise gave rise to optimism. As early as August 1948, the Western Union Chiefs of Staff (WUCOS) had come to the conclusion that "we should hold the enemy as far east as possible in Germany with the resources available at any given time."[8] This was the principle of forward defense, which was also adopted as the starting point for NATO defense.[9] In the short term, the main defense line would be concentrated along the rivers Rhine and IJssel. The latter part of the defense line had been included in NATO defense plans after strong

Dutch pressure and with British support. The Dutch position was that this defense line was paramount to safeguarding at least the political and economic heart of the country.[10] This situation was far from ideal, as it meant that, in the event of an enemy attack, in the first years to come, the northeastern part of the country would be promptly given up. Still, things were to start looking up in the near future.

As stated earlier, the British, who for centuries had set great store by holding the Low Countries for the purposes of their own defense, supported the idea of a defense line along the river IJssel.[11] This emerged, among others, from a discussion between Field Marshal B.L. Montgomery of Alamein and General J.M.G. de Lattre de Tassigny of France at the end of 1948 on the "alignment of our defences in Holland." Montgomery, then Chairman of the Western Union Commanders in Chief Committee, stated that "it was essential to do everything possible to prevent the Russians overrunning Western Holland. . . . To achieve this object it would be necessary to fight on the IJssel line." De Lattre, then commander of the Western Union's ground forces, also recognized that "the IJssel was the most reasonable line of defense," but he had reservations about the viability of this defense line. The British field marshal's rejoinder was: "In all circumstances, however, [I] would continue to work on the principle that we should never desert the Dutch."[12] At the beginning of 1949, Montgomery went as far as to propose to commit a British infantry brigade for the defense of the IJssel until such time as the Netherlands had raised sufficient troops itself. He was backed by the British Chiefs of Staff. The British Defence Committee, however, was not prepared, as yet, to take such a step. Therefore, in an emergency, it would have been most likely for a brigade from the British Army on the Rhine (BAOR) already stationed in Germany as an occupying force to have been ordered to move to the IJssel line.[13]

The June 1950 outbreak of war in Korea ushered in a new phase in the building of an Allied security system. The invasion of US-backed South Korea by communist North Korea immediately sparked off fears of a Soviet attack on Western Europe. These fears were not entirely unfounded. In the years before, the Cold War had intensified, mainly as a result of the blockade of Berlin and, to a lesser extent, due to reports that the Soviet Union, in addition to the United States, had also acquired nuclear capability. The invasion of South Korea was the first large-scale military operation outside what was considered the Soviet sphere of influence. The common thinking was that what was possible in Asia could also happen in Europe. And who was to guarantee that such a thing would not take place? It is only recently, following examination of records released after the Cold War, that we are virtually certain that Stalin never had the intention of attacking Western Europe. At the time, however, fear predominated as no such assurances were to be had.

From the summer of 1950, NATO, which had been mainly politically oriented at first, rapidly transformed itself into a political and military organization. The most visible sign of this was the establishment of SHAPE. On December 19, 1950, General Dwight D. Eisenhower was appointed the first Supreme Allied

Commander Europe (SACEUR). The "militarization" of NATO was also reflected in the stepping up of the Allied defense effort, mainly at the urgent request of the Americans. Immediately after war had broken out in Korea, there turned out to be various "strings attached" to British support for the IJssel defense line. Montgomery threatened that the Netherlands was to step up the build-up of its troops or lose his support for the defense of the IJssel.[14] This stance, paradoxical though it may sound, was in line with the increase of British involvement in the defense of the Western European continent, which only really took off after the beginning of the Korean War.[15] The situation had become serious now and the British were prepared to come to the aid of their Allies, but only on condition that they stepped up their defense effort.

The Dutch government had trouble reaching a decision to expand its military programs. The country was still recovering from the large-scale military effort in the former Dutch East Indies between 1945 and 1949 in an ultimately fruitless attempt to restore Dutch rule in the former colony by military means in addition to diplomatic resources.[16] These missions, moreover, had precluded an uninterrupted build-up of the armed forces.[17] Following the transfer of sovereignty of Indonesia on December 27, 1949, it was to be almost another eighteen months before the Netherlands was able to resume the build-up of its armed forces in such a way as to meet with the, albeit moderate, approval of the supreme NATO commanders. The defense budget was nearly doubled and the pace of unit formation was stepped up. This did not, however, cause the criticism to die down. The British and the Americans in particular disagreed with Dutch plans to build an extensive navy on top of their proportionally large army and air force.[18] NATO, moreover, found fault with the Dutch mobilization system and the relatively few active units. Hitches in the supply of American equipment supplies – which in itself clearly facilitated the build-up – constituted another delaying factor in the build-up of the Dutch armed forces in those first years.[19] The Dutch government, meanwhile, was leaving no stone unturned in its unflagging efforts at the various international platforms to guarantee the integrity of the entire Dutch territory as soon as possible. Thus, at the NATO Council of September 1950, it was the Dutch government, through Foreign Minister D.U. Stikker, that first raised the delicate issue of the rearmament of Germany. The build-up of German military units would help build a true forward defense in far less time.[20]

Montgomery's shot across the bow demonstrated yet again how important it was for the Netherlands not to waste time over the building of the IJssel defense line. The Dutch government went out of its way to make the IJssel line fully acceptable to all Allies. Within two years, from the beginning of 1951 to the end of 1952 and true to the best Dutch engineering tradition, the Dutch completed a full-scale water defense line. This enabled them to inundate large landmasses on either side of the river in a matter of days.[21] To this end, large weirs were to be moved into the rivers Rhine and IJssel. This engineering feat was meant to convince the remaining skeptics among the Allies.

The Dutch population, meanwhile, was completely unaware of the international debate on the IJssel line. People who read the papers closely might have known of the existence of the defense line. Residents of the area, upon finding that certain parts were restricted, probably realized that something was afoot there that was defense related. Only very few people, however, had detailed information on the exact operation of the water defense line. The construction of the defense line was a highly secret project. The reasons for this secrecy were both military and social. Had it become known that, in the event of a Soviet attack, over 400,000 residents on both sides of the river would have to be evacuated, this would in all likelihood have caused intense unrest among the Dutch population. What was more, operating the weirs would mean that the water supply to the main rivers west of the defense line would be cut off, causing the water management in large parts of the country to be disrupted. These drastic and far-reaching consequences placed the Dutch political and military leadership in a staggering dilemma. On the one hand, given the cataclysmic social and economic consequences, operating the weirs would have to be postponed until the very last moment. On the other hand, from a military-operational perspective, this had to be done at the earliest possible moment, as it would take about one week until complete inundation of the areas in question. This was exactly the time the main enemy force was thought to need to reach the defense line.[22]

The timing of the inundations was not the only uncertainty in the official Allied planning, nor the most important one. In those first years, the official NATO operation plans, as a whole, were not realistic. Frank US and British assessments of the West's defense capability in the face of the anticipated overwhelming superiority of the Soviet conventional armored force tended to be much more somber. This pessimism was mainly based on the fact that the build-up of the Allied forces was progressing much more slowly than planned. The SHAPE Emergency Defense Plan became effective on February 15, 1952. This plan outlined the main principles of NATO defense in Europe in the period prior to the Defense Plan taking effect, then envisaged for July 1, 1954. According to the Emergency Defense Plan, in the Central Sector, "the general line of the IJssel and Rhine Rivers" was to be held.[23] The British Chiefs of Staff, however, deemed this plan "unrealistic because with the forces available... we do not consider that the Rhine Line can be held."[24] The US Joint Outline Emergency War Plan, approved in September 1952, provided for the withdrawal of American troops from the river Rhine to the Pyrenees. Over six months before that, the US Joint Chiefs of Staff had coordinated this plan with General Eisenhower personally. His NATO staff was not informed, only the British were. Both the Americans and the British recognized, however, that General Eisenhower, for political reasons, was forced to take the Continental Strategy as his sole and exclusive starting point in respect of NATO planning. This meant the defense of the Rhine and IJssel line. Any hint at a further withdrawal of troops or any suggestion of a "Peripheral Strategy" would have been unpalatable for the continental European member states. It would shatter Western cohesion and ultimately play into Stalin's hands.[25]

In the early 1950s, then, the situation with respect to Allied planning was anything but straightforward. Although the political and military authorities in the continental Western European member states were not aware of the details of the situation, they realized full well that implementation of the official operation plans depended on the required divisions being raised. They knew that there was a serious conflict between the official position on how, ideally, to operate and the wherewithal to do so. This was a cause for extreme concern. All the more so, as the enemy could be expected to be at the front door at any moment. From the spring of 1951, when Allied defense planning received a strong boost with the newly established European NATO headquarters, Montgomery, the newly appointed Deputy SACEUR at NATO, had got everyone on their toes. He claimed that December 1, 1952 was the "Master Date." "The Russians will have to decide by *then* whether to attack in the West, or not: on the premise that if they waited much longer they would find us too strong."[26] 1952, he felt, was a "a key year," as the German rearmament, which began that year, "may force Russia to strike in the West."[27] He chose December 1, 1952 as the date when "the weapons must be forged and be ready for use," for the simple reason that NATO forces could not achieve full readiness before that date. He further reasoned that

> if the Russians should decide to start World War III they will do so in the winter months: when the Western Air Forces would not be able to operate at maximum efficiency, and when the Western Land Forces would not be in a high state of battle efficiency.[28]

Defense of the Netherlands of marginal concern

Montgomery's declaration of urgency takes us back to the crucial issue, the one that – following the publication of Drew Middleton's article – so occupied the public mind in the Netherlands in the summer of 1952: how would the Allied forces respond in the event of an attack by the Red Army on Europe in the short term? There was room for different interpretations and solutions, which could open the door to widely different national interests. In such a situation, self-interest could become the determining factor in Allied operations. This, precisely, was Holland's worst nightmare. As early as the spring of 1951, when SHAPE defense planning was really taking off, the Dutch Joint Chiefs of Staff Committee – the coordinating body formed by the chiefs of staff of the Services – had observed a serious lack of interest among the Allies in the defense of the Netherlands. The Dutch Defense leadership suspected that the Allied commanders tended to be swayed by the French strategy, which focused on a defense line behind the river Rhine only.[29] This suspicion was based on statements by the chief of the Dutch liaison mission at SHAPE, who warned that Allied headquarters were giving serious thought to a defense line south of the main rivers.[30] The primary task for the French armed forces was "*assurer avec le concours des alliés la couverture de la frontière du Rhin,*" as had been formulated before in the decision by the *Comité de Défense Nationale* of November 30, 1948. The French traditionally considered the river Rhine as their "*frontière naturelle.*"[31] It is interesting to see how the position held by France in this build-up period was both to the advantage and to the disadvantage of the Netherlands. While France was a major ally in that it had always championed and promoted a continental strategy, in an operational sense it had also always done so primarily with a view to the protection of its own territory. This was not necessarily in the best interests of the Netherlands.

The skepticism of the Dutch defense leadership increased in the autumn of 1951 with the appointment of French general Alphonse Juin (from May 1952 *Maréchal de France*) as commander of the Allied Land Forces Central Europe. The Dutch suspicions appeared to be confirmed by various developments. Thus, Marshal Juin's provisional emergency plan had designated both the Ardennes and Holland as firm bases that were to be defended with the greatest tenacity. In his final plan, however, Holland did not feature anymore. The only words in the plan devoted to the Netherlands were that the enemy's advance in the Netherlands would be obstructed through inundation and destruction of infrastructure.[32] The operation plan, however, could easily have turned out even more disastrously for the Netherlands, as becomes clear from the discussions taking place prior to the plan's approval. SHAPE, which was responsible for the coordination and integration of the planning, was obliged to intervene a number of times. At the end of November 1951, the comment from SHAPE on a draft plan was that it agreed that "in first priority a Central Firm Base [fortress] in the area Eifel-Ardennes-Hunsrück" was to be held. In addition, SHAPE commented – and this is of particular interest in this context – that all instances in the draft plan where reference was exclusively made to the 'Rhine', were to be substituted by "IJssel-Rhine."[33] Initially, this instruction had little or no effect. One month later, SHAPE was obliged to issue another request urging the commanding officers of the land, sea, and air forces in the Central Sector to erase "any reference to or inference of withdrawal operations to the west of the IJssel-Rhine" from their draft Central Region Combined Emergency Defense Plan. This was especially true of the paragraph which addressed the "stopline" based on the Vosges-Ardennes-Meuse and Albert Canal.[34]

And there were other ominous signs. There was reason to believe that Rotterdam was no longer considered a major supply port for the purposes of NATO defense planning. This would deflate the importance of the IJssel defense line.[35] There were also indications that the scheduled oil pipeline network in the context of the NATO infrastructure program would stop below the main rivers. In the spring of 1952, the anxiety of the Dutch Defense leadership was fuelled by reports by the commander of the Northern Army Group (NORTHAG), Sir John Harding, who wanted to move the line between the Dutch and the British army corps from the river Waal southward to the Rees-Gogh-Afferden-Boxmeer-Uden-Vught line. He maintained that one Dutch division was to be deployed south of the main rivers, in the vicinity of the Reichswalt.[36] The Chief of the Dutch General Staff, General B.R.P.F. Hasselman, considered this southward move premature. He felt that priority should be given first to raising sufficient troops for the defense of the IJssel sector.[37] Harding's intention to move the NORTHAG Main Headquarters from Eindhoven to Maastricht (the Pietersberg) and the Rear Main Headquarters from Valkenswaard to Fort Eben-Emaël can be seen in the same light.[38] And, to add insult to injury, there were strong indications in the same period that France was lobbying to get Marshal Juin appointed commander of all NATO forces in the Central Sector, a position then held by General Eisenhower in addition to his position as SACEUR.[39] It was suspected that this would have far-reaching consequences for the Netherlands.[40] A Dutch minister stated that "Since the French still hold to the Antwerp-Ardennes line as the main defense line, the appointment of General Juin is dangerous for the Netherlands from a strategic point of view."[41] By the way, it should be observed that Juin repeatedly opposed the designation of Antwerp as the principal supply port for the British troops. He preferred to see one or more French ports on the Channel designated for this purpose.[42]

Indeed, the Dutch Defense leadership was on a different wavelength altogether. Dutch priorities lay with establishing a robust defense line behind the IJssel river. In the event that enemy forces were to break through this line, Allied forces were to be withdrawn to a "firm base Holland," which was to be held at all costs. They pointed out the considerable advantages of preserving a strong bridgehead west of the IJssel and north of the main rivers. In the event of a potential enemy break-through south of these rivers, the Allies would retain air bases, which would enable them to bomb enemy lines of communication. At the same time, the enemy would be denied these air bases. This would be a crucial factor, as the bases were eminently suited to conducting air strikes and attacks with guided missiles, be they atomic warheads or not, against the strategic air bases of the British Isles. In addition, the retention of a firm base Holland would deny the enemy the use of the Dutch coastline with its ports and sea inlets, which would enable the enemy to establish submarine bases and so allow them to take maximum advantage of their superiority in this domain.[43]

These views were more or less in line with the views held by the German military leadership and the approach advocated by General Eisenhower as the most desirable from a military point of view. The starting points were that Denmark and parts of northern Germany were to be held in order to be able to launch a flanking attack on advancing Soviet units. Southern Germany and the Alps were to be held for the same reasons, namely to attack the enemy's other flank.[44] The German view was then known by the name of "the Speidel plan," after the German general Hans Speidel – Rommel's former chief of staff – who first unfolded the German plan at the inaugural negotiations on the European Defence Community in Petersberg (Germany) in the early months of 1951.[45] It was this plan that was frequently advocated in the Dutch media as a viable alternative to the French defense concept. At the end of 1951, the German views and, of course primarily, General Eisenhower's views were reflected in the SHAPE defense plan that was supposed to take effect from July 1, 1954.[46] The Dutch (and the German and Danish) worries, as stated before, concerned the implementation of the Emergency Defense Plan valid until July 1, 1954. As a matter of fact, the Dutch military leadership, at this stage, did not have any serious intentions of linking the Dutch and the German defense lines. A proposal made by an influential Dutch general, possibly in consultation with the Allies and with German help, to extend the IJssel line to the river Ems and the Dortmund-Ems canal, fell on deaf ears with his Dutch colleagues.[47] They felt that the defense of the IJssel line was the most realistic and viable option.

Indications that appeared to corroborate the suspected Allied neglect of the defense of the Netherlands north of the main rivers coincided with the unfavorable assessments by the Allies of the progress of the build-up of the Dutch defense. The Dutch army and its officers in particular got it in the neck, as witnessed by the blistering comment by Montgomery after his visit to the Netherlands at the end of November 1951: "The Dutch Army [is] useless to NATO."[48] This, clearly, did not help matters. "Underperformers" carry little weight. For the moment, the complainant, the Netherlands, had been relegated to the dock.

The Dutch government with its back to the wall

The difficulties and differences of opinion with respect to the build-up of the Dutch armed forces, with particular reference to the army, were common knowledge at the time. In January 1951 this situation had even led to the discharge from office of the internationally respected Chief of the General Staff General H.J. Kruls.[49] Only very few people of the political, diplomatic, and military establishment, however, were aware of the real ins and outs of the international tug-of-war with regard to the strategic position of the Netherlands. This was all the more reason why the chance "discovery" of Drew Middleton's article in the middle of the summer of 1952 had the impact of a meteorite for the vast majority of the Dutch population. It made the headlines in virtually all the newspapers in the Netherlands.[50] The Dutch population had suddenly come face to face with the dangers looming in the distance. Not only would the northern and eastern parts of the Netherlands be given up in the event of a Russian attack – something that few people in the country were aware of in the first place – chances were that the densely populated western part of the Netherlands would follow suit. As I said before, there was even a distinct possibility that the south of the Netherlands would not be defended either. Only very few people were aware of this, however.

Middleton's article prompted the most influential and respected parliamentarian of the time, the leader of the Roman Catholic party, Prof. C.P.M. Romme, to ask the government to disclose the information it had.[51] This greatly embarrassed the government. Almost four weeks went by before parliament had an answer. Although this was understandable, given the fact that a new government was being formed, it did not inspire confidence. The government was in a predicament that can be likened to trying to square the circle. While being aware of the contours of the official Allied defense plans and knowing that there was a considerable gap between these plans and their realization, the government was unable to communicate any information as the plans were cosmic top secret. Even more importantly, the government was *unwilling* to do so, as it feared this information would put an immediate stop to the taxpayers' willingness to foot the astronomical defense bill. And this was necessary if the aforementioned gap was to be bridged within a number of years.[52]

Earlier that summer, the Dutch government had already sought to obtain a definite undertaking from the most senior NATO officials on holding the IJssel line as part of the main defense line and on holding the western part of the Netherlands as a firm base. The new SACEUR, General Matthew B. Ridgway, who had been appointed in April 1952, recognized that there was "cause for misunderstanding regarding intentions" concerning the Emergency Defense Plan. He gave the assurance, however, that

> I am firmly determined (and so is Maréchal Juin), under the Emergency Defense Plan to defend the Rhine-IJssel line to the last. I do not countenance any thought of failure in this strategy and, therefore, no planning for withdrawal into national redoubts is possible.[53]

The Dutch political and military leadership, however, was anything but reassured by this statement. While Eisenhower had expressed his approval of the inundation plan for the River IJssel and appeared to have every intention of holding the part of the Netherlands situated to the west of this river as a firm base,[54] Ridgway was known to be adverse to "fortresses" and "redoubts."[55] Even at his installation, Ridgway had hinted at its being more important, to his mind, to concentrate the armed forces so as to be able to withdraw to a bridgehead and launch a counter-offensive from there, than to attempt to hold, at all costs, the strategically exposed parts of Western Europe.[56] Small wonder, then, that the Dutch were highly skeptical of Ridgway's comments, especially when he said that planning for withdrawal into national redoubts was out of the question. In the same statement, moreover, he commented that, due to the enemy air and mine threat, Rotterdam and Antwerp were not to be counted on as supply ports in times of war. General Hasselman, however, remained adamant in his response. He informed General Ridgway that the Dutch military authorities thought it best to prepare a retreat to a firm base.[57] All in all, these developments had led to a situation in the course of 1952 that was unsatisfactory to all parties concerned. In the last analysis, it boiled down to confidence and capability, both of which were in short supply in the summer of 1952.

What was the government to tell parliament in order to square the circle? The Minister of War and the Navy, Mr Cornelius Staf, as a first step, went to NATO Headquarters in Paris to get first-hand information on the real merits of the situation.[58] This did not get him very far though. The only solution was time and patience, but this would not have done for an answer to parliament at a time of acute threat, as it was then thought. For this reason, the government resorted to more general formulations, hoping that this would be sufficient to contain the unrest.[59] The first drafts of the government's answer to Romme's questions still contained passages such as "the existing plans provide for the defense of the territory of the Netherlands." This was subsequently watered down to "the existing concepts provide for an *adequate* [my italics] protection of Dutch interests." This was rephrased once more as: "The existing plans, given the limited means, are taking Dutch interests into account."[60] The government's ultimate answer to parliament was worded as follows: "The government does not think that it is in the public interest to disclose the existing military-strategic plans." It went on by saying that:

> The Dutch government holds that the enormous Dutch defense efforts in the context of Allied defense plans *ought to be* [my italics] accompanied by the absolute assurance that, in the event of an attack, the territory of the Netherlands will be defended. In light of the information the government has on Allied military-strategic concepts, this standpoint leads to the undiminished continuation of the Dutch defense effort.[61]

Outsiders had no option but to take the government's word for it, in the same way as the government had to trust SACEUR. Romme appreciated the government's predicament. He felt that it had spoken clearly, "as clearly as one could wish for under the circumstances, and in words that are meant to set our minds at ease."[62]

Doubts persisted, however. This went as far as Atlantic solidarity itself being called into question. Prof. F.C. Gerretson, a member of the Senate of the States-General for the Christian Historical Union, a former Protestant Christian political party, asked the government if it had any assurances that, if the Netherlands were to be occupied after an unsuccessful Allied defense, none of the Allies would make a separate peace before the whole of the Netherlands had been liberated. The government answered that it felt this was sufficiently covered by Article 5 of the North Atlantic Treaty.[63]

The Dutch government was meanwhile trying to find a willing ear at the highest levels for the issue of the Allied defense planning concerning continental Western Europe, with special emphasis on the Netherlands. Initially, it even contemplated raising the issue of the Emergency Defense Plan in the highest military body of NATO, the Military Committee, or in the permanent representation of this committee, the Military Representative Committee.[64] The US State and Defense Departments showed more than the usual attention for the Dutch concern and wondered what issue it was exactly that the Dutch government wished to raise.[65] With hindsight, it is easier to see what interest this was to the Americans. As stated before, the US forces' planning process in those months was completely focused on a peripheral strategy. Their interest will not have diminished when a short time after that the Dutch government decided to take the matter up at the highest level, namely the North Atlantic Council and the Standing Group. Minister Staf drew up a short and succinct memorandum for the members of the two NATO bodies for the purposes of these meetings.[66] In addition, the Joint Chiefs of Staff Committee was engaged in drawing up a draft telegram to the Dutch Permanent Representative in the North Atlantic Council, Mr A.W.L. Tjarda van Starkenborgh Stachouwer, which accurately reflected the Dutch position with regard to NATO strategy.[67] The two Ministers of Foreign Affairs, Mr J.W. Beyen and Mr J.M.A.H. Luns, finally, briefed the Dutch ambassador in Washington in regard to the stance he should take in his interviews with US policy makers.[68] All this was done pending the results of an interview with Field Marshal Juin.

The interview took place in The Hague on October 22, 1952 and with positive results. Marshal Juin appeared to have convinced his discussion partners of the fact that he "most emphatically did not favor the defense of France above everything else."[69] Other senior NATO authorities were also going out of their way to calm things down and to allay the Dutch concerns. General Ridgway and the NATO Secretary-General, Sir Hastings Lionel Ismay, in short succession, visited the Netherlands for consultations.[70] The SHAPE Chief of Staff, the US general A.M. Gruenther, made the following statement in *Elsevier's Weekblad*, a highly respected Dutch weekly:

> Let me make this clear once and for all: there can be no doubt that the area that relies on SHAPE for its defense will be defended *as a whole*. By the same token, there is no plan whatsoever that would entail even the smallest part of that area to be given up.[71]

This was the best the Netherlands could do for the moment. No absolute guarantees were to be given as long as there were insufficient troops. All hopes were pinned on the German military contribution to the Western defense effort. This was the subject of arduous negotiations in the framework of the European Defense Community (EDC) taking place in those months. Most members of parliament shared this view: "Unless Germany were to be involved in the EDC, the defense of the northwestern corner of Europe would be up in the air." This observation, however, did not in their view alter the fact that the government needed to observe "undiminished diligence."[72] While Minister Staf wholeheartedly agreed with the members of parliament, he also emphasized that he saw certain objections to "conceiving an individual strategy." Although the Netherlands was free to present its own views, what should be first and foremost was "our willingness to give our full cooperation to a communal stance and the implementation of communal plans."[73] While recognizing that various plans had been considered, he was now fully convinced that

> what can possibly be done to defend the entire NATO territory is now being done. What can possibly be done, as...it needs to be feasible. And it becomes more feasible with a further defense effort.... This also means that it will not be possible to stick to one's own ultimate goals. A defense line further to the west [in which case the territory of the Netherlands would not be defended as a whole] will therefore have to be considered.[74]

The statements by the Dutch government and senior NATO officials did not fail to produce their effect. Over two months after the publication of Middleton's article, domestic emotions had calmed somewhat and the Allies had once again closed ranks. Although the Dutch government did show "undiminished diligence" as far as this strategic issue was concerned, it was relatively reticent in other matters. It realized that, being a minor ally, it did not for the time being command a great deal of influence. The planned intervention during the joint meeting of the

North Atlantic Council and the Standing Group, which was also attended by Ismay and Ridgway, was abandoned. At the eleventh hour the Dutch permanent representative at NATO refrained from raising the Dutch issues. The three members of the Standing Group limited themselves to generalizations. Van Starkenborgh concluded that presenting specifically Dutch issues would not be productive. He also dissuaded his Belgian colleague from raising specific issues on the use of the ports of Rotterdam, Antwerp, and Le Havre. He feared that the matter would only be dealt with "in passing" with the added risk that the "unprepared Secretary-General would be drawn into making inconvenient statements."[75] From that moment, the Dutch government confined itself to making a number of critical comments in the margin of major debates on strategy.[76]

A less pressing matter

From 1953 onwards, it looks as though the volatile issue of the defense of the Netherlands was becoming less and less of an issue in the public and political debate. Various factors contributed to this process. At the end of 1952, the IJssel defense line had been completed and various Allied commanders had expressed their satisfaction about this fact. Also, the Allies were generally speaking a great deal more positive about the progress of the Dutch defense build-up than before. This was greatly helped by the fact that the US equipment supplies were not fraught with as many difficulties as they had been at the outset. An even more important factor in this context was the prospect of a sizeable German contribution to the Western defense effort in the context of the European Defense Community. This would enable a veritable forward defense. Arguably the crucial factor was the death of the Soviet leader Stalin in 1953. All things considered, there appeared to be time for a short breathing space.

Concerns had not been taken away completely. The fact that the northeastern part of the Netherlands would be given up without further ado in the event of an enemy advance remained hard to swallow. What the Dutch people, fortunately, did not know was that the military leadership, at the end of those hectic months, had itself begun to entertain serious doubts as to the feasibility of a "firm base Holland!"[77] At the most senior military and political levels, highly somber scenarios continued to circulate internally for a number of years to come. At the beginning of 1954, Mr Beyen and Mr Luns, in a memorandum to the Minister of Defense, stated that in the absence of the planned twelve German divisions "NATO forces will not be able to do more than hold up the advance of Soviet forces. At best, this delaying operation will result in a bridgehead being held in southwestern France." They were under the impression that holding a "bridgehead Holland [. . .] would be unfeasible from a military point of view."[78] Minister Staf, likewise, had ceased to believe it was possible.[79] Things remained difficult for a while. As late as February 1957, the then Commander in Chief Allied Forces Central Europe, the French general Jean Valluy, concluded that the strategic concept then valid was "doubtless the least unsatisfactory, but one which gives no real protection to Western Europe."[80] The fact that people in the Netherlands appeared to be less concerned from 1953 onward is to be attributed to the more positive assessment of the Soviet Union's political intentions, rather than to the military capacities of NATO.

From 1958 onwards the Netherlands was actually reaching smoother waters. 1958, not 1954, as had been intended, witnessed the first concrete steps being taken toward a forward defense. The main defense line shifted from the Rhine-IJssel line to the Weser-Fulda line. This had become possible thanks to the participation of the German armed forces in the NATO defense – the plan for a European army having been rejected in 1954 and the Federal Republic of Germany having joined NATO one year later – and to the positioning of tactical nuclear weapons. In 1963, the line was moved further east, to the river Elbe, along the border between the two German states, the *innerdeutsche Grenze*. That was the end of deeply worrying articles in the papers like Drew Middleton's and the end, too, of practically insurmountable dilemmas facing the Dutch government. The debate about the defense of the Netherlands moved one level up, namely to the credibility of the strategy of massive retaliation adopted by NATO.

Conclusion

In the early 1950s the Netherlands would have been left undefended in the event of a Soviet attack. People with inside information considered this painful scenario more than likely at the time. The build-up of NATO's conventional and nuclear forces had not yet made the progress required to enable a forward defense. The principal question at this stage was which areas were to be held and which were not. The answers to these questions were laid down in operation plans, and, more importantly, in preparatory measures aimed at implementing these plans. Widely different views and interests clashed in the process, particularly those of the French and the Dutch. In the first years, especially, the Dutch government was unable to muster arguments to lend weight to its demands. On the contrary, it found itself in the dock facing charges by NATO authorities of failing to meet the deadlines for the required speedy build-up of the Dutch armed forces. With the appointment of then General Juin as commander in chief of the Allied land forces in Central Europe, French strategic views appeared to be gaining the upper hand. This was a drawback for the Netherlands, because for the French the defense of the IJssel sector was not a first priority. When in the summer of 1952 the Dutch parliament asked the government to clarify the situation with respect to the defense of the Netherlands, the government found itself virtually in checkmate. It was both unable and unwilling to admit that the Allies, in the first stage of a potential war, would not do everything in their power to defend the Netherlands. The government, following the example of NATO, resorted to consciously vague formulations. Although unsatisfactory, this proved to be sufficient, particularly when the immediate threat of an attack had apparently disappeared. From 1953, the defense of the Netherlands was becoming less and less of an issue of public debate. At the end of the 1950s, the focal point of the debate shifted to the credibility of the NATO strategy of massive retaliation.

The conundrum of the main defense line in the NATO Central Sector at the beginning of the 1950s provides a textbook example of NATO's uncertain and tumultuous formative years. NATO's organization and operation plans took shape along the way as it were, tentatively and gropingly. In this process, national interests clashed, sometimes dramatically. In these early years, there was no such thing as an independent NATO or European Headquarters. The statements and actions by these bodies were by definition informed and directed by the said clash of national interests. Naturally, rather than admitting this to be the case, NATO dressed up its decisions with all the paraphernalia of being in the common interest. National governments, consequently, could and indeed were landed in highly awkward positions, as exemplified by the predicament of the Dutch government in the present article. In the circumstances, governments were forced, Janus-like, to adopt two faces. When they were addressing the people, who wanted to be protected and defended, they put on their reassuring face. Another, more assertive one was needed to confront NATO, which was, as yet, incapable of providing the protection. National governments, therefore, pursued a two-track policy. In NATO's decision-making platforms they fought each other tooth and nail to broker the best possible deal for their country, while at the same time reassuring their own people, even though they did not always have reason to do so.

Notes

1 I would like to thank Heleen Heckman (MA) and Karen Rowley BA (Hons) of the Translation Service, Royal Netherlands Army for their kind assistance.
2 Drew Middleton, "French Idea of European Defense Opposed by More Military Leaders," *New York Times*, August 17, 1952.
3 See J.W.L. Brouwer and C.M. Megens, "Het debat in de ministerraad over de Nederlandse militaire bijdrage aan de NAVO, 1949–51" [The Debate in the Council of Ministers on the Dutch Military Contribution to NATO, 1949–51], *Bijdragen en mededelingen betreffende de geschiedenis der Nederlanden* [Contributions and Communications on the History of the Netherlands], 107 (1992): 486–500.
4 J.W. Honig, *Defense Policy in the North Atlantic Alliance. The Case of the Netherlands* (Westport, CT: Praeger, 1993).
5 Jan van der Harst, "European Union and Atlantic Partnership: Political, Military and Economic Aspects of Dutch Defence, 1948–1954, and the Impact of the European Defence Community" (PhD thesis, European University Institute, Florence, 1987), pp. 86–93.
6 I would like to thank Dr Gregory W. Pedlow (SHAPE Historian), Dr Peter Cooper (Assistant SHAPE Historian) and Mr W.F.M. (Bill) Gregoire (Chief Central Records, SHAPE) for their kind assistance.
7 Albert E. Kersten, "Die Außen- und Bündnispolitik der Niederlande 1940–1955," in *Nationale Außen- und Bündnispolitik der NATO-Mitgliedstaaten*, eds, Norbert Wiggershaus and Winfried Heinemann (Munich: Oldenbourg, 2000), pp. 153–75.
8 Minutes of the WUCOS Meeting, August 24, 1948, DG 1/6/36, Archives of the Brussels Treaty Organisation/Western European Union (BTO/WEU), Public Record Office, Kew, Richmond (London), United Kingdom (PRO). The aim to engage a potential enemy from the east offensively outside Dutch territory had been long and widely accepted among the Dutch military leadership. This becomes clear, among others, from the reaction by Colonel M.R.H. Calmeyer, the later State Secretary for

Defense (1959–63) to a memorandum on the structure of the army by the Deputy Chief of the General Staff, Major General A.Q.H. Dijxhoorn, September 24, 1945, File 177/5, Box 177, Institute of Military History, Royal Netherlands Army, The Hague.

9 The NATO member states had accepted the principle of forward defense as early as December 1950 at a meeting of the North Atlantic Council (NAC). Sixth meeting of the NAC, December 1950, C6-D/1, NATO Archives, Brussels. An excellent article on the origins of the forward defense strategy remains: James A. Blackwell Jr., "In the Laps of the Gods: The Origins of NATO Forward Defense," *Parameters, Journal of the U.S. Army War College*, 15, no. 4 (1985): 64–75. The first plan in which forward defense was actually operationalized, albeit in main outline, was the SHAPE Defense Plan, which was disseminated on January 1, 1952. The plan covered "initial operations of Allied Command Europe in the event of war commencing 1 July 1954." The Commander in Chief Land Forces in the Center was charged with conducting "a mobile defense in the North German Plain, trading space for time, inflicting maximum destruction and delay on the Soviets, holding as far east as possible, with a final stop-line not farther west than the IJssel-Rhine." He also had to "defend a position east of the Rhine to include the Ruhr, the hilly country of Central and West Germany, and the Black Forest." "SHAPE History. Plans and Progress 1951–1952," vol. I, Section II, pp. 193–7, Central Records (CR), SHAPE, Mons (Belgium). If the Soviet Union were to attack before July 1, 1954, the SHAPE Emergency Defense Plan that took effect on February 15, 1952 would be used. I shall refer to this plan further in the chapter.

10 M.R.H. Calmeyer, *Herinneringen. Memoires van een christen, militair en politicus* [The Memoirs of a Christian, Soldier and Politician], annotated and with an introduction by J. Hoffenaar (The Hague: Sdu Uitgevers, 1997), p. 426; Jan Schulten, "Die militärische Integration aus der Sicht der Niederlande," in *Die westliche Sicherheitsgemeinschaft 1948–1950. Gemeinsame Probleme und gegensätzliche Nationalinteressen in der Gründungsphase der Nordatlantischen Allianz*, eds, Norbert Wiggershaus and Roland G. Foerster (Boppard am Rhein: Boldt, 1988), p. 95.

11 See for instance "Short Term Strategic Aims in Europe at the Outbreak of War", Report by the Chiefs of Staff, September 8, 1948, COS (48)200(0), Archives Ministry of Defence: Chiefs of Staff Committee, Minutes (DEFE 5), 5/12, PRO.

12 Meeting of the WUCOS and Commanders in Chief Committee, December 15, 1948, FC(48)7, DG1/10/53, BTO/WEU Archives, PRO.

13 "Note for the Record" concerning an interview between General De Lattre de Tassigny and the British defense minister, January 11, 1949, Foreign Office Archives (FO) 371/79248, PRO; Letter from the Chairman of the Western Europe Commanders in Chief, Montgomery, to the Chief of the Imperial General Staff, Field Marshal Sir William J. Slim, January 18, 1949, WE/HQ/1/147, and a letter from Slim to Montgomery, February 2, 1949, CIGS/BM/33/3031, War Office Archives (WO) 216/298, PRO.

14 Minutes of the Dutch Joint Chiefs of Staff Committee, July 7, 1950, Naval Staff Archives, Central Archives Depot of the Ministry of Defense, Rijswijk, Netherlands (CAD).

15 British involvement in the defense of the mainland of Western Europe up until the mid-1950s was mainly characterized by political damage limitation. British security and defense policy in the first five years after the Second World War rested on three tiers: the defense of the United Kingdom, a firm hold on the Middle East, and control of the sea lines of communication. The British viewed European defense as defense of Britain by proxy. They looked upon air power and atomic weapons as being the best means to deter and overcome the Soviet Union. After the outbreak of the Korean War, however, an active military continental commitment was much in evidence, as was most clearly shown by the stationing of a number of divisions in the Federal Republic of Germany. Compare Paul Cornish, *British Military Planning for the Defence of Germany, 1945–1950* (New York: St. Martin's, 1996).

16 Between 1945 and 1949 the Royal Netherlands Army alone sent over 120,000 personnel to the Dutch East Indies. The personnel would stay there for an average period of

three years or more. The last batch left the East in mid-1951. See Jan Hoffenaar, "De terugkeer van de militairen van de Koninklijke Landmacht uit Indonesië (1947–1951)" [The Return of the Service Personnel of the Royal Netherlands Army from Indonesia (1947–51)], *Mededelingen van de Sectie Militaire Geschiedenis Landmachtstaf* [Reports by the Military History Section, Army Staff], 13 (1990): 99–133.

17 Jan Hoffenaar, " 'Hannibal ante portas': The Soviet Military Threat and the Build-up of the Dutch Armed Forces, 1948–1958," *Journal of Military History*, 66 (2002): 163–92.

18 See note 2.

19 C.M. Megens, *American Aid to NATO Allies in the 1950s: The Dutch Case* (Amsterdam: Thesis Publishers, 1994).

20 Fifth meeting NAC, September 15, 1950, C5-VR/2, NATO Archives, Brussels.

21 J. Hoffenaar and B. Schoenmaker, *Met de blik naar het Oosten. De Koninklijke Landmacht 1945–1990* [Looking Eastward. The Royal Netherlands Army, 1945–90] (The Hague: Sdu Uitgevers, 1994), pp. 113–15; J.R. Beekmans and C. Schilt, eds, *Drijvende stuwen voor de landsverdediging. Een geschiedenis van de IJssellinie* [Floating Weirs for the Defense of the Netherlands: A History of the IJssel Line] (Utrecht: Walburg Pers/Stichting Menno van Coehoorn, 1997).

22 Memorandum by the Chief of the General Staff, Netherlands Army, January 29, 1952, Cab. 52/90, File 34/1952, Archives Ministry of War (top secret), CAD; Minutes of the Dutch General Defense Council, May 30, 1952, Box AVR 1952–55, Semi-Static Archives of the Ministry of General Affairs, The Hague (SSAMGA).

23 SHAPE EDP 1-52, code name "Vigilance," February 15, 1952, enclosed with a letter from SACEUR, signed by the Deputy Chief of Staff Plans and Operations, Air Vice Marshal E.C. Hudleston (RAF), and addressed to the Commander in Chief Allied Forces Northern Europe, December 1, 1951, SHAPE 731/51, 1B R-2L-21A, CR, SHAPE.

24 "SHAPE EDP," January 9, 1952, COS (52)26, DEFE 5/36/26, PRO. Although the Commander Allied Land Forces Central Europe, General Juin, was slightly more cautious on the subject of the viability of the Emergency Defense Plan in a letter to Eisenhower (December 31, 1951, 11/ALFCE/SG), he nevertheless stated that "we find ourselves today, and for two more years, in a dangerously precarious situation," 1B R-2L-042, CR, SHAPE.

25 Walter S. Poole, *History of the Joint Chiefs of Staff: the Joint Chiefs of Staff and National Policy*, vol. IV: *The Joint Chiefs of Staff and National Policy 1950–1952* (Washington, DC: US Government Printing Office, 1996), p. 159.

26 "Remarks by Field Marshal Montgomery" at the SHAPE Staff Conference on May 18, 1951, 1B R-2 C-030, CR, SHAPE.

27 "Visits to UK, Belgium, and Holland. Note by Field Marshal Montgomery," June 12, 1951, FM/47, 1B R-3 L-018, CR, SHAPE.

28 "Note by Field Marshal Montgomery, 27 May 1951," 12C R-1L-13, CR, SHAPE.

29 Minutes of the Dutch Joint Chiefs of Staff Committee, June 8, 1951, Naval Staff Archives, CAD.

30 Letter from the Head of the Netherlands Liaison Mission at SHAPE to the Minister of War and others, June 2, 1951, no. U.390-51/M.1, MPA/679, Military Political Matters Archive (MPA), Semi-Static Archives, Royal Netherlands Army, The Hague (SSAKL).

31 Quoted in Pierre Guillen, "La France et la question de la défense de l'Europe occidentale, du Pacte de Bruxelles (mars 1948) au Plan Pleven (octobre 1950)," *Revue d'histoire de la deuxième guerre mondiale et des* conflits contemporains, 144 (1986): 80.

32 This becomes clear from a letter from the Chief of the General Staff, Netherlands Army to SACEUR, June 11, 1952, no. MPA 1492AT/1213–1274, and from a Memorandum from the War Minister for the purposes of the General Defense Council meeting of

September 19, 1952, as previously submitted to the chairman of the Joint Chiefs of Staff Committee for comment, September 11, 1952, no. NAP 52/1173, MPA/1492, MPA, SSAKL. No draft plans have been found in which the west of the Netherlands was explicitly designated as a "hold area" or a "firm base."

33 Letter from Major General P.L. Bodet, Acting Deputy Chief of Staff, Plans, Policy, and Operations, to Commander in Chief Allied Land Forces Central Europe, November 28, 1951, PPO 1241, 1B R-2 C-11, CR, SHAPE.

34 Letter from SACEUR, signed by Major General P.L. Bodet, Acting Deputy Chief of Staff Plans, Policy and Operations, to the Commander in Chief Allied Land Forces Central Europe, the Commander in Chief Allied Air Forces Central Europe, and the Flag Officer Central Europe, December 28, 1951, SHAPE 801/51, 1B R-2 C-13, CR, SHAPE.

35 Van der Harst, "European Union and Atlantic Partnership," p. 90. The military appraisal of Rotterdam was hotly debated during these first years of the build-up. An early example of this is the extreme lengths to which the then Chief of the General Staff, General H.J. Kruls, had to go in 1949 to get Rotterdam accepted as a "port of stores" beside Antwerp for the purposes of the Short Term Plan of the Western Union. See Minutes of the WUCOS meeting, September 27, 1949, DG 1/6/36, BTO/WEU Archives, PRO.

36 Letter from the Head of the Netherlands National Section at the British Army on the Rhine (BAOR), Major A.A. Paessens to the Chief of the General Staff, Netherlands Army, May 6, 1952, no. BAOR 4022 Plans and letter from Harding to the Chief of the General Staff, August 22, 1952, no. BAOR 1053, Netherlands Detachment NORTHAG Archives, CAD.

37 Letter from Hasselman to Harding, September 1, 1952, no. MPA 1629 N/1213–1274, MPA/1629, MPA, CAD.

38 Letter from the Head of the Netherlands Liaison Section at NORTHAG, Colonel A.D.C. van der Voort van Zijp, to the Chief of the General Staff, c. August 6, 1952, no. 1118 ZG, Netherlands Detachment NORTHAG Archives, CAD.

39 SACEUR was also Commander in Chief of the US Armed Forces in Europe.

40 Letter from the Minister of Foreign Affairs, signed by the Secretary-General for Foreign Affairs, to the ambassador extraordinary and plenipotentiary in London, April 18, 1952, no. N 4349, File NAVO/1945–54/00269, Archive NATO 1948 and Directorate of Military Affairs (NATO/DMA), Foreign Affairs Archives (FA), The Hague.

41 Minutes of the Council of Ministers, April 21, 1952, File 396, 2.02.05.02, Council of Ministers Archive (CMA), National Archives (NA), The Hague.

42 See the letter from Lieutenant General Jean E. Valluy, Deputy Chief of Staff, Logistics and Administration, to SACEUR, November 21, 1952, no. 48/LOG/DCLS, concerning "Ports for British Forces in Germany in Wartime", 12C R-2L-22, CR, SHAPE. NB: Up until the end of 1951, British troops were supplied through Hamburg. This changed the following year. In peacetime, the British Army on the Rhine (BAOR) was mainly supported through the port of Antwerp, with ammunition coming through Zeebrugge and personnel through the Hook of Holland. The vulnerability of this "Antwerp complex" in wartime soon led to a search being conducted for more southerly alternatives.

43 Memorandum by Minister Staf, September 11, 1952, no. NAP 52/1173, MPA/1492, MPA, SSAKL.

44 See for instance Eisenhower's explanation of his plans at a meeting at the White House on January 31, 1951:

> I want to build a great combination of sea and air strength in the North Sea. I'd make Holland and Denmark a great 'hedgehog' and I'd put 500 or 600 fighters behind them and heavy naval support in the North Sea. I'd do the same sort of thing in the Mediterranean.

Foreign Relations of the United States, vol. 3 (1), p. 452.

The next year, 1952, saw an increasing "opposition between the Eisenhower strategy (hold areas in the north and south) and the French strategy (a possible withdrawal to France)," as the Dutch ambassador in Washington J.H. van Roijen formulated it. See telegram from Van Roijen, June 13, 1952, N 5, File NAVO/1945–54/00269, NATO/DMA, FA.

45 For the development of German military-strategic views see Frank Buchholz, *Strategische und militärpolitische Diskussionen in der Gründungsphase der Bundeswehr 1949–1960* (Frankfurt a.M./Bern/New York/Paris: Europäische Hochschulschriften, 1991).

46 See note 9.

47 Letter from the Head of the Netherlands Liaison Mission at SHAPE, Lieutenant General Th.E.E.H. Mathon, to the War Minister a.o., June 2, 1952, no. U.390–51/M.1, MPA/679, MPA, SSAKL; Letter from Mathon to the Minister of (Foreign Affairs?), August 31, 1952, File 771, Secret Papers Archive I, FA.

48 Report by Montgomery of his "Visit to Holland from 26 to 28 November 1951," November 29, 1951, FM/57, 12C R-1L-14, CR, SHAPE. A Dutch report of the visit stated that according to "Monty" the army was "unfit to fight anybody, today." Folder 771, Secret Papers Archive I, FA.

49 See J.W.L. Brouwer, "Politiek-militaire verhoudingen aan het begin van de koude oorlog: rond het ontslag van generaal H.J. Kruls, januari 1951," [Political-military Relations at the Beginning of the Cold War: The dismissal of General Kruls, Januar 1951] in *De Koude Oorlog. Maatschappij en Krijgsmacht in de jaren '50* [The Cold War: Society and Armed Forces in the 1950s] eds, J. Hoffenaar and G. Teitler (The Hague: Sdu Uitgevers, 1992), pp. 70–86.

50 See among others "Startling disclosure in the *New York Times*: Defense of the Netherlands at Issue," *Volkskrant*, August 19, 1952; "Differences of Opinion on Strategy an Issue Once Again," *Algemeen Handelsblad*, August 19, 1952; "Opposition against French Views," *Nieuwe Rotterdamsche Courant*, August 19, 1952; "Paris Wants Defense Line along the Rivers Rhine and Waal," *Het Vrije Volk*, August 19, 1952; "Is the Netherlands Defended?," *Telegraaf*, August 22, 1952; "Can the Netherlands Count on Allied help?," *Trouw*, August 22, 1952.

51 Appendix to the Proceedings of the House of Representatives of the States-General, Extraordinary Session 1952, question 7 (registered on August 20, 1952).

52 One month later, on September 27, 1952, J.J. Fens, a member of parliament for the Roman Catholic party, raised the issue in the Consultative Assembly of the Council of Europe.

53 Letter from Ridgway to Hasselman, August 14, 1952, no. SHAPE/812/52, AG 1241/5 PPO, 1B R-01L-179, CR, SHAPE.

54 This, at least, was the conclusion drawn by Minister Staf at the end of May 1952, following his last visit to SHAPE. Minutes of the Dutch General Security Council, 30 May 1952, Box AVR 1952–55, SSAMGA.

55 "History of ALFCE 1952," p. 60, 12B R-2L-001, CR, SHAPE. See also Matthew B. Ridgway, *Soldier: The Memoirs of Matthew B. Ridgway*, as told to Harold H. Martin (New York: Harper & Brothers, 1956) p. 248. He wrote there that as SACEUR he would not have given up any territory on the single condition that he would not defend hopeless positions.

56 Minister Staf cited these comments by Ridgway in a memorandum dated February 8, 1954. File 498, CMA, NA.

57 Van der Harst, "European Union and Atlantic Partnership," p. 92.

58 Report from Sir Neville Butler (HM's Ambassador in The Hague) to Lord Hood, August 25, 1952, FO 371/102466, PRO.

59 Council of Ministers meetings of August 25, and September 4, 1952, File 397, CMA, NA.

60 For the various drafts of the government's answer to the questions by Prof. Romme, see File 04335, Code 9 (I) Archive, FA.

61 Appendix to the Proceedings of the House of Representatives of the States-General, Extraordinary Session 1952, answer to question 7 (registered on September 13, 1952).
62 "Equal Right to Defense," *Volkskrant*, September 25, 1952.
63 Appendix to the Proceedings of the Senate of the States-General, 1952–53, question 1 (registered on 1 October and answered on October 21, 1952).
64 Message from Mr. A.W.L. Tjarda van Starckenborch Stachouwer (Dutch Permanent Representative to NATO) to the Minister of Foreign Affairs, September 9, 1952, N 157, MPA/687, MPA, SSAKL.
65 Message from Van Roijen (Dutch Ambassador in Washington) to the Minister of Foreign Affairs, October 2, 1952, N 11, MPA/687, MPA, SSAKL.
66 Message from Mr Staf to Mr Van Starkenborgh, October 10, 1952, MPA/687, MPA, SSAKL.
67 Chief of the General Staff, led by the Deputy-Chief of the General Staff, Colonel C.J. Valk to the chairman of the Joint Chiefs of Staff Committee, October 18, 1952, no. MPA 1899P/1200–1274, MPA/687, MPA, SSAKL.
68 Message from Beyen/Luns to Washington, October 11, 1952, N 8, MPA/687, MPA, SSAKL. This message had been drawn up by the General Staff Headquarters. Draft answer to a telegram from Van Roijen, N 11, MPA/687, MPA, SSAKL.
69 Minutes Defense Committee, October 23, 1952, Defense Committee Archives, CAD.
70 See among others *Het Parool*, October 15, 1952.
71 "Defense of the Netherlands: A Declaration," *Elsevier's Weekblad*, October 18, 1952.
72 Proceedings of the House of Representatives of the States-General, 1952–53, 2800, VIII A, no. 10 (Provisional report, October 21, 1952).
73 Proceedings of the House of Representatives of the States-General, 1952–53, 2800, VIII A, no. 11 (Memorandum of Reply, October 31, 1952).
74 Proceedings of the House of Representatives of the States-General, 1952–53, p. 211.
75 Code message from Van Starkenborgh to the Minister of Foreign Affairs, October 29, 1952, N 275, MPA/687, MPA, SSAKL. Upon conclusion of the meeting, the official press release gave renewed assurances that the NATO strategy "included the defence of all peoples and lands for which NATO bears responsibility." "NATO Purpose Reaffirmed," *The Times*, 29 October 1952.
76 Thus, at a Strategic Guidance meeting (SG 13/25) in the Military Representatives Committee (MRC) of November 18, 1952, Van Foreest stated that this guideline did "not emphasize sufficiently the inter-relation between the defense of Northwest Europe and the defense of the British Isles." MRC-060-52, NATO Archives. When, a few weeks later, on December 9, 1952, the Military Committee (MC) discussed the Strategic Guidance (MC 14/1), Vice Admiral J.E. van Holthe made an important remark concerning "an effort to hold selected key areas as long as possible." MC/CS-007, NATO Archives.
77 "Firm Base Holland Memorandum" (no.7101cf/1213–1901) submitted to the Chief of the Naval Staff, the Chief of the General Staff, and the Chief of the Air Staff by the Chairman of the Joint Chiefs of Staff Committee on November 19, 1952. The conclusion was that withdrawal to and holding of a firm base Holland was impossible. MPA/1492, MPA, SSAKL. Although the committee found that the memorandum was based on the most somber assumptions, what clearly emerged was that the military leadership had little faith in this new Fortress Holland.
78 Draft letter by the Minister of Foreign Affairs and the Minister without portfolio to the Minister of War and the Navy, January 9, 1954, File 771, Secret Papers Archive I, FA.
79 Minutes of the Council of Ministers, February 8, 1954, April 21, 1952, File 399, 2.02.05.02, CMA, NA.
80 Statement by the Commander in Chief Allied Forces Central Europe (CINCENT) at a meeting with his sub-commanders, February 27, 1957, enclosed with a memorandum from CINCENT to SACEUR, April 9, 1957, AFCE/76/57, 1A R-14L-045, CR, SHAPE.

12 McNamara, Vietnam, and the defense of Europe

Lawrence S. Kaplan

The Vietnam War has had an enormous impact on America's history, leaving a legacy that has not been fully digested even after the passage of a generation. While there has been an outpouring of monographs, memoirs, and philippics on all aspects of the war, there has been too little careful study of the complicated relationship between the United States and its European allies in NATO.[1] The relative lack of interest among historians may be attributed to the modest changes it brought to the Atlantic alliance, in striking contrast to the Korean War that transformed the alliance into a military organization. An additional obstacle may have been the absence of documents from NATO whose archives only recently have been opened through 1965.

The intent of this chapter is to examine cognate NATO problems that developed directly from the war, particularly the conflict between US Secretary of Defense Robert McNamara and both the American and European military establishments over US troop redeployment from Europe to Vietnam in the 1960s. This issue had ramifications extending from transatlantic differences over nuclear strategy to European fears of abandonment to congressional resentment over the inequities of burden sharing in the alliance.

European uneasiness over the Vietnam War

During the early phases of the Vietnam War, from 1961 to 1964, the European allies had been supportive of the US aid to South Vietnam. In the confines of the North Atlantic Council meetings and its subordinate committees they professed to recognize that the United States was serving the common cause of containing communism by helping South Vietnam to cope with Viet Cong subversion.[2] This consensus collapsed in the wake of the American decision to dispatch troops to Vietnam in March 1965. The allies' uneasiness had surfaced with the murder of president Diem in November 1963 and with the succession of unstable governments that failed to cope with the increasingly confident Viet Cong insurgents. The Tonkin Gulf resolution that Congress presented to President Johnson in the summer of 1964 had opened the floodgates of American aid to the beleaguered South Vietnamese. But this action raised questions in Europe about the wisdom of the senior partner's support for corrupt as well as inept governments and about the sincerity of America's putative willingness to engage in unrestricted negotiations with Communist North Vietnam.[3] Rather than serving a common cause, the United States was now seen as diverting its energies and resources from its appropriate focus in Europe to an area outside the scope of the alliance. Such were the perceptions of the behavior of the American partner among many of the European members, even if they could not accept the French judgment that America was tainting NATO's integrity by imposing its imperial objectives on a Third World country.[4]

Although it was obvious that the increasing tempo of America's involvement in the Vietnam war in 1964 quickened European opposition to American military policies generally, NATO Europe's uneasiness existed independently of worries over Vietnam. It rested on the larger question of the credibility of the transatlantic ally's commitment to Europe's defense. Was there a possibility that the United States, vulnerable to Soviet intercontinental ballistic missile attack since the success of Sputnik in 1957, would revert to its traditional interests in Asia and the Pacific at the expense of its relatively new obligations to Europe? The Vietnam War could signify the termination of that commitment.

McNamara's Athens speech

From a European perspective, the American guarantee – the pledge under Article 5 of the North Atlantic Treaty – was enshrined in the maintenance of a low nuclear threshold in the event of a Soviet attack in Europe. Anticipation of massive retaliation following any act of Soviet aggression, of whatever magnitude, had been a cardinal feature of NATO's defense posture in the Eisenhower administration. An attack against any ally should trigger a quick nuclear response. In brief, "massive retaliation" was the essence of deterrence throughout the 1950s.

European confidence in this nuclear strategy was shaken early in the Kennedy years when Secretary of Defense McNamara delivered a critical address at the Athens meeting of the North Atlantic Council in May 1962, denigrating the role of nuclear weapons and emphasizing a doctrine of a more flexible response to Soviet aggression.[5] McNamara made a point of downplaying the nuclear component by suggesting that distinctions should be made among Soviet acts of aggression. Initially, the response should be made at the lowest possible level, utilizing conventional forces and escalating to the nuclear only when no other response was credible. This approach reflected the administration's sense of the inadequacy of a major nuclear retaliation against even a minor or inadvertent Soviet violation. The secretary was advocating instead major increases in NATO's conventional forces capable of coping as well as deterring aggression. His speech was essentially a vigorous expression of the administration's challenge to the old orthodoxy rather than a surprise sprung on unsuspecting allies. But McNamara's effort to win support for raising the nuclear threshold directly contradicted Europe's conviction, shared by the US military services, that deterrence required a low nuclear threshold to maintain NATO's defense capability and that ground forces of whatever size would be incapable of coping with a Soviet conventional offensive.

Among the grievances the allies had against the McNamara initiative were his actions in reducing the number of US troops in Europe at the same time he was urging Europeans to increase their force contributions. Granted that American pressure on Europeans to raise their financial commitments to western defense in the 1960s was driven by concerns over dollar losses created by the cost of maintaining a large military presence in Europe. Yet, it was not the cost factor that was primary in McNamara's plans. He was convinced that the current force structure confronting the Soviet challenge was wasteful as well as costly and judged that a more efficient military organization in Europe would reduce costs while enhancing the quality of western defenses.

Significance of the "Big Lift"

By 1963, he felt he had found a way to utilize the latest advances in technology to increase the efficiency of the US military contribution to the alliance without perpetuating the drain on the treasury created by expenditures inherent in the stationing of thousands of American troop in Europe. This was "Exercise Big Lift," the dispatching of troops by air from an American base in Texas to assigned positions in Germany. It involved the airlifting of some 16,000 combat ready tank troops of the 2nd Armored Division to West Germany in more than 200 Air Force transport planes. The secretary of defense found proof that an entire armored division could be flown to Europe, draw its supplies and equipment from depots there, and be ready to participate in NATO maneuvers without delay. This arrangement, celebrated in a Pentagon news brief in September 1963 as the "largest transoceanic Army–Air Force deployment ever made by air," would enable the United States to provide rapid reinforcements in Europe when needed.[6] The divisions in reserve in the United States would save expenses that American forces in Europe imposed on the transatlantic balance of payments.

The Kennedy administration had never recovered from the shock of discovering upon taking office the imbalance of some billion dollars between income from abroad and expenditures lost abroad. Reducing this figure was one of its objectives, and McNamara's program for a more efficient military was welcomed in Washington, even though the Army and Air Force leaders were less enthusiastic about the prospect.

But the Big Lift raised questions among Europeans – particularly Germans, the most vulnerable ally – about just how US flexibility in this matter would affect the US force deployment in Europe. After all, what could be sent quickly, could be removed just as quickly. It required assurances from Secretary McNamara that the exercise did not mean that the United States intended to reduce the actual number of US combat troops in Europe.[7] Within NATO's Military Committee the US member, Admiral John L. Chew, tried to minimize the significance of the airlift by pointing out that the Defense Department had been conducting exercises of this sort for many years, "although not as extensive as this one."[8]

Admiral Chew's fellow members were not comforted by this qualified assurance. The Big Lift had implications disturbing to the allies. Granted that it was a successful exercise, its initiation could not be made in secret and conceivably might raise tensions in a crisis. But this was not the primary caveat at this time. General Adolf Heusinger, chairman of the Military Committee, asserted that "the capability of moving complete major units by airlift across the Atlantic did not replace the need for forward deployed combat-ready ground and air forces which could effectively oppose an attack from the outset."[9]

This was an ongoing concern for German military leaders. In November 1966, General Fritz Berendsen, a member of the Bundestag, gave a moving address before the Military Committee of the NATO Parliamentary Conference. He reminded his audience that while Americans could talk of rapid reinforcements with variations on the Big Lift, Soviet forces had the advantage of proximity to the crisis area. Did the "growing air transport capacity of US forces" genuinely amount to full equivalence of forces on the ground?[10] Heusinger and Berendsen were not alone in their concern. In 1967, Britain's Sir Fitzroy Maclean in his capacity as chairman of the NATO Parliamentary Conference (renamed the North Atlantic Assembly in 1966) warned that "however mobile a force might be, the United States mobile strategic reserve did not have the same effect as uniforms on the street."[11]

US reactions to German concerns

The removal of American "uniforms on the street" was at the heart of German insecurity as the buildup in Vietnam accelerated in the fall and winter of 1965 and 1966. Was the reduction of American military personnel in Germany a symptom of American reduction of concern with Europe? This was a question far more important than the number of troops to be redeployed to the United States for later dispatch to Germany. The extent of Germany's insecurity was reflected in the tenor of the reports of Chancellor Ludwig Erhard's meeting with Johnson and Ambassador Karl Heinrich Knappstein's dispatches from Washington.[12] The ambassador made a point of noting the pressure McNamara was exerting on him over contributions to the Vietnam War effort. In a confidential memorandum on a conversation with Chancellor Erhard in January 1966, unofficial envoy Henry Kissinger reported the chancellor's fears that US involvement in Asia "could reduce its interest in Europe." Erhard had heard that McNamara had urged Knappstein to have the Federal Republic send "at least an engineering battalion" as an earnest sign of the nation's identification with the American cause in Vietnam. The chancellor felt that Germany was demonstrating its support by encouraging the work of a German civilian construction team to help the Vietnamese, and wondered if the increased American pressure was intended to give the United States an alibi to withdraw American units from Vietnam.[13]

German paranoia over the impact of the Vietnam War on the status of US forces in Europe was given impetus by the rumbling both in the Senate and in the administration over the continuing drain American troops in Europe imposed on the balance of payments. While McNamara did not make the cost factor his primary focus, he did note that his plans would reduce the imbalance by $200 million.

At every opportunity the secretary of defense protested the inadequate German military budget. Less than 5 percent of its gross national product was earmarked for defense, as opposed to 8 percent of the US budget, even though West Germany's gross national product grew each year by 5 percent. Moreover, he asserted that the Germans stinted on its reserve stocks; then US kept ninety-day reserves, while the Germans limited theirs to 30 days. If only the Germans would do their part, McNamara claimed, the US could cut its expenses by $200 million without hurting military effectiveness.[14]

McNamara's irritation with German resistance to his program was manifested in an indiscreet interview with the German sensational magazine, *Quick*, in which he castigated German leaders for complaining excessively about American intentions. They were naïve, he insisted, if they believed that in helping other parts of the world we were deserting Europe. He added that they were also naïve if they believed that the United States would invest a larger sum of money in their defense than they did for themselves. This was a heavy-handed reference to German reluctance to increase the nation's defense budget. The president, more discreet in his comments to German visitors, was as unhappy as McNamara about the German propensity for self-pity, for claiming as Chancellor Kurt Georg Kiesinger (Erhard's successor) did, that the United States fails to consult its allies when decisions were made. President Johnson told John McCloy, then negotiating for greater German effort to reduce the payments imbalance, that "If I had a dollar for every time that I consulted the Germans, I'd be a millionaire."[15]

The cost of the US troop commitment to Europe, and particularly to Germany, was never far from McNamara's mind, even as he had other reasons for troop reductions. As he put it to Defense Minister Kai-Uwe von Hassel, the United States would have to reduce its forces to match the lower offset goals the Germans were proposing. He was convinced that American forces in Germany were the principal factor in the balance of payment deficit, a problem that had plagued the Pentagon since 1961 when the first offset agreements were set in motion. The rising costs of the Vietnam War only exacerbated the imbalance.[16] A 30 percent increase in defense expenditures between 1961 and 1965 could be traced to the burden of the Vietnam War. The secretary was not just expressing a personal judgment; two senior administration figures warned President Johnson in November 1965 that "it would be necessary for the government to dramatize the balance of payments problems as *part of the total effort connected with the Vietnam War*"[17] (italics in text).

Still, the secretary had to take into account the serious questions raised by Germans and other Europeans about the significance of the rapid increase of US forces in Vietnam. The figures themselves were striking. In stark terms McNamara outlined the change from Americans serving as advisers to the Vietnamese forces to active combatants. It began with the landing of two battalions of Marines at Danang in March 1965 and escalated to 75,000 by mid-June. By the end of July, as he noted at a meeting of the National Security Council that given the continuing successes of the Viet Cong, more combat battalions were needed immediately. The fifteen battalions were not sufficient. Over the next

15 months he estimated that 350,000 additional troops would be added to the US forces in South Vietnam.[18]

It was hardly surprising that Europeans would ask what effect the dispatch of such large numbers of American soldiers to Vietnam would have upon the US troop strength in Europe. The British journal, *The Economist*, for example, assumed as early as July 1965 that the increased American military presence in South Vietnam would force President Johnson to call up specialists to be drawn from the European theater: "The forces in Europe will probably be milked to supply Vietnam and replaced by raw units."[19]

It was speculation of this sort that inspired Senator Leverett Saltonstall of Massachusetts to proclaim in October 1965 that American forces in Europe have not been affected in any way up to the present time by our activities in South Vietnam.[20] Uncharacteristically, McNamara recognized the need to offer the same assurance to uneasy European allies. When asked at a Senate hearing 3 months later if he planned to take troops out of Europe for deployment in Vietnam, he responded that this would not be desirable – or necessary:

> I think the main reason for leaving our combat troops in West Germany at this time is to insure that the Soviets don't embark on some military activity there that would cause us serious pressure and concern at a time we are engaged as deeply as we are in southeast Asia.[21]

This was a valid and credible point, but it did not address the question of how many combat troops would be needed to deter Soviet aggression. The secretary left an escape route in the foregoing statement that he may have foreseen in January 1966. The steady expansion of American involvement in the war in 1966 and 1967, with the rapid increase of troop commitment to Southeast Asia, made it inevitable that questions about the diversion of US forces and consequent thinning of the forces in Europe would persist. There were 267,500 US military personnel in South Vietnam by June 1966, compared with 150,000 in division forces in Central Europe in 1968.[22] Small wonder that the question remained in focus.

McNamara vs. the JCS

For the most part, America's military establishment was as uncomfortable with McNamara's initiatives – and his rationalizations – as were the Europeans. The Army envisioned the drawing down of highly skilled personnel from aviation maintenance, construction, and signal services; the Air Force would have to yield 4 tactical reconnaissance and 6 tactical fighter squadrons comprising 7,000 personnel; and the Navy would have to give up a Marine Corps battalion landing team from the Sixth Fleet. And this was only the beginning, they feared. By mid-1966 a substantial portion, up to two-thirds of USAF reconnaissance aircraft would be removed from NATO assignments, along with 30,000 servicemen with critical skills. The British delegation to NATO worried that the withdrawal of

US troops, even if only temporarily, would give the French military spokesman an opportunity "to make as much political capital as possible" from American redeployment plans.[23]

McNamara had an answer to his critics, one that cast aside the frequent references to costs and imbalance of payments. These were always present in the secretary's mind, considering his penchant for efficiency and his track record in cutting down the size of the Pentagon bureaucracy. But the driving factor in his evaluation of the military structure in Europe was based on efficiency more than on economy. In his review of US forces for the preparation of the fiscal year 1966 budget, he made a case for withdrawing troops from Europe before Europeans had made an issue of troop redeployment to Vietnam. In March 1965, just as the first Marines were landing in Danang, he told General Lyman L. Lemnitzer, then commander of US forces in Europe as well as NATO's supreme allied commander in Europe (SACEUR),

> if the real effectiveness of our divisions and tactical air units is proportional to their costs and personnel strengths, our forces appear to be much more effective relative to those of the [Warsaw] Pact than if one were merely to count numbers of divisions and aircraft.[24]

As redeployments were set in motion over the following year, the secretary claimed that whatever decrease had been made in the numbers of troops in Germany was "offset to a significant degree by reorganization of supply and support units to provide greater efficiency and by far the greater capability to deploy men quickly from CONUS [continental US]."[25]

McNamara was expressing the essence of his position on military organization, which was strongly supported by the youthful civilian corps of defense intellectuals labeled the "Whiz Kids." They joined the secretary in deprecating the size of Soviet conventional forces, emphasizing the technological edge the United States had in coping with Soviet ground forces.[26] It was not that he was opposed to a conventional buildup; this was a centerpiece of his advice to the NATO allies as a means of avoiding nuclear warfare. But numbers of themselves were of less importance. Ever since the success of the Big Lift he believed he had found a more flexible way of utilizing US troops than stationing the American contingent permanently in Europe.

McNamara had his critics in the White House as well as in the military. Presidential envoy, John J. McCloy, reported the negative military effects of force reductions in Europe. Even the removal of one division, he was convinced, would lead to serious cuts in Europe's own contributions. Moreover, he questioned the validity of the Big Lift concept of dual-basing 10–40 percent of US troops. He cited the Joint Chiefs' judgment that the "actual flight time is only a small fraction of the total time needed." It would require 40–45 days, not 30 days after mobilization for two divisions to be combat-ready. And it would take 2 years before new sites were prepared for division equipment, along with specially designed air-conditioned storage depots for stockpiles overseas. In brief, dependence on the airlift would result in a serious reduction in US capability for flexible response. General Earle B. Wheeler, chairman of the Joint Chiefs of Staff in 1967 weighed in forcefully, with a military authority McCloy could not match, when he asserted that "there is no military justification for force reductions in Europe." They would lead to comparable reductions in allied forces, increase Soviet leverage, and ultimately damage US influence in Europe. Wheeler concluded with the observation that if more than 50,000 US troops were removed, the army could not retain tactical integrity sufficient to prevail in combat.[27]

The chairman of the JCS was posing a worst-case scenario. At no time did McNamara propose such drastic measures. The secretary could cite precedents for redeployments. Until the Vietnam War intruded itself into NATO military planning, US requests to the Military Committee for withdrawal of units or equipment were routine. Usually the Standing Group of the Military Committee (composed of Britain, France, and the US) would agree with respect to the temporary withdrawal from Europe of 5 RB-66 aircraft of the 25th Tactical Reconnaissance Wing for "eventual use in meeting operational requirements in Vietnam. Temporary withdrawal of these aircraft would have only a negligible effect."[28]

The Military Committee's complacency in this instance may have been an aberration since the decision was made in November 1965, in the midst of the buildup in Vietnam. Even in May of that year the Supreme Allied Commander, Atlantic (SACLANT) expressed his regrets when the US Permanent Representative on the North Atlantic Council asked for temporary withdrawal of an aircraft carrier assigned to the Atlantic command, deploring "this reduction in the effectiveness of the striking fleet." He made it clear that he could not "view with equanimity the recent pattern of withdrawals and recategorization which is progressively reducing the effectiveness of his forces."[29] And this exchange took place before the administration asked Congress for the first major troop increase for Vietnam operations.

Despite the Defense Department's observations that US forces in Europe were larger in 1965 than they were in 1961, the US contributions did not meet Supreme Head quarters Allied Power in Europe's (SHAPE) force goals. Pointedly, General Lemnitzer (SACEUR from 1963 to 1969) noted in the annual reviews of US commitment to NATO serious shortfalls. In 1965, he was polite but direct in complaining that "the vulnerability of US Air Force units in Europe continues to be a matter of concern."[30] Variations on this theme appeared each year.

No one was more conscious of this problem than the Supreme Allied Commander himself. More forcefully than in the previous year, Lemnitzer criticized McNamara in February 1966 for making once again "an overly optimistic statement regarding tactical air strength."[31] NATO's annual review of the alliance's forces in November 1965 mixed his appreciation for the United States exceeding SACLANT's recommended force goals with a recognition that there were a number of shortages in major weapons categories. The report regretted that only one missile squadron of the six-squadron requirement stated in SACEUR's recommended goals were met. SHAPE was "seriously concerned at the impact of this significant withdrawal."[32]

The US military's disapproval of McNamara's redeployment program expanded over time. It disturbed the Joint Chiefs that the secretary's proposed changes were driven by what they considered to be financial considerations that prevailed over military advice. For a time, France's decision in 1966 to leave the integrated NATO command and force the evacuation of US forces from its territory muted its objections. This drastic action, however, provided McNamara with an opportunity to advance his reformation of American personnel in Europe. He argued that France did NATO a favor by accelerating his plans for a more efficient use of NATO's and America's resources. Given the need for new lines of communication and transportation, he was able to solidify his program for dual-basing of US forces.

The Joint Chiefs did not share McNamara's enthusiasm for dual-basing, and worried over the Vietnam War's impact on NATO's military capabilities. By the beginning of 1968, there were more than 500,000 US personnel in Vietnam whose costs increasingly impinged upon the force levels in Europe. One US general, Bruce Palmer, claimed that the drain of manpower "destroyed the U.S. 7th Army in Germany without the enemy firing a shot. It destroyed that army because we were so strategically out of balance we used the 7th Army as a replacement for Vietnam."[33] Obviously, it was not just the European allies who engaged in hyperbole when troop redeployment was involved.

Just how much damage McNamara's initiatives caused deserves a more objective analysis than they have received in the past. Certainly the loss of specialists weakened NATO defenses, but to what degree? The nightmare scenarios of whole divisions being sent to Vietnam never materialized. Nor did McNamara envision mass redeployment of US troops. But the removal of troops, no matter how few, triggered European fears of abandonment that were unjustified. It also set off alarms about the secretary's disregard for professional military advice and his excessive reliance on civilian aides.

Looking back on the redeployment issue 15 years later, the retired SACEUR recognized the demands that the war in progress in Southeast Asia imposed on the military establishment as opposed to war as a deterrent in Europe. He recalled that the Army "tapped us to move experienced people out and get them to Vietnam.... So our capability went down for the loss of both people and equipment, ammunition and so on." There was no choice, he felt. Vietnam where the fighting was going on had to receive priority. He admitted that combat readiness of American units in NATO was affected: "You just have to accept lower capabilities," something to be accepted "without discussion or argument, because we knew damn well what the requirements were." He emphasized that despite the crisis in Southeast Asia,

> we didn't send units to Vietnam. No[t] that I would have considered [it] a mistake, because I would rather have an American unit of 90 or 75 or 60 per cent strength and not have to change the United States' commitment for that kind of unit being where it was.

Lemnitzer even found some benefits from reverse redeployment, bringing combat veterans in the war against the Viet Cong who would have experience under fire that no NATO unit could claim.[34]

Impact of the Mansfield resolutions

If Lemnitzer's rationalizations for the redeployment of US troops from Europe to Asia were not always coherent, an explanation may be found in the financial pressures exerted by the administration and the Senate as well as by the secretary of defense. There is no question that McNamara used the costs of maintaining a military presence in Europe and the consequent effect they had on the balance of payments as a ploy in countering European discontent with US redeployments as well as in pressing the allies for a greater share of the financial burden. He had considerable support from the administration, which helped to dilute the military opposition to his policies. Further pressure came from rising unhappiness in the Senate, both with the progress of the Vietnam War and the lack of support from the European allies.

There never was a time when senators felt that the allies were paying their fair share of the defense of Europe. Secretary McNamara's selective redeployments were not enough for many senators. In August 1966, Senator Mike Mansfield of Montana gathered forty-three senators to introduce the first of many subsequent resolutions calling for substantial reductions in the size of the American military in Europe unless the allies increased their defense expenditures.[35] His colleagues' concerns were not identical. For some, the main issue was the money; for others, it was the persistent complaints about unequal sacrifices; for still others, it was the lack of European understanding of the stakes of the war in Vietnam.

Mansfield's resolutions were just that an expression of discontent without expectation of any alteration of America's role in Europe. In the next year, though, Senator Stuart Symington of Missouri introduced an amendment to the annual defense procurement bill that would have prohibited the use of funds to support more than 50,000 troops in Europe.[36] If enacted, this bill would have affected the viability of NATO's defense structure. Symington's bill was intended to demonstrate congressional impatience with the partners' behavior. But like Mansfield's resolutions, his action was basically a warning, not a prelude to America's departure from Europe. He withdrew his amendment on the same day that he introduced it. Neither Mansfield nor Symington had any wish to weaken NATO in the face of the Soviet adversary. In this respect the Mansfield and Symington maneuvers reflected the ongoing importance of NATO to America's leaders.

The trilateral negotiations

NATO governments on both sides of the Atlantic took the Senators' message seriously. The immediate response was found in the trilateral negotiations involving three major players – the United States, Britain, and Germany. The offset issue was hardly new. It antedated the Vietnam escalation, and would have embroiled transatlantic relations even if redeployment had not become an issue. From 1961 to 1964, the United States and the Federal Republic had worked out bilateral offset agreements, which mandated the purchase of American military equipment to offset the costs of the American military presence in Germany. By 1966, the financial difficulties of the three major allies reached a point at which the Americans and the British warned that they would not maintain their forces in Germany without new concessions from the Federal Republic.[37]

To resolve these problems President Johnson appointed veteran emissary John J. McCloy to find a way to keep the British army of the Rhine intact by squeezing new concessions from the Germans. On the assumption that Germany would help Britain's serious foreign exchange problems, the Johnson administration promised to raise its purchases of British equipment from $35 million to $40 million worth of orders. Negotiations, however, were complicated by the fall of the Erhard government in October 1966 and the initial belligerence of his successor, Kurt Georg Kiesinger.[38] The new chancellor chafed at German dependence on the United States, but ultimately accepted some dual-basing provided that the decisions were based on common security requirements and not on temporary financial reductions. The Federal Republic also agreed to pledge $500 million in special medium-term US securities. This effort to relieve the balance of payments deficit failed to satisfy Senate critics who claimed that Germany would be winning new profits from their investments rather than bearing a fairer share in the defense of Europe.[39]

McCloy fought a losing battle to stop redeployment. He had to retreat from his basic position that withdrawal of any troops would weaken NATO's defenses. He had little choice. There was no question that dual-basing of US forces was necessary to quiet Senate objections. The question then was how many troops would be involved in the redeployment process. McNamara against the judgment of the Joint Chiefs wanted 4–6 brigades from 2 divisions, while the State Department, always more politically attuned to European sensibilities, recommended half that number. Harlan Cleveland, US ambassador to NATO, wanted only one division involved. In this context McCloy positioned himself as a compromiser. He would bridge the gap by dual-basing 3 of 6 brigades. If necessary, taken them from the 24th division, which he felt was badly deployed in Bavaria.[40]

The result of the negotiations was a US rotation system, involving up to 35,000 troops from the 24th division and including an understanding that at least one brigade would be in Germany at all times. The other two would return annually for maneuvers. The agreement in May 1967 would relocate slightly over 33,000 military personnel and their dependents by September 1968, generating a savings of $70 million.[41] These arrangements did not solve the balance of payments problems any more than they removed the question of burden sharing from the administration's or Senate's agendas. As Under-Secretary of State Nicholas Katzenbach observed in 1968, "the trilateral talks last year brought us some time, but it is important that we begin discussions with the FRG as soon as we can on arrangement for the next two years."[42]

Concluding reflections

McNamara never did convince the Joint Chiefs or the SACEUR of the wisdom of his approach to the structure of NATO forces in Europe. But he did not have to win his case with them. While Congress was increasingly critical of the secretary's conduct of the Vietnam War, its pressure for reducing the number of US troops in Europe helped to ensure the success of dual-basing even after McNamara left office in 1968. Six months after he resigned, his successor, Clark Clifford, was advised by the director of his Office of International Security Affairs to

> tell the Chiefs that in our opinion it will be necessary to make a fairly strong commitment to the Congressional leaders that of the total of 330,000 military personnel in Europe and adjacent areas, a total of 100,000 will be redeployed to CONUS [continental United States] or otherwise withdrawn within the next year or two, counting in that total 34,000 from...the "rotational" division force now being brought back from Germany.[43]

McNamara left the Pentagon in 1968 discredited for his conduct of the Vietnam War and disheartened by his sense of its futility. As his memoirs have disclosed, he remains haunted by a war that he belatedly recognized as a tragic mistake. The tendency of critics and of McNamara himself to concentrate on this facet of his career has helped to obscure the bold initiatives he had taken in NATO military affairs. His brashness offended the allies, and his arrogance repelled the professional military men, but the substantial inroads – exemplified by dual-basing of troops – that he had made into what hitherto had been the realm of the men in uniform remained in place even if he did not.

If the European allies accepted a dual-basing formula that legitimized redeployment of US troops, it was not because they too had accepted McNamara's judgments. A number of factors were in play by the end of the Johnson administration that affected NATO's views on the flexibility of US troop disposition in Europe. A critical element in their acquiescence was the removal of Vietnam from the European scene. The fear of abandonment that had agitated Germans in the middle of the decade had dissipated with the recognition that US forces in Europe were not being dismantled. Their numbers did decline from over 400,000 in 1962 to a little under 300,000 in 1968, but this reduction did not signal their ultimate removal from Europe to serve in Southeast Asia.

That the United States was moving toward de-escalation in Vietnam was a further indication that Asia was not to replace Europe in America's scheme of things. A third factor in Europe's acceptance of the McNamara strategy was the Czechoslovak Crisis in the summer of 1968. The Warsaw Pact's brutal suppression of the Czechoslovak heresy was a sober reminder of the importance of US troops in Europe. The invasion "tended to get the Europeans to pull their socks up a little more," as the State Department's John Leddy noted, although he was not sure "how long this is going to last."[44] The crisis induced Germans to put off their intended budget reductions for defense as well as to slow down the Senate's drive for troop reductions. But European hopes for détente with the Soviet bloc revived quickly, as did Senate complaints against Europeans. It is more noteworthy that McNamara's program of dual-basing that had begun with the Big Lift of 1963 continued long after he had been removed from the scene.

Acknowledgments

I should like to express my appreciation to the Commission for Educational Exchange for the Fulbright Research Award in Belgium and to the Lyndon B. Johnson Foundation in Austin for a Moody Grant which advanced my studies, respectively, in the NATO archives and in the Lyndon B. Johnson Library in 2002.

Notes

 1 Prominent exceptions include Frank Costigliola, "The Vietnam War and the Challenges to American Power in Europe," *International Perspectives on Vietnam*, eds, Lloyd C. Gardner and Ted Gittinger (College Station: Texas A&M Press, 2000), pp. 143–53; Fredrik Logevall, *Choosing War: The Lost Chance for Peace and the Escalation in Vietnam* (Berkeley, CA: University of California Press, 1999); Thomas A. Schwartz, *Lyndon Johnson and Europe* (Cambridge, MA: Harvard University Press, 2003). See articles on "The International Dimension of the Vietnam War," *Diplomatic History*, vol. 27 (January 2003): 35–151; see also Leopoldo Nuti, "Transatlantic Relations in the Era of Vietnam: Western Europe and the Escalation of the War, 1965–1968," paper presented at an international conference on "NATO, the Warsaw Pact, and the Rise of Détente," Dobbiaco, September 26–28, 2002.
 2 Lawrence S. Kaplan, "The Vietnam War and Europe: The View from NATO," in *La guerre du Vietnam et l'Europe, 1963–1973*, eds, Christopher Goscha & Maurice Vaïsse (Brussels: Bruylant, 2003), pp. 90–6.
 3 Ibid., pp. 96–7.
 4 Ibid., p. 98.
 5 McNamara address, Ministerial Meeting of North Atlantic Council, May 5, 1962, *Foreign Relations of the United States, 1961–1963*, National Security Policy VIII, 275–81.
 6 Department of Defense News Release, Office of Public Affairs, No. 1273–63, 23.
 7 *Baltimore Sun*, October 22, 1963.
 8 Summary Record, 116th Meeting of the Military Committee in Permanent Session, Paris, November 7, 1963, MC/PS 116, p. 3, NATO Archives, Brussels.
 9 Summary Record of a Meeting of the North Atlantic Council, Paris, December 17, 1963, C-R (63) 75, p. 10, NATO Archives, Brussels.
10 Minutes of the Meeting of the Military Committee, Paris, November 15, 1966 MC (67) 1, vol. 42, pp. 2–3A, NATO Parliamentarians' Conference, Brussels, NATO Parliamentary Assembly Library, Brussels.
11 Minutes of the Meeting of the Military Committee, Brussels, November 17, 1967, MC (68) 1, vol. 49, pp. 2–3A, North Atlantic Assembly, NATO Parliamentary Assembly Library, Brussels.
12 Minister von Lilienfeld to Foreign Office, September 19, 1966; Ambassador Knappstein to Bundesminister Schroeder, June 10, 1966, subject: Visit of Chancellor Erhard to Washington, *Akten zur auswärtigen Politik der Bundesrepublik Deutschland 1966* (Munich: Verlag R Oldenbourg, 1997), pp. 1266ff; 802ff.

13 Memcon Kissinger with Chancellor Erhard, January 28, 1966, papers of Francis Bator, box 28, Lyndon B. Johnson Library, Austin, Texas (hereafter cited as LBJL).

14 McNamara memorandum for president, September 19, 1965, Trilateral Negotiations and NATO, National Security Files, National Security Council Histories, box 50, LBJL.

15 David Klein memorandum for McGeorge Bundy, January 27, 1965, National Security File, Country File – Europe and USSR, box 184, LBJL; Bonn cable 10131 to State Department, subject: Chancellor Kiesinger's comments on US–German relations to CDU editors, March 2, 1967, Trilateral Negotiations and NATO, tabs 53–57, box 2, LBJL; Memrcd Bator, LBJ Conversation with McCloy, March 1, 1967, March 2, 1967, box 2, LBJL.

16 Edward Drea, "The McNamara Era," in *A History of NATO – the First Fifty Years*, ed. Gustav Schmidt (3 vols, Basingstoke, UK: Palgrave, 2001), vol. 3, p. 190; Hubert Zimmermann, *Money and Security: Troops. Monetary Policy, and West Germany's Relations with the United States and Britain, 1950–1971* (Cambridge: Cambridge University Press, 2002), pp. 164–6.

17 Diane Kunz, "Cold War Diplomacy," in *Diplomacy of the Crucial Decade: American Foreign Relations during the 1960s*, ed., Diane Kunz (New York: Columbia University Press, 1994), p. 98.

18 Summary Notes of 553rd NSC Meeting, July 27, 1965, subject: Deployment of Additional U.S. Troops to Vietnam, NSC Meetings File, National Security File, box 1, LBJL.

19 *The Economist*, July 31, 1955.

20 11th Annual Conference, October 7, 1965, NATO Parliamentarians' Conference, Brussels, NATO Parliamentary Assembly Library, Brussels.

21 US Congress, Senate McNamara testimony, US Senate Subcommittee on Appropriations and Committee on Armed Services, January 21, 1966, *Supplemental Procurement and Construction Authorizations, Fiscal Year 1966: Hearings*, 89 Congress, 2nd session, January 21, 1966, pp. 30–1.

22 *Annual Report* of the Secretary of Defense, Fiscal Year 1966, Table on US personnel in Vietnam, p. 36; McNamara draft memorandum for president, [June–July] subject: The Balance-of-Payments and Forces in Europe, Papers of Clark Clifford, box 17, LBJL.

23 Drea, "The McNamara Era," vol. 3, pp. 192–3; A.G. Draper, UK delegate to NATO to W.H. Harbord, Ministry of Defence, April 19, 1966, Western Organisations and Coordination Department, WU11918/6. FO 371, Public Record Office, Kew.

24 McNamara's letter to Lemnitzer, EUCOM, March 3, 1965, McNamara Papers, box 122, RG 200, National Archives and Records Administration, Washington, DC.

25 Text of McNamara speech, *New York* Times, March 3, 1966.

26 See Alain Enthoven and K.Wayne Smith, *How Much Is Enough? Shaping the Defense Program, 1961–1969* (New York: Harper & Row, 1971), pp. 132–42.

27 McCloy's letter to president, September 21, 1966, subject: The Military Effects of US Force Changes in Europe, Trilateral Negotiations and NATO, National Security File – National Security Council Histories, box 50, LBJL; Wheeler memo for Secretary of Defense, February 2, 1967, JCSM 60–67, subject: Military Deployment from Europe, box 51, LBJL.

28 Memo Secretary-General to Permanent Representatives, November 19, 1965, PO/65/567, subject: Withdrawal of United States Aircraft from Europe, NATO Archives, Brussels.

29 Memo Secretary-General to Permanent Representatives, May 26, 1965, PO/65/567, subject: Change of Category of a United States Aircraft Carrier Earmarked to SACLANT, NATO Archives, Brussels.

30 Memo General T.W. Parker, US Army Chief of Staff for SACEUR to Chairman, Standing Group, NATO, October 22, 1965, SHAPE/152/65-2102/21, subject: Annual Review 1965: Evaluation of the Reply of the United States to ARQ 1965, NATO Archives, Brussels.

31 Lemnitzer to Brigadier General Norman Orwat, USAF, Executive Assistant to SACEUR, February 25, 1966, L-3471-71, box 141, National Defense University Library, Washington, DC.
32 1965 Annual Review: Draft Chapter on the United States – Addendum 2 to AR (65) United States-D/3, November 8, 1965, pp. 3–4, NATO Archives, Brussels.
33 Quoted in *The Second Indochina War*, ed., John Schlicht, Proceedings of a Symposium held at Arlie, Virginia, November 7–9, 1984 (Washington, DC: Center of Military History), p. 266.
34 General Lyman L. Lemnitzer. Interview by Ted Gittinger, Washington, DC, March 3, 1982, pp. 35–6, LBJL.
35 Phil Williams, *The Senate and U.S. Troops to Europe* (New York: St Martin's Press, 1985), pp. 143–5.
36 John S. Duffield, *Power Rules: The Evolution of NATO's Conventional Force Posture* (Stanford, CA: Stanford University Press, 1995), p. 188.
37 Background to the Negotiations, nd, NSC paper, p. 1, Trilateral Negotiations and NATO, Book 1, NSC History, box 50, LBJL.
38 Bonn cable 10131 to State Department, subject: Chancellor Kiesinger comments on US–German relations to CDU editors, March 2, 1967, Trilateral Negotiations and NATO, tabs 53–57, box 2, LBJL.
39 US Congress, Senate, Combined Subcommittees of Foreign Relations and Armed Services Committees Report to the Committees of Foreign Relations and Armed Services, *United States Troops in Europe*, 90 Congress, 2nd session, October 15, 1968, pp. 88–9.
40 Memo State, Defense, and Treasury for president, nd, subject: Force Levels in Europe, Trilateral Negotiations and NATO, book 2, 45–652, box 50, LBJL; Memo Cleveland to Rusk, February 7, 1967, National Security File – Agency File, NATO General, vol. 4, box 36, LBJL; McCloy to president, February 23, 1967, subject: Force Levels in Europe, National Security File – National Security Council Histories-Trilateral Negotiations, box 50, LBJL.
41 Background paper: Trilateral talks and NATO force planning, NATO Ministerial Meeting, Luxembourg, June 13–15, 1967, National Security File – Europe and USSR, box 35, LBJL.
42 Memo Katzenbach, Deming, and Roth for president, January 7, 1968, subject: Report of our European Balance of Payments, National Security File – Subject file, box 3, LBJL.
43 Memo Warnke for Secretary of Defense, July 8, 1968, subject: Discussion with JCS on July 8 of US Troop Levels in Europe, Papers of Clark Clifford, box 17, LBJL.
44 John Leddy, interview by Paige Mulhollen, March 12, 1969, p. 19, LBJL.

Index

LaVergne, TN USA
11 April 2010
178874LV00001B/10/A